The Essential Guide™ to Walt Disney World®

2023

Executive Editor: Suzanne Albright

Primary Author: Jessie Sparks

Contributing Author: Melissa Moore

Cover Design: Suzanne Albright

Cover & Interior Artist: Gary Bilodeaux

Credit is given on individual images where appropriate.

To buy books in quantity for corporate use or incentives, email us at travelmadeeasyguide@gmail.com.

Retail Price: $24.99

Commercial Pricing Available

Limit of Liability/Disclaimer of Warranty

We make no representations or warranties with respect to the accuracy of completeness of the contents of this work and specifically disclaim all warranties, including without limitation warranties of fitness for a particular purpose.

The publisher, authors, and editors disclaim any liability to any party, for any loss or damages that may have erroneously been published herein, whether due to accident, negligence, or other cause. We cannot be held responsible for any time, labor, or travel costs. Neither the publisher nor the author shall be liable for damages arising from relying on any information contained herein.

No warranty may be created or extended by sales or promotional materials. The advice and strategies contained herein may not be suitable for every situation. This work is sold with the understanding that the publisher is not engaged in rendering legal, accounting, or other professional services. If professional assistance is required, the services of a competent professional person should be sought. The fact that an organization or website is referred to in this work as a citation and/or a potential source of further information does not mean that the author or the publisher endorses the information the organization or web site may provide or recommendations it may make. Further, readers should be aware that internet web sites listed in this work may have changed or disappeared between when this work was written and when it is read.

Please be advised that travel information is subject to change at any time, and this is especially true of prices. We therefore suggest that readers write or call ahead for confirmation when making travel plans. The author and the publisher cannot be held responsible for the experiences of readers while traveling.

Information is published in a variety of electronic formats. Some content that appears in print may differ from that found in electronic books.

ISBN: 978-1-956532-08-1

Manufactured in the United States of America

10 9 8 7 6 5 4 3 2 1

Table of Contents

Adults are only kids grown up, anyway.

- Walt Disney

Dedication & Acknowledgments

To kids young and old-from one to 100...planning their first visit or their hundredth.

We graciously thank all the people who took time out of their busy schedules to help put all this information together.

We especially appreciate the assistance we received from the Orlando/Orange County Convention & Visitors Bureau and the multitude of Walt Disney World Cast Members and all the other hard-working folks at the Walt Disney World Resort.

Many individuals provided assistance in the research and development of this wonder- and magic-filled book. It would take too much time and fill many pages to create a proper "Acknowledgments" section that would do justice to each single person who deserves to be mentioned. We thank them all for their encouragement and enthusiasm.

Editorial Staff
Executive Editor: Suzanne Albright
Editorial Assistant: Jessie Sparks
Production Editor: Janet Albright
Project Editor: Thomas Uebelman
Copy Editor: Sammi Yuzko

Composition Services
Project Coordinator: Jessie Sparks
Layout and Graphics: Gilbert Koenig
Proofreader: Sammi Yuzko

Publishing and Editorial Management
Editorial Director: Thomas Brenenstahl

Notes from the Editor

The writers and editors make every effort to ensure the integrity and accuracy of information gathered from many sources. Every effort has been made to produce the most up-to-date resource with information designed to educate readers and potential tourists. Any information presented herein may require updates or correction at any time. Register online to get email updates of important information as it happens.

The rates, prices, and daily schedules are current as of the date of publication date for each seasonal edition, and are subject to more-frequent revisions as we may deem necessary.

We recommend that you contact any establishment to verify pricing prior to your trip. Phone numbers or other contact information are prominently incorporated. Please refer to the in-depth Contact List that we provide, beginning on Page 1.

Please call Walt Disney World at (407) W-DISNEY or visit their web pages to confirm any information found in these pages before your visit. We recommend that readers install the My Disney Experience App to make it easy to check online.

Disney occasionally makes last minute schedule changes. The day before you visit each park, verify the exact time that it opens and closes. If you don't want to use the app, look online at disneyworld.disney.go.com/calendars or call Walt Disney World at (407) 824-4321.

If we missed anything, or if there is a new development that hasn't yet gotten integrated, please email us that information. Upon verification, we will provide you with a free copy of this book.

We welcome reader feedback.
Please send us comments about your experiences and observations. We will add you to our mailing list if you want to stay on top of Walt Disney World information.

How to Contact Us:

Email us: travelmadeeasyguide@gmail.com

Preface

Disney World is the family vacation of a lifetime! Everyone should experience it the way it is meant to be experienced: full of *Magic and Wonder*.

Some people may value a spontaneous trip over an overly-planned and controlled experience. Other people just want an easy vacation that is filled with as much fun as possible. Our tips help you strike whatever balance you desire.

A Walt Disney World vacation requires the right preparation and forethought, and the quality of your information is important. This guide offers the best way to easily plan a great trip.

All good vacations take time to research. For many people, planning is half the fun. *Following the information in this book will guarantee the vacation of a lifetime.* Our only goal is to make certain you will enjoy your visit.

Maximize the Value of Your Vacation for Your Entire Party

Inside this book, you will learn how to navigate the parks, regardless of whether you are traveling as a couple, as an extended family, or as an entire tour group.

After learning about all your available options, think about what you want out of your trip. Then think about how your goals compare with others who are traveling with you. We help you work with each member of your party so that you won't find yourself in a mad rush each day trying to accommodate everyone's personalities and interests.

Time & Money Saving Tips

No advice book would be worthwhile without tips to save time and money.

We offer more advice than any other book to help you maximize value while getting the most exciting experience. This how we've become the most sought-after book on the market!

Guide Book Benefits for Everyone

This book was written for the first-time visitor who does not know what to expect. However, even the most seasoned Disney World guest will find interesting facts, as

Insider's Tip!

If you're staying on Disney property with a large group (eight or more members), ask for Grand Gatherings when you make your reservation. This is Disney's team that handles larger parties. Make sure to tell them all the events you are celebrating during your visit. They offer excellent service.

What is at stake?

Factoring in travel costs to Orlando, along with local transportation, hotels, meals, and park passes, your <u>per person</u> price for your special holiday can easily top $1,000!

well as cost- and time-saving benefits, just by skimming through it.

From a touring perspective, this guidebook is just like those available when traveling foreign countries worldwide. Be prepared for a level of detail perfect for new fans, and something that the biggest, return fan will also appreciate!

How This Guidebook is Better

- Low Price
- Regular Updates - More Often than Any Other Guidebook!
- More Complete and Detailed

We offer the most time- and money-saving tips in a guide that easily fits anyone's budget.

We update it whenever a major change happens, so you know you have the most current information available.

We take pride that this book is 100% complete, offering the highest level of detail anywhere!

Experience Disney Like a Local

Our writers and editors live and breathe nothing but Disney.

This book was developed by local Orlando residents, including Walt Disney World Annual Passholders, former Cast

Insider's Tip!

Look at our optimized sections designed especially to maximize the comfort and fun for youngsters. We provide safety tips followed by a comprehensive guide to character meet-and-greet experiences and character dining.

Members, and theme-park insiders. We all experience Disney on a daily basis.

This book could not have been completed without the generous support of Disney Cast Members, each contributing anonymously and off-the-record to make sure you are reading the best information available.

We also thank the hundreds of families we've interviewed in order to integrate visitors' viewpoints into one optimized format. We extensively researched what could be done to improve experiences of disenchanted guests. You'll find out exactly how to avoid the frustrations that make costly family trips less than ideal. Our goal is to make sure you know how to get the most out of your vacation without suffering frustration and disappointment.

Independent, Honest and Straightforward Advice

The publisher is <u>not officially associated with Disney</u> or any of its affiliated companies. Thoughts and opinions do not represent the Disney Corporation in any way. Advice is honest and straightforward, designed to help visitors save time, money, and hassles.

We visit parks, restaurants, and hotels on a regular basis to observe what is happening, what is new, and to find out what is being planned.

We especially value our conversations with students and the input from local and international Cast Members (who work for Disney, either during their studies or immediately after graduation). Like us, they continually see how visitors respond to the Disney experience.

Preface

Live Internet Cameras

While you are planning your visit to Disney World (or other Disney resorts and theme parks around the globe), take a look around the resort with Disney Live Cams (disneylivecams.com). The camera feeds on this site bring live Disney magic directly to you through the internet. It is also available as an iPhone app.

Daily Cam Events (disneylivecams.com):

- <u>WDW Property webcam</u> features Epcot's nighttime light show each evening, live from the Epcot theme park.
- <u>Disneyland webcam</u> – This web cam is always on the move and has a variety of sights throughout the day. You will see views of the Disneyland Resort, California Adventure park, and some park rides.
- <u>Disneyland Paris Balloon webcam</u> – Experience daily rides with this one-of-a-kind view of Disneyland Paris.
- <u>Animal Kingdom Lodge</u> – Check in with your favorite African animals, as they roam one of Disney's premier resorts.

When inspecting properties, we appear as normal tourists and ask enthusiastic and interested questions. We don't identify who we are to encourage honest views and opinions from Cast Members and guests.

We enjoy Disney World very much and gain great pleasure from the environment, or this effort would not have been possible. The information is provided with upbeat descriptions, yet tempered with honest evaluations to prepare you with what you can realistically expect.

Never disparaging, we administer eye-opening warnings as needed to protect your vacation investment, while directing you toward ways to optimize your cherished memories.

50th Anniversary Edition!

A GOLDEN CELEBRATION

October 1, 2021 marked the beginning of the golden 50th anniversary of the Walt Disney World Resort (and the fifth anniversary of our book series)! Disney World is in the midst of an epic 18-month celebration, titled *The World's Most Magical Celebration*. Attractions, such as Guardians of the Galaxy: Cosmic Rewind and Remy's Ratatouille Adenture, recently opened. In addition, discontinued services, such as FastPass+ and Extra Magic Hours, have been replaced with new programs to coincide with the event.

The biggest change for guests is that you must now make an advanced reservation for each park you wish to visit. Without a reservation, there is no guarantee you will get entry on the dates of your visit.

Extra Magic Hours has been replaced with Early Theme Park Entry. Gone are the days when Disney chose a single park to open early or stay open late for its onsite hotel guests. Instead, those staying on-property are treated to a 30-minute early entry into the park of their choosing each day, as well as occasional after-closing park hours.

Disney replaced its (formerly free) FastPass+ reservation service with a new paid attraction reservation system. You can now purchase reservations to gain Lightning Lane access for select attractions and entertainment. (See our section on Lightning Lanes (LL) and Genie+ in the Tools and How to Use Them chapter.)

A golden transformation has taken place over Magic Kingdom and Cinderella's Castle. This transformation extends into the night as the Happily Ever After fireworks show has been replaced with Disney Enchantment. This fireworks show uses lights to bring stories of love and friendship over the castle and down all of Main Street, U.S.A., in a golden celebration that leaves guests in awe and wonder.

Fans are most excited about the May opening of Guardians of the Galaxy: Cosmic Rewind and the upcoming opening of Tron Lightcycle Run, which should happen by the end of Fall 2022.

For those who haven't visited Epcot in a while, some magical changes have been underway with a complete revamp of the park entrance and Future World. With a fresh look and the recent openings of Remy's Ratatouille Adventure and Guardians of the Galaxy: Cosmic Rewind, it's magnafique!

Epcot also has a new, nighttime lagoon show, called Harmonious, which replaced Illuminations. Disney's signature use of lasers and fireworks are combined with incredible music scores and awesome technology. You won't want to miss it!

For the first time in its history, Walt Disney World has a nighttime show that spans all four theme parks. Beacons of Magic debuted October 1, 2021. Using lights and music, each of the park icons gets an evening 50th anniversary transformation.

Make your reservations now to ensure you don't miss taking part in the festivities, as parks are more popular than ever, though capacity is still limited.

50th Anniversary Edition!

Covid-19: What to Expect

(UPDATED SEPTEMBER 01, 2022)

Walt Disney World is still understaffed following mass layoffs due to the global pandemic known as Covid-19. While Disney is actively hiring and working to open all of its operations, certain services, restaurants, and attractions may be unavailable during your visit.

Walt Disney World follows CDC guidance for setting their Covid-19 policies.

As updates to attraction/show availability and restaurant openings are being made on almost a daily basis, it is impossible to always have the most current information in our publication.

Please check our recommended blog and Facebook resources for regular updates. Below is a summary of what you can expect.

Crowds at the Parks

Disney World crowds are back and bigger than ever! People are ready to get on with their lives and are heading to Disney in droves. While Disney claims it is operating at reduced capacity, guests are noticing a lot of congestion in walkways and queues. With the loosened social distancing and mask requirements, those who are still high risk may want to avoid the parks.

As the 50th Anniversary Celebration is being held through March 31, 2023, expect some of the largest crowds ever seen at the parks. Will you be there?

Theme Park Operational Changes

Don't plan to purchase a last-minute park pass and gain entry into the parks. Walt Disney World Resort now requires an advanced reservation before entering any of the theme parks. (This is a permanent change.)

Visitors must obtain tickets in advance, set up an account (either online or through the My Disney Experience app), and make a reservation for the desired day through their account.

Park hopping is available but limited (with a valid Park Hopper pass). Guests must make a reservation for the first park they plan to visit each day. No reservation is required for the second park. However, you must wait until 2 pm to change parks, and you may be turned away if that park is at capacity. (You can check the app for availability before changing parks.)

FastPass+ reservations have been replaced with the paid Lightning Lane reservation system. This means, if you don't pay for Disney's Genie+ day-of reservation system (Tier 2 attractions) or pre-reserve a paid time for Tier 1 attractions, you must wait in a stand-by queue for each attraction (or use a virtual queue for select new attractions). With large crowds and limited options, the lines for attractions may appear much longer than in the past. The lines move much quicker than you might think, though (and often quicker than the posted wait times).

Parks hours are back to normal. However, park hours may change, so verify the hours of the parks you wish to visit in the days and weeks leading up to your trip.

Many character dining restaurants do not have characters right now. (Check the individual restaurant on disneyworld.disney.go.com/dining to see if the particular restaurant you are interested in has characters on the date of your visit.)

Buffet meals have been temporarily changed to family-style. They are still all-you-care-to-eat, but you must order extras from a server.

Many special guided tours and paid events are also suspended right now. Private, VIP tours are still operating. You can schedule these directly with Disney.

Disney Pass & Ticketing Options

Certain types of annual passes and ticket upgrades are not being offered right now. For instance, the popular Dining Plan option is not available for vacation packages. This is likely due to reduced availability of certain restaurants.

The popular Tables in Wonderland, which is a dining and entertainment discount membership for Florida residents and Disney Vacation Club members, is also not being offered.

Disney Hotels

While many hotels were closed through 2021, all Disney World hotels and most area hotels are now open and accepting reservations for future bookings.

Resort hotels that are open may not be completely open. In other words, some pools and restaurants remain closed. However, at least one dining establishment and swimming pool will be open at whichever Disney hotel in which you're staying.

Disney Transportation Changes

Parking lot shuttles are only running at Magic Kingdom and Animal Kingdom. Other Disney transportation options are open, but they have reduced frequency. Because of this, plan a delay of 15-30 minutes (depending on crowd size) into your schedule if you're using any Disney transportation.

Health & Security Screenings

Visitors are no longer required to go through a temperature/health screening to enter each Walt Disney World property.

Standard security screenings are still in place. If you have visited Walt Disney World in recent years, you are already familiar with these standard security protocols, such as walking through a metal detector and the possibility of security checking purses, backpacks, strollers, etc. for prohibited items.

Mask Requirements

Masks are optional on Disney property, except inside of First Aid centers. Disney recommends that unvaccinated guests continue to wear masks indoors, though it is not required.

Disney Sanitation & Social Distancing in Attractions

Social distancing does not exist at Walt Disney World Resort (or any other area theme parks).

If there's one thing that is virtually guaranteed at theme parks, it's that you will come into contact with numerous touch points with which many others have been in contact. This is enough to keep many germaphobes from visiting theme parks, even without a global pandemic.

Disney is once again using biometric (fingerprint) scanners when you enter the parks. (Speak to Guest Relations prior to entry for an alternative entry method.)

Single rider lines have been reopened, and Disney is back to filling up rows by placing strangers together. You will be sitting close to other people at attractions.

Shows & Character Greetings

A few indoor theater shows are currently shut down, but most are now open in some capacity. Magic Kingdom parades have also returned, and each park has at least one evening projection or fireworks show to commemorate the 50th Anniversary celebration.

Character hugs and autographs are back! You can also see your favorites in parades and Character Processionals held throughout the parks.

Non-Theme Park Activities

External Disney activity options have returned, including golf, boat rentals, fishing, and horseback riding. See our Other (Non-Park) Fun & Activities section in the About the World chapter for more information.

Reasons to Use a Travel Agent

Did you know?

A travel agent's planning services are free for travelers staying at a Disney hotel (and many major chains). Booking with an agent costs you the same as if you had to plan everything by yourself, but you get all their services, expertise, and advise, WITHOUT CHARGE.

Specialized Disney Agents earn a commission from the companies whose services they sell, which is embedded in the price you pay. Since you're paying this fee already, there is every reason to rely on yor travel professional.

What to expect from a travel agent.

Their expertise is invaluable to customize each trip to your needs. This expertise can be invaluable if someone in your party has food allergies, mobility needs, or a child with a disability. Agents also have exclusive access to multiple databases of hotel rooms and packages that go beyond what is available to the average tourist.

If you are someone who loves planning your own trips, just let the travel agent take care of the aspects you don't want to do. A good travel agent assists with as much or as little of the planning as you like.

Plus, should an unexpected issue arise, your agent is always on-call, even during your vacation and willingly steps in to help you, right up until you return home.

Special Credentials

With a quick search, you can find an agent who specializes in all things Disney. Look for "Authorized Disney Vacation Planners" to ensure your journey is memorable and hassle-free. Agents who sell Disney vacations are required to become experts in the "College of Disney Knowledge," an ongoing training program. Through this onsite training and first-hand experiences, they are your best Disney resource. Always ask to see your agent's College of Disney Knowledge Certificate!

> **Look for the following logo when selecting a travel agent for your Walt Disney World vacation:**
>
>

College of Disney Knowledge Training Modules

The program includes five mandatory training courses:
- Adventures by Disney
- Discover the Enchantment of Aulani
- Discovering Disney Cruise Line
- Disneyland Resort Basics
- Exploring the Walt Disney World Resort

Disney offers the following advanced training topics:
- Webcasts direct from Disney
- Effective Use of Disney Destinations Videos
- Getting to Know the Client
- Understanding the Client's Needs
- Matching Disney Destinations to the Client's Needs

When people laugh at Mickey Mouse it's because he's so human; and that is the secret of his popularity.

- Walt Disney

Disney World Contact Information

Guest/Consumer Inquiries

Walt Disney World Resort Guest Relations

General Information Including Tickets By Phone:	(407) 824-4321 (includes Spanish option) or (407) 824-2222 (direct operator assistance)
Mailing Address:	Walt Disney World Ticket Mail Order PO Box 10140 Lake Buena Vista, FL 32830
Walt Disney World Resort Guest Website	DisneyWorld.Disney.Go.com
Resort Room-Only Bookings	(407) 939-7429
Vacation Package Booking	(407) 939-7675
Tickets	(407) 939-1289
Canada Guest Information	(407) 939-6244
Disney Parks Vacation Planning Information Line	(800) 205-3002
Disney Passholder Information and Reservations	(407) 560-PASS or (407) 827-7200
Disney Tours: (Keys to the Kingdom, etc)	(407) WDW-TOUR (939-8687)
Hotel Reservations (Disney Properties): Group Reservations (10 rooms or more)	(407) 934-7639 (407) 828-3318
Disney Central Reservations Mailing Address:	Walt Disney World Central Reservations P.O. Box 10100 Lake Buena Vista, FL 32830
Magical Gatherings (for family reunions)	(407) 934-7639
Walt Disney Travel Company:	Toll Free: (800) 828-0228 Florida: (407) 828-3232
Walt Disney Travel Company Mailing Address:	Walt Disney World Travel Company P.O. Box 22094 Lake Buena Vista, FL 32830
Accommodations:	(407) 934-7639 or (407) 824-8000

Convention Information:	(407) 828-3200
Convention and Banquet Information Mailing Address:	Convention and Banquet Information Walt Disney World Resort South PO Box 10000 Lake Buena Vista 32830-1000
Dining Reservations:	(407) WDW-DINE (939-3463)
Resort Recreation Information:	(407) 939-3463

Special Activities and Sports

Golf:	(407) 939-4653
Fishing:	(407) 939-7529
Tennis:	(407) 939-7529
Boat Rentals:	(407) 939-7529
Surfing:	(407) 939-7873
Carriage Rides:	(407) 939-7529
Electric Cart (sightseeing):	(407) 824-2742
Trail Rides: (90-day advance schedule)	(407) 939-7529
Wagon Rides:	(407) 824-2734
Disabled Requests:	(407) 939-7807
General Information for the Hearing Impaired:	(407) 939-8255
Telecommunication for Deaf Reservations:	(407) 939-7670
Lost & Found Theme Parks Blizzard Beach Water Park Typhoon Lagoon Water Park	(407) 824-4245 (407) 560-5408 (407) 560-6296
Merchandise Guest Services: 9:00am-8:00pm EST Monday – Friday	Florida: (407) 363-6200 or Toll Free: (877) 560-6477 (international callers) (407) 934-6111
Mail order inquiries: Walt Disney World Park merchandise including Aulani and Disney Cruise Line	Email: Merchandise.Guest.Services@ DisneyParks.com
Merchandise Mail Order Guest Service	Walt Disney World PO Box 10070 Lake Buena Vista, Florida, 32830-0070
Attraction Refurbishment Schedule:	(407) 824-4321
Weddings:	(407) 828-3400
Honeymoon:	Toll Free: (877) 566-0969
Weather Information:	(407) 824-4104

Walt Disney World Entertainment

Magic Kingdom Schedule:	(407) 824-4321
Epcot Schedule:	(407) 824-4321
Epcot Holiday Entertainment:	(407) 824-4321
Hollywood Studios Schedule:	(407) 824-4321
Cirque Du Soleil: (tickets 6 months in advance)	(407) 939-7600
House of Blues box office:	(407) 934-2583

Walt Disney World Resort   Hotels

Property Name	Phone	Fax
Disney's All-Star Movies Resort	(407) 939-7000	(407) 939-7111
Disney's All-Star Music Resort	(407) 939-6000	(407) 939-7222
Disney's All-Star Sports Resort	(407) 939-5000	(407) 939-7333
Disney's Animal Kingdom Lodge	(407) 938-3000	
Disney's Art of Animation Resort	(407) 938-7000	
Disney's Beach Club	(407) 934-8000	(407) 934-3850
Disney's Beach Club Villas	(407) 934-2175	(407) 934-3850
Disney's Boardwalk Villas	(407) 939-5100	(407) 939-5150
Disney's Boardwalk Inn	(407) 939-5100	(407) 939-5150
Disney's Caribbean Beach Resort	(407) 934-3400	(407) 934-3288
Disney's Contemporary Resort	(407) 824-1000	(407) 824-3539
Disney's Coronado Springs Resort	(407) 939-1000	(407) 939-1003
Disney's Fort Wilderness Resort and Campground	(407) 824-2900	(407) 824-3508
Disney's Grand Floridian Resort & Spa	(407) 824-3000	(407) 824-3186
Disney's Old Key West Resort	(407) 827-7700	(407) 827-7710
Disney's Polynesian Resort	(407) 824-2000	(407) 824-3174
Disney's Pop Century Resort	(407) 938-4000	(407) 938-4040
Disney's Port Orleans Resort – Riverside	(407) 934-6000	(407) 934-5777
Disney's Port Orleans Resort – French Quarter	(407) 934-5000	(407) 934-5353
Disney's Saratoga Springs Resort & Spa	(407) 827-1100	(407) 827-4444
Walt Disney World Swan	(407) 934-3000	(407) 934-4499
Walt Disney World Dolphin	(407) 934-4000	(407) 934-4099
Disney's Wilderness Lodge	(407) 824-3200	(407) 824-3232
Villas at Disney's Wilderness Lodge	(407) 824-3200	(407) 824-3232
Disney's Yacht Club	(407) 934-7000	(407) 934-3450
Shades of Green (US active and retired Military personnel & their families only)	(888) 593-2242 (CONUS) (407) 824-3600 (OCONUS)	(407) 824-3665

Walt Disney Contact Information

Compliments, Complaints, Suggestions

Walt Disney World Guest
Communications
PO Box 10040
Lake Buena Vista, Florida 32830

Note Regarding Complaints: You're not likely to get feedback, however Disney works hard behind the scenes to cure any problems.

If you wish to write to the CEO of the Walt Disney World Company or the Chairman of Walt Disney World Parks & Resorts, both can be reached at 500 S. Buena Vista Street, Burbank, CA 91521. (You can also write directly to the President of Walt Disney World at the above address.)

If your complaint is egregious enough, warn that you plan to write a letter to the editor at the *Orlando Sentinel* (orlandosentinal.com) or share negative reviews online if you do not get a satisfactory resolution from company officials. Disney does not like negative press!

If your complaint has to do with service or accommodations at a resort, hold the manager's feet to the fire. Let him know you expect a reasonable resolution. Be pleasant, but firm with your complaint, and give the manager a reasonable amount of time to respond before going higher up the chain of command.

Walt Disney World Educational Programs

Write to: PO Box 10000, Lake Buena Vista, Florida 32830

Epcot Discovery Center (for Teachers)

Call (407) 824-4321

Walt Disney World Guest Letters and Letters to Mickey Mouse

PO Box 10040
Lake Buena Vista, Florida 32830

Orlando Area Visitor Resources

Orlando Official Visitor Center – If you plan to stay off-property or visit other area attractions or restaurants, contact the Orange County Convention and Visitors Bureau. They can provide a complimentary vacation planning app and the *Orlando Official Vacation Guide* (allow two to three weeks for delivery). Call (800) 643-9492 or (407) 363-5872, 9 am – 3 pm (Eastern Time) or go to visitorlando.com.

Hotelcoupons.com – Order a copy of the *Florida Guide* for discounts on lodgings restaurants and attractions statewide. Sign up to get this monthly guide by email. A printed copy can be requested by calling (800) 222-3948 (M-F, 8 am – 5 pm Eastern). There is a $3 charge for sending each hardcopy booklet.

Kissimmee Visitor's Guide – Kissimmee is the nearest tourist area to Disney World. It is located just south of the property. The *Kissimmee Visitor's Guide* has a directory of attractions, restaurants, special events, and other useful info. It also offers discounts for hotels and advertisements for rental houses, timeshares, and condominiums. Call Kissimmee Convention and Visitors Bureau at (800) 327-9159 or (407) 944-2400 or reach them online at floridakiss.com.

Helpful Internet Websites

Facebook has official Disney sites for each resort location for fans to comment and connect. Just do a quick search to find them.

If you have a Disney-related question, consider using an Internet discussion forum. Disney Park's Mom's Panel (disneyworldmoms.com) is officially sponsored by Walt Disney World and was chosen from among over 10,000 applicants who competed to win the sponsorship.

It offers tips and discussions relevant to a Walt Disney World vacation, including Disney Cruise Line, runDisney, and traveling with sports groups. The site is in English, but some members speak Spanish. The moms are unpaid volunteers who take the time to respond to queries. Expect them to speak candidly and openly about their experiences.

Best Unofficial Disney Websites, Blogs and Discussion Boards

TouringPlans.com – Sponsored by the writers of *Unofficial Guide to Walt Disney World*, this site has a small fee to use.

WDWHints.com – A Walt Disney World Blog bringing its readers excellent "HINTS", which stands for Helpful Information, News, Tips, & Secrets. It publishes all-things related to Disney, and their team of writers especially enjoys researching tips, tricks, and little known things about the Disney parks (and then sharing them with you!)

Allears.net – Updated weekly with news, photos, menus, and tips for guests with special needs.

Disboards.com – This is a very active Internet forum.

Kenny the Pirate – kennythepirate.com provides up-to-date character listings with an associated character locator app. They also provide custom travel/touring plans and a crowd calendar.

Wdwmagic.com – Includes news and current information with a related Internet forum at forums.wdwmagic.com.

micechat.com – This is a long-running blog with a forum for discussions.

World of Walt (worldofwalt.com) – The site is dedicated to providing timely and entertaining information about The Walt Disney Company – and specifically about the Walt Disney World Resort. They have useful information on Disney tickets, Disney resorts, Disney vacation planning, and the Disney Cruise Lines.

The Dibb (thedibb.co.uk) – Bulletin board with information directed towards visitors from the United Kingdom.

wdw360.com/forums – An active forum for questions and advice.

themainstreetmouse.com – A blog with a discussion forum (though you must wade through a lot of advertising).

Mousepad (mousepad.mouseplanet.com) – This is an active discussion forum with related blog postings.

MouseSavers.com – Offers the best money saving tips in a newsletter. It includes lists of discount and reservation codes for use at Disney resorts. Sign up for their email list to receive notice of savings (up to 40% in some cases). They also include discount codes for car rental and non-Disney hotels.

distripplanner.com – Calculate the cost of using Disney's Dining Plan to help determine if it's worth it.

Resortfeechecker.com – Search their database of Orlando resorts to compare fees.

Resortfees.com - Search their databse of Orlando resorts to compare fees.

Best Social Media Pages

Im So Disney Facebook Page – A place to connect with other Disney fans to ask questions, post pictures, etc.

Walt Disney World Annual Passholders Facebook Page – A place to connect with other Disney fans to ask questions, post pictures, etc.

Mickey's Not So Secret Disney Fan Facebook Page – Sponsored by Disney Made Easy, this page allows Disney fans to connect with one another and the authors of this guide book.

Disney Made Easy - Walt Disney World Tips & Tricks Facebook Page (facebook. com/groups/disneymadeeasytips) - A place for Disney fans to read and share tips, as well as ask travel questions directly to the authors of this Walt Disney World guide book

Ticketing Resellers and Travel Agencies

Build a Better Mouse Trip (buildabettermousetrip.com) – A travel agency with a number of planning and travel resources listed on their website.

Mickeytravels.com – An authorized Disney vacation travel planner.

Smallworldvacations.com – An authorized Disney vacation travel planner.

Undercovertourist.com – This ticket reseller often provides park tickets to Walt Disney World and other area attractions at a discount.

Videos, Photographs and Radio Stations

YouTube is a great resource to see what the parks look like. Just type in the name of the attraction you wish to see. You can often find night-vision videos to see what some of the dark rides are like, although most of the videos are amateur quality.

Martinsvids.net is an excellent website that contains pictures and videos, including many bygone attractions.

MouseWorld Radio at mouseworldradio.com is an internet radio station that plays sound clips, theme songs, etc.

Walt Disney World Today is a podcast on iTunes and at wdwtoday.com.

Best Site for Food Allergies:

Allergyeats.com/Disney

Best Apps to Download:

MousePerks+ identifies property-wide discounts available for Tables in Wonderland cardholders, Annual Passholders, Disney Vacation Club members, and Disney Visa cardholders.

MyDisneyExperience is the official app of Walt Disney World. Track queue lengths, look up park hours, find character meeting locations, make dining and Lightning Lane reservations, or even pre-order meals from select Disney dining locations directly through the app.

Disney World Contact Information

Accepted Currencies & Making Purchases

Once you've looked through this book, we hope you'll be ready to pull out your credit card and book your Walt Disney World vacation!

Fortunately, <u>all major credit cards are accepted</u> throughout Walt Disney World. These include Visa, Master Card, Discover Card, American Express, Diner's Club, and Japan Credit Bureau.

When determining which credit card to use for your Disney vacation, consider the perks or rewards each card offers. Check to see if there are travel advantages, such as insurance coverage on car rentals. Some cards even offer cash back or cheap financing options for large purchases.

In order to get new customers and provide an added financial incentive to visit their resorts, Disney Visa has a 0%

financing offer for 6 months when you use it to purchase your Disney vacation package (all at once, directly from Disney). We like this card, as it gives you reward dollars to use on food or souvenir purchases *during* your vacation. Apply for this card from the Disney World web site (disneyworld.disney.go.com) and get a statement credit after your first purchase.

If you are staying at a Disney hotel, Disney allows you to link a credit card to your MagicBand, so all of your purchases can be made directly with it. (We provide more details about MagicBands in the Tools and How to Use Them chapter.) Keep in mind, though, Disney has done a lot of research to determine that you are more likely to spend on *average $200* *more* during your vacation for this added "convenience."

For those who prefer to use cash, Chase ATMs are available at each Disney park. (Their locations can be found on the Disney Park Maps.) They are also at Disney hotels, shopping, and entertainment locations. If your card doesn't work in one of these, there are several nearby Sun Trust banks, the most convenient of which is an easy walk across the street from Disney Springs. Go to suntrust.com for a list of all their locations.

Walt Disney World also accepts *Google Pay* and *Apple Pay* as an added convenience for those who have this feature set up on their smart device.

Disney Dollars

There are other fun options for making purchases at Disney. Disney Dollars used to be the "official currency" of Walt Disney World. Disney discontinued the printing and sales of these fabulous bills in May of 2016, though they are still an accepted form of currency.

It is actual paper money you can use at the parks, though most who purchased them kept them as souvenirs. The currency can still be found in $1, $5, and $10 denominations (and a special $50 option that was printed for Disneyland's 50th anniversary in 2005). Each different denomination has a different character on it, like real currency. Kids love using these bills.

Since this currency is discontinued for purchase, you can only buy Disney Dollars second-hand. Ebay is an excellent resource, but be sure it is the actual Disney Dollars currency being purchased and not just "funny money!" Disneydollars.net shows each design that was produced, so check there to be sure it's authentic before buying.

Disney Gift Cards

Disney Gift Cards provide a convenient payment option. You can select from among a wide variety of unique gift card designs online at disneygiftcard.com. If you prefer, pick one up in person at any Disney retail location, including local Disney Stores in communities throughout the world.

Accepted Currencies & Making Purchases

Insider's Tip!

Package Pickup. As you make purchases at a park, there is no need for you to carry them with you all day long.

Guests staying on Disney property can have their purchases (including photos) delivered directly to their hotels.

Are you staying at an off-property hotel? No problem! You can also have your purchases held at a package pickup location (near Guest Relations just inside the entrance of each park and also at the International Gateway exit in Epcot) for easy retrieval on your way out of the park. Allow a minimum of 3 hours for purchased items to be delivered to the park entrance.

Insider's Tip!

One perk to the Disney Chase card is that you get one free printed photo each day with select Disney characters at Epcot and Hollywood Studios. At Epcot, there is a special photo shoot location in the Innoventions West building especially for this perk, and a special Star Wars meet-and-greet is in the Star Wars Launch Bay at Hollywood Studios. As this has become more popular over the past couple of years, the lines have grown, so plan to visit early in the day if you want to take advantage of this awesome bonus.

Insider's Tip!

It's a good idea for you to call and notify your credit card company of your out-of-country or out-of-state travel plans. Many credit card companies, particularly American Express, require prior notification when you are traveling. Take the time to call the one(s) you'll be using to make sure your card doesn't get put on hold during your vacation.

About the World

The Walt Disney World Resort, informally known as Walt Disney World (or just Disney World) is the largest single entertainment complex on Earth. It is located in Lake Buena Vista, Florida, just south of Orlando.

Walt Disney World has been synonymous with family fun for about 50 years. Opened on October 1, 1971, Walt Disney World Resort is the most visited vacation resort – and the largest recreational property – in the world. A phenomenal nearly <u>60 million annual visitors</u> make the trek to enjoy fun in the sun and to experience the magic this travel destination offers.

The Walt Disney World Resort has been described as exceedingly creative and meticulously clean.

Its overall design reflects a phenomenal attention to detail that has a way of making guests feel like they've been transported away from reality – much more so than any other theme park located anywhere else in the world.

Spread over more than 43 square miles (greater than 27,000 acres), Disney World spans an area larger than the island of Manhattan! In fact, the resort contains the four biggest Disney Parks ever built.

What is Disney World?

Did you know that Disney World is much more than just those four amusement parks (Magic Kingdom, Epcot, Hollywood Studios, and Animal Kingdom)?

In addition, the property abounds with fun things to do. You can cool off in the hot summer sun at two exciting water parks. Golfers can choose between four professional golf courses or two fun-themed miniature golf courses. Lovers of the outdoors appreciate the recreational vehicle campground and an equestrian facility known as Triple-D Ranch.

There is <u>little that *cannot* be done</u> on Disney property, including hiking, horseback riding, tennis, boating, and even water sports.

Sports fanatics enjoy the ESPN Wide World of Sports Complex. Disney's

Wedding Pavilion is available for those planning their nuptials (and is just one of numerous dream-wedding locations). Disney also sponsors a wildlife preserve a few miles away from the main property. This is a hidden gem, perfect for strolling around when you have a free afternoon. With all there is to do, it's no wonder some guests return year after year!

Resort Housing

You can sleep at one of 30 themed resort hotels (including Disney Vacation Club properties and villas).

Disney also maintains and runs ancillary properties, including restaurant and retail venues at Disney Springs and Disney's BoardWalk.

An astonishing number of dining and lounge facilities (close to 300!) dot across the property, including everything from snack booths to signature dining locations and numerous nightlife spots.

Transportation

Connecting all the fun, Disney's property has its own multi-lane highways, monorail, and a waterway (lake and canal) transportation system.

Brief History of Walt Disney (1901-1966)

Walter Elias Disney was born in Chicago, Illinois, on December 5, 1901. When Walt was four, he and his family moved to a farm in Marceline, Missouri, where his brother purchased some farmland.

It was here that a neighbor paid him for his first cartoon gig – he drew pictures of his neighbor's horses! Throughout his childhood, copying front-page cartoons from the newspaper honed Walt's technical skills and cemented his interest in the field. Thanks to these early childhood experiences, Walt eventually pursued the arts of animation and entertainment that we associate with the man today.

Walt's other great love was trains. His interest in locomotives began in Marceline, as well, where Walt's uncle was a railway engineer who often rambled through town on his regular run. Walt and his brother would listen closely for a special signal to know when their uncle was manning the engine.

In the early 1920s, Walt began cartooning in earnest. While his first company, *Iwerks - Disney Commercial Artists*, was short-lived, he and his brother Roy were undeterred. They landed in Hollywood three years later where they set up the cartoon studio that would eventually bring them great success.

Where did Walt's idea originate?

Walt took his family out for a fun-filled day at an amusement park one day, an experience that turned out less than spectacular. The park did not meet his personal standards or expectations, given the prices and the value received.

The idea was born to eventually develop his own family-centric entertainment venue that would have top-notch attractions and maintain the absolute highest operational standards. This dream inspired him for the rest of his life.

Because of the visit to the park earlier in his life, he was certain to keep his park spotlessly clean – which is why you will see trash cans every few steps.

Almost anywhere you look in the parks, you find employees (Cast Members) scanning for anything that needs to be tidied up. To this day, Cast Members strive to live up to Walt's dream.

Walt planned his amusement park over a period of several years as he continued to build his animation business. His dream finally morphed into the 160-acre Disneyland site in Anaheim, California.

Huge Success at Disneyland Leads to Walt Disney World Resort

Disneyland quickly became a top tourist attraction and Walt Disney dreamed of expanding on the success of his wildly popular California location. The immense – and instantaneous – commercial success of this first park sparked the visionary within Walt. He wanted to grow his revolutionary ideas and create something even bigger.

Just four years after the 1955 opening of Disneyland Resort, Walt Disney Productions started acquiring land for a second development.

Walt's concept would supplement, and build on, Disneyland's existing popularity. Once they had control of the land, they immediately began building Walt Disney World® Resort – which was to become *exponentially-larger* than Disneyland. Its flagship park, Magic Kingdom®, led the charge when it opened on October 1, 1971.

Unfortunately, Walt passed away in 1966, five years before he could see his dream fulfilled.

Insider's Note! The first edition of this book was published on October 1, 2016, which marks the first day of Walt Disney World's 45th year.

Park Expansions

Like Disneyland, the Magic Kingdom Park was also an instant success, leading to the quick planning and development of additional parks and expansions over time.

The entire recreational complex eventually became four separate park venues. The second park, Epcot, finally became a reality in 1981. The two remaining parks

"If you can dream it, you can do it."
- Tom Fitzgerald, Imagineer

opened in later years. Updates, additions, and expansions have taken place ever since, proving Walt's dream is still alive and growing.

Walt's second park vision, Epcot® Park or the "Experimental Prototype Community of Tomorrow," was an idea for a completely new "planned (utopian) community." Although the final design did not mirror Walt's original futuristic dream, Epcot was heavily-influenced by his ideas. In fact, components of the initial plans for Epcot helped designers create a real community, Celebration, Florida, in 1996. It is located just a few miles from Disney World (though no longer owned or controlled by Disney).

Disney Imagineers stayed true to Walt's design concepts for the final two theme parks, Disney's Hollywood Studios™ and Disney's Animal Kingdom® Theme Park. While one reflects Walt's love of show business, the latter reflects his admiration for live animals.

Since Disneyland opened, Disney has built and operates nine other parks and resorts *worldwide*!

Theme Park Details

MAGIC KINGDOM

There are so many fun things to do at the Magic Kingdom that you could spend all day and still not see and experience everything. This park features the most rides of all of Disney World's parks. Many people plan to spend two or three days of their vacation at the Magic Kingdom.

The Magic Kingdom follows the same model as Disneyland in California, and it has a similar layout. Prepare to be

About the World

impressed as you get to stroll down a real American Main Street (Main Street, U.S.A.) that was plucked from days gone by, over a century ago.

You will see the iconic Cinderella Castle towering above its surroundings at the far end of the street (similar to Sleeping Beauty's castle at Disneyland). If you are up for a treat, eating at Cinderella's Royal Table inside the castle will be a memorable family experience.

Your adventure continues as you travel through an exotic tropical paradise (Adventureland).

You can visit the real Old West (Frontierland), then head east along the mighty Mississippi River before finding yourself at the political foundation of the country (Liberty Square).

Next along the promenade, (or if you walk right through the castle rather than turn left at the central court) you'll enter Fantasyland, where you'll want to ride the Carrousel, catch Peter Pan's Flight, and meet your favorite princesses.

The final stop on your journey is a land (Tomorrowland) that reflects Walt's fascination with technology – including space exploration.

Fantasyland

The 2012 expansion of Fantasyland exploded the realm of make-believe, and was the largest in Disney's history. It added classic castles and brand-new adventures. You can now visit with characters like The Little Mermaid, Gaston, and Belle. The expansion included Storybook Circus, a circus-themed area with attractions like Disney's iconic Dumbo the Flying Elephant and The Great Goofini's Barnstormer, a small roller coaster perfect for youngsters. You can even meet Goofini (Goofy) across the way at Pete's Silly Sideshow character meet-and-greet.

All of the newer attractions are worth the visit. The most popular of these is The Seven Dwarfs Mine Train, a tame, though extremely fun, roller coaster. Like most primary attractions, the line will be long if you don't use Lightning Lane.

Of course, there were new dining options developed within the expansion. Most notably, the excellent Be Our Guest restaurant (inside of Beast's Castle!) is a must-do if you can get dining reservations in advance. The food is top-notch, and the atmosphere is unlike anywhere else at Walt Disney World.

The Three Mountains

Don't forget the three mountain roller coasters (those with "mountain" in the title): Space Mountain (Tomorrowland), Splash Mountain, and Big Thunder Mountain Railroad (both in Frontierland).

It is common to hear people refer to the five mountains, which include Seven Dwarfs Mine Train and Expedition Everest (Animal Kingdom). Note: You will need to have Lightning Lane reservations for Seven Dwarfs Mine Train and Space Mountain if you can't get to the park first thing in the morning. Line waits can be up to two hours on busy summer days.

EPCOT

The second Disney World theme park, Epcot, is divided into two distinct sections, Future World and World Showcase.

Future World has several educational exhibits of thrilling technologies. But it also has some very fun things. For example, you can take a ride on Test Track or experience the thrill of space exploration on Mission: Space. Small children immensely enjoy The Seas with Nemo and Friends, an underwater journey in a clam-mobile!

Travel around World Showcase in Epcot to experience the culture and cuisine of 11 different countries. It is also where kids can defeat villains in Duck Tales World Showcase Adventure (opening soon). This adventure gives kids smart phone devices to embark on an interactive scavenger hunt.

Harmonious

Don't miss the spectacular show that incorporates music, lights, lasers, drones, and fireworks each evening.

HOLLYWOOD STUDIOS

Lights, camera, action! Big screen movie magic comes to life at Disney's Hollywood Studios. Down at the end of Sunset Boulevard, look for The Twilight Zone Tower of Terror and Rock 'n' Roller Coaster Starring Aerosmith. These attractions are two of Disney World's most thrilling and exhilarating rides.

Toy Story Land is where you will meet up with Woody, Buzz, and the gang on Toy Story Midway Mania, a moving 4-D video game adventure.

Of course, no adventure is more thrilling than Star Wars. Hollywood Studios has an entire land dedicated to the franchise, called Star Wars: Galaxy's Edge, which includes one of the most innovative rides in the world, Star Wars: rise of the Resistance.

Don't forget to make dining reservations for the Sci-Fi Dine-In Theater or the high-end Hollywood Brown Derby. Children will enjoy eating at the Prime Time Cafe or the Hollywood and Vine character buffet.

At the end of your day, don't miss the must-see, nighttime Fantasmic water show and the spectacular Star Wars extravaganza, each with fantastic flames and fireworks!

ANIMAL KINGDOM

Animal Kingdom's incredible icon is the elaborately-carved Tree of Life. The trunk of the gigantic tree is home to "A Bug's Life" 3-D show. Its two primary attractions, Avatar Flight of Passage and Kilimanjaro Safaris, are real crowd-pleasers.

The most-thrilling attraction is Expedition Everest, which is a fast and exciting train-coaster that travels up snow-capped mountain peaks before heading through the dark center of the summit, bringing you face-to-face with the Abominable Snowman (also known as the Yeti). This coaster offers a couple of unique features that are unlike anything you have ever

Disney's Blizzard Beach Water Park

Blizzard Beach is a water park modeled after a winter ski resort. Its theme is that a freak snowstorm has hit Central Florida. The resulting "snow melt" makes for some of the world's most exhilarating water rides.

Guests can either ride solo or with a friend down Runoff Rapids or on one of three thrilling inner-tube slides. You can also race to the finish line on the

About the World

The Florida Project

Walt envisioned a "world" where guests could completely get away from aspects of the day-to-day grind. The idea was based on the realization that vehicle traffic and other non-Disney realities were still visible from the highest rides within the extremely popular Disneyland in Anaheim, California.

To correct this, Walt secretly purchased large tracts of land in Florida that he could combine to create an all-encompassing resort, which he called "The Florida Project." Walt Disney World is therefore an oasis from the seediness that is often associated with popular tourist areas.

Construction on the "Florida Project" ultimately began in the 1960s. Initial plans included a futuristic city called the "Experimental Prototype Community of Tomorrow," or *EPCOT*, which would have been located close to what eventually became Downtown Disney (now redeveloped into Disney Springs). However, those plans were put on hold, and the first incarnation of Walt Disney World was limited to Magic Kingdom and some hotels.

Sadly, Walt Disney died in 1966, but his dream became reality when Magic Kingdom opened in 1971. In honor of the visionary, Roy Disney named the entire "Florida Project" complex Walt Disney World.

Finding the Right Location for Disney's New World

The company performed market surveys revealing that only five percent of Disneyland's visitors came from east of the Mississippi River, where 75% of the United States population was concentrated.

Additionally, because Walt Disney did not control the property surrounding Disneyland, and because he disliked the myriad businesses springing up nearby, he was intent on finding property that would provide him exclusive control of the entire project and surrounding areas.

The new development was to be a private haven where visitors could leave the worries of their day-to-day lives. He wanted them to live – if even just during their vacation – in a dream world that could be completely orchestrated.

Walt scoped out several potential properties in the Sunshine State. He ruled out the coastal cities of Tampa and Miami due to the threat of hurricanes and the damage they cause when they first make landfall.

In November 1963, he explored the center of the state. Disney eventually settled on the Orlando-area after he flew over huge swaths of undeveloped land that had great transportation connections.

Walt ultimately selected a site near Bay Lake in the heart of Central Florida. His decision was partially based on a well-developed transportation network, including a location near the intersection of two major highways. Local governments were in the planning stages of Interstate 4, a major interstate highway, and Florida's Turnpike (toll road system). The McCoy Air Force Base (which later became Orlando International Airport) was located just east.

While most people consider the city of Orlando the home to Disney World, the resort property is actually located in the municipality of Lake Buena Vista, Florida, about 20 miles away.

Through some creative lobbying, Disney was able to form the Reedy Creek Improvement District. Consolidating the new land he had purchased under the jurisdiction of a formal government – completely governed by Walt Disney World – afforded the company rights of an incorporated Florida city.

Disney announced the plans for his revolutionary concept in the late 1960s. In order to keep land owners from withholding their property or trying to sell for more than the property was worth, he set up several companies and aliases to conduct real estate negotiations in strict privacy. The last thing he wanted was for competitors or land speculators to pick up land that adjoined his property and begin causing the problems he experienced in Anaheim.

Ultimately, Disney was able to assemble a total contiguous property of about 43 square miles (27,000 acres!) to form Walt Disney World – about the size of San Francisco (and about one and a half times the size of Manhattan Island)!

Oswald the Lucky Rabbit was created by Walt Disney and Ub Iwerks in 1927 for Universal Pictures.

Toboggan Racers. Slush Gusher is a high-speed, 90-foot-long thrilling ride for big kids. Youngsters have their own special area for splashing around, complete with waterslides and a snow-castle fountain. The park's chairlift takes you up to the top of the mountain where you can choose from several water slides, including Summit Plummet, with its 120-foot drop – the world's tallest body slide and one of the steepest anywhere on Earth!

Disney's Typhoon Lagoon Water Park

Typhoon Lagoon's backstory is that a typhoon raged through a tropical oasis, leaving shipwrecked vessels littering the area.

The park has 23 waterslides and is home to the Surf Pool, its signature attraction. Spanning a full acre, this is the largest wave pool in North America. Listen for the sound of thunder!

The waves are so big that even surfers can enjoy it. Before the park opens each morning, group surfing lessons are offered for ages eight and up. Typhoon Lagoon boasts some other popular attractions, including the brand new family ride, Miss Adventure Falls, and Humunga

Kowabunga with its extreme – near-vertical – five-story drop. Younger children love the water play area designed just for them, including Ketchakiddee Creek with its spray and play, tot-friendly action.

Other (Non-Park) Fun & Activities

In addition to their four theme parks and two water parks, Disney has many other recreational facilities.

Disney Springs

Disney Springs® is a huge shopping complex with fast service restaurants and themed, sit-down dining and entertainment. There is something to do for everyone in the family, including riding around the lake in floating cars and hovering high overhead in giant balloons. It is split into four parts: Marketplace, Town Center, The Landing, and West Side.

Cirque du Soleil performs their resident show on a nightly basis. One of the biggest draws, House of Blues, has an exciting concert venue, large restaurant, and bar.

ESPN Wide World of Sports® Complex

This huge sporting facility is a major draw for athletes and fans alike. It is where Disney hosts hundreds of professional and amateur athletic events each year. It is also the site for the Atlanta Braves' spring training, and it is home to national AAU events every summer.

Other Relaxing Recreation

Disney has championship golf courses, miniature golf courses, health and beauty spas, boating, and fishing opportunities. These activities can keep your family entertained on days you don't want to visit the theme parks.

Fort Wilderness

Fort Wilderness is Disney's campground area. It's located in a wooded area close to Wilderness Lodge, a huge resort.

Families can stay at the campgrounds overnight or just show up for a day. Some people stay for months-on-end!

If you love animals and nature, you should visit the ranch. There are wild deer roaming the property and a real ranch with horses. It's free to stop by and look.

Fort Wilderness is a tranquil, relaxing place to get away from the noise and "hustle and bustle" of the theme parks.

Tri-Circle-D Ranch

https://disneyworld.disney.go.com/recreation/tri-circle-d-ranch/

Kids of all ages love riding painted ponies on the Magic Kingdom's Prince Charming Regal Carrousel. Most have no idea they can hop into the saddles of real ponies and horses at the Tri-Circle-D Ranch at Fort Wilderness.

Have you ever wondered where the horses that pull the trolley around the Magic Kingdom live? They live in a large barn near Pioneer Hall. You can show up to say hello to them. Kids older than nine years old can also ride a trail on horseback (for a fee)!

These horses also pull horse-drawn wagons and the carriages at some of the resorts.

Adults often take romantic carriage rides on special occasions. (Around Halloween and Christmas, there is a particularly special ride on a horse-drawn wagon that is made especially for families.)

The Tri-Circle-D Ranch is located along the canals that feed into Bay Lake and the Seven Seas Lagoon. This is close to where you can rent a motorboat or canoe to play on the water. It's also a great place to fish (catch-and-release only).

Chip 'n' Dale's Campfire Sing-A-Long

This (completely free!) show is one of Disney's best kept secrets.

Each night your family can gather around a campfire, sing songs and meet Chip and Dale. There is a small fee for supplies if you'd like to join in a marsh-mallow roast and make tasty s'mores.

Bay Lake Water Fun
https://disneyworld.disney.go.com/recreation/motorized-boats

Your family can rent boats and zip around the lake. Take a mini speed boat (called a "Sea Raycer") for a spin, or get a larger pontoon boat for a relaxing day on the water.

Minimum Height and Age Required

You must be 18 years or older to rent a boat by yourself. Children 12 years old and 60 inches (5 feet tall) can steer the boat with adult supervision.
Rentals cost about $45 per half hour.

Fishing
https://disneyworld.disney.go.com/recreation/fishing/

Walt Disney World offers guided fishing excursions as well as dockside fishing. It's catch-and-release only. Give it a try. Just don't let Nemo or Dory know!

Golf, FootGolf, & Miniature Golf
https://disneyworld.disney.go.com/recreation/#/golf

If you have a passion for golf, Disney has a selection of four beginner and championship golf courses.

Reservation availability and fees vary based on the season and time of day.

The latest golf trend is footgolf — a combination of soccer and golf. Disney has a course for that!

Reservations are limited and require 90 days advanced notice. The cost starts at $20 and goes up from there.

There are also two themed mini-golf attractions, which are fun for the entire family. Winter Summerland has a Christmas-theme, while Fantasia Gardens patterns itself on the classic Disney animated film.

Each has two separate 18-hole courses for a great challenge.

Disney's Winter Summerland

When Santa Claus and his elves need to vacation, this is where they visit. Santa built these mini-golf courses as a place to relax when Christmas is over.

There are two Christmas-themed courses: Summer or Winter!

The Summer course is beach themed, complete with surf boards and castles.

It has the more challenging, trickier holes. First-timers might want to start with the easier Winter course.

As a reminder of their home at the North Pole, the elves built a second course that looks like it is covered in snow. Putt your ball around (or through) Igloos, snowmen, and even holes for ice fishing!

There is a small fee to play:

$12 for one round for kids 3-9
$14 for 10 years and older

Fantasia Gardens

Only one of the mini-golf courses here is based on the classic Disney film named Fantasia. Around the course are dancing mushrooms, hippos dancing ballet on their tiptoes, stairs made of xylophones, and even holes grouped by musical themes.

If you're up for a unique mini golf experience, the second course is specially designed to challenge even golf pros. It's a real golf course made miniature. It even has real grass and sand!

There is a small fee to play:

$12 for one round for kids 3-9
$14 for 10 years and older

Sports

If you love to play sports, there are lots of things to do around Disney World. You can stay active by riding bikes, exploring playgrounds, trekking through the forest trails at Fort Wilderness or jogging around the Boardwalk.

ESPN Wide World of Sports Complex

Sports nuts won't want to miss seeing this huge facility. It was designed as a place to play almost any sport you can imagine.

In fact, the Atlanta Braves make the baseball diamonds their spring training home. They hold games there every year in March. (And, yes, you can watch if you're in town!)

Show up any other day to watch amateur sporting events that are taking place. Tickets cost about $12 for kids 3-9 and $17 for anyone 10 years or older.

If you want to see a Major League game, you need advanced tickets. Prices vary, so have a parent call for information (407-939-4263).

The Baseball stadium has lawn seating. Bring a blanket and picnic lunch to enjoy the game.

Disney Resort Hotels

Because Disney World was designed to be fully integrated, the best way to enjoy all its offerings is to stay at one of the many hotels "on property." There are prices and amenities to fit any family budget.

High-quality furnishings, immaculately clean grounds and facilities, and attention to details will make your hotel stay feel like a home away from home.

Staying right on Disney property gives great guest benefits, including free transportation to and from the Orlando International Airport.

Free Transportation

Disney's free airport shuttle service ended in 2021. However, Disney still provides free boat, bus, monorail, or Skyliner transportation to the parks and other attractions. They even transfer your purchased merchandise from the parks directly to your room for free. Using package delivery empties your arms so that you are not weighed-down with souvenirs.

Early Theme Park Entry Benefit

Probably the best thing about staying on property is the Early Theme Park Entry (which replaced the Extra Magic Hours benefit). This perk gives you and other resort guests early access to any one of the four theme parks of your choosing for 30 minutes each morning. This allows you to get to the popular rides before other guests (who are staying at non-Disney hotels).

Disney Deluxe Resorts

Disney has nine high-end resort properties that offer uniquely-themed accommodations. Each of these provide top-notch accommodations and fine dining. Their premium recreational activities complete any vacation experience.

- Disney's Animal Kingdom Lodge
- Disney's Beach Club Resort
- Disney's BoardWalk Inn
- Disney's Contemporary Resort
- Disney's Grand Floridian Resort & Spa
- Disney's Polynesian Resort
- Disney's Wilderness Lodge
- Disney's Yacht Club Resor
- Star Wars: Galactic Starcruiser

Disney Deluxe Villa Resorts

Disney Deluxe Villa Resorts (part of the Disney Vacation Club) feature spacious accommodations. They offer amenities including living rooms and either full kitchens or kitchenettes.

- Bay Lake Tower at Disney's Contemporary Resort

- Disney's Saratoga Springs Resort & Spa
- Disney's Old Key West Resort
- Disney's Animal Kingdom Villas — Jambo House & Kidani Village
- Disney's Beach Club Villas
- Disney's BoardWalk Villas
- Boulder Ridge Villas at Disney's Wilderness Lodge
- Copper Creek Villas & Cabins at Disney's Wilderness Lodge
- Disney's Polynesian Villas & Bungalows
- Disney's Riviera Resort
- The Villas at Disney's Grand Floridian Resort & Spa

Moderate Resorts and Value Resorts

If you plan to spend all your days at the parks, you don't need to spend a lot on your hotel accommodations. The final two classes of resorts will save you money.

These resorts offer the exact same finishing touches at a fraction of the price — and customer service is just as great! Because they tend to attract families, the noise level may be higher, particularly at the Value resorts where kids are encouraged to run around and play.

Moderate Resorts

- Disney's Caribbean Beach Resort
- Disney's Coronado Springs Resort
- Disney's Port Orleans Resort – French Quarter
- Disney's Port Orleans Resort – Riverside
- The Cabins at Disney's Fort Wilderness Resort (The associated Campsites technically fall under a separate Campsite category)

Value Resorts

- Disney's All-Star Movies, Sports and Music Resorts

TRIVIAL FACTS!

- Disney washes 16,000 loads of clothing a day and dry cleans 30,000 garments.
- Each year, they serve up 10 million burgers and 6 million hotdogs, 9 million pounds of french fries and 150 tons of popcorn, and guests guzzle 75 million Coca-Cola beverages to wash it all down!
- Mickey has almost 300 different costumes.
- With over 70,000 employees, Walt Disney World is the largest single-site employer in the U.S.

- Disney's Pop Century Resort
- Disney's Art of Animation Resort

Using Your Own Car

If you decide to drive during your Disney World vacation, there are a couple of important things to know. While guests staying at any Disney resort or hotel must pay a daily parking fee, it includes standard parking at any of the theme parks.

Otherwise, parking costs $25 per day for standard spaces at the four main theme parks ($30 per day for recreational vehicles; $45-50 for preferred parking spaces).

While expensive, parking is transferable to other parks during the same day. So if you purchase Park Hopper passes, you won't have to worry about paying more than once per day for parking everywhere.

Parking at the remaining Disney recreational facilities is always free.

If you're driving your own vehicle to enjoy non-Disney experiences, remember to bring change for toll roads (or purchase a toll pass).

Sea World Orlando, Legoland Orlando, Busch Gardens Tampa, and Universal Orlando all charge a daily parking fee, which is comparable to Disney prices.

However, Universal Orlando allows guests arriving at 6 p.m. or later to park for free, except on special event evenings. This means you can enjoy Universal CityWalk (Universal's shopping, dining, and entertainment venue) in the evenings without paying for parking.

Disney Transportation Options

Boat

Disney has an extensive water transportation system. Water taxis and ferryboats are an excellent and fun way to travel around the resorts and theme parks. Magic Kingdom is accessible via water taxi from several hotel properties, including Disney's Grand Floridian Resort & Spa and Disney's Polynesian Resort. Epcot is also accessible by ferryboat from numerous resorts, including Disney's Beach Club Resort, Disney's Boardwalk Inn and Villas Resort, and the Walt Disney World Swan and Dolphin Hotels. The fun at Disney Springs is accessible by ferryboat from Disney's Port Orleans Resort, Disney's Old Key West Resort, and Disney's Saratoga Springs Resort.

Bus

Disney's convenient and complementary bus transportation system provides easy access around its massive property. Every 20 minutes, you can hop on a bus from your resort and travel to any of the theme parks or Disney Springs. While most trips are direct, there are a couple of journeys that require bus-to-bus transfers.

Monorail

A ride on the Walt Disney World Monorail System is worth the experience, even if you arrive in Orlando with your own automobile. The three-rail system makes several stops, taking guests between Epcot and Magic Kingdom, and provides transportation to the Magic Kingdom resort hotels.

Disney Skyliner

Disney created a gondola transportation system in the sky to take guests between the Hollywood Studios/Epcot area and Disney's Art of Animation, Pop Century, Riviera, and Caribbean Beach resorts.

Minnie Vans

Getting from place to place on Disney property can take quite a bit of time if you don't have your own vehicle. Disney has its own taxi service, Minnie Vans. For a fee based on distance, hire a driver with one of these whimsical 6-person vans to shuttle your party from one Disney location to another. Order your Minnie Van using the Lyft app.

About the World

About the World

Who Runs the Show?

When the Magic Kingdom opened in 1971, the Walt Disney World Resort employed about 5,500 employees. They are known as *Cast Members*, to keep employees mindful of Walt's idea that the parks would be an extension of the big screen.

Today, more than 70,000 Cast Members work together to make the magic happen. Disney World is, by far, the largest single-site employer in the United States, with around 3,700 different job classifications. Disney spends well over a billion dollars on annual payroll (almost two billion when considering added benefits).

College Students and International Support

Anyone visiting Disney will instantly recognize the huge number of college-aged and international employees. In order to meet their on-going needs, the company has a couple of related programs.

Walt Disney World College Program

Many college-aged employees are contract employees working under the *Walt Disney World College Program*. This is a Disney-sponsored college internship that is available to American college students. It is designed to help keep the Disney dream alive at a low cost while giving students real-world business experience. This program employs much of the theme park and resort "front line" Cast Members.

While working in positions related to their degree majors, students give up two semesters in college for the opportunity to travel to Orlando and help with operations.

Disney established four off-property housing communities (apartments) within 15 miles (24 km) around Walt Disney World, which are owned and operated by the company. Most students, along with other Cast Members, live in these apartment complexes while they work at the resort. The company provides efficient bus transportation between their job locations and housing. The residential needs of Cast Members are taken care of in a safe, strictly-controlled environment with tight security measures.

Walt Disney World Academic Exchange and Cultural Exchange Programs

There is also the Walt Disney World International College Program, an internship program that offers international college students (ICP's) from all over the world the same opportunity, and shared housing, just mentioned.

The Cultural Exchange Program is a 12-month exchange program that allows people from all over the world to live in America and work at one of the Disney World parks. Most of the Cast Members in Epcot's World Showcase work under this program.

Introduction

Theme parks are filled with people – just like you and your family – who took the time to book their perfect Disney vacation. Yet standing in long lines throughout the day is where you see them, hot and miserable. They spend a fortune and only make it on a handful of rides, all while baking in the Florida sun (or soaking from an unexpected downpour)!

- **The Crowds** – There are ways to get around crowds to let you see more without standing in lines. Read our valuable tips and discover how the traffic patterns within the parks vary depending on the time of day and the season you're visiting.
- **Park Fatigue** – You may not have considered how a long day in the park will affect you and your children. Learn how to prevent anyone in your party from getting exhausted.
- **The Weather** – Unless you've experienced Disney and all of its seasons, it's difficult to understand how the extreme weather can vary. Time your visit to avoid severe conditions, and prepare to deal with the heat or the occasional cold snap.
- **Hotel Accommodations** – We provide clear details and comparisons of on-property versus off-property hotels. You will easily understand what is included with the rate and which option best suits your vacation needs. Most importantly, we identify the hidden costs that can squeeze your budget and cause you to miss out on other experiences.
- **Transportation** – Use our pointers to navigate around Orlando. Learn how to get around Walt Disney World property with ease.

Guide Book Layout

This book is organized into several sections. We start off with pre-vacation planning and preparation advice. To get you started thinking about your upcoming fun, we share over **50 free** (yes, *free!*) things you can do that can be an integral part of your overall experience. We even share information about non-theme park fun to include in your vacation.

You will be amazed at all the things you can do without ever leaving Disney property. Tourists are often surprised to find out the many free or very low-cost options that can consume entire days of their vacation without having to set foot inside one of Disney's parks.

Additionally, look for our *Insider's Tips* throughout the book. These provide valuable insights and advice.

If you have young children, you will want to review our *Traveling with Small Children* section. We take great care to address the needs of families with smaller children. If you are traveling with family members who have special needs, you will find that Disney specializes in accommodating them all.

Each theme park is detailed in its own section. The summary of each park is followed by a brief description of its attractions, shows, and events. Discover behind the scenes tours and activities designed to entertain adults and children alike, including special games. Use our easy restaurant guide to learn where to eat and what you can expect to pay for your meals.

Introduction

Of course, no park visit would be complete without meeting characters. We share current character meet-and-greets in each park, so you know where to find your favorites.

Guests with special interests will find that Walt Disney World is far more than just its four main theme parks. Our remaining sections cover all of the great sports and entertainment options on-property. In Volume II, we provide detailed walkthrough descriptions to enhance your experience.

Prepare to Explore

Keep in mind that Walt Disney World, with its vast and expansive properties, is designed for explorers. Unlike Disney parks elsewhere, Walt Disney World offers fun and entertainment in unlikely places, even outside of their paid admission venues. We share where readers can find all the hidden gems.

Disney is really a great big show. As part of the "production," they use words and phrases unique to the theme park culture. The next page provides some terms that are particular to Disney. They are words that you might read in this book or hear during your visit.

Happy planning!

Insider Tips to Get You Started with Your Vacation

What To Know Before You Go!

The tips we share are to *improve* your experience. However, there are some global guidelines that everybody should try to follow. These are the overriding rules to guide your initial planning and ensure you are well prepared for your trip.

Research When to Visit

Figure out the best days and seasons to visit the park. See our Crowds at the Parks section. In it, we help you narrow

Disney Credit Card

Consider obtaining a Disney *Chase* credit card. These credit cards offer some great perks for Disney guests. You will get very favorable 6-month, 0%-financing for your dream vacation.

Chase includes a nice added bonus that is a deal-maker: a free printed character photo each day you visit **Epcot and Hollywood Studios**! Your Epcot meet-and-greet picture will be with one of the original, "Fab Five" characters (Mickey, Minnie, Donald, Goofy, and Pluto) in the Innoventions building. You also get to meet one of your favorite Star Wars characters for a photo opportunity in the new Star Wars Launch Bay at Hollywood Studios. Keep in mind, this is an exclusive meet-and-greet (with free printed photo) reserved only for Disney Chase card holders.

Your card also gets you discounts at select merchandise locations, along with Disney Reward Dollars you can use to pay for food and souvenirs on your trip. The Disney Chase debit card also includes most of these benefits. To apply, visit disneyworld.disney.go.com/visa-card/promotion.

Finally, expect to get a credit of $50 to $200 on your first statement (depending on which card option you choose), after your initial purchases.

Helpful Glossary of Disney Slang

Adventure or Attraction	Ride or Theater Show
Attraction Host	Ride Operator
Audience	Crowd
Backstage	Behind the scenes area (for Cast Members only) and out of view of guests
Cast Member	Disney Employee
Character	Disney character played by a Cast Member
Costume	Attire or Uniform
Dark Ride	Indoor Attraction
Day Guest or General Public	Any guest not staying at Disney resort
Face character	Face is not covered by costume
Fur	Head-covered costume
Greeter	Cast Member at the attraction entrance or supporting a character at a meet-and-greet
Guest	Disney Customer
Hidden Mickeys	Silhouette or "front outline" of Mickey's face that is located subtly in a building, ride, or other design. These can be found almost anywhere.
Lightning Lane	A separate attraction entrance that allows you to bypass the standby lines, available for purchase individually (Tier 1 attractions) or through the Genie+ system (Tier 2 attractions)
On Stage	In view of customers
Pre-show	Entertainment that takes place prior to feature presentation
Resort Guest	Guest staying "on property" at a Disney resort
Role	Cast Member's Position or Job
Soft opening	Opening of a park attraction prior to its stated opening date
Transitional Experience	The element of a queue or pre-show that provides a storyline or information that complements the attraction or is essential to fully understanding the attraction

down – to the week – a time that works for you while avoiding the crowds and (hopefully!) inclement weather. The calendars we provide can be printed out to keep handy while you confer with others in your party.

Considering school and work schedules, some families have strict limits on the dates they can take their vacations. Don't worry if your visit won't coincide with our recommended dates. We will help you navigate the parks even during the busiest season.

Seven Ways to Save

Disney World isn't cheap, but there are plenty of ways to save on everything from accommodations to meals with your favorite characters.

1. Visit during the Off-peak Season

During the slow season, Disney offers up to 30 percent discounts (or even free dining!) for standard packages. Discount packages are usually advertised during the month of January for stays into spring, and early fall for stays into November. Visit disneyworld.disney.go.com/special-offers to see the current featured offer.

2. Stay in a Room with a Kitchen

While you will probably pay a little more for a suite or villa with a kitchen, you'll save by eating in your room – or by preparing meals to take with you into the park.

3. Eat Outside the World

If you have your own vehicle, you can take a break away from the hustle and bustle of the parks and go to a nearby restaurant. Off-property restaurants are generally less costly. Consider buffets, sandwiches, or take out ("take away") to get your belly filled at a low price. You'll save by avoiding some costly meals at restaurants throughout Disney World, and unlike eating at a full-service establishment,

you'll be able to save an additional 20% from expected gratuities!

4. Stay at a Value Resort

Disney's Value Resorts (Pop Century Resort and All Star Movies Resort) offer on-property accommodations at the most reasonable rates for families of four or less.

5. Save on Disney Character Breakfasts

If you are going to have a meal with Disney characters, remember that it is always cheaper at breakfast time than dinner. Children are fresh, the meal gets you going for the day, and you are up bright and early to start your day!

6. Set a Strict Souvenir Budget

Even though everyone wants a monogrammed Mickey hat, Elsa dress, or Cinderella slippers, set a reasonable amount for each child (and adult) and stick to those limits! There are things you will need to buy, such as a character autograph book, if you don't bring one with you. Keep in mind, Disney has merchandise that is unique to their parks, such as themed commemorative picture frames, that are designed to grab your purse strings (or tug at your MagicBand)!

7. Find the Deals

Disney World hotel deals sometimes include discounted theme park tickets or meals. Many off-property hotels offer complimentary transportation. Pay attention to discounts, and don't be afraid to ask about deals when you call any local business you plan on using during your stay.

Over 50 Freebies to Start Your Vacation

There are not many things that Disney gives away absolutely free. The following is a comprehensive list of the wallet-saving and fun things you can do for no additional cost. Read through the guidebook if you need more specific details.

Included with Park Admission

Water – Simply ask for a cup of ice water at any Disney-owned location that serves fountain beverages. The water comes from the beverage machine filtered and chilled. The alternative is expensive at $3 per bottle (+ tax!) or $5.50 for premium Smart Water. This adds up fast for a family of four or five to rehydrate a few times per day!

Colorful Disney Souvenir Pins – You can request a free souvenir pin/ button to attach to your lapel or hat that commemorates the purpose of your vacation. They are available at any Guest Relations location and in some retail shops. You just have to ask.

Special Occasions
- 1st Visit!
- Happily Ever After
- I'm Celebrating!
- Happy Birthday!

Character Phone Calls – While you're picking up your pins at Guest Relations, ask if you can get a phone call for whatever occasion you're celebrating. The Cast Member will get a character on the line to give you a very "special" greeting.

Professional Photography – Disney *PhotoPass* photographers are everywhere throughout Disney parks. While the system is designed to sell you additional pictures, they will also snap a family photograph using your personal camera. That means you get the same professional-quality poses at the **best photo opp locations**, without having to pay for a Memory Maker package. If you want a photograph taken almost anywhere of the entire family, don't hesitate to ask any Cast Member. They are always accommodating. Barring one of them, most other guests will certainly oblige your request.

Character Autographs – You don't need to purchase an expensive autograph book to take advantage of this benefit. In fact, if you print out your favorite princess or character picture at home to have it signed, you are likely to get more face time with the characters of choice. In our Traveling with Small Children section, we give complete details on how to enhance this experience for youngsters. We offer tips and tricks to make signature collecting fun and exciting for the entire family. We also provide a detailed listing of all the characters, including where – and when – you can find them. (If you miss a character autograph, you can contact Disney after your vacation and ask them to send a signed photo of that important character!)

Nikon Fun Spots – Look for specially marked locations that are ideal for taking pictures. These signs highlight the best scenery to stage a memorable photograph.

Vacation Planning App – The MyDisneyExperience app is completely free. It is an all-in-one tool that allows you to reserve your vacation, Lightning Lane selections, dining, and more. (See our Tools and How to Use Them section for more details.) Included in the app is Disney's MagicMobile, a free tool you can use as your park ticket, hotel key, and more. You can even customize the look of it!

Play Disney Parks App – The Play Disney Parks app is another free perk. This one is used to unlock special trivia and adventures in each of the theme parks. Just check the app as you walk through the property to see what's available (such as Duck Tales World Showcase Adventure in Epcot)!

Just for Kids

Free Theme Park Admission for Tots – Children two years old and younger get free theme park admission. While they may not remember the experience, there is plenty to entertain the wee ones, and our next freebie makes bringing them along a potential huge advantage to families

with older children. Also, when your child is older, these pictures may become his or her most cherished "baby" photos. Our special *Traveling with Small Children* section shows you how to maximize the safety, comfort, and overall experience for the little ones.

Rider Switch – If you have a child in your family who is *too small* – or *becomes too afraid* – to go on a ride, don't fret. Disney has a program that allows one parent to wait with the child while the rest of the party goes on any ride. This is actually a huge benefit, as the first adult who goes on a ride then switches with the other parent. The rest of the party gets to go on the ride with the second parent **again** <u>WITHOUT the extra wait in line</u>.

Stickers – Certain locations, such as **Cosmic Ray's Starlight Café** and **Monsters Inc. Laugh Floor** at Magic Kingdom and the Fort Wilderness boats sometimes have stickers to hand out. And you can always get complementary stickers from any <u>Disney Vacation Club</u> kiosk throughout the property.

Epcot Exclusives

Soda Samples – Club Cool in Epcot has samples of soda from around the world, and there's no limit to how many samples you are allowed to enjoy.

E-Postcards –Locations throughout Epcot let you send either a picture or video postcard via email. Look for the kiosks after riding Spaceship Earth, Mission: Space, and Test Track, as well as inside the Mexico Pavilion. Children tend to enjoy taking time working with the kiosks and developing a proper family message.

While these are a great way to remember a trip, they do not replace text messaging for speed. Just be aware that, for whatever technical or business reasons, it often takes days (and sometimes weeks!) to receive your postcard, so this is better suited as a memento of your trip, rather than a "Wish You Were Here" postcard to a friend.

KidCot **Cards** – KidCot is a program of fun and educational things for kids to do. Children receive a Ziploc bag with commemorative fact card at each KidCot location that is found in each of the Epcot World Showcase pavilions.

The Cast Member manning the station will also put a stamp on the card. In China, Japan, and Morocco, they'll even spell your child's name in their foreign alphabet. We provide more information about this and other special attractions for children in the *Epcot* section.

Magic Kingdom Exclusives

Sparkling Hair Glitter – Your little prince or princess can look especially regal if you go to Harmony Barber Shop or Castle Couture and ask to get sprinkled with pixie dust. If it is not too busy, your children will enjoy the diversion, and there is no cost. You can also go to Guest Relations and ask for a bag of pixie dust to do your own sprinkling.

Candy Samples – At the **Magic Kingdom Confectionary** on Main Street, you sometimes find a sign up, near the cotton candy maker, with a "secret" password. Say the word to the cotton candy maker to receive a free sample. The **Ghirardelli** chocolate shop at Disney Springs also offers free chocolate samples each time you enter the door.

Jungle Cruise Map – When your boat returns to the station after the ride and you disembark, ask a nearby Cast Member about getting a map of the ride. There are a limited number available each day, so it's best to ask for it as early in the day as

possible. Make sure you ask for the Guest Skipper Card (see below) at the same time.

Specialty Ride Cards – At the Barnstormer roller coaster within the Magic Kingdom, tell the Cast Member if it's your child's first roller coaster experience. They sometimes have a commemorative card to hand out. Other specialty cards you can request (but aren't always available) include a "Guest Skipper" card on the Jungle Cruise (just for helping to drive the boat) and an authentic "driver's license" at Tomorrowland Speedway.

Hollywood Studios Exclusives

Disney Historian Magical Moment – Visit the *Walt Disney Presents* attraction in Hollywood Studios. As you enter, ask the Cast Member if he has any trivia for you. He will produce a card with questions for you to complete while discovering details about Walt's life throughout the museum. Once you have answered all of the questions, proceed to the back, and give your completed form to the Cast Member located there. You will receive a nice "Disney Historian Magical Moment" card as a memento, and you will be allowed to sign a very exclusive guest book to commemorate the moment.

Free Dessert – Visit *Backlot Express* for a meal at any time throughout the day. If you receive a rare "magic tray" with your meal, you will also be given a free dessert! (This only happens to a handful of lucky guests each day.)

Animal Kingdom Exclusives

Wilderness Explorer Club – Kids and adults can join this special club at several kiosk locations throughout the Animal Kingdom. You get a free booklet to help you complete tasks, which ends up being a great commemorative souvenir of your trip.

No Park Admission Required!

Transportation/Trading Cards – These are small trading cards (similar to baseball cards) that Disney's transportation drivers have available to hand out to guests. They are one of Disney's best kept secrets. Check with transportation drivers on Disney buses, boats, etc. to see if they have any available cards with them that day. You can also catch African "Goodwill Ambassadors" at the Animal Kingdom Lodge Hotel who sometimes carry free trading cards to give out with information about their homeland.

Disney Boat, Monorail, & Bus Transportation for Fun – Disney provides some unique transportation choices for no charge to visitors. Aside from the buses, which you can pick up at any hotel, park, or Disney Springs, you can also ride the Disney boat and monorail transportation. There is no better way to cool off and relax after a hot day than a jaunt across the lake. Additionally, the Epcot monorail provides a stunning overhead view from inside the park, and you don't need to pay for park admission to see it! In case you missed where we mentioned in above, don't forget to ask Disney's transportation drivers if they have any *trading cards* available to give out to youngsters.

Park Guidemaps – You can pick up a *Guidemap* for each park (and Disney Springs) at any Guest Relations or Disney resort lobby. Of course, they are also available at stations as you enter the parks. Not only do the maps guide you through your vacation, they also make great mementos.

Autographed Photos – If you don't have the time to meet each character, contact Walt Disney World Guest Relations (see contact info above) and ask them to send you an autographed photo of your favorite character.

Disney Resort Extras

Hotel Recreation – Check with the front desk of each Disney hotel for a *Recreation and Activity Guide*, which outlines fun events held each day at that hotel. For instance, Port Orleans French Quarter Hotel holds a daily *Mardi Gras* parade. If you want a set of authentic Mardi Gras beads for the parade, you can often find a Cast Member giving them out around the hotel. While these activities are designed for the benefit of hotel and resort guests, many of them can be experienced when you visit a property for your meal reservations or other scheduled event (no questions asked).

Fireworks – You don't have to pay park admission to experience some of the nightly fireworks shows. The monorail hotels and Disney's BoardWalk have excellent viewing locations for the Magic Kingdom and Epcot fireworks, respectively. Additionally, the audio from the Magic Kingdom show is piped in for visitors sitting along the beaches at Disney's Polynesian and Grand Floridian properties to enjoy. (You do not need to be a guest staying at the hotel to take part.)

Electric Water Pageant – One of the advantages of watching the Magic Kingdom fireworks from a monorail hotel is the opportunity to watch the nightly parade of lighted floats on the Seven Seas Lagoon. Depending on the resort from which you choose to view the parade, this water show can be seen shortly before or shortly after the fireworks.

Holiday Decorations – It's not just the parks that get decked out for the holidays.

The resorts also get in on the action. For instance, Disney's Contemporary, Grand Floridian, BoardWalk Inn, and Beach Club Hotels all have giant gingerbread displays, most of which also offer sweet treats for sale. Fort Wilderness Campground is also aglow each year from tourists decorating their RVs and camping spaces. Anyone can visit and walk around to see the displays, but you can also pay to go on a wagon or sleigh ride that shows you around the property.

New Year's Eve Souvenirs – Several locations both inside the parks and at the hotels, including Port Orleans French Quarter Hotel, have New Year's Eve parties, where you can celebrate in a gloriously festive fashion. You may get free hats, beads, and other trinkets at these parties to commemorate the annual event.

Other Entertainment – Three hotels (Disney's Grand Floridian, Port Orleans French Quarter, and Port Orleans Riverside hotels) offer live music and entertainment on select evenings in their lounges. There is also a piano entertainer in the lobby of Disney's Grand Floridian Resort hotel who plays most days (no purchase necessary).

Resort Maps – Ask the lobby Cast Member of any hotel for a map of the resort property. Each property has a colorful map with its own personality, which makes a great scrapbooking keepsake. They also depict the location of the nearest bus stops.

Parking – It's always free for non-hotel guests to park at Disney Resort hotels with a valid dining reservation (excluding *Swan* & *Dolphin*), making each unique property an excellent choice for exploration and dining when you're not in the parks. In addition, the two Disney water parks, both Disney miniature golf courses, conventional golf locations, Disney Springs, and Disney's BoardWalk also offer free parking.

Valet Parking for Disabled Guests – The only thing better than free parking is free valet parking! Guests with a disabled parking pass (permit) can receive complementary valet parking at the Deluxe Disney hotels. Of course, you may feel obligated to tip the valet attendant (standard $2 to $5), but this is a great option if disabled parking spaces are scarce.

Marshmallow Roasts – Several Disney Resort hotels have evening campfires where guests can enjoy free roasted marshmallows. These events happen just before the "Movies Under the Stars" begin at the following resorts:
- Animal Kingdom Lodge
- Animal Kingdom Villas – Jambo House
- Animal Kingdom Villas – Kidani Village
- Beach Club
- Boardwalk Inn
- Caribbean Beach
- Contemporary
- Coronado Springs
- Grand Floridian
- Old Key West
- Polynesian Village
- Port Orleans French Quarter
- Port Orleans Riverside
- Saratoga Springs
- Wilderness Lodge
- Yacht Club
- The Cabins at Fort Wilderness
- The Campsites at Fort Wilderness

Movies Under the Stars – Each Disney Resort hotel plays an outdoor movie on select nights (weather permitting). Anybody visiting the hotel can sit down and enjoy the movie free of charge. Find the current schedule

Over 50 Freebies to Start Your Vacation

at buildabettermousetrip.com/wdw-outdoor-movie-schedule.

Animal Kingdom Lodge Hotel Exclusives

Day & Night Vision Viewing of Wild Animals – Many people don't realize the Animal Kingdom Lodge Hotel has real live African animals roaming around on-property. Anybody can stop in to see them (from a safe distance). And after dusk, a host provides high-tech night vision goggles to watch nocturnal activities.

Fort Wilderness Campground Exclusives

Campfire Sing-Along with Chip 'n' Dale – Sit around the campfire and enjoy singing and dancing with these loveable characters each evening at Fort Wilderness Campground.

Walking/Jogging/Wilderness Trails – Many of the Disney Resort Hotels have excellent trails. The Wilderness Trail from Wilderness Lodge to Fort Wilderness Campground is especially nice. Not only can you expect to see non-aggressive live animals along the way, including families of wild deer, but the trail ends at the **Tri-circle D Ranch** horse stables and outdoor stalls located at the Fort Wilderness Campground. You can view live horses and ponies and maybe even pet one (or pay a little extra money to go on a ride).

Real Horses – Fort Wilderness is where all the beautiful Disney World horses are kept and maintained. If you go early in the day, most of them are still on hand before they have started their daily chores around the property. However, you will find some horses at the outdoor stalls at any time of the day. If you are lucky, you will be able to pet one on the nose. Cast

Members are usually not around *in force*, and when they are, they are busy taking care of the animals. If you are there early enough, you will be able to watch as the big animals are loaded up to travel from their homes to Main Street, U.S.A. for their trolley car trips.

(As an aside, the Cast Members who you see actually working with the horses are the same ones responsible for their daily care. Disney horses [and all other animals!] are well-taken care of and quite happy.)

Grand Floridian Hotel Exclusives

Rise & Shine Yoga Classes – At 8:15 am each Tuesday and Thursday, guests can enjoy a free yoga class near Building 8 at Disney's premier deluxe resort.

Non-Resort Entertainment, Tours, Events, and Excursions

Entertainment, Dining, & Shopping – Visiting **Disney Springs** and **Disney's BoardWalk** is free. (Parking at the BoardWalk may be limited to paid valet parking during busy times if you don't have a valid dining reservation.) Both locations offer excellent options for dining and shopping, along with some free entertainment. Magicians and other performers grace the BoardWalk each evening with multiple performances.

Expect to hear live music or see an amateur act perform while visiting Disney Springs. It even offers free events throughout the year, such as the Festival of Masters Art Weekend in November and holiday entertainment, including a free visit with Santa Claus from mid-November through December.

Guided Tours – The daily BoardWalk Ballyhoo Guided Tour starts at *Disney's BoardWalk Inn* and is absolutely free. It leaves at 9 a.m., so check in no later than

8:45 a.m. at the *Belle Vue Lounge* if you wish to join the tour.

Special Honors

Veterans Honor – Veterans can go to Guest Relations at the Magic Kingdom to request to be the "Veteran of the Day" if one has not already been chosen. The veteran gets to help with the flag lowering ceremony when the formal Disney color guard *retires the colors* (takes down the flag) each evening just before sundown. The honored veteran also receives a certificate to commemorate the occasion.

Special Veterans Honor - On three US federal holidays (Memorial Day, Veterans Day, and Independence Day), Magic Kingdom Cast Members who are also military veterans will come to the flag to be specially honored in a moving ceremony that is worth watching. It is not uncommon for a military fly-over to take place right above Main Street, U.S.A.

Family of the Day – Early birds definitely have it made at Disney. Each park chooses a family of the day just before park opening. The honor includes being part of the opening ceremony and parades (at Magic Kingdom), a picture with opening characters, as well as special ride access. Unfortunately, only one family gets this fun each day.

At the Parks

Baby Care Centers – As a free service to parents with small children, each park has a quiet, air conditioned location where you can take your child to rest or nurse. These centers feature clean changing tables and peaceful nursing rooms. Toddlers enjoy the relaxing storybook area. Diapers and other supplies are available for purchase.

First Aid Centers – You can pick up aspirin and bandages or receive minor first aid care for no charge in every park. Medically-trained staff are on hand to assist guests with special matters. This area also has a very tranquil, cool place for guests who need to relax and get out of the sun.

Wi-Fi & Electronic Device Charging Stations – Free Wi-Fi is now available throughout the parks and hotels on-property. Fortunately, there are also places to plug in your mobile device if the extra usage drains the battery. Just look for an outlet near your table at most counter service restaurants or one of the D-Zones (see next).

Relaxation Areas – Known as *D-Zones*, there are a few areas meant purely for relaxation. They typically include a comfortable place to sit down and take a snack break. These areas may also have food and drink carts or kiosks as well as electronic device charging stations.

The concept for the D-Zone relaxation areas began at Magic Kingdom with the introduction of a *Tangled* area, near the restrooms in *Fantasyland*. There is also an indoor, big top area in *Storybook Circus* (in the newest area of Fantasyland).

The idea is for people to have a space to cool down, charge their all-important devices, and to take a break from some of the hustle and bustle of the park.

Restaurants (Meals and Libations)

Drink Refills – While technically not completely free, given the high price of soft drinks at theme parks, you will appreciate this tip by the end of each day. With your soft drink purchase, at least one location in each park has self-serve beverage stations where you can freely refill your coffee, cocoa, or soda. These are offered at the following restaurants:

Fountain Refill Locations

Animal Kingdom - *Restaurantosaurus* and *Satu'li Canteen*

Hollywood Studios - *Backlot Express*

Epcot - *Sunshine Seasons* and *Electric Umbrella*

Magic Kingdom - Tortuga Tavern

Recipes – If you eat something enjoyable at any restaurant, ask your server if the recipe is available. You can also email Disney customer service after your trip, and someone will let you know in a couple of days whether or not they can give you the recipe. Not all recipes are available, though, as some specialty chefs want to keep theirs secret. There are also websites where visitors share Disney recipes, such as wdwrecipes.com and disneyfoodblog.com.

Free Dessert – If you're celebrating an anniversary or birthday, check with Sunshine Seasons and Liberty Inn at Epcot. You may find a Cast Member willing to give you a free treat.

Free Birthday Meals! – While not technically a Disney-specific tip, and one that most readers may also be aware of, many restaurants in the area around Disney World offer free birthday meals if you sign up for their e-clubs. Most notably, Landry's Select Club provides $25 to use at any of its restaurants (including Rainforest Café and T-Rex at Disney Springs!) There is a $25 membership fee, which you get back immediately as a credit to use at the restaurant. Earl of Sandwich at Disney Springs also offers a free brownie to the birthday boy or girl. Of course, it does not hurt to mention your special day (e.g. birthday, anniversary or other) at any restaurant. You may be surprised at what special treatment you get.

Download Our Free, Comprehensive Budget/Planning Tools At:

bit.ly/DisneyPlanners

First Considerations

Planning a vacation to Walt Disney World brings with it many decisions. Once you choose your travel dates, start with the next most important questions.

- Where will you stay?
- How many days will you want to visit the parks?
- Will you go to the parks every day?
- What will you include in your daily plan?
- Will you get up early to get to the parks at opening time?

Advance Planning is Key - The Early Bird Catches the Mouse

Start planning your trip at least seven months in advance. It doesn't take seven months to actually plan it – *we promise* – but that gives you time to take full advantage of all the benefits if staying on-property.

There are many benefits to staying on Disney property. Complete details are provided later, so we won't delve into them all here. You will pay a premium for your hotel stay, but you will save in time, hassle, and parking fees. (Guests staying on-property get to use free Disney transportation – even to and from the airport!)

On-site guests can also start reserving portions of their vacation as much as 60 days in advance (2 months and 10 days). If you choose to stay on-property, this advanced planning will pay off handsomely.

Plan to have restaurant reservations in place up to 60 days in advance (especially necessary for signature and premium restaurants). You may need to keep checking daily to get special restaurant reservations, especially if you are traveling during a peak period and want seating at popular restaurants at busy daily mealtimes.

Regardless of where you stay, you must purchase park admission long before your trip to ensure you get park reservations on the days you want. This requires you to determine the total number of days you plan to visit and know which parks you intend to see.

Plan to schedule your park reservations as far in advance as possible. This is especially important if you're traveling during any holiday, as park reservations fille up fast!

Park reservations can be made very early. The system currently allows reservations for about a year in advance. You can only reserve as many days as the number of days on your park pass. If you have an annual pass, you are limited to three to five reservations at any one time, depending on the type of annual pass.

Have a Daily Plan

There is so very much to see and do. Have your notes and plans ready to go so that you don't find yourself wasting time making decisions throughout the day.

Give copies of your notes and schedules to everyone in your party.

A plan will make it easy to meet up if adults and teen children want to split off from the rest of the group. There is no reason to be confused about what it is everyone wants to experience. It will also make it easy for alternate plans to mesh together so that family time is maximized.

- Plan when you will be waking up and when you need to be on your way each day.
  - If you're a family of early birds, be familiar with each park's opening process. (See each theme park's section for details about when to arrive and what to expect first thing in the morning.) Know how to navigate the parks.
- Have your transportation method (with times and pick-up locations) figured out.
- Include the times and types of meals you want to eat, and figure

into your schedule time for rest and snack breaks.

- When creating your daily schedule, have alternates available, including what happens if you get to a park late. (What will you skip without regret or leave to experience on a subsequent visit?)
- Make sure your young children have sufficient times scheduled for taking potty, snack, and water breaks.
- Schedule down times to rest and relax away from the hustle and bustle.
- Determine if your children are tall enough to go on all the rides or are old enough to ride alone. This will greatly affect your travel plans. Children seven and under are not allowed to go on any ride alone, but some rides (such as Kali River Rapids at the Animal Kingdom) require *one adult per child*.
- If anyone in your party has physical limitations, help them understand the process for moving about the parks.

Create a Budget

Start a detailed list of vacation expenses as soon as possible. The earlier you do this,

Insider's Tip!

If you choose to stay off-property, pay attention to how you will get to the parks. Most "free" shuttle buses don't even pick you up until the parks are already opening, and then most of them only travel to the Ticket and Transportation Center. This means you must transfer to yet another bus to make it to your park of choice each day! In fact, the vast majority of Disney-area hotels charge a "resort fee" of $15 or more (up to $40 per night!) to cover the cost of this mode of transportation. So, you'll be paying for it in addition to your hotel rates. Check the fine print when comparing final prices.

Insider's Tip!

If you don't get the estaurant reservations you really want on your first try, check back once (or twice) each day. Reservations often open up, as other families modify their plans. If you missed out on any Lightning Lane reservation for a ride that you simply have to do, plan to visit those attractions very early in the day, before the wait times get too long.

the earlier you can begin a savings plan to reduce monetary stress.

Download our free budget worksheet at: bit.ly/DisneyPlanners

Make the Most of Your Days

There is nothing worse than feeling like your entire day was wasted waiting in queues. To that end, sleeping in late is never a good idea. You will end up getting to the parks each day when the crowds are building and heat is at its worst and, therefore, only experience a fraction of what you could if you had just gotten up earlier. When it comes to Disney, the early mouse definitely gets the worm!

Eat breakfast early, well before the park is scheduled to open. While character breakfasts are a better value than other character meals, they take a long time and typically cost you the chance to get to the park before the crowd rushes in. (Save your character meal for a non-park day.)

Be prepared to get to the park gates about 30 minutes before the scheduled park opening (45-60 minutes during peak periods). This means you need to account for transportation time, parking time, and time to take the tram (plus the monorail in the case of the Magic Kingdom).

Guests of the Magic Kingdom monorail resorts have a bit of an advantage here. The monorail typically starts running from The Transportation and Ticket Center (TTC) an hour before park opening. The Resort monorail (which takes guests from those hotels to the park) usually starts running around 6:30 a.m., though, or roughly 90 minutes prior to park opening, giving those guests a full 30-minute advantage (not to mention their early entry advantage).

There's a separate line at the TTC for the Resort monorail you can use, or if that line is too long, take the short walk over to the adjacent Polynesian Resort, where you can usually get on the monorail with little or no wait.

Of course, the other big advantage Disney hotel guests have is the Early Theme Park Entry option. Every day, on-site guests get into one of the parks 30 minutes before anybody else. This gives them a chance to experience several rides with virtually no wait.

When it is time for the park to open to the public, Disney sometimes opens the gates a little early to allow guests to shop before the rides are active, giving you a little bonus time in the parks. (The gates always open early at Magic Kingdom, so guests can view the Opening Ceremony in front of the castle.)

The reason you want to be at the park so early is because there is generally a two hour window from 8 a.m. to 10 a.m. when the park is only a small fraction of its capacity. You nearly always get more rides done within this two hour window than the entire rest of the day. No joke.

Epcot's opening is different than the other parks, as its two sections open at different times. Future World opens earlier in the morning (usually 8 or 9 a.m.), whereas World Showcase doesn't open until 11 a.m. Conversely, some of the Future World attractions, such as those in Innoventions close early, at 7 p.m.

During off-season, parks may not open until 9 or 10 a.m., in which case the amount of time to enjoy the parks to yourself is limited, but the overall lighter crowd often makes up for this.

It can take three times longer to get on a ride after 10:30 a.m. than before 10:00 a.m, and the crowds hit their peak beginning around 1 p.m.

Eat snacks throughout the morning and early afternoon, rather than sit down for a meal. Restaurants get busiest for lunch between 11:30 a.m. and 2:15 p.m., so plan to eat a late lunch/early dinner, then snack your way through the evening.

Plan to break for your sit-down meal mid-afternoon (around 4 to 4:30 p.m.) to get away from the crowds and heat. You will come back refreshed and ready for more, while the other guests have worn themselves out.

Most people take a dinner break around 6 p.m., and restaurants are busiest from about 6 to 9 p.m. This is a great time for you to start getting back on rides. The lines will still be fairly long on busy days, but the heat will be less intense. (The hottest part of the day is around 3 to 5 p.m.)

Other great ride times are during parades and fireworks, as the crowds congregate on the streets, leaving many popular attractions wide open!

For Hollywood Studios, this often means you can get on Tower of Terror with little to no wait, while people are in the early evening showing of Fantasmic.

For Magic Kingdom, nearly every ride but Seven Dwarfs Mine Train and Space Mountain clears out while people watch fireworks.

Unfortunately, Epcot's fireworks start when the park closes, so there is no ride opportunity there.

Animal Kingdom doesn't have fireworks, but it does have an evening show at the Tree of Life that can help clear out the queues.

If you plan to leave a park immediately after a parade or fireworks show, or if you plan to close out a park, expect to get caught in huge crowds leaving at the same time. You may wait up to an hour to get on a bus or monorail. In extreme circumstances, the wait can be much longer. If you rely on off-property shuttle transportation, this could mean you will miss your shuttle.

However, parks always leave their merchandise locations open later than park hours. We recommend you stroll through the shops and enjoy yourself while waiting for the crowds to clear, rather than try to fight your way through. Keep in mind, the shops will be busy as shoppers make last-minute purchases, but those frenzied people clear out fairly quickly.

If you're leaving the park earlier, right after a parade or fireworks, position yourself near the park exit to make sure you're at the front of the crowd.

Typical Daily Schedule

Arrive Early – Get a Good Night's Rest and Don't Sleep In (Too Late)!

After waking up and getting a filling breakfast, plan to arrive early at the park – even before opening. We know it's your vacation, but this one tip will vastly improve your experience.

As mentioned previously, early morning hours are the best for getting on popular rides without Lightning Lane reservations with little wait.

Get to sleep early at night so that rising early is not a hassle for your family. Stay well-rested. There is nothing worse than starting a day off with parents and children already getting tense and on one-anothers' nerves. And, it is not fair to

Insider's Tip!

There are times when an attraction's stand-by queue is just as quick as its Lightning Lane queue. If that's the case, use the stand-by queue, so you can see any unique features built in for waiting guests. (Lightning Lane queues usually bypass these neat interactive features.) If you love the ride, you can still use your Genie+ reservation to experience it a second time!

Insider's Tip!

Buffet restaurants at Disney that serve both lunch and dinner typically allow their last lunch reservations just after 3 p.m. If you get one of these late lunch reservations and linger a bit over your meal, you will see the more expensive dinner items put out within the hour. You will be able to eat off the full dinner menu for the price of lunch!

Insider's Tip!

Most people with smaller children leave the Magic Kingdom immediately after the evening fireworks show, leaving the park nearly (but not quite) as quiet as the early morning hours of the day. On nights when the Magic Kingdom stays open particularly late (sometimes as late as 3 a.m.), you will see the rest of the families leave by midnight. If you can, plan for a non-activity day for the following day and close out the park. These are the rare days when you might be able to do the best rides multiple times.

force children to "have fun" when they are exhausted.

Get to a park to see the opening ceremony (if any) and be at the "rope-drop"

Even if you aren't morning people, at least at the beginning of your vacation consider getting to the Magic Kingdom Park early to see the opening ceremony. We discuss the ceremony in detail in Volume II. It is worth catching in person. The entire audience is properly warmed up and excited to start the day.

If you are staying on-property, always plan to make use of the Early Theme Park Entry. Even if you show up a little late, you will be miles ahead of regular-admission guests.

Getting to a park early gives you the reward of small crowds (and shorter wait

times) that make the experience a blast! You can hit the most popular attractions with very little delay, moving at least twice as fast as someone who arrives three or four hours later. Who would rather spend 90 minutes in a stand-by line to get onto Toy Story Mania, when you could otherwise walk on in less than 10 minutes?

And, of course, the mornings are the coolest part of the hot Orlando days. In this book you'll learn all about using Genie+ and have reserved *other* times to get right onto the rides and attractions you really want to experience. But there is no reason not to go on them again nice and

You may wonder how Disney determines attraction wait times. Gone are the days when somebody would estimate based on how far back a line stretched. Nowadays an attendant will give random guests a red plastic card on a lanyard as the guests enter a queue. A guest with a card hands it in to the person loading the ride, and the card gets scanned to determine the exact length of time the guest actually had to wait.

This means the posted wait times are very accurate. However, late in the evening, wait times can vary dramatically from the posted times. Within the last hour that the park is open, for instance, you will often find wait times are about half those posted.

Insider's Tip!

If there is an important ride you haven't been able to get on all day, try within the last hour the park is open. Most posted wait times that late in the day are longer than the actual wait, but check with the attendant to be sure. If all else fails, get in the ride queue just before the park closes. Disney closes down attraction queues at park closing, but they keep the rides open long enough to get through everybody waiting in line. This is also a fun way to see what a park looks like after closing!

early in the morning when there is no line and no crowds.

Take a Mid-Day Break

When the crowds swell and the lines start crawling by mid-afternoon, it is time to relax and take it easy with a daily break. Midday can be especially brutal in the spring and summer months. (During the rainy season that starts in June, it might also rain for two or three hours.) Rather than suffer through it at the parks, unwind! Take two to four hours and have a cool dip in the hotel pool. Or nap and rejuvenate along with the kids.

Insider's Tip!

At Magic Kingdom, if the Express Monorail has a huge line, check the Resorts Monorail. It also makes a stop at the TTC. If the line is too long there, consider making the short 5-minute walk to Contemporary Resort and taking the monorail from there, often with little to no wait in line (but not always)!

Insider's Tip!

Magic Kingdom fireworks can be viewed from the hotels across the lagoon, and any music or dialogue from the show is played for hotel guests to hear outside the park. If you plan to leave immediately after fireworks, we recommend you take the monorail to Polynesian Resort before the show and find a place to watch on the beach. You'll also get to see the Electric Water Pageant, and you can easily walk back to the TTC from Polynesian without waiting for a packed monorail.

Plan to Stay Late

Your entire family will like getting back to the park, rested and cool, for the evening fun to come. After it gets dark, The Magic Kingdom takes on a truly different vibe. It has specially-lighted night shows and fireworks to excite the crowds.

The weather may start out still a little high, but it will moderate and then cool down. By 8 or 9 p.m. you will get to see nighttime entertainment without worrying about all the rides. But if you do want to get on more rides, it is during these shows when lines thin out again. After the first nighttime show, the crowds will start to leave the park.

Before Leaving Your Hotel to Travel to a Park

No matter how great you might plan, leave room for contingencies. Although it is very rare, Disney can change its times without explanation. The day before you will be at any park, verify the exact time that it opens and closes. You can look online at disneyworld.disney.go.com/calendars or call (407) 824-4321. We also have the direct phone numbers for each of the parks in the previous pages.

Stay Relaxed and Have Fun (& Don't Neglect Nap Time)

If you're overheated and tired, scrap your planned schedule for a few hours. Take an unscheduled midday break and come back in the evening. Families with smaller children often leave the parks early, so night owls will benefit from wait times on family rides that are nearly as short as early morning hours.

Unless everyone in your party agrees, don't force them to become "Themepark Commandos." Running from attraction to attraction in order to see everything as fast as possible will not only be stressful, but the memories will become blurred. There are those who work so hard at having fun that, as soon as the last explosion of the fireworks show is done, they get back to their hotel and collapse. They then wake up the next day, still reeling from exhaustion, and have another action-packed day planned.

Insider's Tip!

If you plan to stay super late one day, plan to take it easy the next morning. This method of touring is why we think that park visits are best handled every other day.

The fact is that you will need at least two days to leisurely visit each park and see the vast majority of the shows. If you want to see other things at Disney World, plan for an even longer vacation. Or come back again – most likely, plenty will change between visits, making each magical trip a new experience.

If you have many people in your party, including young children, it is a very smart idea to plan for a free, relaxed day after the first park visit. The emotional energy that it takes to stay on-the-go is simply too much for very young people. Take the journey slow and easy, and you won't need a vacation when you get home from your trip!

First Considerations

PRE-TRIP PLANNING CHECKLIST		
Planning Timeline	**Action Needed**	**Date Completed**
9 Months or Sooner	Set Up Account on MyDisneyExperience App	
7 Months or Sooner	Purchase Theme Park Tickets	
6 Months or Sooner	Make Individual Theme Park Reservations	
90 Days in Advance	Make Hotel Reservations	
90 Days in Advance	Make Airline Reservations	
60 Days in Advance	Make Dining Reservations	
60 Days in Advance	Make Special Event Reservations (Tours, Lightsaber Builds, Robot Builds, Etc.)	
60 Days in Advance	Modify Theme Park Reservations as Needed	
30 Days in Advance	Make Transportation Reservations	
14 Days in Advance	Confirm Special Requests with Hotel	
7 Days in Advance	Purchase Memory Maker	
1 Day in Advance	Complete Hotel Advanced Check-In	

Download Our Free, Comprehensive Budget/Planning Tools At:

bit.ly/DisneyPlanners

Tools and How to Use Them

If you don't know about the available tools and how to properly utilize them, you won't get the most out of your vacation. There are tricks and techniques without which you are likely to find your well-intentioned plans fall apart and your family unable to do much of what you actually intended.

Get These Vacation Planning Kits

The first thing anyone should do is request a copy of the free Disney vacation planning video from the Disney Parks Vacation Planning Information Line to better help you make your decisions. You can get an immediate download of the video at disneyvacations.com/all-parks, or Disney will send a DVD to you in the mail if you prefer. [Request your DVD at the same website or by calling (800) 205-3002 any time of day.] It contains a complete tour of the four theme parks, two water parks, and over 20 on-property resorts. The video includes affordable ways to play and stay during your Disney vacation, plus personalized tips and information on special events.

The next step is to call the Orlando/Orange County Convention and Visitors Bureau to request both a complimentary vacation planning kit and the Orlando Official Vacation Guide. Keep in mind that they will take two to three weeks to arrive. Call (800) 643-9492 or (407) 363-5872 (9 a.m. to 3 p.m. Eastern Time), or go to visitorlando.com. They also have a website that provides discounts for non-Disney hotels, restaurants, ground transportation, shopping malls, dinner theaters, and other theme parks and attractions (visitorlando.com/offers).

Disney's My Disney Experience

While you are online, sign up for an account with Disney's My Disney Experience and download the My Disney Experience app (disneyworld.com) onto your smartphone or tablet. Once you have established your account, use it to augment what you are reading about as you go through this book.

Disney's MagicMobile

Included in the My Disney Experience app is MagicMobile. If you have a Google Pay or Apple Pay enabled smart device, you can activate the MagicMobile feature,

What is Disney's MyDisney Experience?

Disney's My Disney Experience is the name of an integrated vacation planning and management system. Within the system, Disney has incorporated many different online management tools. These include:

- My Disney Experience app that allows you to reserve a park, purchase park tickets, and make other trip plans in a single location;
- PhotoPass that allows you to manage your vacation photos; and
- Genie that allows you to manage your itinerary, restaurant, show, and attraction reservations.

My Disney Experience includes a collection of high-tech, wireless enhancements for the theme parks, such as MagicBands which act as hotel room keys and also replace the need for credit cards at restaurant and retail locations. Everything integrates with the online programs and app.

allowing you to use your smart device as your park ticket and PhotoPass tracker.

MagicBands

The My Disney Experience system centers around the use of MagicBands, which are rubber wristbands – available in a variety of colors – that are embedded with electronic RFID (radio-frequency-identification) microchips. They are designed to be durable and reusable from one trip to the next.

These bands are used for park admission, for the Lightning Lane and PhotoPass systems, for Disney Dining Plan, as hotel room keys, and for restaurant reservations. Disney hotel guests can also register a P.I.N. and credit card number to use their MagicBands for the purchase of meals and merchandise while on Disney property. (The option to link a credit card is currently unavailable for guests staying off-property.)

MagicBand+ options are also available, which vibrate and light up to interact with select objects and events (such as the evening fireworks shows at Magic Kingdom and Epcot).

Lightning Lanes (LL) and Genie+ (G+)

Disney World replaced its free FastPass+ queues with paid Lightning Lanes. Lightning Lane reservations for the most popular Tier 1 attractions at each park may be purchased separately through your My Disney Experience account on the day of your visit. You can reserve two of these **Tier 1 Lightning Lane (*LL*)** reservations per day.

Current Tier 1 Attractions:
- Magic Kingdom - Seven Dwarfs Mine Train & Tron Lightcycle Power Run
- Epcot - Guardians of the Galaxy: Cosmic Rewind
- Hollywood Studios - Star Wars: Rise of the Resistance
- Animal Kingdom - Avatar Flight of Passage

These popular rides are not available for reservation through Disney's paid Genie+ app (see below). The price for a reservation varies based on the ride and the day of visit. Expect between $9 and $15 (plus tax) per person per attraction.

To reserve the less popular Tier 2 attractions that have Lightning Lanes, you can sign up for Disney's paid **Genie+ (*G+*)** system. Genie+ costs $15 (plus tax) per person per day that you wish to use it. Reservations through the app must be made one-at-a-time on the day of your visit. You can make the first reservation as early as 7 a.m. that day. Once you use a reservation, you can make the next reservation.

Keep in mind that both reservation systems are based on ride availability, so booking as early as possible is vital. With Genie+, you may not be able to get the Lightning Lane reservations you want on particularly busy days.

Note: There are no re-rides allowed with the Genie+ system. Make sure you use each Lightning Lane reservation or cancel it. Once you book an attraction, you can't book it a second time that day. If you love it and want to ride again, you must wait in the stand-by queue.

Tools and How to Use Them

Insider's Tip!

Disney has done extensive research about the purchasing habits of guests and has determined you are more likely to make a purchase if it's extra convenient. Disney makes it easy to spend with reckless abandon by allowing guests to link their credit cards to their MagicBands.

Because studies suggest that people are less likely to make a purchase with cash than a credit card (or MagicBand), we strongly recommend you bring a set amount of cash for purchases. Try to avoid any credit card use during your stay if it is very important to stay within a fixed budget!

Disney hotel guests and annual passholders receive discounts on MagicBand purchases through their My Disney Experience accounts. All other visitors can purchase a MagicBand online, or they can pick one up when they get to the parks.

Standard colors cost $19.99, while *designer styles*, including limited edition bands that play a little tune when used or customized bands (available in Tomorrowland at Magic Kingdom or at Disney Springs), cost a little extra.

Of course, Disney offers the ability to spend more to personalize your MagicBand by adding cute charms and other accessories. These rubberized bracelets last a very long time and can be enjoyed well after your vacation ends.

MagicBands are not required to take advantage of My Disney Experience benefits. Even on-property guests have the option of requesting standard passes (formerly called *Key to the World* passes) if they are not comfortable with the long-range RFID tracking technology used within the MagicBands. These standard passes link to your account and can still be used for most of the above-mentioned benefits.

How Genie Operates to Enhance Your Visit

When you register your trip plans, you can enter detailed information about the entire party with whom you are traveling directly into the Genie portion of the My Disney Experience system. This allows you to manage everybody's plans, individually or as a group.

Genie allows you to make restaurant reservations and even place amusement ride or show reservations at the parks (Lightning Lane). Several counter-service restaurants now take advanced, same-day orders through the system, allowing guests to bypass the standard lines.

Step-by-step Instructions

To sign up for My Disney Experience, go to the Walt Disney World website (disneyworld.com) and hover your mouse over the "My Disney Experience" menu option (in the upper right-hand corner of the home page). When the dropdown menu appears, click on "Create an Account." You will be prompted to provide your name, address, and other pertinent information. Be sure to add other members of your party to your account in order to use the advance reservation system for everyone.

Click on the "My Plans" link for a calendar display of everything you have included in your plans. This page displays all your reservations and plans for each day, including hotel reservations, the park you plan to visit, its operating hours, as well as your Lightning Lane and dining reservations. You also have the option of adding to those plans and reservations using the links on the page.

The Genie itinerary planner is also an excellent tool to use once you have your Lightning Lane selections. We suggest using the tool on Disney's Apple or Android app, rather than on the website, as the app is more streamlined and appears to have more dedicated bandwidth than the website. (The website is subject to errors and crashes, making trip planning frustrating.)

How to Set Up a My Disney Experience Account

You can create a My Disney Experience account through the Walt Disney World website even before you have scheduled your vacation or ordered your park passes. To sign up for My Disney Experience on the the Walt Disney World website, simply register with your email address and choose a password. This will create a profile and give you basic privileges to help you organize your trip itinerary.

You can reserve times for recreational activities and events, book your stay at a Disney hotel, make dining reservations, and even buy advanced tickets to the parks and special ticketed events. Any purchases or reservations you then make through the website will automatically populate into the My Disney Experience system and the associated mobile app and vice versa.

Insider's Tip!

When you purchase your park passes, request to have them mailed to you immediately. You can reserve your park choices up to approximately one year in advance. To get the best park availability for a hassle-free trip, have your park tickets delivered to you at least 180 days in advance.

To start making reservations from home, you need a MagicBand linked to your reservation or the *numbers* located on the back of your park pass.

Insider's Tip!

Guests can purchase a MagicBand for as little as $19.99. This rubber bracelet uses wireless technology to replace all plastic passes you might be used to, including hotel room keys and park admission passes. You can also link these to your credit card and use them for purchases throughout your entire stay if you are staying on-property. MagicBands have Radio Frequency Identification (RFID) chips in them to track and link everything together.

My Disney Experience

Once you have Disney hotel reservations or add park passes to your My Disney Experience account, you can sign up for the enhanced My Disney Experience, called Genie, which then allows you to make park reservations, create a daily itinerary and make (paid) Lightning Lane reservations.

Advanced My Disney Experience (Genie) Information

The following sections go into even more detail about using My Disney Experience features, such as Genie+. Check the detailed information for each theme park to see our recommendations on which rides and restaurants for which you need advance reservations.

Insider's Tip!

Try to reserve your first Genie+ Lightning Lane time for early in the day (beginning at 10 am), as you will be able to get a new Lightning Lane time as soon as the first is used.

Insider's Tip!

You can select everyone in your travel party to make sure you all ride an attraction at the same time, or you can choose to make separate attraction reservations for different members of your party. You can also make changes to each person's Genie+ Tier 2 Lightning Lane reservation.

Disney's Free Genie vs. Disney's Paid Genie+ System

Genie is a planning tool included in Disney's My Disney Experience app. In it, there are free and paid services available. The paid services include individual pre-paid Lightning Lane reservations and the Genie+ system.

The free portion of the app allows guests to create a customized itinerary that automatically updates throughout the day. In it, Disney makes recommendations for attractions, dining, entertainment, and other experiences you may want to experience. They also provided suggested times for you to do these experiences based on their own forecasted lowest wait times.

Through Genie, you can purchase up to two individual Lightning Lane reservations each day for the most popular (Tier 1) attractions in each park, until each is sold out (available beginning at 7 a.m. the day of your visit for on-property guests or at park opening for off-property guests).

With the Genie+ service, you can reserve Lightning Lane return time windows for the less popular (Tier 2) attractions in each park. You can make the first reservation at 7 a.m. the day of your visit. Reservations are one-at-a-time and based on availability, so there's no guarantee that you will get a reservation for each of your desired attractions, particularly on busy days. However, your time waiting in line should be vastly reduced with it.

There are some other features included with Genie+, such as the ability to take Magic Shots (special, interactive photos) directly through the app.

Disney's Free Genie System Tutorial:

In addition to the paid Genie+ system, which allows guests to reserve Lightning Lane reservations for attractions, Disney has created a free system called Disney's Genie.

Genie is a very helpful system that helps guests create an online itinerary and even provides suggested times to go to attractions for which you don't have Lightning Lane reservations.

To use Disney's Genie, open the My Disney Experience app on your smart device. Look for the "Get Started with Disney Genie!" prompt under Today's Plans (found at the top of the Home Page).

Click on "Get Started Now" to begin planning your daily itinerary.

Be prepared to enter the attractions, entertainment, and dining choices which most interest you for the day. Click the "Start Now" button when you're ready with your favorite options.

Choose the date and park for which you're making plans. If you already have a park reservation for the date selected, that park will appear automatically when you select the associated date on the calendar.

Now select the members of your party for whom you want to make plans on that day. Each person you previously linked to your My Disney Experience account who has a valid park pass for that date will appear in the list.

Finally, you get to the fun part - entering your top choices for the day!

At the top of the page, choose between Attractions, Entertainment, Dining, and Enchanting Extras.

Under each menu options, a list of available options appears. Simply choose each option you're interested in experiencing that day. Select "Continue" to go to the next page, My Interests.

On the next page, click each Interest to help Disney Genie customize plans and recommendations based on your personal preferences. These include the types of Characters you prefer, such as Villains or Star Wars, as well as the types of activities you like. Select "Continue" to go to the next page, My Display Preferences.

On this page, move the toggle button next to the options you wish to see for each Disney Genie recommedation. For instance, if you wish to see what height requirements each suggested attraction has, move the toggle to the "on" position next to that option.

On the next page, you can choose to purchase individual Lightning Lane reservations (if available) for Tier 1 attractions. If you don't want to purchase any, choose the "Skip for Now" option at the bottom of the screen.

You can now choose to purchase Disney's paid Genie+ service for $15 (plus tax) per person for that day by selecting "Get Disney Genie+ Service." If you want to continue with the free service, select "Skip for Now" at the bottom of the screen.

Now, sit back and allow the magic to happen! A customized itinerary will pop up on the next screen, titled "My Day." The itinerary will include top attractions, entertainment, and dining recommendations, including the suggested times to go based on Disney's own forecasted lowest wait times.

If you don't like a recommendation, simply click on the three ellipses at the top right corner of each suggestion and make your desired changes.

Your customized itinerary will automatically update throughout the day, as you either go on rides or expected wait times change, so check it often.

To access your itinerary throughout the day, open the My Disney Experience app. Click on the three bars located on the bottom right of the screen. This opens the Welcome menu.

Click on My Genie Day to open your menu and make changes.

NOTE: If you are using Disney's paid Genie+ system or Disney's Disabled Access Service (DAS), you can reserve your next Lightning Lane reserve time window by clicking on the desired attraction in your itinerary.

If the attraction is not on your itinerary list yet, swap a recommendation by clicking on the three ellipses at the top right of a selction you wish to remove from the itinerary to make room for the desired attraction. Click on "Swap Recommendation" when the popup menu appears and choose the desired attraction.

You must be in the park already to select a DAS Pass return time window.

Tools and How to Use Them

Lightning Lane Reservations

Lightning Lanes have replaced Disney's FastPass+ service. Unlike the old service, **GUESTS MUST WAIT UNTIL THE DAY OF THEIR VISIT TO MAKE A LIGHTNING LANE RESERVATION.**

If you are staying on Disney property, one of the biggest advantages is the ability to get the exact times you want for your favorite rides and attractions. Why is this? Unlike guests staying off-property, Disney allows their on-property guests to reserve their Tier 1 pre-paid Lightning Lane reservations for the two most popular attractions at each park **AS EARLY AS 7 A.M. THE MORNING OF YOUR VISIT.**

While off-property guests can still reserve their Tier 1 Lightning Lane times on the app prior to entering the park, they must wait until the park officially opens for the day to do so.

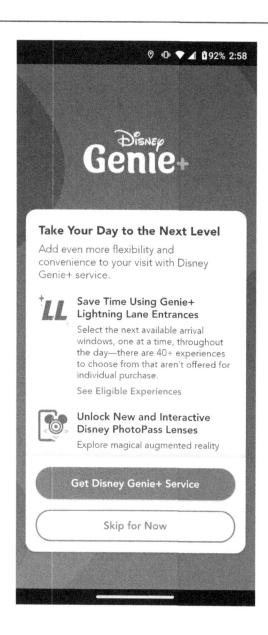

Insider's Tip!

There is no way to cancel or modify your individual paid (Tier 1) Lightning Lane reservations, so make sure you choose a time when everyone in your party will be available.

If the attraction for which you have a reservation goes down during your return time window, your return window will automatically be extended for the remainder of the day. If it stays down the entire day, Disney will automatically refund the purchase price to your account.

How the Paid Genie+ System Works

For the price of $15 (plus tax) per person per day, visitors can reserve one Tier 2 Lightning Lane attraction at a time, beginning at 7 a.m. the morning of the park visit. Park hoppers are not limited to reservations in a single park. Guests can choose from any of the Tier 2 attractions in each park. To get reservations for a Tier 1 attraction, you must pay a separate reservation fee for each (up to two per day).

You will need to wait in standby queues or enter a virtual queue (if available) to get into all of the other prime attractions you want to experience. The worst-case scenario is that you might miss something altogether if wait times are too long to fit into the rest of your schedule.

Most attractions and Character Meet-and-Greets have Lightning Lanes (formerly FastPass+) available. Check the attraction information for each park in this guide to find out which attractions are available for Lightning Lane reservations. See our detailed attraction descriptions to find out when might be a good time to get on a popular ride without a Lightning Lane reservation.

Insider's Tip!

The Seven Dwarfs Mine Train books up quicker than other rides in Magic Kingdom. If you can't get a reservation for this attraction, plan to race to the ride as soon as the park opens.

Once you have used each Genie+ Lightning Lane reservation, the hour-long "return window" has expired, or two hours (120 minutes) have passed from the time you booked your last reservation (whichever occurs first), you can reserve another attraction time. (Note: If you booked your first reservation at 7 a.m., the two-hour countdown to book your next reservation begins at park opening, not 7 a.m.)

Tools and How to Use Them

From making theme park reservations to creating personalized itineraries to ordering food at the parks, at least one guest in each party must link everyone's tickets (and MagicBands, if using them) to a My Disney Experience account. To do so, login to the account you previously created (or create a new one if you haven't already done so). You can then add your entire travel party's passes to the account under Tickets and Passes. (Look for the ticket/pass number on that back of your park ticket.)

From here, on-property Disney hotel guests can link a credit card to park passes and MagicBands and create a P.I.N. for each person to use them to make purchases during your trip. (Disney currently only offers this feature of linking credit cards to MagicBands to their on-site hotel guests.)

Genie & Genie+

Once the passes are linked into your account, you can reserve specific dates to visit each park for <u>everyone</u> in your party through Disney's Genie system (part of the My Disney Experience app). Choose the desired date of visit on the calendar, then select each person in the party whom you wish to include on that day. The list of available parks will appear, and you can select which one you plan to visit. (You can modify it later.)

Create Your Itinerary & Make Lightning Lane Reservations

Paid Lightning Lanes replaced the former free FastPass+ system. Disney offers guests the ability to purchase individual reservations for its two most popular (Tier 1) attractions in each park (up to two per day) or to purchase the Genie+ reservation system for the less popular (Tier 2) attractions.

Guests with Lightning Lane reservations have a distinct advantage over those who don't, as approximately four Lightning Lane guests are allowed onto each ride for every one waiting in the stand-by queue. If the Lightning Lane is particularly busy, though, Cast Members will often allow many more Lightning Lane guests onto the ride over stand-by guests, leaving stand-by guests waiting in line for a long time.

To take full advantage of Lightning Lane reservations, set up your itinerary early and be prepared to make your reservations as soon as the system opens on the morning of your park visit. With Genie+, the reservation system opens at 7 a.m. for all guests. With individual Tier 1 Lightning Lane reservations, the system opens at 7 a.m. for Disney on-property hotel guests and at park opening for off-property day guests.

Prior to 7 a.m., log into the app and select My Genie Day from the menu. Select the prompt to "Get Started Now" with the Genie planning tool. (You can also make reservations through your My Disney Experience account on the disneyworld.com website. However, we recommend using the app, as it seems to work far better with fewer errors.)

Follow the prompts to create your daily itinerary. When the reservation system opens, check the individual attractions to see if Lightning Lane reservations are available.

Click on the link to purchase individual reservations or Genie+ and follow the prompts to select an available time for your party.

Tier 1 reservation prices vary based on the ride's popularity and the date of visit, but you can expect to pay between $7 and $20 per person for each Lightning Lane reservation.

We strongly recommend you request your Tier 1 Lightning Lane times as early in the day as they become available, since the best rides are typically booked early. (The most popular attractions are sometimes completely sold out by the time the reservation system opens to off-property guests.)

If you are not able to reserve your desired Lightning Lane times in advance, once you enter the park using your admission pass, look for a member of Disney's Guest Experience Team to assist you with reservations. These Cast Members wear blue shirts and are usually located on the main pathways of each park. If your top choice is not available, check throughout the day to see if someone may have canceled, opening a spot for you. Otherwise, you'll have to ride using standby lines.

Make Dining Reservations & Modify Your Daily Genie Itinerary

Now that you have your Lightning Lane reservations scheduled, it's time to figure out where to eat.

Disney provides suggested restaurants in your previously created itinerary, but you may want to fine-tune it and make dining reservations for table-service locations.

Open the app or go to the Walt Disney World website (disneyworld.com) and sign in to your account. Select "My Genie Day" from the menu.

This page shows you what you have planned on a selected day of your vacation. To change the day you are viewing, click on the calendar and choose the date you want.

You have the option of modifying or adding to your itinerary for that day by choosing the link for either Genie+, dining reservations, shows you want to see, or characters you wish to meet.

To make dining reservations using the app, select "Check Dining Availability" from the menu, or search individual restaurants online by going to disneyworld.

disney.go.com/dining/#/reservations-accepted. From this page, you can filter your results further by location, date, and time. You will see a list of available restaurants that meet your criteria. Select any restaurant to view menu and pricing information. On the restaurant's page, verify the date and time you want, then click on "Find a Table."

You will be given time options that are close to your search criteria. Select the one that works best for you. (You will be asked to log in again to verify it is you.) On the next page, you will select the name of the person authorized to manage the reservation, as well as identify the other members of your dining party.

The next page requests your credit card information to hold the reservation. Disney uses this credit card to charge you a cancellation fee if you don't show up for your meal and didn't cancel at least 24 hours in advance for most restaurants. Complete the information, click "Next," and Disney will confirm your reservation, which will now show up on your itinerary for the day.

You can also add restaurants, particularly counter-services restaurants, to your daily agenda without a reservation.

The option to add rides, entertainment, and character meet-and-greets for which you don't have Lightning Lane reservations is also available. (If you take the time to fill out your preferences, Disney will automatically make recommendations for you.)

Read our Disney Genie Tutorial for specific instructions on how to make changes to Disney's recommended attractions, dining, and entertainment.

Sample Itineraries

We provide sample itineraries at the end of each park section to give you an idea of what to include. Readers who want help

Insider's Tip!

Many locals love to take pictures of vacationing families. You can often spot the locals or frequent Disney visitors, as they generally don't carry cameras and aren't looking around the theme parks in wonder. You can also stop a Disney Cast Member who is not helping another guest to ask to have your picture taken – even as you get on a ride. You don't even need to speak the language to make yourself understood. Simply hold your camera out and point to yourself.

We've never seen anybody refuse to take a picture for a tourist. Don't hesitate to ask someone, whether that person appears to be a local or not, to take a picture of your entire family. In fact, offering to take a picture of another family is a great way to open the door to ask them to reciprocate!

When you request that someone takes your photo, ask to have multiple pictures taken from different angles and change your poses slightly each time. Don't just smile. Try a kiss on the cheek or holding hands in the air. Remember that memory cards have a lot of room, and you will better be able to cherish those amazing memories if you have all the pictures you can take the time to snap.

Importantly, make sure you offer to *do the same for others*, and ask that partners give a quick smooch to each other when you snap the picture!

developing one for themselves are invited to email us using the contact information provided at the beginning of this book.

You can use our sample itinerary as a good basis for which Lightning Lane selections to choose and the order in which you should see rides to hit most, if not all, of your must-see attractions in a single day at Magic Kingdom.

Professional Camera Insider's Tip!

- Have everyone say "Mickey!" to be sure you see smiles in every photo!
- When in doubt about light levels, use your flash. This will help prevent graininess from poor quality image sensors that don't have a high ISO setting. (This is camera speak for level of light sensitivity. The higher the number, the darker the scene can be and still appear clear in the photo.)
- Try not to zoom in too much. You can always crop a photo later, but try to let each picture tell the entire story. Take a moment to look at the scene and get as much surrounding background as possible so that someone looking at your picture will see where you are and what you are doing.
- Try to avoid clutter in the foreground so your eyes focus on what is important.
- Don't be afraid to take many snapshots, but take time to check your settings and scene when it really matters!
- Please be aware that **"selfie sticks"** are prohibited in the Parks.

Keep in mind, though, the timing and order of everything in our sample itineraries will depend greatly on crowd sizes and availability of Lightning Lane reservations.

Capturing Your Memories

Before your Disney vacation begins, think about how you plan to take pictures and videos to memorialize your trip. Consider the size and weight of your camera and/or camcorder and how many hours you will be carrying it around each day. Will your family split up during your vacation, requiring multiple cameras? Can your camera slip inside your pocket when you're not using it? Does it take good shots in low-light conditions, such as on a moving dark ride or at a nighttime parade?

Many vacationers like to use smartphones for all of their pictures and videos. This can be a great, convenient option. Before using this as your primary picture-taking mechanism, be sure to test the camera in various lighting and action circumstances. Many take very

Leave your "selfie sticks" at home. They are banned in Disney parks.

poor pictures and video in dark conditions, making them virtually useless on dark indoor rides and anywhere else after dark (which is when much of the action happens at Disney).

You should also consider who will be taking pictures during your trip. You might be surprised how often a single person, such as the father of a family, is unofficially designated the photographer and rarely, if ever, shows up in the vacation photos!

Disney Camera Shops

If you forget to bring your own camera, you can pick up a disposable camera at

Insider's Tip!

Even if you don't think you'll want to purchase any of the PhotoPass pictures, it's still a good idea to get a PhotoPass card (or register a MagicBand or MagicMobile account) in case you change your mind later.

Insider's Tip!

If you have several members of your family who want to share photos, make sure someone takes the initiative to collect copies of everyone's pictures to compile into a shared DVD, either by the end of your trip or after you return home. A large party can have hundreds of pictures, but more importantly, there may be hours of video documenting everyone's visit. Gigabytes of video can take a very long time to send over the Internet.

Insider's Tip!

You can use multiple MagicBands linked to a single MyMagic+ account or get multiple PhotoPass cards, but be sure to register your cards online using the instructions on the card before losing any of them!

Insider's Tip!

If you won't be able to go online soon, write down the PhotoPass number in a secondary location in case you lose the actual card.

Tools and How to Use Them

Insider's Tip!

If you decide to use this service, remember to check disneyphotopass.com for the digital photos taken on attractions and taken by PhotoPass photographers in the parks. If you are using a PhotoPass card, rather than your MagicBand to track those photos (see below), be sure to log in immediately and link the card.

many gift shops inside the parks. The best selection of disposable cameras at each park is found at its Photo Center. They also sell additional memory cards and batteries. Additionally, this is where you can get printed copies of attraction photos or PhotoPass pictures taken by Cast Members that day.

If you need printed pictures to share with your tour group before your trip ends, nearby drug stores, including Walgreens and CVS, offer photo printing services. They also have the equipment to burn the images digitally to DVDs within about an hour.

Helpful Hint: Be sure you have a spare memory card available in case you choose to drop off your memory card to have your photos processed.

Insider's Tip!

Most of the rides that get the best pictures are fast, bumpy, or wet. This makes it difficult – or dangerous – to try to operate a camera while properly bracing yourself. If you try to do so, make sure you have a proper strap and can maintain a firm grip at all times!

Insider's Tip!

If you are taking a conventional D-SLR (digital) camera, have a few rubber bands around and a plastic bag. Wrap the camera, up to the end of the lens, so that only the glass is exposed to any water.

Disney PhotoPass Service

Fortunately, Disney offers ample options to capture photographic memories with their PhotoPass service (DisneyPhotoPass.com). If you decide on a character meal or any other premium experience, you'll appreciate how nice it is to have so many professional photographers around.

We'll tell you how to use these services to ensure you capture great photos of your entire family. Keep in mind that most families eventually decide to make at least a couple of purchases, so don't disregard the idea of using the service until you get to the parks.

Even if you don't initially plan to buy any of these pictures, there is no cost to you for having the photos taken unless you choose to order a print or download individual images later on. You can also order all your photos on a disc to take somewhere more reasonably-priced to print out yourself. This is a decision you can make in the comfort of your own home after your trip.

Insider's Tip!

In just a bit, we'll go over the details about Disney's Memory Maker package that provides a great all-for-one-price option. While the price is high, the memories are priceless.

Insider's Tip!

If you have your camera ready, you may have time to snap a *blurry* shot of the preview photo. On purpose, the display system makes it impossible to get a clean photographic copy. However, even if it's not a great snapshot, getting to laugh for a bit about funny and frightened faces (you would not otherwise want around forever, anyway!) is worthwhile. (Disney couldn't expect otherwise.) But if you think you will only buy a couple of the official pictures, it's worth trying.

Attraction Photos

Some of the very best moments of a Walt Disney World vacation are experienced on the thrilling attractions. You may want snapshots that allow you to relive your favorite thrill rides. Unfortunately, there's no practical way for you to take your own family photo while doing so, and it could be difficult or dangerous to attempt capturing your own photographs on some of the attractions.

Disney captures fantastic pictures of your entire party *enjoying* rides at the most memorable moments. One fan-favorite picture catches guests as they rocket forward during the Rock 'n' Roller Coaster's insanely fast take off (zero to 60 miles per hour in just a couple of seconds)! What's more is that Disney is now starting to integrate videos into their top-notch technology.

Getting to look at the facial expressions of your friends or family can be priceless, which is why Disney can sell these photos for a hefty price. It is not particularly surprising that guests are willing to pay a premium for these memories to be caught on camera. After all, you will get to relive that magical moment for years to come!

You get to see a preview of the picture for sale immediately upon exiting the rides that offer souvenir photos (on your way to the attraction's attached retail shop).

While the kiosks at the end of each ride let you review your picture and make a purchase if you want a print

then-and-there, there is absolutely no sales pressure to do so. Chances are good that you will choose to purchase at least one of these photos on your vacation for a minimum of $15 plus tax.

If you're wearing a MagicBand, the technology is *supposed* to automatically link attraction photos to your account. Unfortunately, the pictures don't always link properly. If there is a particular picture you know you will want to buy later, don't trust that the long-range MagicBand RFID chip will work. To be certain it registers into your account, link the attraction photo to the MagicBand or to your park pass manually by pressing the band (or pass) against the Mickey emblem under the attraction photo at the preview station.

Remember! If you don't have a Magic-Mobile account or MagicBand, pick up a PhotoPass card for free from any PhotoPass Cast Member you see stationed throughout each park.

There are 13 select attractions that automatically link the on-ride PhotoPass pictures (or video in the case of the Seven Dwarfs Mine Train! and Twilight Zone Tower of Terror) to the My Disney Experience account for each guest rider. As just mentioned, they pick up the MagicBand signal when you hop aboard. A big advantage to the system is that you don't have to take time to review them on-the-spot, but

Insider's Tip!

In addition to the official Disney photos that are added to your PhotoPass account, you are welcome to ask PhotoPass photographers to use your *own personal camera* to take pictures that you can enjoy right away.

They will gladly help out, and you can be assured that they know how to operate your camera. It is by far the best way to get great shots of your entire family at some of the prime locations these professionals have chosen.

The system makes a lot of money for Disney, so they aren't stingy. This is a great way to make sure you have photos of the entire family together at the end of your vacation.

can look at them with other family members when you want to take a break.

Magic Kingdom

- Seven Dwarfs Mine Train
- Buzz Lightyear Space Ranger Spin
- Pirates of the Caribbean
- Space Mountain
- Splash Mountain

Epcot

- Test Track
- Frozen Ever After
- Guardians of the Galaxy: Cosmic Rewind

Hollywood Studios

- Rock'n' Roller Coaster
- Slinky Dog Dash
- Tower of Terror

Animal Kingdom

- Dinosaur
- Expedition Everest

Park Photos

Disney's PhotoPass service is not limited to capturing pictures of your attraction experiences. You'll find professional Disney photographers (equipped with the best Nikon camera equipment) along the promenade, at every iconic, picture-taking location throughout the four main theme parks. They

also trail along with most characters at each meet-and-greet location. During peak periods they may appear at Disney Springs and the water parks.

How the PhotoPass Service Works

Simply walk up to the photographer (or get in line if there are others in front of you). When it's your turn, he/she will ask you if you have a MagicMobile enabled smart device, MagicBand, or PhotoPass card. Don't have either? No problem. The Cast Member will give you a PhotoPass card as soon as the pictures are taken. And as you already know, you can use your MagicMobile account or MagicBand in lieu of having to hold onto a separate card. How easy is that?

The Cast Member will direct you on where to stand and how to pose, then send the data electronically to their network.

Insider's Tip!

Because it takes a while to review and choose prints, and because of all the available printing options, expect long wait times near park closing when families are picking out their photos on the way out of the park.

Getting Prints at the Park

You have the option of purchasing hard copies of one or more of these professionally taken photos at various locations throughout Disney property, or as we already indicated, you can order digital or hard copies online when you get home from your vacation.

The attractions with souvenir photos have sales counters set up to print pictures, but there are central photo centers in each park where all of your other PhotoPass pictures can also be printed. If you choose to have your photos printed at one of these locations, know that the lines can get long. This is especially true towards the end of the day as guests get ready to leave. On a good day, a small group of people can easily have a couple dozen pictures taken.

Ordering Prints from Home

Ordering your prints from home allows you more time to view options and decide exactly what you want. You will find your pictures online at disneyphotopass.com. If you used MagicMobile on your smart device or a MagicBand, your pictures should automatically show up when you log into your account. If you used one or more PhotoPass cards, though, be sure to log into your Disney account as soon as possible to link the card to your account.

PhotoPass Picture Features

There are some PhotoPass features you may consider worthwhile. These include special Disney borders that you can easily change which identify the season, park, or special occasion you're celebrating. The system is optimized for an easy and fun experience.

Possibly the biggest draw to purchasing PhotoPass pictures, though, is Disney's Magic Shots. These are special photos where Disney adds in a little magic, such as Tinker Bell standing in the palm of your hand!

Don't Forget! There are disadvantages to using PhotoPass as your sole source of vacation pictures.

- The pictures expire 45 days after they're taken (unless you have already purchased Memory Maker, which we explain below), so they must be purchased and downloaded quickly, *or you will lose your memories forever!*
- PhotoPass is great with the variety of photos from posed shots taken in fixed locations; spontaneous photos at events; and "gotcha" pictures on thrill rides at the peak of fear and fun.
  - Still, if you rely only on Photo-Pass, you'll miss out on a lot of opportunities for candid action-photos. Remember to take some of these yourself...
  - And, pictures are no substitute for memorable videos of particularly special moments. (We can't wait for Disney to roll out more video options!)

Insider's Tip!

Remember, Disney's Memory Maker entitles you only to electronic copies of your vacation photos, while you can purchase individual pictures for print from home or at the park. When you get a printed attraction photo at the actual attraction, you also get a unique cardboard photograph frame that represents that ride.

Disney's Memory Maker

While you are likely to purchase at least one or two attraction photos, Disney offers the Memory Maker package for guests who want multiple pictures. With this package, you can download _all_ PhotoPass pictures and videos, including those taken on attractions, for a single price.

Importantly, it allows you to link all of the PhotoPass and attraction photos <u>for your entire party</u> to a single account and download digital copies of <u>each and every picture</u> for the same price.

You don't have to decide to purchase Disney's Memory Maker ahead of time, but if you do order it before you're trip, you'll save money!

> _How it Works:_ You can purchase Disney's Memory Maker through the PhotoPass section of your MyMagic+ account online. The price is $199 (or $169 if you purchase it _at least three days in advance of your trip_).

> You already know that before you get to Disney World, you can link every MagicBand and theme park ticket for everyone in your party. Either of these will then be available to use

throughout your visit. (Theme park tickets can be used in lieu of Photo-Pass cards.) And when you get to the park, you or members of your group have the option of adding additional PhotoPass cards. When you are at a park, if members of your party forget their tickets or MagicBands, they can just pick up a PhotoPass card and you can add it into your account later.

This will automatically link all of your vacation photos to your account, making them available immediately to review online to add custom borders and download.

Once you purchase Memory Maker, you have a year to download – from the date a photo was taken – all the pictures you are interested in keeping (along with the variety of borders you might select). And as we said previously, as with all PhotoPass accounts, be sure to purchase Memory Maker or individual pictures within 45 days of your photos being taken, as the pictures completely disappear from your account after that length of time. Don't risk losing your memories forever!

Picture Spot Locations

Picture Spot signs are located in ideal places throughout the theme parks. These extremely popular photo locations are set against backdrops such as Cinderella's Castle in the Magic Kingdom and the Tree of Life in Disney's Animal Kingdom.

These photo opps are noted on park maps and with signs throughout the parks.

When you arrive at a Picture Spot, check the sample photo below the sign for ideas on how to frame your perfect family photo!

Insider's Trivia!

Eastman Kodak Company was one of the original sponsors when Disneyland opened in 1955. Until late 2013, Picture Spots were branded as Kodak Photo Spots. That sponsorship deal ended when Kodak filed for bankruptcy.

The Seasons of Disney: Hot, Hotter, & Hottest

When to Travel & What to Wear

Visit Off-peak Season – Save Money by Avoiding Peak Periods

The amount of flexibility you have for your trip increases during the slower seasons (known as Value Seasons) when lines and crowds are more manageable. And unlike the jacked up hotel rates you'll find during peak periods, area hotels, including Disney lodgings, offer considerable discounts for room prices and travel packages.

After Winter Break – Low Tempersture and Limited Crowds

Wait until <u>after the winter break</u> to head to the parks, when American kids go back to school. Temperatures are lowest during the <u>second week in January through the first week or so of February</u> (the period leading up to President's Day, other than MLK weekend). This also happens to be the same time crowds tend to be the thinnest. If you have to visit earlier in January, try to arrive any time after New Year's Day. However, check in advance for scheduled ride closures at this time. Some rides are likely to be closed for repairs between early January and mid-February.

Early Summer – Rising Temperatures and Manageable Crowds

The temperatures may be on the upswing from May through mid-June (until Summer Break begins), but the crowds are generally moderate. Expect busy weekends, as locals enjoy the longer days and special events during this period.

Late Summer Lull until the Holiday Season Begins

Temperatures are still somewhat high when the next lull begins, starting in mid-August and running through mid-October. Moving into November (except for Thanksgiving week) through the first two weeks of December, you will find lighter crowds and cooling temps – though some days can still be hot and muggy.

International Visitors

Historically, September has been the absolute best time to visit Disney Parks, when youngsters from the United States are back in school and the lines are thinner. However, Disney has been working hard to change that over the past decade.

International marketing efforts have drastically increased international tourism. During this season, it's still relatively slow, but not like in past years.

This timing coincides with the end of hurricane season, and even though it is much lower than the summer peaks, the temperature can still get pretty high. Keep an eye on the weather forecasts, because while rare, severe storms can happen this late in the season. It is also not uncommon for it to rain an hour or more daily several times a week.

Remember that Disney typically uses this off-season period to close down rides for refurbishment, as they keep all attractions open during peak seasons.

Also, if parades and fireworks shows are important to you, they may be limited or not available during off-season days, as the parks tend to have shorter evening hours. For instance, Fantasmic (Hollywood Studios) is only performed on certain evenings during the off-season, while it is often shown twice per evening during the longer summer hours.

Still, with the cooler temperatures, lower hotel prices, and lighter crowds, we think the trade-offs are worth it to visit during off-season.

Summertime

Most people visit Walt Disney World during the summer months (June to August). This is the period when hotel prices are at their peaks and parks are filled with people, particularly since students in the U.S. are all out of school. The summer tourist season brings with it many guests from the Southern Hemisphere, where they are experiencing winter chills, as well as those enjoying summer breaks from Canada and Europe. In short, this is an extremely busy, peak season.

If you're visiting Florida during this time primarily for the beaches, water parks and nightlife, Orlando is an excellent choice. Unfortunately, it's the *worst time of year* to come if you plan to visit theme parks.

Summers at Disney World are very hot. But it is not *dry heat*. It's very humid. In a place known for its intense heat and unrelenting humidity, the summer months become unbearable for spending time outdoors, even for most local residents.

Without proper preparation, the energy and fun can be zapped out of even the most hardy adult, let alone the smallest child. Even fans of the great outdoors will be crying. If you are not conditioned for the heat, it can be dangerous.

Seasonal Ride Closures

Part of the magical experience Disney provides to guests is the impeccable cleanliness level and top-notch maintenance throughout the parks. Nobody wants to see peeling paint or rusty tracks that detract from an attraction's overall appearance. With its regularly-scheduled maintenance, Disney makes sure you never will.

Many rides must be shut down annually for overhauls. These down-periods can be for several weeks, although they are generally scheduled during non-peak seasons. (Major changes to an attraction may cause closures of several months any time of year, though.)

This is how Disney keeps rides performing and looking great, without delays or breakdowns. For instance, Splash Mountain typically closes in early January each year and doesn't re-open until mid-March!

Fortunately, Disney usually schedules ride closures far enough in advance that you can find out if your favorite attraction will be open during your anticipated trip dates. While there is no longer an easy way to check ride closures on Disney's website, there are other online places to find this information. Here's a good resource to see which rides are scheduled to close for refurbishment: wdwinfo.com/wdwinfo/rehab.htm. Alternatively, contact Disney directly at (407) 939-2273 to verify the dates of scheduled attraction maintenance.

Be especially careful to avoid serious sunburns and heat strokes.

Finally, summer marks the rainy (and peak hurricane!) season, when long and steamy days are often punctuated with thunderstorms. We're not talking about the steady drizzle common in other parts of the U.S., like the Pacific Northwest. These torrential downpours accompany extremely dangerous lightning strikes, high winds, and sometimes (though weak and extremely rare) tornadoes.

However, if you can only come during this time of year, read our following tips to help make your visit bearable and enjoyable.

Beat the Heat – Tips for Keeping Cool in the Subtropics

- What to Wear for Comfort.
  - Wear light-colored and lightweight, moisture-wicking clothes made with breathable materials, such as cotton (but not tightly-woven fabrics like denim). Moisture-wicking underwear can also be quite helpful.
  - Shorts and t-shirts are fine during the summer, as long as you are wearing plenty of sunblock, though we recommend loose, lightweight pants or dresses that provide some protection from the sun.
  - The nights stay hot and steamy, so you won't need to pack sweaters for the evenings.
  - Most importantly, do not let your fashion sense get in the way of wearing comfortable clothing. You may be stuck in these clothes for hours at a time with no way to change them if you become uncomfortable. The vast majority of park-goers will be wearing casual, comfortable clothes, so

The climate brings with it lots of sweat. In fact, Orlando is ranked as number one of the top "10 Sweatiest Cities in America," according to a 2022 study conducted by MyDating-Adviser.com, in collaboration with a team of scientists. The study looked at how much heat is trapped in each metropolitan area during summer months. Three other Florida cities made the list: Tallahassee, Cape Coral, and Jacksonville.

there is no reason to try to make a fashion statement.

- Plan daytime special events which require dressing up at cooler, indoor locations. Late evenings are better suited to outdoor venues. Short outdoor activities during the mid-day sun can be tolerated for about 30 minutes before you will have to retreat back into the A/C.

- Make sure everyone is wearing sunglasses with UV protection. Keep in mind that children's eyes are particularly sensitive, even if they don't show it.

- During the days, wear a hat with a wide brim to block the sun from your face, eyes, and neck. Disney sells a lot of great souvenir hats that meet this need, including safari-style hats at the Animal Kingdom. You may wish to make this the one item you intend to purchase directly from Disney, as they have a number of fun and unique styles at fairly-reasonable prices. (You can expect to spend about $20-$25 on many designs.)
  - You might find a suitable option at the Disney Outlet (mentioned in our saving money section).

- People with electric scooters or wheelchairs often choose to use

a sun blocking umbrella that can be attached to the vehicle in lieu of a hat, which is also an excellent option.

- Sunscreen and insect repellants are absolute musts, and you need to reapply several times throughout the day. Disney provides insect repellant for free, but not the "natural" kind. Be sure to stock up, especially with sunblock, before going to the park. If you run out, of course Disney will sell you some, but it's at a premium. Unless you are going to remain exclusively indoors, be sure to wear sunblock, even if you don't normally use it. Apply it often, use it liberally, and don't forget to put it on your face.

- During the peak daily heat, make plans that will keep you indoors as much as possible. If you are outdoors, take plenty of breaks in the shade (or better – indoors!) and drink four to six ounces of water every 15 to 20 minutes.
  - If you are taking your own water and have access to a freezer, try freezing your water bottles the night before so that they remain cool in your bag or backpack.
  - Alternatively, remember our tip from above: any kiosk or fast-serve restaurant that has fountain drinks will give you a free cup of ice water. When the water or soda you bring from home gets warm in your backpack or stroller – and on hot Florida Summer days, it will get warm! – you can use this ice to refresh it.

- If you're staying at a hotel on Disney property, take advantage of it by taking refuge during the hottest hours. Visit the parks early in the morning, take a break during the most intense heat when the sun is directly overhead from about 1 p.m. to *at least* 5 p.m. in the afternoon. Plan to return to the theme parks during the cooler evening hours. (Wait until the sun starts to go down, if possible.)

- Consider buying a neck fan or misting fan filled with ice water. (Have a dry towel available to wipe your brow.)

- Try wearing a bandanna soaked in ice water around your neck. If you feel the effects of the heat, cover your head in a towel soaked in ice water for a few minutes. If you don't feel better, seek attention from the First Aid center.

- Body powders, such as those with corn starch (e.g. Gold Bond), can help reduce chafing and absorb excess body moisture. This is especially important if you sweat excessively or have sensitive skin that can get irritated from body moisture and humidity.

- A menthol-based lotion may provide a cooling sensation to those who are extra sensitive to the heat.

- Have a change of clothes – even an alternate hat – handy. There are few things more miserable than walking

around for hours in damp clothing. A quick rinse in a bathroom with a fresh shirt, hat, and underwear can do wonders to make you feel better on a hot day. And don't forget a change of clothes for your children. They get sweaty, too! Even one change of clothes halfway through your day (every four hours or so) will do wonders to increase your comfort level.

- Finally, be considerate of others. If you are sweating, chances are you don't smell pleasant. Standing in a crowded line with others who have body odor can make the long waits unbearable. Even if you come from a culture that doesn't normally use anti-perspirant and deodorants, use it on your trip to Disney World. Anti-perspirant will actually help reduce sweating, and you can put it anywhere on your body to stop unwanted moisture.

Shoe Wear

Have you ever noticed local Floridians always wear flip flops? This isn't because we're lazy slobs — although that may also be true! It's actually because we're practical. We've experienced the pain and discomfort related to swollen feet in regular shoes, which include nasty blisters that can ruin a day out in the theme parks.

Floridians often use high quality sandals or flip flops during the summer (such as Merrell) that have natural materials and minimal places for feet to rub and chafe.

Many people make the mistake of thinking shoes that are comfortable for walking around back home will be suitable for walking around Disney. This might be true in the coldest months, but your feet are bound to swell in Florida's hotter months. A pair of shoes that can

Insider's Tip!

There are a few places you can get your name embroidered on a hat or set of mouse ears on Disney property (for a fee). These are *Adrian and Edith's Head to Toe* in Hollywood Studios, *Mouse Gear* in Epcot, *The Chapeau* in Magic Kingdom, and *Disney's Days of Christmas* in Disney Springs. However, if you find a hat you like at another Disney retailer, you can take it to any of these locations to have the embroidery done for an additional charge.

be adjusted throughout the day is vital. Good arch support and cushioned insoles are also important in any walking shoe.

Finally, shoes with high heels are not appropriate for a day at a theme park. If you only plan to go out for a couple of hours to eat dinner, they are fine, but remember you will be walking quite some distance to get to any restaurant inside one of the parks. Consider attractive sandals, instead. You won't be out of place in even the nicest theme park restaurants, and your time spent will be much more enjoyable.

Summertime Visits

During the summer months, the parks are open longer hours than other times of year. Go first thing in the morning and enjoy popular outdoor rides. When it starts to get too hot, do not try to push yourself.

If you can afford to do so, rely heavily on Lightning Lane reservations. Even with them, when planning your schedule from the late morning until the late afternoon, look for (indoor and air-conditioned) "dark rides."

Keep in mind: Without Lightning Lane reservations, stand-by lines can be ninety minutes (or longer!) during the day, leaving you hot and dehydrated. The heat can also make you and your children very cranky. If you cannot find indoor queues for rides, this would be the best time to head back to your hotel, even if it is not on-property. Take advantage of the refreshing pool or take a rejuvenating nap. This can also be a great time to hit a water park if you have tickets.

Don't go back to the park until evening, after you've eaten and the sun is going down. Now is the time when others who weren't as smart as you are likely to take a break for dinner, so the crowds thin out a bit. You, however, will be well-rested, well-fed, and able to enjoy yourself until the park closes.

Embrace the Rain – Don't Fight It!

Disney World enjoys a unique sub-tropical climate unlike anywhere else in the United States. Peak summer weather brings somewhat random downpours many days per week. If you visit during this time, keep a close eye on the weather forecasts. The hardest rains can absolutely drench those who are unprotected in a matter of seconds. Though you may not want to carry an umbrella all day long for sun protection, plan to keep one with you

Insider's Tip!

1. Don't make the mistake of wearing brand-new shoes on your trip. Give yourself time to break them in properly. Plan to walk for several miles per day a few times before your trip to see how your feet hold up in your shoes. Remember, you can expect to walk four to seven miles daily on your Disney vacation, which is a lot different on your feet than a 20-minute walk back home!
2. If you decide to wear tennis shoes, it's a good idea to use athletic, moisture-wicking socks and foot powder.
3. Find a place to sit down and take your shoes off (away from other people, preferably!) a few times throughout the day to reduce swelling and to reapply powder. Also, bring blister bandages along (the thick, waterproof kind) just in case. Your feet will thank you!

if you don't want to risk getting caught in a downpour.

The Poncho – Versatile and Easy to Carry

If you are traveling as part of a large group or family, umbrellas may not be an efficient choice. Alternatively, bring an easier-to-carry, lightweight poncho. They can be bundled together to make taking several of them convenient.

Not only does the poncho protect you the instant a storm hits, it has added benefits. When the air cools down, a poncho can act as a wind-breaker. Best yet: ponchos protect you from getting too wet on a couple of rides, such as Kali River Rapids (Animal Kingdom) and Splash Mountain (Magic Kingdom). For obvious reasons, Disney won't let you use an umbrella on a ride or during outdoor shows, so the poncho wins in versatility, hands-down.

The ponchos sold anywhere on Disney property will cost more than twice the price of ones purchased off-property. A large family can easily drop $50 when it is time to outfit themselves during an emergency downpour. The Mickey-branded throw-away ponchos sell for nearly $10 (each!) compared to the plain, un-branded versions that can be purchased for only a buck at the discount 99¢ or "dollar" stores. Disney ponchos available on-property are not only more expensive, they also lack durability. However, if a poncho purchased at the parks rips, Disney will replace it for free.

Since you love Disney as much as we do, you may want a poncho that has your favorite characters on it. Fortunately, many area stores, such as at Target and Walmart, sell Disney-branded ones that are both less expensive and more durable than those sold inside the theme parks. The whole family can have fun wearing their favorite Disney characters at a fraction of the price that Disney charges.

Summer-time Storm Tips

- Longer storms that last a couple of hours or more are great for clearing out the crowds at all of the Disney theme parks, and especially at the water parks.
- You might find you have a water park nearly to yourself if you go there following a downpour.

Autumn

Each year has different trends. One year you may find the weather cooling down to bearable temperatures as early as September, while the stifling heat can last through October other years. (In 2015 and 2016, the weather stayed in the 80s through nearly all of December!) During the months of September through November, expect relatively warm days and potentially cool nights.

This means your daytime wear should be similar to what's needed in the summer, but you may want to change into long pants for the evening with sweaters or light jackets available in case the temperature cools. Disney makes a lot of money on unexpected sweater and blanket purchases in the evenings from people who did not plan accordingly. And just because one evening is warm doesn't mean the next one will be. Wear layers of clothing every night.

You will still want to carry an umbrella or poncho through about mid-October,

Insider's Tip!

Ponchos should definitely be part of your family's wardrobe, especially to wear on wet outdoor rides in the evening.

Insider's Caution!

If you are in a pool when a thunderstorm starts, get out immediately. If you see lightning, find shelter. People get hit by lightning every year in Florida.

though the chances of actually needing it will be less.

The big plus to Disney in the autumn is the lack of crowds. You may have missed what we said earlier: Disney does a great deal of marketing to South American tourists, so the off-seasons aren't as dead as they were just a few years ago. But compared to the summer crowds, there are a lot less people to fight to get to the front of a line.

Overall, Orlando has much better weather and smaller crowds in the fall season. While it may seem like the best time of year to go, there is a slight catch. Disney uses the off-season to refurbish its rides, which can sometimes mean a ride is shut down for months. They also use the off-season to refurbish the water parks, so only one is open from October to February. This means you may miss out on a ride or two that you really wanted to experience if you're not careful. Fortunately, Disney always advertises these planned closures well in advance, so a simple check of the park calendars will tell you if your favorite rides will be available when you want to travel.

Winter

Humidity and temperatures are both at their lowest levels during the winter months of December through February, with the months of January and February getting the coldest. While there is an occasional frigid streak, the days are typically still warm during the winter,

often reaching 80°F (26.7°C) or higher. Thanks to the lower humidity, you should be comfortable in jeans, which you will definitely want to wear when the cooler temperatures of the evenings hit. Carrying along a reasonably warm windbreaker will be sufficient during the days.

Winter evenings can be chilly, though, and night time temperatures often drop to near-freezing. Plan on wearing layers that you can add or remove throughout the day. Include a sweater and heavier coat in your travel wardrobe. Children and adults who are particularly sensitive to the cold should have gloves, a scarf, and a hat just in case. During these months, it is very important to <u>wear something waterproof on all water rides</u>, such as a coat or poncho. Even if it *seems* hot, cool breezes can pick up and temperatures can drop rapidly. You do not want to be stuck in wet clothes when that happens! Wet and cold clothing will bring your fun to an immediate halt.

Best Disney Travel Times for Each Season

Weather is not the only factor to consider when making travel plans. Just as important are the crowds and events. Let's go over details that will help you determine when to visit Disney and what will be going on at different times of the year.

Enjoy Lighter Crowds

The week after Labor Day until the week before Thanksgiving (but not the week of Thanksgiving!) is generally slow – in other words, most of the fall season. Just bear in mind that this is still the end of the hurricane season and temperatures are quite high.

The least busy period generally starts the day after Labor Day through the first couple of weeks in October. Disney begins

The Seasons of Disney: Hot, Hotter, & Hottest

to get quite busy again the week leading up to Thanksgiving Day.

From mid-November on, Christmas decorations are up in the parks, and the special holiday shows and parades are under way. The festive spirit in the air makes the holidays particularly enchanting at Disney World. People seem to be more courteous and tend to act more friendly and cordial during the Christmas holidays, which is a nice change from the summer months when tempers can flare.

Late Fall to Winter – Visiting the Parks for the Holidays

There is nothing more magical than entering the Magic Kingdom on an 80 degree day and finding yourself in the middle of a winter wonderland, snow and all!

The Disney holiday season isn't just Christmas. In fact, it starts during the fall and goes all the way through the first part of January. There are some variations in the seasonal festivities, though.

During September, the Magic Kingdom begins its autumn transformation with Jack-o-lanterns and hay bales galore. This is also when Disney begins celebrating Halloween (as early as August!)

Disney After Hours Boo Bash (August through October)

On select nights, the Magic Kingdom closes its gates early to general admission guests at 7 p.m., so those with a special pass to the Disney After Hours Boo Bash can enjoy the park all to themselves. Party passes are linked directly to your Magic Band or park pass.

In an attempt to control crowds, the number of attendees is limited for each party, so attraction wait times are typically much shorter than during the day. Going to a Halloween party in September or early October usually means the party will not be sold out, so there will be even fewer guests, and it can almost feel like you have the park to yourself.

What's so special about these parties that would make someone want to shell out the extra cash to attend?

Each year, Disney transforms the park, including certain rides, into a Halloween "spooktacular." You won't see any of these transformations until the party actually begins, meaning you can't "sneak a peak" without the wristband.

This is the best trick-or-treat party you'll ever see. If your children love sweets, they won't be disappointed. We're

The Seasons of Disney: Hot, Hotter, & Hottest

Insider's Tip!

Certain rides, such as Splash Mountain, and one of the water parks are closed for part of the winter while they are refurbished. Others are closed for refurbishment during other off-seasons. Always check the refurbishment list before planning your vacation to make sure you will be able to experience the attractions you want.

Insider's Tip!

One favorite time of year to visit the parks is *the week prior to Thanksgiving week*. However, visiting anytime *after Thanksgiving week* until *the week before Christmas* is more festive, as holiday decorations abound. The first week of December is particularly good, and the crowds are again moderately thin. Hotel prices drop and the weather cools to bearable temperatures without being too chilly.

The Seasons of Disney: Hot, Hotter, & Hottest

talking about buckets of candy for those who want it!

In addition to taking part in everyone's favorite Halloween pastime of begging for sweets, there are special events, such as a Halloween stage show, parade, and fireworks. One more thing to look forward to is rare meet-and-greet opportunities with characters you're unlikely to see any other time: villains!

Because the Magic Kingdom is the only park that transforms itself especially for Halloween, it causes another phenomenon to happen on party nights: busy crowds at other parks (and Disney Springs).

This means whichever park stays open the latest on party nights (usually Epcot) gets flooded with all the remaining guests that have the park hopper option.

Since autumn is the off-season, this isn't usually too bad (except on Fridays and Saturdays). To avoid crowds, find non-themepark-related things to do on party nights.

Thanksgiving and Christmas: When to Make a Holiday Visit

If a trip to Walt Disney World seems like a great way to get into the holiday spirit – and trust us, it is – a great time to visit can be the week *before* Thanksgiving week. People flood the parks during the actual week of Thanksgiving, but it can be quite slow the <u>week prior</u>. All of the holiday decorations are up and the seasonal shows and special events are already running.

If you want to wait until December to celebrate Christmas, try the first half of the month. It gets busier and busier the closer it gets to the actual holiday.

During the Christmas season (mid-November to the first week of January), all of the parks make an amazing transformation. The theme parks get amazing trees each year, each several stories tall

Insider's Tip!

How do special event passes work? The pass is linked to your My Disney Experience account and any passes or MagicBands assigned to you. Upon entry into the park, you will receive a color-coded bracelet to wear throughout the evening. (The wristband's color is specific to your evening to keep guests from reusing them to gain entry to an event on another evening.) Cast Members check for these bracelets throughout the night, and guests without one are gently funneled out of the park.

and uniquely-themed for its park. Characters dress in their winter garb for photos and parades, and the entire resort has an incredible, festive atmosphere.

Disney Very Merriest After Hours (mid-November through late-December)

Similar to its Halloween Party, the Magic Kingdom also holds a Christmas celebration called Disney Very Merriest After Hours. There are a couple of

Insider's Tip!

Don't waste the daily admission price for a regular park pass on the day you plan to attend a paid special event like the Disney After Hours Boo Bash. Those with the special Halloween Party pass can enter the gates early at 4 p.m., and the party doesn't end until midnight, giving you plenty of hours at the park <u>for less money than it costs for a one-day pass</u>.

differences. No rides are transformed (and of course, no trick-or-treat stations).

Party-goers are offered unlimited holiday beverages, such as eggnog and hot cocoa, and cookies throughout the party (along with healthier apple slices and juice), several dance parties break out, and it may be the rare time you get to see certain characters in the park, including Uncle Scrooge, Peter Pan and Wendy, and the Seven Dwarfs. The Mayor of the Magic Kingdom usually makes an appearance on Main Street, as well.

Of course, no Christmas party would be complete without snowfall, which Disney magically delivers on Main Street.

Christmas at Epcot

As a park known for its food, try some of the fun holiday options Epcot has to offer, such as *Gluhwein* in the Germany Pavilion and gingerbread men sold in the American Adventure Pavilion.

Candlelight Processional

The America Pavilion also hosts the seasonal Candlelight Processional. See the Special Annual Events section for more details about this special (and unbelievably popular) Christmas event.

> What is amazing is how quickly a change can happen at Disney. You could be attending the Disney After Hours Boo Bash party on Halloween night, then enter the Magic Kingdom the next morning to find it's suddenly winter. Actually, the transformation takes place over the first couple of weeks in November, but since all the work happens at night when the parks are closed and empty, the change can be drastic from day-to-day.

Holiday Dining – Thanksgiving or Christmas Reservations

If you want to share a special holiday meal with your family and friends, dining at Disney can be memorable. Planning your special meal for Thanksgiving rather than Christmas tends to be easier. More than 35 different specialty dining choices abound on Thanksgiving Day, allowing you to bask in a traditional culinary experience throughout Walt Disney World Resort. Traditional Christmas meals are somewhat more scarce. Liberty Tree Tavern in Magic Kingdom provides a turkey-rich feast, while 50's Prime Time Café in Hollywood Studios is another favorite for those seeking the holiday's favorite fowl.

Christmas Day at the Magic Kingdom

Is anything more festive than the Magic Kingdom on Christmas day? Just be prepared for crowds of epic proportions! However, there is a little known secret about Christmas day that can make the experience much more enjoyable. While it does not last for long, the Magic Kingdom is typically nearly empty first thing in the morning until about 10 a.m., as even vacationers are back in their hotel rooms opening presents and enjoying a Christmas breakfast. You can enjoy nearly all of the popular rides with very little wait if you get to the park at opening.

Christmas Day at Other Parks

Animal Kingdom often fills to capacity on Christmas, and the crowds clamor to Epcot to eat a special dinner and watch the Candlelight Processional later in the day. However, Hollywood Studios tends to be slow on Christmas day. We have enjoyed several nice, quiet Christmases at Hollywood Studios in the past.

The Seasons of Disney: Hot, Hotter, & Hottest

Televised Christmas Holiday Parade

Have you seen the Christmas parade Disney broadcasts on Christmas day each year? That's actually filmed at the Magic Kingdom during regular hours, some time in late-November or early-December. Each year, Disney has a different way of soliciting people to be in the video, but regular guests can usually view the proceedings from afar, including the concert events.

CROWDS AT THE PARKS

Off Season – Lowest Attendance Levels (Best Time to Visit)

January (except New Year's Day) until just prior to Presidents' Week in February

The week following Labor Day (September) until the week prior to Thanksgiving (November)

The week following Thanksgiving (last Thursday in November) until mid-December

Moderate Attendance Levels

After Presidents' week in mid-February through early March

Late April through early June (except Memorial Day weekend)

Columbus Day Weekend (October)

The week of Halloween (surrounding October 31st)

The first part of Thanksgiving week

The last two weeks of the U.S. Summer Break – mid-August through Labor Day

Peak Season – Highest Attendance Levels (Best Time to Avoid)

Presidents' week in mid-February

Spring Break season – Mid-March through Late April

Memorial Day weekend (May)

Mid-June through mid-August (Summer Break, especially 4th of July weekend)

Thanksgiving Day and weekend (late November)

Christmas week through New Year's Day

Rules to Avoid Crowds

We know it's not always possible to schedule your vacation during the off-season, unless it coincides with a holiday, so we've created this section to give you an idea of what to expect during the various months.

The slowest off-season periods may have only 10,000 guests visiting the Magic Kingdom per day. Compare this to peak periods, when the parks can be expected to

Insider's Tip!

If you don't know exactly where you want to eat, make reservations an hour or so apart at different restaurants. As the day approaches and you have firmed up your plans, you can cancel whichever reservations you don't need. (Double check any cancellation policies!)

The Seasons of Disney: Hot, Hotter, & Hottest

Insider's Tip!

If you plan to be at any park on the actual day of Thanksgiving, Christmas Eve, or Christmas, get dining reservations early. You can get them as much as 180 days in advance (plus ten days for on-property guests), and certain places, such as the Liberty Tree Tavern in the Magic Kingdom, fill up immediately. However, Disney always keeps a certain number of seats available for walk-ins, so if you find yourself in a park without reservations, go to Guest Relations first thing in the morning to ask if you can get into the restaurant of your choice. You may need to wait until the restaurant you want to eat at actually opens for the day and immediately get your name on the list.

approach capacity. That's about 90,000 people a day (or nine times as many visitors) in Magic Kingdom alone! During peak periods, hours are extended, and any on-going ride maintenance will be complete so that the parks are ready for the anticipated turnout. (If you missed our earlier warning: Beware that slow periods are when some rides are closed for refurbishment. Disney also closes one of its water parks during the slow season.)

Avoid Heavy Holiday Crowds

There are a few general rules to avoiding crowds at Disney.

Stay out of the parks during United States holidays. Never come on any holiday weekend or the week(s) surrounding major holidays (Thanksgiving, Christmas, and New Year's Day).

Particularly avoid Labor Day (September), Independence Day (July 4th), the week of Thanksgiving Day (and the following weekend), Christmas through the New Year's Day (if New Year's Day falls before the weekend, avoid the following weekend), Easter, Martin Luther King Day weekend, Memorial Day weekend, the week of President's Day (mid-February) until after Easter – the busiest day ever recorded at the Magic Kingdom was during the Easter holiday in April of 2013!

The last two weeks of December through the first Sunday of January are particularly bustling with guests coming from all over the world to experience Disney's holiday magic. In fact, the week of Christmas through New Year's Day is the busiest period at Walt Disney World. Christmas Day will have you standing shoulder-to-shoulder and moving down Main Street, U.S.A. at a snail's pace. It might be fun for a few minutes, but it quickly becomes a major ordeal, especially for parents pushing strollers. Just trying to disperse after a fireworks show in the Magic Kingdom leads to congestion and slow-moving lines.

Avoid School Breaks

Avoid the summer months (Summer Break) when children are out of school, particularly mid-June through mid-August. Summer season, while not quite as busy as Christmas, is generally the worst time of year to visit. School-age families pour in from all over the United States, and the South American tour season is at its peak (as they're escaping the dead of winter down there). The crowds combined with the heat and difficulty of navigating the large tour groups make this our least favorite time of year to visit.

The last half of August leading to Labor Day weekend is the best time to

The Seasons of Disney: Hot, Hotter, & Hottest

visit for families that can only visit during the summer break but want to beat the intense heat and crowds of the summer. Most U.S. families are finished with their fun for the season.

Spring Break season is also very busy, seeing crowds from all over the United States, Canada, and Europe, as school breaks stagger throughout March and April. The busy Easter holiday falls within the same season.

If you decide to book your trip during school breaks, you will be going with the masses. Still, it might be the only way to schedule your vacation. If that is the case, be certain to read through all of our advice relating to maneuvering around the crowds.

Taking Children Out of Class

Many parents plan to take their children out of school for their Disney trip, using the week following Christmas or after Spring Break ends. The week following Labor Day (in September) is also excellent, particularly as the subject matters kids learn during that week in school aren't likely to be as intense as those later in the school year. This is a fantastic time to miss the crowds and (usually) avoid a busy school schedule.

Visiting outside designated school breaks is a must if your family does not have school-age children or if you're close enough to Orlando for a weekend getaway.

Touring the area after Spring Break will allow you to benefit from Florida's fabulous spring weather. The timing will also let you see Epcot's International Flower and Garden Festival. Consider the first three weeks of May, before Memorial Day.

And, while it's not a complete substitution for school, there are many educational aspects of Disney, particularly at the Animal Kingdom and Epcot. When considering whether or not to take your children out of school to visit Disney during lighter crowds, it's important to discuss scheduled curricula with teachers to see if there is anything the child shouldn't miss.

Avoid Big Conventions

Consider whether there are any large conventions happening in Orlando the week of your visit. Conventions can cause area hotel rates to skyrocket up to triple the price of value season rates, and conventioneers tend to flood the parks between sessions. Check out the website at ccc.net/globalcalendar to see the list of events happening at the Orlando County Convention Center (which is the area's largest venue, located in the tourist center on International Drive).

Some of the popular events include:
- National Cheerleading Competitions
- High School Marching Band Competitions
- High School Sporting Events

Insider's Tip!

If you are planning to visit on Christmas, make your day extra special by visiting the Magic Kingdom at opening time. Crowds are almost non-existent early in the morning, allowing you to experience all of the best attractions with little wait.

That all changes around 10 a.m. when you can expect huge crowds to enter the parks. Unimaginable waves of guests begin to press in on the park, as it fills to capacity.

If you want to visit the Magic Kingdom on Christmas day, stay at one of the Disney hotels, so you can get Early Theme Park Entry to the park at 7:30 a.m. Get your rides out of the way and plan to leave when crowds flood in. Eat a Christmas brunch or take a break in your hotel room and enjoy opening your presents!

- Professional Sports Competitions at ESPN
- Charity Events

Guests Can Be Turned Away

Parks sometimes reach capacity and close to further incoming guests, particularly on holidays. Because of this, it is imperative that you make a park reservation as early as possible, prior to your vacation.

Prior to the park reservation system, Disney closures operated on a phased system, which gave priority to on-property guests and those with dining reservations.

While the phased closure system is technically a thing of the past, guests staying at Disney resorts still have an advantage in the form of Disney hotel concierges, who can sometimes make magic happen for guests in the form of last-minute park reservations.

Insider's Tip!

Talk to your child's teacher about an alternative project that reflects real-world things that your child will benefit from experiencing. Perhaps developing a well-written report about things your children learned during their trip can be substituted for their missed coursework.

Insider's Warning!

The immense crowds around Christmas are heel-to-toe and claustrophobic. Guests who aren't prepared for what to expect can become angry or disillusioned. Lines are much longer than during off-peak periods and can easily reach two hours or longer (for a three-minute ride)!

The Seasons of Disney: Hot, Hotter, & Hottest

Best Times to Visit, by Month and Day of the Week

This information can be used as a general planning guide so you will know what to expect on the exact days of your visit.

Best Months to Plan a Visit

Here is a quick trip planning guide by month for your reference. Remember that hurricane season goes from the beginning of June to the end of November.

MONTHLY ATTENDANCE GUIDE

Month	Expected Crowds	Special Exceptions
January	Low	High on New Year's Day and through weekend if New Year's Day is near a weekend; WDW Marathon weekend is very busy; Tinker Bell Half Marathon weekend is very busy (runDisney.com)
February	Low before week of President's Day; High week of President's Day; Medium following week of President's Day	
March	Medium first two weeks; High last two weeks	
April	High	Highest on Easter weekend and the following week
May	Medium	High during Memorial Day weekend
June	Medium first two weeks; High last two weeks	Gay Days increases attendance for a week beginning the first weekend of June
July	High	July 4th is one of the busiest days of the year
August	High first three weeks; Medium last week	Crowds taper slightly at end of the month, as locals go back to school
September	Medium through Labor Day; Low beginning week after Labor Day	

October	Low	Halloween Event closes MK early on certain evenings, pushing crowds to other parks; Food & Wine Festival draws additional crowds to Epcot
November	Low through week before Thanksgiving week; High Thanksgiving week; Low beginning Monday after Thanksgiving	Christmas Event closes MK early on certain evenings, pushing crowds to other parks
December	Low first two weeks; Medium third week; High Christmas week through New Year's Eve	Christmas Event closes MK early on certain evenings, pushing crowds to other parks; Certain celebrity visits to Epcot draw higher than normal crowds

Best Days to Plan a Visit

Regardless of season, the number of visitors at each park varies by the day of the week. Here is a quick trip planning guide for expected crowds by day of week for your reference. Attendance is highly variable, so use this as a general guide only.

Keep in mind that weekends are always relatively busier than weekdays, so guests staying off-property should plan to visit mid-week. Monday through Wednesday are generally the slowest days for all parks,

and you can expect Magic Kingdom to be busier than other parks, unless the other park is hosting a special event, such as Epcot's Food & Wine Festival.

Remember, certain special events, such as holiday parties at Magic Kingdom or a popular musical guest at Epcot's International Food & Wine Festival, affect crowds and create a lot of extra tourist and local traffic.

Days to Enjoy Lower Crowds at the Parks: By Park

Magic Kingdom	When to Enjoy	Tuesday
	Days to Avoid:	Monday, Wednesday & Weekend
Epcot	When to Enjoy:	Monday
	Days to Avoid:	Tuesday, Thursday & Fridays
Hollywood Studios	When to Enjoy:	Tuesday
	Days to Avoid:	Wednesday & Sunday
Animal Kingdom	When to Enjoy:	Thursday & Friday
	Days to Avoid:	Monday & Saturday

The Seasons of Disney: Hot, Hotter, & Hottest

Days to Enjoy Lower Crowds at the Parks (By Day of the Week)	Sunday	Monday	Tuesday	Wednesday	Thursday	Friday	Saturday
Magic Kingdom			X				
Epcot		X					
Hollywood Studios			X				
Animal Kingdom					X	X	

Daily Park Attendance Guide

	Magic Kingdom	Epcot	Hollywood Studios	Animal Kingdom
Monday	High	Low	Medium	High
Tuesday	Low	High	Low	Medium
Wednesday	High	Medium	High	Medium
Thursday	Medium	High	Medium	Low
Friday	High	High	Medium	Low
Saturday	High	Medium	Medium	High
Sunday	Medium	Medium	High	Medium

There's no way to predict exactly what will happen at a park on a particular day. Take, for example, Disney's shocking lack of preparedness (in 2013) for Hollywood Studios' *Friday the 13th Villains* event. Portions of the park were closed for the evening as the park filled to capacity, creating hours-long gridlock in and around the parking lots, as well as extreme waits at restaurants around the park. (The event was held as a separately-ticketed event the following summer, similar to the Christmas and Halloween parties at Magic Kingdom, and there is no indication that it will be held again in the future.)

Wait Times During Your Visit

While you should use Lightning Lane reservations for the most popular attractions, there are many that you will likely wait to experience in standby queues. Keep in mind that the wait times for queues fluctuate throughout the day, so check the times often to catch a ride during slower periods.

We recommend you monitor expected wait times with the official Disney My Disney Experience app, which is updated regularly by Disney employees. Each time you get off of a ride, it's fast and easy to check wait times to determine which attraction to experience next.

Crowd Calendar Advice from Private Companies

There are many apps that are not owned or operated by Disney. These companies use past data as a fairly accurately way to predict crowds on specific days of the year.

Others try to rely on users to upload wait time information while they are at the parks, meaning their actual hour-to-hour accuracy is hit-or-miss.

Touring Plans (touringplans.com) is one website that attempts to take all the guess work out of visiting the parks with a crowd calendar and itinerary planning tool. They charge a fee for a subscription to their services. Many guests believe the information is reliable.

Why pay money when you can get virtually the same calendar for free and use Disney's Genie to create a completely free itinerary? Undercover Tourist (this company also sells discounted Disney tickets!) has a completely free crowd calendar online at undercovertourist.com/planning/when-to-visit.html.

Insider's Tip!

Use the theme park reservation system as a gauge to determine how busy a particular park will be on the day of your visit. (Be sure to make your reservations early - you can change them later!) If you see the park you've booked fill up with reservations, but other parks are available, you may want to switch your reservations to the available park. You must cancel your current park reservation, then reserve a new one, so be sure to check reservation ability on the park reservation calendar before doing so.

Keep in mind, though, that Disney's pre-planning tools (such as Lightning Lane reservations) are constantly changing, making predictions difficult. Fortunately, with the Genie+ system in place, you have the ability to schedule most rides on the same day, regardless of what the wait times are expected to be in stand-by queues...for an additional fee.

Insider's Tip!

A rainy or drizzly day is a good time to visit any park, as the weather literally and figuratively puts a damper on the crowds. After thunderstorms, all parks thin out, and the water parks are often almost empty – even at the peak periods.

Insider's Tip!

Early Theme Park Entry benefit is wonderful if you're a Disney hotel guest, particularly in the early morning hours when you can walk on to almost any ride without a wait.

However, this perk has changed. While resort guests used to get one- to two-hour early or late entry into a specific park each day, it is now 30 minutes of early entry into any park of your choosing.

The Seasons of Disney: Hot, Hotter, & Hottest

Special Annual Events (List Ordered by Date)

Epcot International Festival of the Arts – Mid-January through mid-February

Epcot International Festival of the Arts made its debut in 2017. It is included with your Epcot park admission. During the festival, artists display their wares, celebrating art in all its forms. To the delight of patrons, edible art can be enjoyed from booths throughout World Showcase. The event is daily starting in January and running into February. Musical acts feature Broadway performers who entertain crowds with Disney Broadway showtunes.

- Specialty venues with experts may require reservations and an additional fee.

Mighty St. Patrick's Festival – March

Mighty St. Patrick's Festival at Disney Springs celebrates Irish culture for the two weekends leading up to St. Patrick's Day each year. Irish dancing and live music, along with lots of alcohol, are the key features of this event. Disney picks up its visible security presence during the festival, and incidents are rare. The atmosphere, especially during the evening, is not always family friendly, though. Aside from increased traffic at an already overly-busy venue, Disney Springs special events don't generally draw additional tourists to Disney World.

- Held in March at Disney Springs
- Free Entry

America Gardens Theatre Concert Tips!

The *Garden Rocks* and *Eat to the Beat* concert series are held at the America Gardens Theatre at the center of World Showcase. This is an open-air venue with a lot of seating, but not all of it is under cover.

You can watch the show while sitting in whatever seats you find available after the line is seated, or stand at the edge of the venue.

Plan to show up early to get the best "stand-by" seats, though. There is a roped-off (but unmarked) queue that forms on the Italy-side of the venue. There will be Cast Members nearby if you need directions.

Locals often line up an hour or more before a show to get the best seats for the most popular bands. (Many local families get annual passes just for these great concerts!)

To get a great seat for one of the last two shows of the evening, wait in the line during the previous show. As the line moves forward, you can simply stop when you reach the front of the line, allowing the people behind you to proceed past you into the concert. You'll be at (or very near) the front of the line for the following show, and you'll be able to watch the current one from your stand-by line location!

The stand-by queue is seated 15-20 minutes prior to each show. You can nearly always find seating (even if it's near the back) if you arrive before the line is seated. No matter how busy a concert gets, standing room is always available (albeit behind the seating area and along the promenade).

Note: You are free to photograph and video these concerts (as you can virtually all performances at Disney property venues).

Epcot International Flower & Garden Festival – Early-March through Early-July

Epcot International Flower & Garden Festival is included with your Epcot park admission. The park gets decked out in its flowery finery to showcase incredible plants from around the world and topiaries with very familiar Disney character faces. Various experts and horticulture celebrities are on-hand to teach you everything you need to know about beautifying the inside and outside of your home. The event starts in March and runs into May. This is the less crazy of Epcot's two prime annual festivals.

Garden Rocks Concert Series

The highlight of the event is the Garden Rocks Concert Series (formerly the Flower Power Concert Series), held Fridays, Saturdays, and Sundays throughout the festival. Epcot draws a different line-up of bands from the 60s, 70s, and 80s each year, such as Starship, Herman's Hermits, and many more. Each weekend highlights a different band, which plays three different 30-minute "mini" concerts (playing the same or similar set) per day.

Be sure to check Disney's website to find out who will be playing during your visit (disneyworld. disney.go.com/entertainment/epcot/flower-garden-rocks-concert-series/).

The Garden Rocks Concert Series, held at the America Gardens Theatre at the center of World Showcase, is an open-air and open-seating venue (subject to specially-reserved areas for groups).

The peak Spring Break season brings more visitors to Epcot and other parks from March through April, but you can avoid the crowds by visiting the festival in early May. Of course, weekend evenings tend to be more crowded than other days due to the concerts and locals visiting the park.

- Specialty venues with experts may require reservations and an additional fee.

Independence Day – July 4th

Independence Day is celebrated at Magic Kingdom with specialty fireworks and a parade. Epcot holds a special fireworks event after the evening's Harmonious show. While July is always busy, the 4th of July can have claustrophobic crowds. Consider enjoying the Magic Kingdom fireworks from the beach at the Polynesian Resort or from a nearby high-rise hotel, such as the Blue Heron Beach Resort, located on SR-535 just south of the I-4 interchange.

Dapper Day – Multiple Days April and November (Magic Kingdom and Epcot)

Dapper Day is a "fan-driven" event held each spring and fall at one or more parks. This is an informal event where people meet at the park dressed in stylish clothing, often from a retro period. Anybody can dress up or sponsor a group to meet at the park informally. Go to dapperday.com to see details about dates and how the event began.

- Note: This informal event is included with your park admission.

Insider's Tip!

If you missed the call out box on the prior page (America Gardens Theatre Concert Tips!), review what we said about how to get good seats.

The Seasons of Disney: Hot, Hotter, & Hottest

Epcot International Food & Wine Festival – Mid-July through Mid-November

Epcot International Food & Wine Festival is Epcot's second and more popular large, annual event, held mid-September through mid-November of each year. In addition to the regular country pavilions within World Showcase, Epcot lines the area with nearly 30 food and wine booths from other countries throughout the world. You can also pay extra for special culinary experiences with celebrity chefs.

The highlight of this festival is the Eat to the Beat Concert Series, held *every night* of the festival. There are a wide variety of bands, mostly from the 1980s and 1990s (though some are newer), who each play three concerts every evening for two-three nights during the festival. Disney guests and locals often flock to the park after work, and weekend evenings get particularly crazy with the alcohol and crowds. If you don't like crowds, we suggest you attend the event earlier in the day and leave after the first of the three concerts held each evening.

- Note: This event is included with your Epcot park admission.
- Celebrity chefs host events at specialty venues that may require reservations and an additional fee.

Disney After Hours Boo Bash – Select Nights August through October (Magic Kingdom)

Disney After Hours Boo Bash is a child-friendly Halloween celebration held at the Magic Kingdom each year on select nights from September through October. It's a specially-ticketed event that closes down the park early to guests without a ticket. There are many highlights, which include: villain and specially-costumed Disney character

Insider's Tip!

The Eat to the Beat Concert Series draws a different line-up of bands each year. Each band plays two to three days in a row, and they put on three different 30-minute concerts each evening. Be sure to check Disney's website to find out who will be playing during your visit or visit their Facebook page at www.facebook.com/EpcotFoodandWine.

meet-and-greets; Halloween-themed parades, entertainment, and fireworks; and unlimited trick-or-treating to obtain as many sweets as you can eat for no additional charge at multiple locations throughout the park. Certain attractions close during this event, but most stay open and have much shorter lines than during the day. However, the increased price and lack of special touches this event had in past years means this is a one-time splurge. If you've done it before, you may not find it worth the higher prices to do it again. Adult ticket prices for this event start at $129 plus tax.

- Separate Event Admission Required

Insider's Tip!

The Halloween Party is one of the rare occasions where adult guests are allowed to dress up as their favorite Disney characters. Any other day, adults (ages 14 and up) who look too much like the official characters get turned away at the gates to avoid confusion. (Disney wouldn't want unauthorized people representing themselves as beloved characters.)

The Seasons of Disney: Hot, Hotter, & Hottest

Disney Very Merriest After Hours— Select Nights November through December (Magic Kingdom)

Disney Very Merriest After Hours is an annual celebration at the Magic Kingdom. The parties are held on select nights in November and December, leading to the week before Christmas. It's a specially-ticketed event that closes down the park early to guests without a ticket. There are many highlights, which include: rare and specially-costumed Disney character meet-and-greets; a Christmas parade complete with Santa; and as much holiday beverages and cookies as you can eat! Certain attractions close during this event, but most stay open. Due to the limited capacity of this party, and because so much of the party is held at special events, conventional rides and attractions have much shorter lines than during the day, prior to when the party begins. However, the increased price and lack of special touches this event had in past years means this is a one-time splurge. Like many special events, most people only need to experience it once and probably won't find it worth the price for

an additional time. Adult ticket prices for this event start at $129 plus tax.

- Separate Event Admission Required

Candlelight Processional – Late-November through Late-December

The Candlelight Processional is held nightly during the holiday season at Epcot. A celebrity tells the *Story of the Nativity* backed by a "singing Christmas tree" choir that adds to the festive atmosphere. The celebrities are the big draw at this event, and the lineup changes each year. Celebrities such as Neil Patrick Harris, Whoopi Goldberg, and Trace Adkins have been known to host this popular event to standing-room only crowds.

The processional is extremely popular for locals and returning guests, and getting a stand-by seat to watch is quite difficult. Most stand-by guests

Insider's Tip!

Check Disney's website for the lineup of celebrities and the date each will be reading the nativity story. The schedule is not available until the event nears.

The Seasons of Disney: Hot, Hotter, & Hottest

Insider's Tip!

- One of the special features of Disney Very Merriest After Hours is fake snow falling on Main Street. Guests who haven't paid to stay late can linger around Main Street when the park closes to them (7 p.m.) and experience the snow and holiday lighting.
- Be on the lookout for the Mayor of the Magic Kingdom on Main Street during Disney Very Merriest After Hours. Other special guests of the evening typically include The Seven Dwarfs, Cinderella's Wicked Stepmother & Stepsisters, and the iconic Scrooge McDuck!
- Don't pay for Disney Very Merriest After Hours just to allow your child to get a holiday picture with Santa. Santa shows up at the Magic Kingdom, Epcot (with Mrs. Claus!), and Disney Springs every day from mid-November to early-January. There's no extra charge to meet Santa and get a picture with your own camera (even at Disney Springs!)

Insider's Tip!

Ensure a seat at the Candlelight Processional by making a dinner and show reservation. Because seating is very limited, many people opt to pay for a dinner and show package that ensures priority seating in the theater. If you want a special Christmas celebration with a specific celebrity, this is a memorable experience.

Note: This event is included with your Epcot park admission

Insider's Tip!

In some cases, festivities take place during the days leading up to New Year's Eve. For example, Magic Kingdom and Epcot usually hold their special New Year's firework events for the three to four days leading up to the night, giving you time to see each show.

end up standing at the back, along the promenade. The venue is small enough, however, that even standing in the back provides a fairly decent view of the show.

Festival of the Seasons – Mid-November to Early-January (Disney Springs)

Festival of the Seasons is held annually at Disney Springs from mid-November to early-January. Disney Springs transforms with Christmas decorations, festive live music, and, of course, Santa for the little ones to meet. Crowds don't necessarily flock to Disney Springs just to attend this nightly event. However, locals often bring their children to meet Santa closer to Christmas, so weekends late in December can be even more crowded than usual.

- Free Entry: Open to the Public.

New Year's Eve – December 31st

New Year's Eve is a special night at every Disney park (except Animal Kingdom), Disney Springs, and each resort. You will find music, dancing, fireworks, and celebrations no matter where you choose to spend the evening. Aside from Animal

Kingdom, each park stays open until after midnight and has specialty fireworks just for the occasion. Expect huge crowds, as this is one of the busiest days (and weeks) of the year at Walt Disney World.

- This event is included with your park admission and is open to the general public (Disney Springs) and to resort guests.

Disney Marathons and Half Marathons – Multiple Times Year-round

Disney Marathons and Half Marathons are held throughout the year. Each event has its own special theme. They also include shorter running and walking venues, so children can take part. Marathons start at one park and wind through Disney's property, ending at another park. Go to RunDisney.com or call (407) 939-iRun to get an up-to-date schedule and reserve a spot. Expect park and vehicle traffic to be heavy during these events. Avoid crowds by visiting whichever park(s) is not hosting runners on a specific day.

- Each event requires a reservation and advanced ticket purchase (cost varies)

Disney H2O Glow Nights

Water park fans will love this after-hours event held during the summer months at Typhoon Lagoon. Toy Story characters abound at this glow party for kids and adults. Adult ticket prices for this event are currently $59 plus tax.

Other After-Hour Events

Throughout the year, Disney offers themed and non-themed before- or after-hour events to each park, allowing guests the opportunity to enjoy lighter crowds. Adult ticket prices for these events are generally $125 plus tax.

Specially-ticketed events, such as Disney Very Merriest After Hours and Disney After Hours Boo Bash close down the Magic Kingdom at 7 p.m. on event evenings. Don't waste a regular park pass to visit a theme park earlier in the day. Guests with tickets for those special events can gain access to the park as early as 4 p.m. (The events run until midnight, giving you a full 8 hours of fun!) Though a few attractions may close during special events, the majority of rides are open and typically have shorter wait times after the park closes to non-ticketed guests (especially as the evening goes on and guests are busy with event parades and shows). Event tickets generally start at $129 and up (plus tax). Attending a specially-ticketed event is a great way to experience the Magic Kingdom for much cheaper than a 1-day pass to the park.

The Seasons of Disney: Hot, Hotter, & Hottest

Vacation Transportation

Insider's Tip!

Find a travel website (such as CheapTickets.com) to search multiple days and find the best fare. Use it to find the cheapest day of the week to travel during your possible vacation dates, and then comparison shop on different sites to find the best deal for those days. Don't forget to factor in the price of hauling your luggage when comparing rates! Southwest Airlines still allows you to bring two pieces of luggage for no additional cost, while most other airlines in the United States make you pay extra for each checked bag.

Orlando International Airport (MCO)

Getting to Orlando means choosing between driving from your hometown or flying on an airplane. If you come by plane, you'll most likely land at Orlando International Airport (known locally as OIA), which is the third largest airport in the U.S. (Airline Code: MCO; In addition to your flight planning, you'll need this code to look for auto rentals, which is a topic we discuss shortly.)

After arriving at the airport, you'll hop aboard the "People Mover," a monorail which will take you to baggage claim and transportation.

This is a world class airport offering free wi-fi, extensive shopping & restaurants, as well as banking and mailing services. Visit their website (orlandoairports.net) or mobile app for terminal maps. While you are there, you can see the airport's permanent art collection that includes a unique statue of a tourist napping. This statue is so realistic that many people assume it's a real person!

Airfare prices vary with the season. In most cases, February through March airfares are relatively low compared to peak late-November through December travel, when rates can double. Midweek flights are usually the cheapest. Check

Insider's Tip!

Foreign Language Assistance: Multi-lingual tourist information centers, located by the security checkpoints, are open from 7 a.m. to 11 p.m.

Vacation Transportation

Insider's Tip!

Complete a rate comparison of taxi (and alternatives) versus car rental and parking. Use the websites listed in this section to do a fare calculation for taxis and shuttles to/from your chosen hotel.

Insider's Tip!

Travel discounts are commonly offered around mid-January.

online for the best deals not available through travel agents.

If traveling by plane, keep in mind FAA restrictions when purchasing souvenirs that you plan to take home on your return flight. For example, snow globes larger than a tennis ball are prohibited as carry-ons because they contain liquid.

Getting Around Orlando – Car Rental, Taxi, and Shuttle Transfers

Getting to Orlando is only a small part of your vacation battle. Once you have flown in or arrived here in your own vehicle, you must understand how to get around.

Even if your hotel has a shuttle to the theme parks, you may need an alternative form of transportation for a portion of your vacation, including getting to your hotel from the airport.

Hotels in the Disney area don't routinely offer free shuttles to and from the airport. Mears and other providers

Insider's Tip!

Taxis and shuttles are near the baggage claim, while car rentals are on the lower level.

Insider's Tip!

If you are visiting from outside of the country, please remember that taxi drivers expect tips in the United States. It is considered bad form not to tip approximately 15%.

offer paid shuttle service directly to Disney resorts and other hotels in the area (see Shuttle Transfers below).

Disney wants you to think of their vacation package as all-inclusive, while staying at a non-Disney (off-property) hotel is ala carte. Therefore, Disney offers free transportation around its property.

Those who like to get the best travel value will compare off-property prices while adding in the costs Disney absorbs into their rates, especially including calculating the costs of transportation to and from the theme park each day. (Add another $25 per vehicle per day for parking.)

Getting To/From the Airport

If you're like most travelers, your transportation adventure will begin once you reach the Orlando International Airport. If free transportation is not provided by your hotel, you will have three primary options of getting there: taxi cab, shuttle, or car rental. There are other, more luxurious options, but if your concern is price, we'll stick to these three.

It's best to know which you plan to use before your trip. (Definitely book your car rental ahead of time.) When you get to the airport, you will take a monorail from your gate to the main hub of the airport. From there, follow the signs to gather your luggage and then to find your taxi, shuttle, or car rental location.

Tourist Trap!

Most legitimate taxi cab companies have comparable rates, but check before you agree to a ride.

Remember: Legitimate taxi cabs are required by Florida law to post their fares clearly on the outside door of the vehicles, along with valid license numbers. If you don't see the fare or license number posted prominently, do not get in that cab!

Beware of hiring any of the "gypsy" cabs that may not be properly licensed (or insured). While some may be honest and fair, others are known to be unscrupulous and may charge you several times what the actual fare is worth. Sadly, there are many unlicensed taxi cabs running around Orlando who tell potential fares one price, then hit them with a much higher price later.

If you are in doubt, do not use the service. Some illegitimate services may put your luggage in their trunk and hold it hostage until you agree to their exorbitant fees. Call the police immediately if you feel pressured by a taxi or feel you are being scammed, and you may want to stay in the cab and on the phone with police until they arrive.

Taxi Cabs

At the airport, taxis are available at both Terminal A and B, just outside baggage claim on Level 1.

If you travel in a large party, hiring a taxi can be more economical than paying the per person charge for a shuttle (see below). To avoid costly metered fares, look for a yellow Mears cab with posted flat-rate fares to Walt Disney World.

Mears and Yellow Cab

Owned by Mears, Yellow Cab is the largest taxi company in Orlando. It provides a metered fare that is based on the distance traveled. In fact, this is the only legitimate taxi cab service that operates on Disney resort property with official permission.

The larger area hotels and theme parks have Mears Taxi Dispatch areas (painted orange to make them easy to find). Contact Mears Taxicab Dispatch (407) 422-2222. Cabs accept credit cards.

Mears now has a smart phone app, similar to Uber, which includes an online map that lets you verify exactly how far away your cab is. Additionally, their drivers have background checks and pay government licensing fees. This doesn't mean their drivers have no criminal backgrounds – some of them do – but it is supposed to weed out any violent offenders. The biggest complaint with any taxi company is that non-American born drivers do not speak fluent English. This creates a further communication barrier to visitors who also don't speak English as their primary language.

Mears and Yellow Cab are the most popular taxi option and both have solid overall reputations for providing trustworthy service. Unfortunately, this translates to long wait times to get a driver to your location during peak periods, and tourists commonly complain about rude behavior and bad attitudes from *some* drivers who don't really need to compete for their fares.

STAY SAFE: All legitimate services will allow you to reserve at the airport or via cell phone and will give you the option of paying via credit card.

Taxi Alternatives – Ride-sharing Services

Uber and Lyft are popular ride-sharing programs where vehicle owners agree to provide rides to strangers for a fare. Prices are usually a bit lower than a standard taxi, as drivers don't pay the same licensing fees or airport access fees. Using one of these ride-sharing programs generally allows for a faster arrival time than hiring a taxi. Also, service tends to be a bit better, as customers provide immediate ratings for drivers, which affect their ability to continue offering services.

Uber (uber.com): (tipping suggested)

Lyft (lyft.com): (tipping suggest) This app also allows guests to order a Minnie Van for paid transportation around Disney property.

The apps for these services are also more sophisticated than the one offered by Mears. They include an estimated wait time for your car to get to you.

While traditional taxis are required to offer service to anyone, these alternative services tend to cater to a more sophisticated client, partly because they require their fares to use the smart phone app for reservations and set up pre-payment with a registered credit card. The fare for you trip is automatically charged to your credit card or an assigned Paypal account when signing up for the service. Tourists must have a payment option on file in the app to use either service.

Importantly, while criminal background checks are not required for their drivers, most ride-sharing companies tend to perform those checks to protect their customers, since their reputation is extremely important. You can easily check

the ratings for available drivers. Their feedback system is designed to weed out drivers (and customers!) who have a reputation for complaints.

The companies also require drivers to have a $1 million insurance policy which helps eliminate unsavory characters.

Shuttle Transfers

You may only have a few people in your party, or perhaps just don't want to deal with negotiating fares with a taxi driver. In this case, a shuttle transfer may be a good option for you. Mears is the largest purveyor of shuttles and you can estimate costs at: mearstransportation.com/orlando-shuttle-service/.

Mears Connect (mearsconnect.com) is Mears' Disney-specific shuttle service that provides shared or direct transportation to hotels on Disney property, including non-Disney branded hotels in the Disney Springs area [(407) 423-5566].

Shared shuttle buses hold many groups of people and will stop at several hotels during the journey. Depending on where your hotel is along the route, these stops can easily add 30 minutes or more to your ride.

Shuttle vans are smaller vehicles that take a single large party directly to their destination. These vans can accommodate up to nine people and cost about $17 per person to get to Disney.

There is a lot of competition for shuttles, so shop around to make sure you're getting the best price. Don't forget to make sure all fees and taxes are included in the final price you're given. Those additional costs have a way of creeping up on you, causing your vacation price to skyrocket!

Some major hotel chains offer shuttle vans and buses from the airport to their resorts. Check to see if one is included in your hotel rate.

Car Rentals

Finally, consider car rentals. Car rental kiosks are located at the Orlando International Airport adjacent to Baggage Claim.

Before we discuss specifics, consider two important notes:

- If you plan to rent a car, a GPS is an absolute must for Orlando driving. If you don't have one on your phone, you can rent one from the car rental agency.
- Florida laws require all vehicle occupants 6-years or older to wear seatbelts, and children up to 5 must be secured in a crash-tested child restraint seat.

Orlando car rental rates are among the lowest in the U.S. Multiple-day packages that include a weekend are usually the best deals, and base rates can be as low as $10 per day. This is due to the extremely high supply and competition for the more than 50 million visitors who visit the city each year. Still, prices can vary wildly from company to company. To find the best rates, be sure to shop around. Arranging your deal before arriving in Orlando will garner you the best savings.

Start with a website like Priceline.com to get a general idea of car rental rates. After comparing base prices, consider discounts that may be available, including membership in a buying club such as Costco or Sam's Club. If you're renting a car only because you need one later on during your trip, be sure to check the cost of the rental at the airport against the cost of renting a car in town. You may find the rates in town are much cheaper even when you factor in the cost of an airport transfer – though this is not always the case.

Enterprise (enterprise.com) and Budget (budget.com) are generally cost-competitive, and both will pick you up at your hotel to take you to the car rental agency when you need to get your wheels.

If you are dropping off your vehicle at a different location than you're picking it up, Budget may be the cheaper option. When looking around on different websites, don't forget to start the reservation process and put the vehicle you want into your online shopping cart to get an estimate of additional fees and taxes you can expect to pay with your rental.

Also, don't forget to check the current price of gas and toll routes around town (gasbuddy.com; sunpass.com/tollcalculator).

Added car rental insurance (Collision Damage Waiver or CDW) costs more, but it may cover damage to a vehicle that your existing automobile insurance policy will not, even if damage is caused by an accident through no fault of your own. Check with your existing car insurance for rental coverage before signing any contract. Also contact your credit card companies about rental car coverage, as some provide insurance if you pay for the rental with that card.

Many agencies offer extra compensation to their employees when they get renters to agree to a policy, so you may feel pressured. If you feel pushed to agree to additional coverage that you don't really want, simply assert that you have all the coverage you need.

Here are other considerations if you plan to rent a car at the airport:

1) Car rental companies often charge premium rates for pick-up and drop-off at the airport, whereas if you need a car later in your trip, you can usually rent it for less in town and have the rental company pick you up and drop you off at your hotel. Because of this, it may be cheaper to get one-way car rentals to/from the airport and a separate rental for only the

Tourist Trap!

Gas prices tend to be shockingly high in the immediate area around the airport. They are also raised around some tourist areas, sometimes as much as $2 to $3 higher per gallon than other areas of town! Not only do some gas stations charge outrageously high per gallon prices, a common practice in Orlando is for gas stations to advertise only their cash or company-specific credit card price on their street signs. After you are lured in, they charge an additional amount to use your personal credit or debit card. These aren't small mom & pop gas stations, either. Shell and Chevron are a couple of the big name corporations who we've seen employ this shady technique.

Worse yet, some unscrupulous gas stations may intentionally have very poor signage regarding the cost per gallon altogether. Once an unsuspecting tourist fills their tank, they find out just how extreme the actual price is. These companies rely on visitors who presume that the price is competitive with no more than a few cents variation. Remember, the actual cost per gallon should be clearly posted on the pump at each filling station. Verify that the price is within the range expected before you insert your credit card.

For these reasons, we recommend you only use **RaceTrac, Speedway, or 7-11 gas stations** while in Orlando, as they have the same price for cash or credit card payments and tend to be reasonably priced. Competitively-priced Speedway service stations are available around Disney. Alternatively, you can drive to the nearby Walmart on Vineland Rd (SR 535) and get good rates from the Speedway, RaceTrac, and Walmart gas stations nearby.

portion of the trip you need. Weigh the cost savings versus the hassle and time it takes to deal with the rental agency to determine if it's worth the effort;

2) Getting to or from the airport is a time-consuming challenge for even the most experienced local driver. Always use a GPS, particularly if you want to avoid the toll roads that are found along the only clearly marked route to Disney (Current toll rates are approximately $2.25 each way);

3) Rental companies have differing policies regarding gasoline: some charge you for what you actually use, while others allow you to pre-pay for an entire tank when you rent the car; and still others simply require that

you return the vehicle with a filled tank, and they charge you a high penalty if you do not.

Private Car Rental: One notable alternative to standard car rental companies is **Turo** (turo.com). This is a private car rental service, where you rent a vehicle directly from its owner, rather than a company. Users of this service often find great deals, especially on larger-capacity vehicles.

You can find vehicles available for pick up at the airport or in town. Just like a standard car rental company, you have the option of purchasing additional insurance.

Insider's Tip!

Epcot is known for its alcoholic beverage options. If you plan to drink, make transportation plans to get safely back to your hotel before heading to the park. Keep in mind that the heat can cause alcohol to affect people differently.

Do NOT drink even one alcoholic beverage if you are going to drive. Police are vigilant and know that tourists will pay the fine rather than absorb the cost of traveling back to the area to stand trial. You can be charged for DUI (driving under the influence) if your blood alcohol level is 0.08% or more. Don't ruin your vacation (and possibly your life) by drinking and driving!

City Bus

If you have plenty of time to kill and don't mind the atmosphere on a city bus, you can save a few dollars by taking a LYNX bus from the airport. This option is probably only reasonable for single or double travelers without children or baggage.

It takes about 60 minutes to get from the airport to International Drive, and costs only about $2. If you are staying off-property, this is an inexpensive way to get around town. Going by LYNX bus costs $4.50 for a single-day pass, weekly passes are $16, and monthly passes are $50. Passes can be purchased on the LYNX website (golynx.com), and daily passes are available from the driver upon boarding. (407) 841-5969. Beware, you cannot take luggage on the bus and you must have exact fare (transfers to connecting buses are free).

Disabled Transportation

Discount Mobility USA, Inc. (discountmobilityusa.com) provides vehicles for hire for the disabled. (800) 308-2503, (407) 438-8010.

Car Breakdowns and Service Stations

For 24-hour roadside assistance, contact AAA at (800) 222-4357 or (800) AAA-4357.

The AAA Car Center is on-site near the Magic Kingdom for serious vehicle issues. They charge a high price but provide good service. Their facilities are usually busy, so plan to leave your car for repairs while you enjoy your day at a park [(407) 824-0976].

The Maingate CITGO on 192 is also available for vehicle repairs. It is close to the property but off-site [(407) 396-2721].

A cheaper alternative, if you can wait a couple of days for repairs, is Your Mechanic (yourmechanic.com). You can schedule a mobile mechanic to come to you and fix your car, usually for a fraction of the cost. However, this option may take days for a repair, especially if you need diagnostics.

Parking Security patrols in parking lots can help you out with minor car problems such as keys locked inside your car and dead batteries. They can also help you locate your car if you have a problem.

Driving laws

Don't forget to wear your safety belt at all times. It's Florida law.

Texting while driving is also illegal in Florida, not to mention that it is extremely

Vacation Transportation

dangerous even around areas you know. It is exceedingly difficult when driving through heavily congested areas. Please don't do it!

Children's car seats are required for kids who are five years or younger. Please don't leave your child (or pet!) unattended in the car. It is very dangerous in the Florida heat, not to mention illegal.

Stop for school buses when the stop sign is extended from the vehicle regardless of your direction of travel relative to the bus (unless it is going the opposite direction on a multi-lane highway a or there is a center island separating traffic).

U-turns and left turns are allowed at all intersections that are not otherwise posted. Don't make a U-turn if the sign posted says it is not allowed – these signs are only placed at locations that are extremely busy and potentially dangerous. There will be another intersection very soon where you will be allowed to make your U-turn safely.

Never drive straight through or turn left on a red light. That can cause an accident and result in a traffic ticket. Many intersections throughout the Orlando area have red light cameras that will catch you even if a police officer isn't present.

You may turn right at a red light, though, unless there is a sign that specifically prohibits that action. Stop at the intersection first before turning to make sure it is safe to go. Please do not hold up other drivers by waiting for the light to turn green if you can safely make your turn.

Insider's Trivia!

The term "turnpike" comes from older days when drivers had to pay a toll to pass a pike (i.e., a poll), which would be raised, or turned, upon collection of the fare.

Orlando Traffic

Metropolitan Orlando is the crossroads of one of Florida's busiest highway systems, located where the north-south Florida Turnpike connects with the east-west Interstate I-4. (Although I-4 runs in a general NE to SW direction through much of Orlando.)

Partly due to the sheer number of travelers from around the globe, driving around Orlando can be a frightening experience, particularly for people not used to big cities. Drivers seldom use turn signals when changing lanes, and accidents staged by criminals trying to commit insurance fraud are more common here than most cities in the country.

As you might expect, the low season is usually the best time for traffic and driving, while holidays and the entire summer season are punctuated with heavy traffic patterns.

During the morning and evening commute in any season, though, highways can slow to a virtual standstill, so plan your travels accordingly. Fortunately, like any other big city, you can usually avoid the worst of the traffic by not driving during rush hours. Generally speaking, 7 a.m. to 9 a.m. and 4 p.m. to 6:30 p.m. are the worst travel times. Friday and Saturday evenings are also high-traffic periods.

Provided there are no accidents, plan for an additional twenty minutes to get around town if you need to drive during these times. While this may not seem like a long time, if you have a busy schedule planned, even traveling between two or three venues can take up a couple of hours.

When preparing your schedule, add an hour extra to and from each location to give sufficient padding (even if you are going to rely on a taxi or alternative transportation, such as Uber or Lyft).

Driving from the Airport

The Central Florida Greenway (State Road 417) runs south and east into Walt Disney World from the Airport. Tolls range between $0.50 and $1.50 per station. They take cash and they also operate on an electronic system called a SunPass, with transmitters that can be purchased locally at grocery and drug stores. (Cash is generally a better option for short-term visitors.) Tollbooths do not take currency larger than $20.

As a general rule of thumb, we recommend using toll roads when driving to or from the airport. The toll roads are faster than alternatives, since they offer a more direct route and are the least traveled due to their premium cost. However, unless traffic is gridlocked at peak periods during the day, there are no real time savings to using toll roads directly around the Orlando tourist attractions. Similar to some cities, Orlando toll roads are also collectively referred to as the "turnpike."

It's worth noting again that you should use GPS while driving in Orlando. Standard GPS settings will often send you on a toll road. Be sure to verify which options are chosen on your GPS to allow you to avoid tolls if you don't wish to pay extra or if you don't have cash on-hand.

Getting to the Parks

Before we discuss the specific benefits of on-property versus off-property hotels, let's discuss the logistics of getting to and around the Disney property.

Traveling to Disney's Theme Parks and Area Hotels

In this section, we'll share information about getting to the parks. Our tips will

Insider's Tip!

When using any bus or shuttle, get a seat as close to the door as possible. You'll be one of the first off the bus, putting you at the head of the crowd to get through security or other transportation queues.

benefit you regardless of whether you plan to stay on Disney property or at an off-property hotel.

Off-Disney Property Guests

If you are not staying on Disney property or using their transportation system, pay attention to the following money-saving advice to make sure getting around and parking does not become a surprise expense during your stay.

Many area hotels offer a free shuttle to Disney. If a hotel you're considering has an offered shuttle, it's imperative you request a full schedule before booking, including a breakdown of how many hotels the shuttle services and which stop your hotel is on the schedule.

Insider's Caution!

Don't ruin your trip with a costly speeding ticket. Just because you're on vacation doesn't mean you get to take a break from traffic laws, even on Disney property. The Orange County Sheriff's Department patrols Disney property. While they aren't putting out speed traps (which Disney would not allow!), they do pull over speeders and reckless drivers. Also, drive defensively. Unaware tourists and Cast Members speeding to make their shifts on time can make for dangerous road conditions!

Vacation Transportation

Vacation Transportation

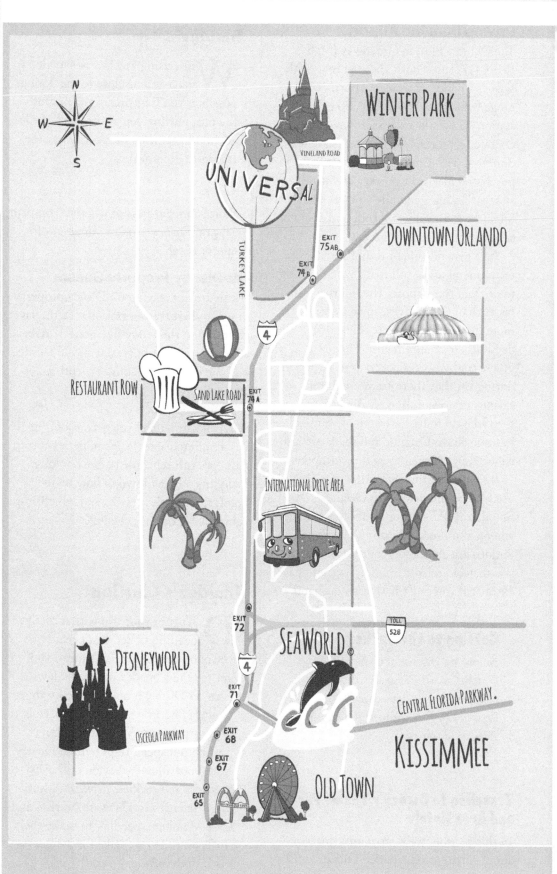

Insider's Tip!

Buena Vista Drive, the street that runs in front of Disney Springs and its area hotels, is notoriously bad for traffic delays. At the best of times, you can expect 15-20 minute delays on this stretch during the evening, especially on the weekend. Fortunately, there is a brand-new exit right off the highway that leads directly into a huge, state-of-the art parking garage to make visiting Disney Springs an easy choice.

We recommend you avoid the State Road (SR) 535 and Buena Vista Drive entrance to Disney Properties by taking Exit 67 off of I-4 West from Orlando to bypass the Disney Springs traffic. This is true even if Disney Springs is your destination, as its most available parking garage is at the end closest to Exit 67.

Taking a right off of Exit 67 leads to Typhoon Lagoon and Hotel Plaza Boulevard, where several non-Disney hotels are located. Take a left to go to Disney's BoardWalk.

Off-property shuttles typically provide service to several hotels, so unless you are lucky enough to be the last stop for the morning pick-up and the first stop for drop-off in the evening, it will likely take a very long time to get to the park. And with most hotel shuttles you can forget about getting to the parks before opening, which we recommend to get the most out of your day.

Add to the late arrival the inconvenience of early pick-up times to return you back to your hotel, it's easy to realize that your days can be shortened by quite a bit. If you consider that admission prices average about *$10 per person for each hour you spend in the park each day*, you can see how much you're losing if you miss a couple of hours that you could otherwise be exploring.

Insider's Tip!

Each entrance to Disney property has a large banner across the highway with Mickey and Minnie on either end to greet guests. Many visitors are tempted to stop their vehicles to take pictures when seeing these welcoming entrances. Do not pull off the side of the road or stop your car to take pictures. It's unsafe and you will get ticketed if seen by authorities.

If you really want this photo, go to the SR 535 and Buena Vista Drive entrance where you can park across the street at Crossroads Shopping Center. Use the traffic lights at the intersection to walk across to the entrance for a safer method of capturing your photographs. At the same time, you can enjoy the many dining options at the shopping center!

Vacation Transportation

Insider's Tip!

Each year, usually during the slow season, the monorail is refurbished. During this time, it will have modified service or routes. Check on the day of travel the best option to use. Other transportation options may be faster.

Also, shuttles that serve multiple hotels often fill up in the first couple of stops, so if your hotel is later on the pick-up list, you may find yourself out of luck and waiting for the next shuttle. In some cases, it may be reasonable to walk to a nearby hotel with an earlier pick-up time, but adding walking to an already full day at the parks is generally not a great idea.

When it comes to off-property hotel shuttles, most run no more than twice in the morning to a single location (see below) on Disney property and twice in the evening back to the hotel, meaning there is no way to take a midday break and return to the park later without spending a small fortune on cab fare or alternative transportation. Not only that, they often require you to return to your hotel long before the theme parks close (which can be as late as 3 a.m. during the summer).

Another consideration is the shuttles typically only drop-off and pick-up at a single Disney World location: the Transportation and Ticket Center. This means you will need to take Disney's free transportation to your final destination if it

Insider's Tip!

As we've noted, here is a site to determine how much you can expect to pay for shuttle and taxi cab services from your chosen hotel: MearsTransportation.com

is not the Magic Kingdom, adding even more time to your trip. (And don't forget how stressful it can be to wait around and load hot and tired children on the bus as they get fussy at the end of the day!)

As a general rule of thumb, when traveling with children ages 10 or younger, this option will not work for you. (Don't worry, though, we'll give you tips later on how to take breaks on-property.)

If you're staying off-site, renting a car or driving your own vehicle are more convenient options. Just be sure to factor the gasoline and parking costs into your equation. (If you are skimming through this book, make sure to see our above tips about how to make sure you get a fair price on gas.)

Traffic is another consideration in the "driving-versus-shuttle" versus staying on-property decision. If you missed our earlier discussion, during peak times, traffic can come to a complete stand-still around town. You may think your hotel that's only two miles away is a short, five-minute drive. During peak traffic times, though, it can be thirty to forty-five minutes either way for that stop-and-go journey.

Disney's On-Property Guests

If you don't plan to drive into Orlando and don't want to stick exclusively to Disney property, the most cost-effective and convenient choice is to rent a car. We provided details about this in the *"Getting from the Airport"* section above. Keep in mind, however, that all of the major area theme parks and beaches charge for parking.

Parking

If you decide to stay on-property and have a car, Disney charges a nightly fee to park at its hotels: $15 (Value Resorts), $20 (Moderate Resorts), or $25 (Deluxe Resorts) . You will be relieved to know there is no additional fee to park at the theme parks - it's included in your nightly parking fee.

Parking Lot Trams

Disney's parking lots are exceedingly large. But if you choose to drive, there are parking lot trams that pick you up near your parking space and take you to the entrance of each park.

By the time you trek through the parking lot and take the tram, you may find you prefer Disney's free transportation alternatives from each resort which takes guests directly to the park entrances.

This is especially true for the Magic Kingdom, where anybody driving must park at the Transportation and Ticket Center and then use a boat or monorail to get to the park. This can add as much as 20 to 30 minutes each way during peak periods due to congestion. There is nothing worse than having to wait in a long line just to get back to your car after leaving the park at the end of a busy day.

Free Buses and Other Transportation

If you choose to use buses, they will drop you off near the front entrance of each park. Disney's buses run frequently, a few trips per hour all day long until well after all the fun dies down. They are exceptionally clean and efficient. Still, many people feel there are time savings to driving (and parking) and choose to do so rather than use Disney's free transportation.

Aside from the buses every hotel offers, certain Disney hotels offer boat or monorail transportation alternatives.

- The Contemporary, Polynesian, and Grand Floridian resorts all offer both monorail and boat transportation directly to the Magic Kingdom.
- The Wilderness Lodge and Fort Wilderness Campground resorts also offer boats to the Magic Kingdom.
- The Boardwalk, Yacht & Beach Club, and Swan & Dolphin resorts

Vacation Transportation

provide boat transportation to both Hollywood Studios and Epcot. You can also walk to the two parks from those hotels.

- Port Orleans, Key West, Treehouse Villas, and Saratoga Springs also offer boat transportation to Disney Springs (formerly Downtown Disney). There is also a Nature Trail (walking/biking path) that goes between Disney Springs and all of these resorts, except for Port Orleans. (Exploring via the boats and trail can be a fun way to spend a day out of the parks, which we discuss further in a later section.)
- Art of Animation, Pop Century, Caribbean Beach, Yacht Club, Beach Club, BoardWalk Inn, and the Riviera Resort have service to Epcot and Hollywood Studios via the Disney Skyliner gondola system.

We recommend you use Disney trans-

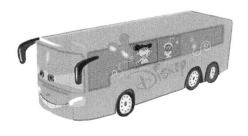

portation to get to the Magic Kingdom. For the other parks, either driving or using Disney transportation is quite efficient.

Minnie Vans

Minnie Vans are Disney's own taxi-type service. For a fee (based on distance), your party (up to eight) can catch a direct ride from one property location to another or even get a ride to the airport.

Guests may book a ride with this service using the Lyft app.

Other Area Attractions & Getting Around Orlando

Up to now, you might see more benefits to staying on-property than off. However, if you plan to spend time at the other theme parks and beaches around Florida, it can make a lot of sense to stay at an off-property hotel or home rental.

By design, Disney wants all of their visitors to stay within the confines of Disney property (and spend their money there). Because of this, Disney offers nothing to help visitors get around the rest of Orlando. In fact, Disney does such a great job of advertising their property as an all-inclusive destination, some visitors are not even aware of the other amazing things to do around Orlando and Central Florida.

Day Trips Around Central Florida

Central Florida is known as the theme park capitol of the world for a reason. You can find everything from small, local attractions, such as **Old Town** and **Fun Spot** (on Highway 192 and on International Drive) to large theme parks that offer major competition for Disney.

Other theme parks include **Busch Gardens** in Tampa (about an hour drive to the west), **Legoland** in nearby

Traffic gets very busy on Sand Lake Road. If you plan to eat dinner at a restaurant on Sand Lake, it's best to determine which of the other main thoroughfares is closest to your location and get onto Sand Lake from there to minimize the amount of time spent sitting in traffic.

Winter Haven, as well as **Sea World** and **Universal Studio**'s two theme parks in Orlando.

Many people also come to Orlando for events at the Orlando Convention Center on International Drive. Check their website (occc.net/Global/calendar.asp) to see what will be happening during your stay.

If you are interested in exploring local culture and wildlife, you may enjoy a trip to Orlando's alligator farm, **Gatorland Zoo**. Additionally, keep an eye out on Groupon and Living Social for great deals on attractions you can only find in Florida, such as swimming with manatees in Crystal River or airboat rides on gator-infested lakes.

Adventure junkies have unique options, such as shooting automatic firearms at **Machine Gun America** in Kissimmee or traversing a zipline "roller coaster" at **Forever Florida** (about an hour away).

If you prefer to stay close to Disney and see reproductions of Florida's nature parks while inside a comfortable air conditioned

environment, **Gaylord Palms**, a nearby hotel and convention center, features exhibitions of the Everglades, Key West, and even the Spanish-infused St. Augustine.

Sun worshippers love to visit Clearwater Beach, one of the world's consistently top-ranked white sand beaches, which is only about a 90-minute drive away on Florida's west coast. It has some of the finest and most beautiful sand in the world, along with its own hub of attractions, including the **Clearwater Marine Aquarium**, home to Winter the dolphin, star of the movie *Dolphin Tale* and its sequel, *Dolphin Tale 2.*

There are two entrances to Disney property on SR 535. One is near the south end of the highway: World Center Drive entrance. The other, close to the I-4 exit, takes you directly to Disney Springs. If you don't mind walking a bit, you can walk to Disney Springs (and the Orlando Premium Outlet Mall) from many hotels along SR 535, avoiding vehicle traffic altogether. From Disney Springs, you can take free Disney transportation anywhere on-property. This is the only entrance to Disney property accessible by foot.

Vacation Transportation

On the opposite coastline, in less than an hour you can reach Cocoa Beach and visit the world-famous **Kennedy Space Center**. You can head up the coastline a few more miles to reach the world famous Daytona Beach, home to the Daytona 500.

There are also ample places to play in the water in the Orlando Metropolitan area. Lake Bryan is a large lake just a couple of miles from Disney Springs where boats and jet skis can be rented (**Buena Vista Water Sports**). (This is also a great location for weddings!) Legoland and Sea World also have adjacent waterparks (**Legoland Waterpark**, **Aquatica**, and **Discovery Cove**) for those seeking a more controlled environment. For a bigger thrill, try **Fantasy Surf**, an indoor surfing park in Kissimmee.

Transportation around Orlando

There's so much to do outside of Disney property, we can't even begin to touch it all here. Get all the information from the local tourism officials to see that Orlando is truly a mecca for family fun!

The real question is how to get to all of these attractions. The good news is many hotels around the Orlando area offer shuttles to Universal and/or Sea World. Those shuttles usually run only once or twice in the morning or evening, but these

Insider's Tip!

The entrance to Hollywood Studios has moved in the past couple of years.

GPS services have not yet caught up to this change. We recommend you use Google Maps when driving to Hollywood Studios to make sure you don't get lost!

parks tend to have shorter hours than the Disney parks.

You might decide for the reasons we listed above that using a hotel shuttle is just not the right option. If you don't want to deal with Orlando traffic, there are many other shuttle and taxi cab options. However, shuttles are limited to major theme parks, and a taxi is completely cost prohibitive for anything outside Orlando.

One great option for people staying off-site along International Drive is the area's own transportation system, the **I-Ride Trolley** (iridetrolley.com). The trolley offers regular service to Universal, Sea World, and a number of shopping and dining options for travelers along its route. Unlimited daily or weekly passes are very reasonable priced, making this a great option for your non-Disney transportation needs.

Traffic, Parking, & Safety Around Disney World (Off-Property)

What happens when you combine drivers who don't quite know where they're going with those who don't know Florida traffic laws? Let's add impatient locals who refuse to leave room for drivers turning into or out of parking lots and, for fun, we'll throw in one of the largest populations of insurance fraud scammers

Insider's Trivia!

For most of its route, US 192 is known as the Irlo Bronson Memorial Highway. It was named after former state representative, senator, and cattleman Irlo O. Bronson, Sr. It is also known as Space Coast Parkway, as it leads westerly to the Space Coast (where Kennedy Space Center is located).

Tourist Trap!

Towing companies use spotters in parking lots to search for tourists who unwittingly park in a spot designated for one restaurant and eat at another. <u>YOUR CAR MAY BE TOWED IF YOU DO THIS</u>!

The signs can be difficult to understand. It is a good idea to double check with the business or restaurant you are visiting to eliminate any costly risks. When in doubt, do not park on the lot.

Take, for instance, two popular restaurants located across the street from the Orlando Premium Outlet Mall. The parking on the side of Restaurant A appears to be part of the Restaurant B parking lot, but the towing signs are your clue that they are not. Spotters are often on-hand to identify tourist "culprits" eating at Restaurant B but parked in poorly-marked parking spots that belong to Restaurant A. Tow trucks are called in to remove dozens of automobiles each evening, while unsuspecting tourists eat their meals.

Notes on Towing: If you get to your car before they have it attached, they have to release it to you immediately. Otherwise, you can call 911 to report that your car has been stolen. Towing companies have an hour to report a tow to the police after taking your vehicle. You may not immediately know that it was just highjacked for "ransom" by a towing company. While Orange County Commissioners have tried to address the predatory operations with new legislation, it is important to double check for towing signage (that is supposed to be clearly posted along the property).

in the country who set up other vehicles for accidents.

Sprinkle in a dash of international drivers accustomed to the "wrong" side of the road. Put them together, and what do you have? Orlando traffic!

Spring break and summer periods bring many more tourists than fall and winter, so traffic tends to be much more congested during those months. Due to the start of the Christmas shopping season, the last week of November, and the last two weeks of December are also typically very busy, causing a great deal of road congestion. In fact, traffic comes to a standstill starting late in the day on Thanksgiving all the way through the following weekend on the roads leading to outlet malls,

particularly Apopka Vineland Road (SR 535) and International Drive (I-Drive).

Disney property entrances are primarily located off of I-4, Irlo Bronson Memorial Highway (192), and SR 535. There are no toll roads on Disney property, but there are several nearby that will take you through town for a nominal fee.

International Drive (I-Drive)

The three primary Orlando area tourist attractions are Walt Disney World, Sea World, and Universal Orlando. Aside from Interstate 4 (I-4), which is the main freeway through Orlando, International Drive (I-Drive) is a major road through town that connects many of the area's tourist attractions in the vicinity of Disney.

Sea World is located between Disney and Universal in what's known as the I-Drive area of town. The area around Sea World has developed into a major hot spot of hotels, smaller attractions, nightlife, and shopping for tourists.

SAFETY TIP! There are a number of bicycle taxis offering to pick up pedestrians along I-Drive. Be aware, there have been reports of tourists getting scammed or even harmed by these drivers. Physical attacks from these drivers are rare, but there is no licensing system for the bicycle taxis to verify the backgrounds of these drivers. We recommend you don't ride them alone, and clearly define terms, such as whether the price is per person or for the entire group. Walk away if communication seems like it might be an issue.

I-Drive is also convenient to Universal Orlando, although many locals choose to use the Turkey Lake Road entrance. Turkey Lake Road runs parallel to I-4, making it an ideal choice when traffic is backed up on I-4 or I-Drive. There are a few timeshare properties and hotels along Turkey Lake Road, along with a Post Office and Super Walmart. More

importantly, traffic tends to flow steadily on this back route.

Universal Studios Area – Sand Lake Road

Sand Lake Road is another main thoroughfare that runs very close to both Universal and Sea World. It is commonly called Restaurant Row and is very popular with locals and tourists alike for its many eating establishments. Sand Lake can be reached off of both SR 535 and Turkey Lake Road. Turkey Lake Road and SR 535 also come together at one point (though Turkey Lake Road is called Palm Parkway where it meets SR 535), so the three together make a large triangle. Sand Lake Road can also be reached from an exit off of I-4.

Apopka-Vineland / State Road 535 (SR 535)

State Road 535 is a main arterial just east of Disney that connects to the major thoroughfares, Highway 192 and Highway 1-4. The centralized location of its many hotels and restaurants makes it extremely convenient for tourists. Unfortunately, traffic can come to a halt

Keep in mind the general rules you are probably already familiar with:
- Keep valuables out of sight in your car.
- Never leave anything visible on the seats of your rental car.
- Lock all packages in your trunk.
- Don't forget to lock your car when you park.
- Don't walk around alone. The buddy system is the best way to keep someone from hassling you.
- Many nightlife spots along I-Drive and at Universal City Walk are not just for tourists. Locals also frequent these places, and, unlike the Disney lounges, these places are for adults only.
- Though most locals are fun-loving and just out to have a good time, stay away from people who appear drunk or who are getting loud or belligerent.
- Avoid getting into altercations, and contact security for the establishment immediately if anybody starts bothering you.

during peak periods, particularly near I-4 adjacent to Disney.

CAUTION! Most roads in Orlando have sidewalks and pedestrian crossing signals. NEVER walk across a road unless you are in a designated crosswalk and have the signal to walk. Even so, look both ways before crossing and be extremely cautious, as many cars will turn corners without looking out for pedestrians. Pedestrians are hit regularly in Orlando, mostly when crossing a busy road outside of a crosswalk.

Highway 192

Irlo Bronson Memorial Highway (Highway 192) is the other major road worth mentioning. There is a 12-mile stretch of Highway 192, heading East-West between SR 535 (Apopka-Vineland) and Highway 27 (where 192 terminates).

Highway 192 (commonly called just "192") is a major tourist strip in the area around the Walt Disney World Resort and it provides very convenient access to Disney property. It has "mile markers" that help tourists locate businesses.

In addition to Hwy 192's convenient location to Disney, it is also known for its discount hotel properties and nearby vacation homes available to rent. Traffic jams don't seem to be much of a problem in this area, and there are restaurants within walking distance from anywhere you may be staying along this highway.

On this section of Highway 192, you also have quick access to I-4 and I-Drive. Other well-known destinations, such as Old Town (which houses a Fun Spot amusement park) and the town of Celebration are also located there.

Traffic can get congested near the intersection with SR 535, heading east.

SR 535 meets Highway 192 where SR 535 terminates, and Disney visitors can use the World Center Drive entrance to Disney property located just a couple miles north of this intersection.

Bicycling

Orlando is not a bicycle-friendly city. There are virtually no bike paths on the roads around Disney or around the other tourist areas. If you choose to use a bicycle to get around near your hotel, stick to the sidewalks. Do not ride your bicycle on the streets. Follow crosswalk signals as though you are a pedestrian; wait for the signal to walk, and carefully check traffic before crossing the street on your bicycle.

Parking around Orlando

Parking around Orlando is fairly straight forward. Most retail locations have either a paid parking garage, a free parking lot, or street parking with parking meters. They are generally well marked.

However, be careful to look for towing signs when you park. Some outside malls with multiple shops and restaurants appear to all use the same parking lot. Upon closer inspection, you may find certain areas are designated only for one restaurant or shop.

Dangerous Neighborhoods

You may be interested in visiting other areas of Orlando than we already mentioned during your vacation. Unfortunately, many bad areas of town are right next to nicer areas, and it's not always obvious when you've entered one or have left the other. Here's a brief rundown of things to be aware of throughout the city.

You are generally safe around major tourist areas during the day and in the early evening. Most threats happen long after dark.

Downtown Orlando is a common destination. It is generally safe during the day, though it can be dangerous at night. If you plan to attend an event or dinner there, park in a well-lit and crowded area, and never walk to your car alone.

Orange Blossom Trail is a main road through town where Costco and Sam's Club are located, but so are many drug dealers and street-walking prostitutes. **Despite the attractive-sounding name, this is a dangerous area to be walking around at any time, and it should be avoided after dark.**

Probably the worst area of town is called *Pine Hills.* You are generally safe to drive through, but don't stop anywhere.

SAFETY TIP! When outside of Disney property and away from high tourist areas, avoid looking like a tourist. You don't want to make yourself an easy mark for criminals. In other words, dress nicely, but without expensive jewelry or purses, when going out for dinner or drinks. Wearing shorts and an Aloha shirt is a dead giveaway that you are a tourist. Don't wear a large camera hanging around your neck.

Disney (World) has that thing—the imagination and the feeling of happy excitement—I knew when I was a kid.

- Walt Disney

Cost Vs. Convenience
Deciding to Stay on Disney Property or at An Area Hotel

This is perhaps the biggest and most difficult decision regarding your vacation. A savvy traveler can save money by staying off-property, provided she takes into consideration all of the fees and add-on expenses when comparing prices.

We'll also explore whether the advantages of staying on Disney property outweigh the higher costs of the rooms. The answer to this depends on your vacation plans and goals...and whether or not you're traveling with small children.

Comparing prices of hotels can be difficult if you don't have exact dates yet.

Often, on the main page of a hotel or booking site, you'll see terms like, "Rates ranging from $39 per night!" It can be a shock, then, to discover your $39 room is actually $139 when you try to book it. That's because rates vary greatly depending on the season, whether it's a weekday or weekend, and many other factors.

Disney is just as guilty as "other guys" for advertising this way, and the worst part is, there's no set off-season "value season" nor "peak season" which are the same across the board for all Orlando hotels. Because of this, it's vital that you do a comparison check of actual dates to determine the real nightly value of the properties you're considering.

Hidden Costs to Calculate

Unfortunately, the price comparisons don't stop with just the nightly rate. You must consider the add-on costs that many off-site hotels charge around Orlando to properly compare against the more inclusive costs of staying at a Disney hotel. Here is a quick checklist of additional costs you are likely to find at an off-site hotel:

- Daily Resort Fees – These are fees which most area hotels charge that are designed to recover the costs for specific amenities and services. These include shuttle transportation to Disney or other parks and recreational facilities, swimming pools, and gyms or weight rooms.

  Unfortunately, even guests who don't plan to use these facilities or services are charged these fees, and there's no way to get them waived.

  Always check directly with the hotel to find out the current daily resort fee. Don't rely on what their website says, as they are subject to change at any time and may be hidden in the fine print. Once you are checking in at the front desk, it may be too late to complain (though you can argue they are using deceptive pricing practices if there is no mention of a resort fee on their website or during your booking process).

  You may also check websites such as resortfeechecker.com or resortfees.com to find if your prospective hotel is included in their lists, although checking directly with the source is usually the most accurate option.

- **Daily Mini-Fridge Fees** – Check to see if your hotel includes mini-fridges in the room and if there's a charge to get one. All Disney rooms include a mini-fridge at no additional cost. Beware, though! Many hotels include pre-stocked mini-fridges and will charge you FOR REMOVING EVEN A SINGLE ITEM – even if it's just to make room for items of your own. Call the front desk and request that someone come out and clear out the fridge for you if you wish to avoid this cost. This is important especially if you have children that may not understand why they can't get a snack when they feel hungry.

- **Daily Hotel Parking Fees** – Many area hotels, including Disney Resort hotels, charge a daily parking fee to guests who have a vehicle. Be sure to find out what that fee is and if the hotel offers a way to waive the fee (such as by dining at one of their restaurants).

- **Parking Fees at the Disney Parks** – Disney waives this fee for its hotel guests, but if you're staying off-site and plan to drive, expect to pay $25 per day for parking ($30 if you have an RV).

- **Gasoline** – When you're considering which hotel to stay in, don't rely on that hotel's "estimated" distance to the Disney parks. Do a MapQuest or Google Maps search for directions to each of the Disney parks to find out how much additional driving you'll be doing each day. If you plan to go back to your hotel for midday breaks, remember to calculate that additional mileage.

- **Cost of Transportation to/from Airport** – Whether you're taking a shuttle or renting a car, this is an

Cost Vs. Convenience

expense non-Disney guests need to calculate.

- **Daily Shuttle/Taxi Fees** – If you're planning on using a resort shuttle, rather than driving, find out if there is any charge for taking it and if gratuities are expected. You should also calculate the cost of taking a taxi cab or alternative (such as Uber or Lyft) in case you find yourself in the position of needing to get back to your hotel at a time when your hotel shuttle isn't running.

- **Internet** – Many area hotels provide some sort of free Internet, but you have to be careful about what is actually being offered. Some charge extra for in-room Internet, and some still require you to use a (CAT5) cable. Most portable devices only work with WiFi, so check with your hotel to make sure they are actually offering free service INSIDE your room. If they only have a hardwired system, ask if they provide use of a cable for free or if you should bring one from home. And remember that any information broadcast over a

public Internet can be intercepted. Use proper encryption.

- **Telephone Calls** – Most Orlando hotels will allow you to make local calls from your room for free, but there are still some that charge per call. If you don't have a cell phone to use for phone calls, be sure to verify that your hotel allows you to call local and toll-free numbers for no additional fee.

On-Property Disney Resort Benefits

Disney offers several hotel options, each uniquely themed and categorized into deluxe, moderate, or value classes. The price per room varies based on the time of year with higher prices during Spring Break, summer months, and holidays. This is also true of off-property hotels.

Staying on-property provides a definite convenience that off-property hotels can't match if most of your trip will be spent at Disney. To encourage guests to spend their entire vacation on-property, Disney provides free transportation between the parks and hotels regularly and frequently throughout each day.

If you have a vehicle and are staying on-property, the cost of parking at the parks is included (though you will pay a nightly fee for hotel parking). If you don't have a car and want to spend some time off-property, don't worry. Some car rental companies will actually come to your hotel and pick you up to rent a car, then drop you off when you're done with the car.

Note that there are some added expenses to calculate if staying on Disney property:

- **Parking Fees.** Disney charges its hotel guests a per night parking fee of $15 for Value Resorts, $20 for Moderate Resorts, and $25 for Deluxe Resorts and Villas. However,

Insider's Tip!

All of Disney's resorts are unique and fun, but there is one that we think is absolutely the best for families with pre-teen children: Disney's Art of Animation Resort. Except for The Little Mermaid rooms, every room is a family-sized suite with kitchenette. Each section is uniquely themed, including an incredible Cars Movie area and Lion King area, complete with fun play areas. Add to that a swimming pool with underwater music, and you have a complete children's fantasy land.

Insider's Tip!

Kitchenette does not mean the same thing as a full kitchen in hotel terms. A kitchenette typically includes a sink, microwave, mini-refrigerator, and coffee maker. Don't expect to be able to prepare and cook complete meals in a room with a kitchenette. A full kitchen typically has a full-sized refrigerator, stove, oven, and dishwasher, as well as cookware and dishes.

this fee includes parking at the theme parks.

- **No Off-property Transportation.** Disney does not provide transportation to other area attractions or shopping. That means that you have to hire a car to get to any off-property location.

Bringing Your Dogs

Certain Disney hotels allow dogs. These dog-friendly resorts (along with their pet-cleaning rates) are:

- Disney's Art of Animation Resort ($50/night)
- Disney's Port Orleans Riverside Resort ($50/night)
- Disney's Yacht Club Resort ($75/night)
- Cabins at Disney's Ft. Wilderness Resort ($50/night)

Insider's Tip!

Some great resources for inexpensive vacation rentals in Orlando are Airbnb (airbnb.com) and Sky Auction (skyauction.com). You may find large rooms with full kitchens for a fraction of what you would pay for a smaller hotel.

You can bring up to two dogs per guest room with no weight or breed restrictions.

Disney does not have specific rooms designated for dogs, but certain areas of each resort are "dog-friendly," including outdoor pet exercise and relief areas.

Disney understands that a dog is part of the family, so they provide some extra-special touches just for these four-legged friends. Dogs receive Pluto's Welcome Kit, which includes a mat, bowls, a pet ID tag, courtesy plastic disposable bags, puppy pads and dog walking maps. A Pluto "Do Not Disturb" door hanger is also provided to let hotel staff know a pet is in the room.

Your dog must stay at a leash whenever outside of your room and needs to be well-behaved (no barking, jumping on people, etc.), and you will need to have paperwork available to show proper vaccinations.

Fortunately, your dog can use most Disney transportation, including buses, Minnie Vans, and Magical Express, provided you keep your furry friend in a pet carrier. Monorails and boats do not allow dogs at this time.

As your canine can't join you at the park, day care and other pet services are available on-property at Best Friends, the full-service pet care facility (fees apply).

As part of their kennel service, Best Friends offers live "Pet Care Cams" on their website or via smartphone app that auto-refresh every 60 seconds. Being able to see that your little, loved friend is being taken well-care of can reassure nervous human-companions.

Off-Property Cost Savings

Is it cheaper to stay off-property? Possibly, but you need to take into consideration all of the costs and the convenience factor before making an informed decision. Also, consider that nearly all off-site hotels charge a daily *resort fee* that's not included in the published daily rate, and some charge an additional fee for parking at their property. **Don't forget:** all hotels, including the Disney hotels, are subject to additional tourist-related taxes, though Disney will give you a clear total cost that includes everything. Be sure to check into all those fees before committing to another hotel.

When thinking about an off-property suite with a kitchen or a vacation home, there are a few things to consider in order to be realistic about the potential savings in food costs:

- Will you have a vehicle to go to the store for groceries?
- Are you willing to make breakfast every morning?
- Are you really going to leave the parks at lunch and dinner to go back to your hotel to make a meal?
- If you plan to make meals to bring along to the parks, is it worth it to carry them around with you all day in coolers?

The answers for many of these questions may be yes for you, especially if you don't plan to spend each day at a park.

Suites with Kitchens

If you have several people in your party or wish to make many of your own meals and snacks to cut down on cost, an off-property suite hotel with a kitchen can be a great option for you. Though Disney now has some room options with kitchenettes and multiple bedrooms for large families, it will cost you. While most Disney rentals are limited to four people per room, off-property suites may allow six or eight people per room, virtually halving your cost of housing.

The Holiday Inn Resort Orlando Suites - Waterpark offers a fun environment very close to the Disney property and has full kitchens in some of its suites. It has among the highest daily resort fee of any hotel in Orlando, but the highly interactive pool/play area means most guests won't feel the need to pay additional moeny to visit a water park.

Another great budget option is the limited service Blue Heron Beach Resort on SR 535. These full sized one- and two-bedroom condos have full kitchens, washers and dryers, and two full bathrooms in each room.

You may also rent rooms at timeshare properties without purchasing a timeshare, such as Westage Resorts. Keep in mind when booking that any time you stay at a timeshare property, you are likely to be pressured to attend a presentation. If you are someone who doesn't like the sales pressure, the easiest way to stop them from pestering you is to schedule to attend a presentation on the last day of your visit and simply cancel at the last minute or just not show up.

Because the larger companies are used to this tactic, they actually require a "refundable deposit" that will be held hostage after a longer-than-expected presentation (as they continually try to force a sale). If you

Cost Vs. Convenience

Insider's Tip!

You can often get great deals on rooms at the Other Disney Property Hotels, which are sometimes even cheaper than Disney's value resorts. They offer many of the benefits of the Disney resorts (though not all). Staying at the Swan and Dolphin, for instance, will get you free parking at the theme parks, advanced Lightning Lane reservations, Early Theme Park Entry benefits, and complimentary delivery of merchandise purchases directly to your room.

Reasons to Stay at a Disney Resort Hotel

Here is a list of advantages to staying on-property for you to consider when calculating the total cost/value of an on-property versus off-property hotel:

- The biggest reason to stay at a Disney hotel is to gain early access to individual Lightning Lane reservations (including Swan and Dolphin hotels). On-property guests can purchase the two daily Tier 1 Lightning Lane reservations as early as 7 a.m. on the morning of their park visit. (Off-property guests must wait until the park officially opens for the day to make these reservations, and the most popular ones are often sold out by that time.)

- Early Theme Park Entry. This perk replaced Extra Magic Hours. To enjoy the parks longer, guests get an extra 30 minutes in the morning. Guests are also occasionally offered the option to stay after-hours at select theme parks. These benefits are generally <u>only</u> provided to guests at Disney hotels, including Swan and Dolphin and Shades of Green. However, Disney-affiliated hotels in the Disney Springs area occasionally offer this same benefits. Guests get to choose from any of the four main theme parks for early entry when it is not open to the general public. Considering how busy the parks can get, that extra time without crowds can be worth a great deal.

- Free airport check-in and baggage transfer to/from the airport for most major airlines. There's no need to wait around baggage claim. You can start your vacation right away and let Disney worry about your luggage.

- Free transportation around Disney property (including Swan and Dolphin hotels). Buses usually pick up every fifteen minutes or so at each location to take you directly to the park of your choice. Some hotels also provide regular boat and/or monorail transportation to the parks. Compare this to off-property hotels. Those that do offer free transportation to Disney typically only pick up once or twice in the morning and evening, dropping you at a single location on Disney property. From there, you must still find your way to park of your choice. (Include a rate comparison of taxi versus car rental & parking.)

- The cost of theme park parking is included with your daily hotel parking fee, if you are driving your own vehicle. While most Orlando-area hotels charge a parking fee (and a daily resort fee, which may include parking),

Insider's Tip!

As a way to just relax when the crowds are lighter, many people use Early Theme Park Entry time to stroll through shops and linger over a meal.

For those who love photography, this is the best time to get great photos of the parks and your family without crowds blocking the background and landmarks.

off-property guests must also pay a separate fee to park at each theme park or Disney's Transportation and Ticket Center (Disney World's transportation hub and the parking area for the Magic Kingdom).

- Advanced dining reservations. On-property guests receive up to an additional 10 days to reserve dining prior to the 60-day advanced reservations open to everyone else. For instance, if you are booked for a 10-day vacation at a Disney hotel, you can begin booking dining reservations for ever day of your trip 60 days prior to the first day of your vacation. Off-property guests must wait to book 60 days in advance of each day of their trip. This is a huge advantage for popular venues, such as Be Our Guest and Liberty Tree Tavern (particularly for Thanksgiving or Christmas reservations).

- Advanced tee times at Disney golf courses (including Swan and Dolphin hotels).

- Complimentary delivery of purchases made within the theme parks or at Disney Springs to your hotel room (including Swan and Dolphin hotels). Don't carry your purchases around all day. Buy what you want and find it waiting for you when you return to your room that evening. Off-property guests have the option to have purchases held at the front of the park for them, which is also nice.

- On-site Disney ticket and concierge desks (including Swan and Dolphin hotels). These people can help you with everything from reserving Lightning Lane times to dining reservations to finding transportation at no extra charge, a service you likely won't find off-property.

- On-site, coin-operated laundry facilities.

- Free Wi-Fi in rooms and in guest areas.

- Free notary services to guests. Just check with the lobby concierge for availability.

- Complimentary wheelchairs for use during your stay (based on limited availability, with a $315 deposit).

- All rooms include mini-refrigerators. (These refrigerators are more coolers than true refrigerators. While they keep items chilled, they do not get as cold as true refrigerators, nor do they have freezers.)

accept discounts to sit through a presentation, DO NOT AGREE TO ANY UPFRONT DEPOSITS no matter the promise of getting your money back easily.

Other Disney Property Hotels

Consider some of the most convenient non-Disney hotels which are located within easy walking distance to Disney Springs. **Disney Springs Resort Area Hotels** are still considered "official" Walt Disney World hotels because they technically are located on Disney property. They can offer great convenience and better prices along with a few Disney perks.

Disney Springs Resort Area Hotels

- DoubleTree Suites by Hilton Orlando – Lake Buena Vista
- Best Western Lake Buena Vista Resort Hotel
- Holiday Inn Orlando - Lake Buena Vista
- Wyndham Lake Buena Vista Resort
- Hilton Orlando Lake Buena Vista
- Buena Vista Palace Hotel & Spa
- B Resort & Spa Lake Buena Vista

Each Disney Springs Resort Area Hotel offers complimentary shuttle service to the Disney parks, leaving every 30 minutes. This is a much more convenient schedule than virtually any non-Disney resort (which may only offer a couple morning and late afternoon trips). They also offer guests preferred tee times at the Disney golf courses, and advanced dining reservations at Disney restaurants and dinner shows.

Additionally, these hotels sometimes offer packages with Disney perks, such as Early Theme Park Entry and early Lightning Lane purchases.

Insider's Tip!

One cost-saving perk the Disney Springs hotels have that even Disney hotels don't offer is a coupon booklet for Disney Springs shopping. Don't expect huge discounts, but you might get 10% off of your bill at Rainforest Café and other meal options.

BoardWalk Area Hotels (Walt Disney World Swan and Dolphin)

Arguably the two best-located, non-Disney-brand hotels are the Walt Disney World Swan and Dolphin. Even though "Walt Disney" is included in their moniker and they are on Disney property, both the Walt Disney World Swan and Dolphin hotels are not officially Disney hotels. Located just a short stroll away from Disney's Boardwalk, you can easily walk to both Hollywood Studios (about 10 minutes) and Epcot (about 15 minutes) from these hotels! These properties also offer easy water transportation to the two parks. Early Theme Park Entry are available to guests of these hotels.

Other Hotels on Disney Property

The newest non-Disney hotel on Disney property is the Four Seasons Resort at Walt Disney World. This is a deluxe hotel that includes a Tom Fazio-designed Four Seasons Championship Golf Course, tennis courts, and water park-like complex complete with underwater-audio swimming pools, lazy river, water slides, splash zone, and even a movie screen with floating chairs!

Children will love the Pirate or Princess In-Room Celebrations option. The princess option includes a "royal princess proclamation" letter from Fairy Godmother and large pink box filled with princess treasures. The hotel even

Cost Vs. Convenience

Guests of Shades of Green, Disney's Swan & Dolphin Hotels, and the Disney Springs Resort Area Hotels benefit from Disney's Early Theme Park Entry just like those staying at any of the other Disney Hotels. If you are going to the parks during any peak period, this is a benefit that you will want to use.

offers a twice-weekly Disney character breakfast!

Military Guests – Shades of Green

There is a hotel just for active and service-retired military personnel and their families on Disney property called Shades of Green (shadesofgreen.org). Shades of Green is located very close to the Magic Kingdom and offers many of the same benefits as a Disney hotel, including complimentary shuttle service and Early Theme Park Entry.

For other veterans, Shades of Green offers open eligibility two months out of the year (usually January and September) to allow all honorably discharged veterans with a DD-214 and their families to stay in this property.

Good Neighbor Hotels off Disney Property

Disney partners with a number of Orlando area hotels, called Good Neighbor Hotels. Disney has screened each to ensure they meet Disney's quality and cleanliness standards.

Good Neighbor hotels do not have Early Theme Park Entry benefits. However, these properties offer a safe alternative if you don't want to stay at a Disney hotel. You can often get deluxe accommodations at them for less than the price of a Disney Value Resort. All Good

Neighbor hotels offer shuttle transportation to the parks, but not necessarily as often as Disney's transportation and not always for free.

Some are pet friendly and offer benefits that range from free parking at the hotel to complimentary breakfasts. One of the Good Neighbor Hotels is even within easy walking distance to Disney Springs.

Good Neighbor Hotels' Amenities

- Buena Vista Suites
  - **No Internet Access Available**
  - **No Pets**
  - Free Disney Shuttle
  - Free Hotel Parking
  - Complimentary Breakfast
  - In-Room Microwave & Refrigerator
- Caribe Royale Orlando
  - **No Internet Access Available**
  - **No Pets**
  - Free Disney Shuttle
  - Free Hotel Parking
  - In-Room Microwave & Refrigerator
- Champions World Resort
  - Pet Friendly
  - Free Area Attractions Shuttle
  - Free Hotel Parking
  - Complimentary Internet
  - In-Room Microwave & Refrigerator
- Clarion Inn Lake Buena Vista
  - Pet Friendly
  - Free Disney Shuttle
  - Free Hotel Parking
  - Complimentary Internet
  - In-Room Microwave & Refrigerator
- Clarion Suites Maingate
  - **No Pets**
  - Free Disney Shuttle
  - Free Hotel Parking
  - Complimentary Breakfast
  - Complimentary Internet

- In-Room Microwave & Refrigerator
- Comfort Inn Maingate
  - **No Pets**
  - Free Disney Shuttle
  - Free Hotel Parking
  - Complimentary Breakfast
  - Complimentary Internet
  - In-Room Microwave & Refrigerator
- Courtyard by Marriott Lake Buena Vista at Vista Centre
  - **No Pets**
  - Walking Distance to Disney Springs
  - Free Disney Shuttle
  - Free Hotel Parking
  - Complimentary Internet
  - In-Room Microwave & Refrigerator
- Embassy Suites Lake Buena Vista
  - **No Pets**
  - Free Disney Shuttle
  - Free Hotel Parking
  - Complimentary Cooked to Order Breakfast
  - Complimentary Internet (in Lobby only)
  - In-Room Microwave & Refrigerator
- Embassy Suites Lake Buena Vista South
  - **No Pets**
  - Disney Shuttle (Additional Fee)
  - Free Hotel Parking
  - Complimentary Cooked to Order Breakfast
  - In-Room Microwave & Refrigerator
- Fairfield Inn & Suites by Marriott
  - **No Pets**
  - Free Disney Shuttle
  - Free Hotel Parking
  - Free Local Phone Calls
  - Complimentary Breakfast
  - Complimentary Internet

- In-Room Microwave & Refrigerator
- Holiday Inn Express & Suites Lake Buena Vista East
  - **No Pets**
  - Free Area Attractions Shuttle
  - Free Hotel Parking
  - Complimentary Breakfast
  - Complimentary Internet
  - In-Room Microwave & Refrigerator
- Sheraton Lake Buena Vista Resort
  - Pet Friendly
  - Free Disney Shuttle
  - Car Rental Facility
  - Complimentary Internet
  - In-Room Refrigerator
- Sheraton Vistana Resort Villas
  - **No Pets**
  - Free Disney Shuttle
  - Free Hotel Parking
  - Complimentary Internet
  - Full Kitchen or Kitchenette
- Staybridge Suites Orlando - Lake Buena Vista
  - **No Pets**
  - Free Disney Shuttle
  - Free Hotel Parking
  - Complimentary Breakfast
  - Complimentary Internet
  - Full Kitchen
- The Palms Hotel & Villas
  - Pet Friendly
  - Free Area Attractions Shuttle
  - Complimentary Breakfast
  - Full Kitchen
- WorldQuest Orlando Resort
  - **No Pets**
  - Free Disney Shuttle
  - Free Hotel Parking
  - Complimentary Light Breakfast
  - Complimentary Wifi
  - Full Kitchen
  - In-Room Washer & Dryer

Maingate Hotels off Disney Property

When looking at hotels on-line, it is important to note that many area hotels advertise themselves as "maingate" resorts. This term can be misleading for people familiar with Disneyland, as it is used to refer to hotels within walking distance to that park.

In Orlando, the self-designated "maingate" hotels are **nowhere** near *walking distance* to the Walt Disney World theme parks. Driving to the parks from each area can actually vary from 20 to 45 minutes!

"Maingate West" usually means the hotel is located within a fairly close driving distance to the Disney property entrance off Irlo Bronson Memorial Highway (US-192), while "Maingate East" refers to hotels closer to one of the Apopka-Vineland Road (SR 535) entrances. However, these terms tend to be used very loosely and should not be used to decide which hotel to book for your stay. Instead, use reviews and maps to determine the right choice for you.

Insects & Other Critters in Orlando Hotels (and Lakes)

Insects are a fact of life in Orlando. Most hotels do an excellent job of keeping the critters out of rooms, but you should always thoroughly inspect <u>BEFORE bringing your luggage inside and opening it</u>! This is true even at Disney hotels, as bugs can get into the nicest properties. The last thing you want is to inadvertently bring an infestation from your vacation home with you.

Bedbugs

While bedbugs are now a fact of life in the United States, they rarely affect Disney properties. When they do, they are are dealt with swiftly, as you would expect at any self-respecting hotel.

Upon entering your hotel room, check the bed mattresses, particularly near the head of the bed. Be sure to remove the sheets and any mattress covers, so you're looking directly at the mattress. Look closely for any sign of bed bugs, which are very small, though visible to the naked eye.

There are online registries you can research regardless of which final accommodations you select. Double check either of the two following Bed Bug Registry sites: bedbugregistry.com or registry.bedbugs.net. These sites report many users' experiences in Orlando properties.

Also check the room for cockroaches, particularly around window sills, behind any easily moveable furniture (don't hurt yourself!), and around the base of the walls. Finding a single dead or dying cockroach isn't out of the ordinary and likely means the hotel is doing its job of keeping the property properly sprayed (though it may say something else about the property's housekeeping), but a live and scurrying critter is a very bad sign!

If you notice any live insects, use your smartphone to take pictures and then notify the front desk immediately. Depending on the level of infestation and the hotel layout, you may want to move to a separate building or cancel your reservation altogether and find new lodgings.

Swimming Pools and Area Lakes

Florida has many interesting creatures. Unfortunately, many of them are drawn to water features and swimming pools at area hotels. Be on the lookout for cloudy water which indicates that a pool is not being properly cleaned and maintained. Opaque water can also conceal snakes and alligators. If your hotel pool is cloudy, don't swim in it.

Cost Vs. Convenience

Insider's Tip!

It's important to take pictures of an insect infestation if you plan to cancel your hotel reservation due to it. This gives you proof to provide to your credit card company in case the hotel tries to charge you cancellation fees.

You may even experience unwanted visitors in and around well-maintained pool, such as lizards, frogs, possums, and raccoons. Avoid and leave them alone; they are part of the local wildlife and do not pose a threat to humans. If you see the rare snake in your pool, alert the front desk and stay away.

However, if you see a large insect with pincers, watch out! Waterbugs are common to the region. They are often two to four inches in length and look similar to the Egyptian beetles commonly seen in mummy movies. These aggressive bugs are excellent swimmers and have an unusual behavior: they like to swim in water and pinch unsuspecting people. And yes, their pinch is quite painful!

Snakes and Alligators

Unless you are familiar with which snakes are venomous and which are not, we suggest you avoid swimming with snakes – and avoid all alligators! – in Orlando.

Area lakes often have alligators - even if you don't see them. Due to risks, there are not many lakes that allow swimming (though some lake-front businesses offer boat rentals for fishing and equipment for water sports, such as water-skis, kayaks, canoes, and stand-up paddle boards).

Disney is like Alice stepping through the looking glass; to step through the portals of Disney will be like entering another world.

- Walt Disney

Disney World Dining

Walt Disney World has a variety of restaurant experiences. There are many types and cuisines with something for everyone, available almost any time of the day and evening.

While you'll be able to find nearly anything that suits your fancy, some of the better locations will take some travel time to get to. But the best of them are part of an overall experience that you will easily remember.

Most people are familiar with dining options inside of the theme parks, water parks, and at Disney Springs. In addition, there are also a number of options at or near Disney hotels, all of which are available for anyone to eat at, even guests not staying at a Disney hotel.

In all, there are nearly 300 restaurants on Walt Disney World property and just over 60 lounges. Of those, more than 100 can be found inside the four main theme parks. That's a lot of choices!

There are a few notes about Disney dining to get started. All of Disney's indoor restaurants are non-smoking. If you must eat and smoke, you will need to get your meal to go and take it to a designated smoking area.

You can get alcohol with your meal at most table-service restaurants. In the Magic Kingdom, the only locations that serve alcohol are: Be Our Guest, Cinderella's Royal Table, Jungle Navigation Co. Ltd. Skipper Canteen, Liberty Tree Tavern, and Tony's Town Square Restaurant.

Keep in mind when dining with smaller children that the desirability of the nicer or more unique restaurants are often lost on them. Aside from character dining, children at Disney don't seem to be overly concerned with ambiance.

Most restaurants have children's menus for ages three to nine, as well as booster and high chairs. Disney also tries to provide quicker service to families with children. Don't try to take your young child to Victoria & Albert's, though; they have a minimum age of 10.

Now that we're ready to get to the meat of the dining section, we will start by providing you with an overview of the types of restaurants you will find at Disney, as well as the relative time-versus-money savings.

Restaurants are either table-service, buffet, family style, or counter-service. Family style means the server brings out food to the table for all members to share. For instance, Liberty Tree Tavern in Magic Kingdom is popular for its family style dinners.

Counter-service Restaurants

At the low end of the dining range are the counter-service restaurants (sometimes referred to as quick service). You order your meal from a Cast Member or automated kiosk and then pick it up from a counter when it's ready.

Many counter-service restaurants now allow for mobile orders through the My

Insider's Tip!

If you accidentally drop food or a beverage, most counter-service restaurants will replace it if you just ask. There's no point in letting your child cry over spilled ice cream!

Disney Experience app with your credit card or Disney Dining points. Use the app to customize and place your complete order. This allows you to skip the ordering line inside the restaurant. Your order is not prepared until you arrive. Upon arrival, simply click the "I'm Here" button within the app to let the kitchen know it is time to prepare your food. It's that easy!

Mobile Ordering Locations

Magic Kingdom:
- Casey's Corner
- Columbia Harbour House
- Cosmic Ray's Starlight Cafe
- Pecos Bill Tall Tale Inn & Cafe
- Pinnochio Village Haus
- Sleepy Hollow
- Sunshine Tree Terrace
- The Friar's Nook
- The Lunching Pad
- Tomorrowland Terrace

Epcot:
- Connections Eatery
- Regal Eagle Smokehouse
- Sommerfest
- Yorkshire County Fish Shop

Animal Kingdom:
- Flame Tree Barbecue
- Harambe Market
- Pizzafari
- Restaurantosaurus
- Satu'li Canteen

Hollywood Studios:
- ABC Commissary
- Backlot Express

Insider's Tip!

Gratuities for good service are expected at standard table-service restaurants, and a gratuity of <u>18% is automatically added to your bill</u> if your dining party has 6 people or more. The same 18% tip is added at Disney buffets, but is not as common at food service locations outside the property.

Reservations are required for all dinner shows and at Cinderella's Royal Table, and they should be made well in advance. Gratuities for good service are expected at dinner shows and Cinderella's Royal Table. Like other Disney's table service restaurants, a gratuity of 18% is automatically added to your bill if your dining party has six people or more.

- Catalina Eddie's
- Dockside Diner
- Docking Bay 7 Food and Cargo
- Fairfax Faire
- Milk Stand
- PizzeRizzo
- Ronto Roasters
- Rosie's All-American Cafe
- Woody's Lunch Box

Blizzard Beach:
- Avalunch
- Lottawatta Lodge
- Warming Hut

Typhoon Lagoon:
- Leaning Palms
- Surf Doggies
- Typhoon Tilly's

Disney Springs:
- D-Luxe Burger

Each Disney hotel also offers mobile ordering at its counter-service restaurant.

The option to pre-order meals at select counter service restaurants using the My Disney Experience app is especially useful during the lunch or dinner rush when you can expect to stand in a long line to place your order.

In all counter-service restaurants, you can choose your own dining location within the restaurant. Counter-service restaurants do not take reservations. Gratuities are never expected at these locations.

Table-Service Restaurants

Next are the standard table-service restaurants, where you are seated and order food from a server who brings it to your table when the food is ready. These are typically a little more expensive than counter-service restaurants. Most table-service restaurants accept reservations and walk-ins. Gratuities are expected.

Insider's Tip!

If guests complain about poor quality or lackluster food, Disney staff will bend over backwards to make things right. *NEVER* accept poor quality food. You are paying premium prices, so if something is cold, dried-out, or doesn't meet your taste, let a server or manager know. Even at a counter-service restaurant, they will re-make your meal to ensure it is fresh. This is especially important when eating at locations that pre-make the food they serve, such as Tangierine Café in the Morocco Pavilion (Epcot).

Buffet Restaurants

Buffet restaurants, including character buffets, are generally more expensive than standard table-service restaurants. These restaurants are all-you-can-eat, and you serve your own food from a wide variety of offerings. This category also includes family-style restaurants, such as Liberty Tree Tavern, where a server brings dishes for the family to share. At all buffets, a server is on-hand to take beverage orders. (Alcoholic beverages and specialty drinks cost extra.) Reservations are accepted at buffet restaurants and are highly recommended. Gratuities are expected.

Dinner Shows

Dinner shows and meals at Cinderella's Royal Table cost more than most buffet restaurants and also require meal reservations and pre-payment. What is and is not included with your meal varies based on the restaurant.

Unlike most restaurant reservations, which get you priority seating at your chosen time, a reservation at a dinner show or Cinderella's Royal Table reserves physical seats within the venue. Thus, depending on location availability, you get to make specific seating requests to enhance your experience.

Disney Signature Dining

Signature Dining restaurants generally have better food and service than others – some even boast celebrity chefs, and the nicest ones have dress codes.

Reservations are nearly always required and should be made well in advance. At a minimum, prices compare to Disney's dinner shows, but some cost much more. Gratuities for good service are expected at Signature Dining locations, and like all table service options, a gratuity of 18% is automatically added to your bill if your dining party has six people or more.

Alcohol Cannot be Found Everywhere!

Alcohol is served at most restaurants, except in the Magic Kingdom where it is

Dress Codes

Victoria & Albert's (Grand Floridian Resort) requires dinner jackets and dress shoes for men, as well as dresses or pant suits for women (no casual clothing allowed).

These other Disney Signature restaurants also have dress codes (khakis, dress slacks, nice jeans, or dress shorts with collared shirts for men; capris, skirts, dresses, nice jeans, or dress shorts for women):

Jiko – The Cooking Place at Animal Kingdom Lodge
Flying Fish Cafe at BoardWalk
California Grill at Contemporary
Bistro de Paris at Epcot
Citricos at Grand Floridian
Narcoossee's at Grand Floridian
Topolino's Terrace at Riviera
Yachtsman Steakhouse at Yacht Club Resort
Todd English's bluezoo & Shula's Steakhouse at WDW Dolphin
Il Mulino New York Trattoria at WDW Swan

Insider's Tip!

The most expensive Disney restaurant, *Victoria & Albert's*, is considered premier among dining locations throughout all of Florida.

served only at Be Our Guest, Cinderella's Royal Table, Jungle Navigation Co. Ltd. Skipper Canteen, Liberty Tree Tavern, and Tony's Town Square Restaurant (dine-in only).

Important Note for Smokers: No smoking is allowed in restaurants.

What to Expect

Now that you are familiar with the dining categories, let's discuss what you can expect when dining on-property.

Eating at Disney restaurants is more about convenience, atmosphere, and experience than it is about the food. If you go to a character meal with the expectation that you are paying for a decent meal with a chance to interact with some of your favorite characters, you won't be disappointed. Likewise, if you go to a dinner show understanding you are paying for the actual show, and the food is there to fill

your belly while watching the performance, you'll be pleased.

Disney might argue that its Signature Dining restaurants *are* about the food; and certain restaurants, such as Victoria & Albert's, Be Our Guest, and California Grill consistently get rave reviews. Even these restaurants have off days, though.

During busy periods, no matter where, you might be rushed through your meal. Just let your server know you need more time if you feel rushed. Unless you have a specific schedule you are following, don't hesitate to take your time and enjoy the experience.

Insider's Tip!

If you must do a character breakfast, either plan it on a day you won't spend at a park, or schedule the latest breakfast reservation you can. This will give you time to catch the attractions early in the morning when crowds are at their lowest levels, and then have your meal as the parks start to get busy. An added bonus if you linger over your meal is that you may get some of the lunch offerings that get laid out without having to pay the additional cost!

Insider's Tip!

We generally recommend snacking your way through the day and only eating a full table-service meal as a late lunch on the days you're visiting a park. Try for a reservation around 3 p.m., especially if you're eating at a buffet restaurant. It will cost you a little more than breakfast, but you will miss the heavy dining rush and the hottest part of the day, coming back rejuvenated for the evening. As with late breakfast buffets, a late lunch reservation at a buffet restaurant means you will also get dinner offerings for no additional cost if you linger over your meal.

Making Your Disney Dining Reservations

As we mentioned before, the My Disney Experience app with its Genie tool aren't just good for managing your park reservations and itinerary. These vacation tools also allow you to purchase Genie+ and individual Lightning Lane reservations, make dining reservations, and make changes to those reservations.

Off-property guests can make dining reservations up to 60 days (2 months) in advance of the actual dining date. On-property guests can make dining reservations up to 60 days in advance plus the length of their stay (up to 10 days), so on-property guests get a few days' advantage to selecting the best times.

All restaurants and dining experiences that accept reservations now require a credit card to hold the reservation. Pay close attention to the cancellation policy, which may be different from one restaurant to the next, in case you can't make your dining time.

Most restaurants require at least 24 hours notice for cancellation or your card will be charged a fee of $10 per person ($25 at Victoria and Albert's).

For restaurants that require prepayment of your entire meal, such as all dinner shows and Cinderella's Royal Table, the cancellation fee can be the total amount of your check!

Insider's Tip!

For holidays, special dining experiences (such as dinner shows), and premium restaurants (particularly Cinderella's Royal Table, Be Our Guest, Le Cellier, and Victoria and Albert's restaurants), be ready at 5:45 a.m. Eastern Time 60 days (+ the length of stay for on-property guests) in advance to make sure you get a table at a time that works for your party. (See the following table for a complete list of restaurants for which we suggest you get reservations.)

The list of restaurants that accept reservations in advance, and their menus, can be found on Disney's site: disneyworld.disney.go.com/dining/#/reservations-accepted. You can make reservations at this same location by clicking on the restaurant at which you wish to eat and choosing the desired date and time. Reservations can also be made by calling (407) WDW-DINE (939-3463) or by using the My Disney Experience app. Be sure to log in when you make your reservations to allow you to manage them online and through the My Disney Experience app.

Note: Disney limits off-property guests to making only one reservation every two hours. This is because unscrupulous companies have tried to abuse the reservation system by hoarding reservations for popular restaurants and selling them to guests for a profit. Disney has done an excellent job shutting down these predatory practices to keep the system fair for actual guests.

Epcot's World Showcase International Cuisine

As you might expect, the World Showcase restaurant offerings reflect authentic cuisine of each of the 11 country pavilions:

- Mexico
- Norway
- China
- Germany
- Italy
- America
- Japan
- Morocco
- France
- United Kingdom
- Canada

How ethnic are Epcot's dining experiences? If there was ever a place for mixed reviews, it would be the restaurants within World Showcase. Some people love them, others hate them.

We asked international Cast Members who work at the restaurants for their "off-the-record" take about how well Disney represents native meals. Thier comments mirror those of Disney guests from the same countries. Most agree that Disney's versions represent good *entry-level* choices for people new to each cuisine.

In other words, if you have eaten at many Moroccan restaurants, you will likely find Disney's offerings within its Morocco Pavilion to be bland and boring. However, if you have never tried this type of food, you'll discover choices that are reasonably common and not so spicy as to be intimidating. This seems true of all the cuisine available in World Showcase.

Insider's Tip!

Go online at 6 a.m. the morning of to try to get cancellations from the previous day. Between 2:30 and 4:30 p.m., or any time on cold and rainy days, speak to the host at the restaurant of your choice in-person. People often cancel reservations in the afternoon and during inclement weather, but only the restaurant host is able to fill those empty spaces.

Value vs. Time

When it comes to value for your dining experience, you must consider your trade-offs. Yes, you can save a lot of money by dining off-site. However, you're paying a lot of money to spend the day inside of a theme park, so is the extra time you're spending away from the park worth the money you might otherwise be saving?

Meal-by-meal Advice

Let's break it down meal-by-meal. If you are staying off-property, we think you'll benefit by eating breakfast off-site (except for your character breakfast). If you're staying on-property and don't have a car, eat at the counter-service restaurant in your hotel. Eat well before the parks open so you can get to the parks early.

Character breakfasts are cheaper than other character meals, but trying to eat a character breakfast before a park opens nearly always means you will arrive to the park a little later, foregoing some of the best opportunities to get on rides.

Insider's Tip!

Lunch is a better option than dinner for dining in parks. Eating a big lunch during the hot daytime hours is much more cost-effective than waiting until dinner time. Not only will a late lunch get you out of the heat, you will be free later in the day when everyone else is heading to a sit-down meal.

Disney World Dining

Disney World Dining

Guaranteed Reservations Required Months in Advance for Best Times

Restaurant (Location)	Reservation Notes
Le Cellier (Epcot, Canada)	Get reservations months in advance for the best times.
Chef Mickey's (Contemporary Resort)	Get reservations months in advance for the best times.
Cinderella's Royal Table	Most difficult reservation is 8 a.m. here due to small restaurant size & high demand to eat with princesses.
Teppan Edo	Reservations are required months in advance to get good times.
Be Our Guest	Get reservations immediately.
Victoria & Albert's	Get reservations immediately.
Biergarten	Get reservations a few weeks early.
Via Napoli	Get reservations a few weeks early.
Liberty Tree Tavern	Easy to get into right away, except on holidays, when demand for classic American cuisine spikes among guests.
Akershus	Get breakfast reservations immediately.

Insider's Tip!

A favorite destination for locals is Beaches & Cream, an old-fashioned ice cream parlor at Disney's Beach Club Resort. Capacity is extremely limited, so reservations are highly recommended, but where else can you eat a kitchen sink dessert and choose songs from a free juke box that plays classic music from the 1950s and 1960s?

Insider's Tip!

Don't limit yourself to eating only at restaurants within the parks. On days when you are not at a park, have fun and explore as many of the Disney properties as you can. Many of Disney's best restaurants are found at their resort hotels, not at the parks. For instance, Boatwright's Dining Hall at Port Orleans Riverside offers excellent Southern fare, and even the quick service restaurants at both Port Orleans hotels are popular meal destinations for locals (thanks in part to the yummy beignets at Port Orleans French Quarter).

Insider's Warning!

Prices can be higher on holidays when surcharges are added and many restaurants modify their menus to celebrate the special day. (Dining Plan members have a different surcharge during holidays/peak times.)

Insider's Tip!

For Kosher counter-service meals, you can go to Cosmic Ray's at the Magic Kingdom, Pizzafari at the Animal Kingdom, ABC Commissary at Hollywood Studios, and Liberty Inn at Epcot.

Insider's Tip!

Disney provides free and easy transportation to each hotel from the parks and Disney Springs. Just ask any Disney employee where to pick up a ride. Getting back to the park is just as easy with Disney's free transportation. If you have your own car, parking is free at the hotels. Explore the many dining possibilities at: disneyworld.disney.go.com/dining.

Quality Coffee

One of the biggest complaints Disney visitors have had over the years has been the inability to get a good cup of coffee. Seeking to improve guest experiences, in 2013 Disney replaced its previous supplier (Nestle) with **Joffrey's Coffee & Tea Company** as the official specialty coffee provider for Walt Disney World parks and hotels.

Joffrey's has several coffee booths, offering specialty coffees and espresso, throughout the four main theme parks. Joffrey's French Roast blend is also the offering at all counter-service and table-service locations throughout Disney properties, and each Disney Signature Dining restaurant has its own original blend of coffee provided by Joffrey's.

If you would prefer something a bit more familiar, **Starbucks** has full-service locations inside of each of the four main theme parks and Disney Springs.

Insider's Tip!

Bring healthy, high protein snacks with you to the parks, since allowing yourself to get hungry leads to poor purchase decisions. You are walking 7-10 miles per day, so expect to eat – and drink – a lot more than usual.

Starbucks is also served in Swan, Dolphin, and Shades of Green hotels. Off-property, but very close to Disney, you can find the busiest Starbucks in all of Florida near the intersection of I-4 and SR 535.

Guests with Special Dining Requirements

We love that Disney enthusiastically strives to meet any special dining needs of its guests. Whether you're a vegetarian, on a strict gluten-free diet, or have certain other allergies, you'll feel like you're receiving the royal treatment at most Disney restaurants when a manager or chef comes out to discuss your specific needs with you.

Review the menu for the restaurant of your choice on the restaurant's web page: disneyworld.disney.go.com/dining. Many meals can be modified for your specific needs. Certain alternative needs are common, such as vegetarian requirements. For instance, the cheese soup at Le Cellier can be made without meat

Insider's Tip!

Freeze your sandwiches and juice boxes overnight. You can use them to keep the rest of your food items cold, and they should be nicely thawed by the time lunch rolls around.

with advanced notice, and the ratatouille at Be Our Guest can be made without mushrooms.

If you have unique meal restrictions, get reservations at sit-down restaurants and then contact the restaurant at least three days in advance to let them know of your specific needs and figure out options. If you plan to eat at a table-service restaurant, contact Disney Dining at (407) 939-3563. You can find out if there are options not listed on the menu that will meet your needs. If not, ask for a restaurant chef to contact you directly. You'll be able to request a modification that meets your approval.

Note that most counter-service restaurants within the parks will not modify food for special needs, such as food allergies, but they may have items that aren't listed on the menu. Counter-service restaurants in the Disney resort hotels make their food to order, though, and managers there are eager to meet special dietary needs.

Savings on Meals and Beverages

Food can be a surprise expense during any vacation. At home, we typically make many of our meals, and people often fail to budget for the cost of dining out for *every meal* each day as part of their vacation expense. Thus, it can be a shock when your credit card statement arrives, and you find your Disney vacation has

Insider's Tip!

Pre-popped popcorn is an excellent snack option to bring to the parks. It weighs very little, and it's something popcorn-lovers are likely to crave throughout the day due to buttery aroma wafting from the many fresh popcorn carts located throughout each park.

Insider's Tip!

While we are certainly not promoting this particularly novel idea, alcoholic beverages can be a big expense at the park. Some people have figured out that replacing water with clear alcohol in their water bottles is an inexpensive way to forego this expense…at least until Disney security starts testing liquids at security checkpoints!

cost you hundreds or even thousands more than you thought.

To make matters worse, restaurants on Disney property generally cost more than similar off-property restaurants. This is, in part, due to the high surcharge (as much as 40% "off the top" of their revenues!) that Disney places on some restaurant owners, who must then pass those costs on to their customers.

It is very easy to spend more than $100 per day for the smallest family. If you don't make firm plans, expect to spend at least $10 to $15 per person, per meal.

Of course, Disney is counting on the convenience factor to keep everyone dining on-property and paying their high

Insider's Tip!

Order take-out. Avoid sitting down at a full-service restaurant. By taking your meal back to your room with you, you'll instantly save the 20% you would otherwise be paying as a gratuity. Table-service restaurants within the parks do not allow take-out (although counter-service locations do!), but this tip will help you save money if you are eating off-property.

prices. After all, do you want to spend hours each day traveling to and from off-property restaurants, or would you rather spend that time getting the most out of the theme parks?

This section offers simple ways to save a little here and there, hopefully adding up to huge savings by the end of your trip. The first tip is the most obvious:

Bring Your Own Meals and Snacks: Many visitors choose to bring their own food to the parks. This can save valuable time and money. However, the weight of carrying beverages, sandwiches, coolers, and ice to keep everything fresh can be a problem over the course of several hours of walking. As we already mentioned, if you choose to bring your own beverages or bottled water, you can ask for a cup of ice at any counter service restaurant that serves fountain beverages. The Disney Cast Member will gladly give you ice and cups.

If you are trying to maintain a strict budget and have too much food to easily carry around in a stroller or backpack, you have a couple of options. These include keeping your snacks in a locker either inside or outside the park, or in your car. Of course, if you are staying at a Disney hotel near the park you are visiting, it might make sense to keep your meals there.

If you choose to keep food inside your automobile (on ice if it is hot outside!), you

Insider's Tip!

Plan to share an entrée with someone else in your party. You can always share a dessert or have a snack later on if you find you're still hungry! You will still come out ahead financially and limit wasted food that would otherwise just get thrown away. This is especially true if you don't have a large appetite.

can take a break or trade-off with other members of your party to bring back additional snacks as they are needed. Taking a break to return to your car (or hotel room) also gives a chance for a short cat nap.

If you don't have an auto, renting a locker may be your best option. Compared to the price of meals, a locker rental is a particularly cost-effective option. Disney rents lockers inside each of its four main theme parks and water parks for $10 to $15 per day, depending on size. In addition, there is a $5 refundable deposit for all locker rentals. If you're park hopping, you only need to pay once, and

Insider's Tip!

Kid's meals also offer a great option for adults. Kid's meals at Disney World counter-service restaurants include an entrée, two sides, and a beverage, all for less than a regular adult entrée. They are technically for children ages three to nine, but Cast Members don't ask if you're ordering for yourself or a child at a counter-service restaurant. Also, people who have had stomach surgery often order from the kid's menu at table-service restaurants. Just let your server know you have a specific need for reduced portions.

Insider's Tip!

What can you do to control any impulse food (and souvenir!) purchases? We suggest you leave the credit cards behind and don't use the charging feature on your MagicBand. Take only your budgeted amount of cash to the park each day, and stick to it!

Great Places for Free Water:

- Magic Kingdom – Pecos Bill Tall Tale Inn and Café; Gaston's Tavern
- Epcot – Sunshine Seasons; Sommerfest
- Hollywood Studios – Coca-Cola Kiosk (Entrance of Park)
- Animal Kingdom – Pizzafari

If you prefer hot beverages, especially after meals or on a cool evening, bring your own insulated mug with instant coffee or tea bags. You can request hot water at the same restaurants noted above. However, some locations may argue that they are unable to provide hot water due to safety reasons. Instead, we recommend you take your mug to restaurant locations with unlimited self-service drink refills, where you can get free hot water out of a spout on the coffee machines – no questions asked!

Restaurants with Unlimited Self-service Beverage Refills:

- Magic Kingdom – Cosmic Ray's Starlight Cafe
- Epcot – Sunshine Seasons; Connections Cafe; Regal Eagle BBQ
- Hollywood Studios – ABC Commissary; Backlot Express
- Animal Kingdom – Restaurantosaurus; Satu'li Canteen

Note: Many people feel uncomfortable asking for free water, especially hot water. If you prefer to use an excuse, simply tell the employee the water is to help you take medication. Disney Cast Members are trained not to question the integrity of their guests, and they will never ask for details about a medical condition.

Insider's Tip!

Free Water – The cheapest way to stay hydrated in the Orlando heat is to simply ask for a cup of ice water from any Disney restaurant that sells fountain beverages. It's Orlando's tap water, which sometimes has a slight sulfur flavor (due to the natural underground aquifer), but it's safe to drink. If you need a flavored drink, bring along Crystal Lite and Kool-Aid flavor packets.

It may not be glamorous, but this little tip can save a family hundreds of dollars over the course of a vacation. Disney charges $3 for a bottle of water, and fountain beverages cost even more. Many people want three or four drinks per day, which can add up for a large family. Consider a four-person family, each buying four bottles of water per day. That's $48 per day plus tax!

Insider's Tip!

Some of the best on-property dining values include **Earl of Sandwich** in Disney Springs (sandwiches from $6.99), **Les Halles Boulangerie Patisserie** in Epcot's France Pavilion (quiche and dessert for about $10), and **Sommerfest** in Epcot's Germany Pavilion (sausage plates for about $10).

Insider's Tip!

Appetizers also make great reduced-size options for dining. Order a few to share among the table, and everybody can enjoy a variety without paying full price. Certain restaurants, such as Rainforest Café and T-Rex (at Disney Springs), have excellent appetizer platters that easily provide enough food for two people and a child - while leaving a little room for dessert - at a much lower cost than two entrees. Staff members are used to people sharing their meals and will gladly bring an extra serving dish and utensils.

Insider's Tip!

When greeting your wait staff, don't forget to tell them if you are celebrating a special occasion, such as a birthday. Most sit down restaurants provide a free birthday dessert, while some of the Disney Signature restaurants provide free desserts for special occasions like anniversaries or honeymoons. Wear your free birthday or anniversary button (available at all Guest Relations offices), and you will find some counter-service restaurants also offer up a free dessert!

you can get another locker for no additional charge after turning in the key to your first locker.

There are also lockers found outside of the theme park entrances and at Disney Springs. These are coin operated and cost $1 each time they're opened. Luggage lockers are also located outside of Epcot for the same $1. These outside lockers can be more cost effective, but remember you will need to go back through security checkpoints each time you exit and wish to re-enter the park.

If you have a stroller, using it to carry heavier items and backpacks is a convenient way to keep your food while not having to transport the bulk of it around with you. You can also easily shift some of the duties to older children. Rolling backpacks can be handy, but remember not to bring anything too large that won't fit on rides with you!

Cash vs. Charge: Create a cash budget for food expenses during your vacation. Buying with cash will help you stay frugal! Impulse purchases can blow those budgets out of the water, and nothing encourages

impulse purchases like a credit card...except perhaps a MagicBand.

One Dun & Bradstreet study shows that consumers are likely to spend 12-18% more when using credit cards than cash. That's about <u>$180 extra</u> if you have budgeted $1,000 for food on your trip!

Even McDonald's notes that the average food purchase in their restaurants went up from $4.50 to $7 with people using credit cards over cash, showing a definite link to credit cards affecting people's food purchases.

Using MagicBands can lead to higher expenditures on food.

With just the wave of a wrist, your MagicBand makes it very easy to charge purchases directly to your hotel room or credit card. Disney has bet more than a *billion-dollars* on this system, planning to make it convenient for you to spend more that you otherwise planned.

Kid's Meals, Appetizers, & Sharing: When you go out at home, you probably order an entrée. Because the portions are larger than many people want to eat for a single meal, most of us take the leftovers home to eat later. However, this is generally not an option when you're out and about during your vacation. It is especially difficult when you have to get back to your fun.

Refillable Beverage Cups: Counter-service restaurants in Disney's resort hotels sell special reusable beverage cups for fountain drinks, hot cocoa, tea bags, and brewed coffee. These durable cups allow unlimited refills of any beverage. They last for several years, making them great mementos to enjoy after you get home from your trip.

While on vacation, you get unlimited refills for your length of stay. Even though they are offered to on-property guests, anyone can purchase these cups for several days' use and then visit counter-service restaurants at various on-property hotels. It's a great way to save money on beverages, plus the counter-service restaurants offer reasonable values for dining on-property. (Remember, transportation to these locations to/from parks and Disney Springs is convenient and free.)

On-property Value Dining

Disney's resort hotels all have food courts, based on the hotel's own unique theme, of course. Counter-service meals typically run in the $10 to $15 per person range, though children's meals are usually less.

Insider's Tip!

There are few restaurants near Disney (or any of the Orlando theme parks) that offer particularly great cuisine, since most are in place for tourists rather than repeat-business diners. We recommend eating at national chains when dining off Disney property to get the same standardized quality and experience available at any of their restaurants.

Insider's Tip!

If you will be traveling during a time that any one in your party will be celebrating a birthday, take advantage of the club memberships that provide free birthday perks available at many chain restaurants. For instance, Earl of Sandwich (Disney Springs) provides a free dessert and Red Robin gives away a free burger, while Landry's restaurants (including Rainforest Café and T-Rex) give you $25 to spend during your birthday month. Many of these clubs are free or charge a nominal fee to sign up. Even if you don't have a membership, mention the special occasion to your server at any restaurant. You might get a free treat!

Theme parks also have counter-service restaurants with similar pricing. While you won't find characters or table service in these restaurants, some counter-service restaurants allow unlimited drink refills.

These locations are great for getting food quickly, so you can get back to playing. Grab a handheld menu, which is available at each counter-service restaurant. This will allow you to peruse all the options and be ready to order when it's your turn. You'll get through the line much faster, and the people in the queue behind you will thank you!

Insider's Tip!

Even a nominal purchase, such as a $3 beverage, is sufficient to save you the $33 cost you'd otherwise pay for valet parking for Tables in Wonderland members.

Tourist Trap!

<u>CAUTION</u>: Rely on information found in your hotel lobby and not on flyers you find under your door. There are some pizza and sandwich companies who slide advertisements for their restaurants directly under your hotel door without permission. Not only is this practice against the law, some companies have very unethical practices. Complaints include very late delivery of terrible food and pizza that is made from commercially-available frozen brands. Even worse are the reports of credit card information being stolen from these unscrupulous establishments.

These companies use names that sound like well-known brands to confuse you if you look on the Internet. Worse yet, they hire criminals to deliver the flyers who cannot find legitimate work and who don't mind that they're breaking the law. Reports of thefts and assaults from these employees are further evidence that you don't want to call and invite these companies to your doorstep.

Disney World Discount Dining Card – "Tables in Wonderland"

(Note: Sales of Tables in Wonderland memberships are not currently available due to COVID-19.) This dining discount card is available to Florida residents, seasonal passholders, and Disney Vacation Club members. For $150 per year, card holders receive 20% off dining purchases for up to 10 people at most Disney restaurants, including alcoholic beverages. Card holders also receive free valet parking at Deluxe Disney resort hotels with any purchase at a participating restaurant at that location.

Off-property Value Dining

You don't need a car to eat off-property. There are a number of restaurants, such as **Moe's Southwest Grill, Fuddrucker's, TGIF,** and **Flippers Pizza,** that are located within an easy 20-minute walk from Disney Springs (which you can get to from any resort property using Disney transportation). These are found just off Disney's property at <u>Crossroads Shopping Center</u> (SR 535 and Hotel Plaza Boulevard).

If you have an automobile, a short drive will take you to one of the area's many **Cici's Pizza** restaurants, which offer pizza buffets or take-out meals for lunch or dinner. Their buffets cost only $5.99 per person, although most coupon books at hotel lobbies include discounts. Just pop into any hotel and ask for them at the front desk.

If you want a little more variety, **Golden Corral** offers an inexpensive buffet at its many area restaurants, and one is a short drive (or long walk) from Disney Springs. They serve all-you-can-eat breakfasts, lunches, or dinners, all for a very reasonable price.

Highway 192 (its formal name is Irlo Bronson Memorial Highway, but people just call it 192) has just as many dining options, most of which are much cheaper

Insider's Warning!

When parking at an off-property restaurant, read signs carefully to ensure your spot is designated for the correct restaurant. Your car can (and likely will) be towed away if you park in a spot designated for a business other than the one you're visiting.

than similar restaurants on Disney property. International Drive also offers several dining choices.

Dining Delivery: Hotels typically have advertising flyers in their lobby and many offer listings of delivery restaurants, the most common choices being pizza and Chinese. After perusing the options, ask the front desk or concierge staff to help narrow down good choices and then check Trip Advisor (tripadvisor.com) for reviews.

If you are staying on-property, WDW generally advises guests to only order pizza from large pizza chains, such as Mod Pizza, Domino's, Papa John's, or Pizza Hut, because some outside companies can not be trusted. These restaurants often offer good deals advertised on their websites. Another pizza restaurant that you will see driving around which gets positive reviews is Flipper's.

Grocery Stores & Delivery: If your hotel offers a refrigerator in your room, you may want to stop by a grocery store or get groceries delivered to prepare your own meals. Make sure you verify the size of refrigerator that will be in your room. When it comes to Disney hotels, only Disney Vacation Club properties, called Villas, have full-size refrigerators. Mini-refrigerators are standard in all other Disney resorts.

On-property Groceries and Sundries. Disney offers some groceries at each of its resorts. Fort Wilderness Resort & Campground has the most extensive selection on-property, partially due to their relative seclusion. However, you can usually get much cheaper grocery prices and a better selection by shopping at one of the area's many grocery stores.

Off-property Groceries and Sundries. The easiest grocery store to reach from Disney property is Goodings Super Market, which is located within walking distance to Disney Springs at the Crossroads Shopping Center located at 12521 South Apopka Vineland Road (SR 535) in Lake Buena Vista. However, this is a very expensive store. We recommend you go elsewhere for groceries if you have a vehicle, but this is a decent option if you're on foot.

Approximately three miles north of the Crossroads Shopping Center is Winn-Dixie, located at 11957 South Apopka Vineland Road (SR 535) in Lake Buena Vista. It's not the cheapest grocery store in the area, but the selection and prices are better than Goodings, and it generally has some of the best produce.

Approximately three miles south of the Crossroads Shopping Center on South Apopka Vineland Road (SR 535) is a Walmart Supercenter, which has even better prices on groceries. This is one of the busiest Walmarts in the country, though, so expect heavy crowds and long checkout lines.

If you prefer SuperTarget for your groceries, keep heading further south along US-192 and turn left at 4795 West Irlo Bronson Memorial Highway, in Kissimmee. Another excellent grocery store, Publix, is located next door!

If you don't have a car, consider a grocery delivery service. These services are great if you want your groceries waiting for you when you check in to your hotel. However, there are some questions you should answer before ordering from one of these services.

Grocery Delivery to Your Hotel

Deliveries to the front desk or directly to your hotel room?

In the case of many hotel and condo properties, delivery drivers will not be able to go directly to your room.

If the front desk must receive your delivery, do they have a refrigerator to use to store your items until you pick them up? Many hotels offer this service, but not all.

Finally, all grocery delivery services require someone be available to receive the delivery. Can you pinpoint a time window for delivery when you know you will be at the hotel to accept delivery if the service delivers directly to your room? Once you know the answers to these questions, you can place your order online.

Here are two companies that deliver groceries to most Orlando area properties:

Orlando Grocery Express is an especially good option if you also plan to rent a stroller on your vacation. They have teamed up with Kingdom Strollers, so people who have already reserved a stroller get a coupon for free grocery delivery. To order groceries, simply go online to orlandogroceryexpress.com and virtually shop their store aisles. For the added convenience, of course you can expect slightly higher prices than you find at discount grocery stores, but they are not unreasonably high. This service has a minimum order of $40 and charges a $14 delivery fee, unless you have a free delivery coupon from Kingdom Strollers. They also waive the delivery fee if your order is more than $200. You must order before 5 a.m. Eastern Time on the day BEFORE your requested delivery time.

Instacart (instacart.com) provides grocery delivery service from major local chains, such as Publix, Costco, Whole Foods, and ABC Fine Wine & Spirits. The prices are close to what you would expect to find in the stores. There is no minimum order, and delivery fees vary based on the size of the order. You can combine orders from any or all of the retailers, though you will pay a delivery fee for each. There

is a 10% gratuity added to your order, which usually must be placed the day before delivery.

Take-out Delivery Services

There are a few options if you want to have restaurant meals delivered to your resort. The following companies provide delivery for several independent restaurants, including Thai, Italian (pizza), Mexican, and American cuisine.

DoorDash (doordash.com) has a good selection of popular ethnic and American food options. Their delivery fee is based on the distance of the restaurant.

Grubhub (grubhub.com) has some limited options. You can find Mediterranean, Japanese, Chinese, Pizza, and sandwiches. They generally have a $15 to $20 minimum order and charge around $3 to $5 for delivery. Be careful, though, because depending on location, the delivery fee from some restaurants can be as much as $15!

UberEATS (uber.com/eats) sends a driver to pick up your food and bring it to you. You can order from a wide variety of restaurants, including popular choices like McDonald's, IHOP, and Tijuana Flats. They generally charge around $5 for delivery. You are limited to ordering from a single restaurant at a time.

Insider's Tip!

When you are leaving the park for a short break (or at the end of the day) order on your way to the hotel and have food waiting for you.

If you are staying around International Drive, **Take Out / Room Service Orlando** provides restaurant delivery service from around 15 establishments: (407) 352-1170; internationaldriveorlando. com/things-to-do/orlando-dining/take-out-express-room-service-orlando.html.

When using any food delivery service, it is important to double check if there is a minimum order and also what is included in the price, as some will automatically add a gratuity to the price of your meal. Be sure not to "double tip" unintentionally. Also, there may be limitations on the hours that they provide service, as most are geared up for dinner operations (starting around 5 p.m.) and stop delivering before midnight.

Travel Guides and Coupon Books

You can find travel guides and coupon books at most grocery stores, inside hotel lobbies, and at the entrance of many chain restaurant locations.

If you are staying at an International Drive hotel, look at internationaldriveorlando.com for their travel guide that includes a coupon book.

Don't forget to check the official visitor's center for additional deals: **Orlando-Orange County Official Visitor**, 8723 International Drive (407) 363-5872, 8:30 a.m. – 6:30 p.m. visitorlando.com.

Buffet Restaurants

Off-property buffets can be quick and inexpensive dining options, especially when you want to catch breakfast early before rushing to a theme park for an early opening. **Ponderosa, Golden Corral, Sizzler, Shoney's** (about 20 in the Orlando area) all offer breakfast buffets at cheap prices. Because of the type of food they offer and the short meal window and large crowds, these meals are usually hot

Insider's Tip!

Most area grocery stores have hot meals available, as well as made-to-order sandwiches. You can save a great deal of time and money by purchasing your food at a grocery store and taking it elsewhere to eat.

and fresh. They are typically good choices for meals throughout the day.

For less-popular restaurants, try not to go during off-peak meal times. Instead, eat as close to dinner time as possible.

Food should be fresh, or don't eat it! All buffet restaurants should allow you to scan the food line before you get seated. If they won't let you take a look before settling on their restaurant, or if it doesn't look hot and fresh, walk away.

Most Chinese or Indian buffets near Disney are mediocre at best. Be sure food is kept piping hot without getting dried out. Look for any dry film forming over soups or stews to be certain you are getting a fresh meal that wasn't re-heated from a prior day. A couple of good options on International Drive are: **Aashirwad Indian Cuisine**, 5748 International Drive (407) 370-9830; and **Punjab Indian Restaurant**, 7451 International Drive (407) 352-7887.

Brazilian cuisine is becoming more common and generally gets positive reviews. **Texas de Brazil** is highly-rated among guests and you'll see their advertising atop yellow taxis throughout the tourist district.

Unless you are certain you are getting it when it's extremely fresh, avoid seafood and lobster buffets. The quality rapidly decreases and is not enjoyable within just a few minutes after cooking.

Insider's Tip!

The most popular food types at buffets tend to have a great deal of turnover, meaning it is constantly being replenished to meet demand. If the place is packed, it is a good sign that the food turnover is keeping things fresh. If the place is virtually empty, beware that food could be stale. Even so, if you can sit near the buffet line, you will be able to see what is being brought out fresh. Just keep in mind that restaurant staff usually puts the older leftover items on the top of the stack, so dig slightly lower to where the food is piping hot and fresh.

View Our Complete Dining/Restaurant Information Tables At:

bit.ly/DisneyPlanners

Dining Guide & Wish List

Place a checkmark next to your favorites, along with the planned date of visit. Use this list to make dining reservations and complete your itinerary.

Disney World Dining

Magic Kingdom Restaurants & Snack Kiosks							
Check Favorites	Planned Date of Visit	Name	Cuisine	Service Type	Cost	Dining Plan Option	Characters
Seven Seas Lagoon							
		Ferrytale Fireworks: A Sparkling Dessert Cruise	American	Table Service, Special Event	$$$	N/A	
Adventureland							
		Adventureland Nut Cart	American	Snack Kiosk	$	Snack*	
		Adventureland Popcorn Cart	American	Snack Kiosk	$	Snack*	
		Aloha Isle	American	Counter Service	$	Snack*	
		Egg Roll Wagon	Multiple Cuisines	Snack Kiosk	$	Snack*	
		Jungle Navigation Co. Ltd. Skipper Canteen	Multiple Cuisines	Table Service	$$	TS	
		Sunshine Tree Terrace	American	Counter Service	$	Snack*	
		Tortuga Tavern	American	Counter Service (Seasonal Only)	$	QS	
Fantasyland							
		Be Our Guest Restaurant	American, French	Table Service	$$$	TS	Y
		Cheshire Cafe	American	Counter Service	$	Snack*	
		Cinderella's Royal Table	American	Signature Dining; Table Service	$$$	TS (2 Credits)	Y
		Disney Early Morning Magic	American	Buffet, Special Event	$$$$	N/A	
		Gaston's Tavern	American	Counter Service	$	Snack*	
		Maurice's Amazing Popping Machine	American	Snack Kiosk	$	Snack*	
		Pinocchio Village Haus	American	Counter Service	$	QS	
		Prince Eric's Village Market	American	Counter Service	$	Snack*	
		Storybook Circus Hot Dogs	American	Snack Kiosk	$	Snack*	
		Storybook Circus Popcorn	American	Snack Kiosk	$	Snack*	
		Storybook Circus Pretzels	American	Snack Kiosk	$	Snack*	

Dining Key

MEAL COST: $ = Low; $$ = Moderate; $$$ = High; $$$ = Premium

$ = $14.99 or less per adult entrée $$$ = $30 - $59.99 per adult entrée
$$ = $15 - $29.99 per adult entrée $$$$ = $60 or above per adult entrée
Characters are available only at the locations noted.
Insider's Tip! Any place that is counter service, you can bring your own meal.

If you can't get into a busy restaurant, consider breaking up your party. They may be able to fit in 2 people, whereas the larger party may get turned away.

Check Favorites	Planned Date of Visit	Name	Cuisine	Service Type	Cost	Dining Plan Option	Characters
		Storybook Treats	American	Counter Service	$	Snack*	
		The Friar's Nook	American	Counter Service	$	QS	
Frontierland							
		Frontierland Churro Cart	Mexican	Snack Kiosk	$	Snack*	
		Golden Oak Outpost	American	Counter Service	$	QS	
		Pecos Bill Tall Tale Inn and Cafe	Mexican	Counter Service	$	QS	
		Westward Ho	American	Counter Service	$	Snack*	
Liberty Square							
		Columbia Harbour House	American	Counter Service	$	QS	
		Liberty Square Hot Sandwich Cart	American	Snack Kiosk	$	Snack*	
		Liberty Square Market	American	Counter Service	$	Snack*	
		Liberty Tree Tavern	American	Table Service (Family Style)	$$-L, $$$-D	TS	
		Sleepy Hollow	American	Counter Service	$	Snack*	
		The Diamond Horseshoe	American	Table Service (Family Style)	$$$	TS	
Main Street U.S.A.							
		Casey's Corner	American	Counter Service	$	QS	
		Main Street Bakery (Starbucks)	American	Counter Service	$	QS for Breakfast	
		Main Street Ice Cold Refreshment Cart	American	Snack Kiosk	$	Snack*	
		Main Street Popcorn Cart	American	Snack Kiosk	$	Snack*	
		Plaza Ice Cream Parlor	American	Counter Service	$	Snack*	
		Taste of Magic Kingdom Park VIP Tour	American	Table Service, Special Event	$$$$	N/A	
		The Crystal Palace	American	Buffet	$$-B, L; $$$-D	TS	Y
		The Plaza Restaurant	American	Table Service	$	TS	
		Tony's Town Square Restaurant	Italian	Table Service	$$	TS	

Disney World Dining

Dining Key

MEAL COST: $ = Low; $$ = Moderate; $$$ = High; $$$ = Premium

    $ = $14.99 or less per adult entrée $$$ = $30 - $59.99 per adult entrée

    $$ = $15 - $29.99 per adult entrée $$$$ = $60 or above per adult entrée

Characters are available only at the locations noted.

Insider's Tip! Any place that is counter service, you can bring your own meal.

If you can't get into a busy restaurant, consider breaking up your party. They may be able to fit in 2 people, whereas the larger party may get turned away.

Check Favorites	Planned Date of Visit	Name	Cuisine	Service Type	Cost	Dining Plan Option	Characters
		Tomorrowland					
		Auntie Gravity's Galactic Goodies	American	Counter Service	$	Snack*	
		Cool Ship	American	Counter Service	$	Snack*	
		Cosmic Ray's Starlight Cafe	American	Counter Service	$	QS	
		Fireworks Dessert Party	American	Table Service, Special Event	$$	N/A	
		Magic Kingdom After Fireworks Dessert Party	American	Table Service, Special Event	$$	N/A	
		Space Dog	American	Snack Kiosk	$	Snack*	
		The Lunching Pad	American	Counter Service	$	QS	
		Tomorrowland Popcorn Cart	American	Snack Kiosk	$	Snack*	
		Tomorrowland Terrace Restaurant	American	Counter Service (Seasonal Only)	$	QS	
		Tomorrowland Turkey Leg Cart	American	Snack Kiosk	$	Snack*	

Dining Key

MEAL COST: $ = Low; $$ = Moderate; $$$ = High; $$$ = Premium

    $ = $14.99 or less per adult entrée $$$ = $30 - $59.99 per adult entrée

    $$ = $15 - $29.99 per adult entrée $$$$ = $60 or above per adult entrée

Characters are available only at the locations noted.

Insider's Tip! Any place that is counter service, you can bring your own meal.

If you can't get into a busy restaurant, consider breaking up your party. They may be able to fit in 2 people, whereas the larger party may get turned away.

Epcot Restaurants & Snack Kiosks

Check Favorites	Planned Date of Visit	Name	Cuisine	Service Type	Cost	Dining Plan Option	Characters
		Future World East					
		Cool Wash	American	Counter Service	$	Snack*	
		Space 220	American	Table Service	$$		
		Taste Track	American	Snack Kiosk	$	QS	
		Future World, Land Pavilion					
		Garden Grill	American	Table Service (Family Style)	$$$	TS	Y
		Sunshine Seasons	Multiple Cuisines	Counter Service	$	QS	
		Future World, The Seas Pavilion					
		Coral Reef Restaurant	American, Seafood	Table Service	$$	TS	
		Future World West					
		The Land Cart	American	Snack Kiosk	$	Snack*	
		World Showcase, African Outpost					
		Refreshment Outpost	American	Counter Service	$	QS	
		World Showcase, American Adventure					
		Block & Hans	American	Counter Service	$	Snack*	
		Fife & Drum Tavern	American	Snack Kiosk	$	QS	
		Funnel Cake	American	Counter Service	$	N/A	
		Regal Eagle Smokehouse	American	Counter Service	$	QS	
		World Showcase, Canada					
		Le Cellier Steakhouse	American, Steakhouse	Signature Dining	$$$	TS (2 Credits)	
		Popcorn in Canada	American	Snack Kiosk	$	Snack*	
		World Showcase, China					
		Joy of Tea	Chinese	Counter Service	$	Snack*	
		Lotus Blossom Cafe	Chinese	Counter Service	$	QS	
		Nine Dragons Restaurant	Chinese	Table Service	$$	TS	
		World Showcase, France					
		Chefs de France	French	Table Service	$$	TS	N*
		Crepes des Chefs de France	French	Snack Kiosk	$	Snack*	

Dining Key

MEAL COST: $ = Low; $$ = Moderate; $$$ = High; $$$ = Premium

$ = $14.99 or less per adult entrée $$$ = $30 - $59.99 per adult entrée

$$ = $15 - $29.99 per adult entrée $$$$ = $60 or above per adult entrée

Characters are available only at the locations noted.

Insider's Tip! Any place that is counter service, you can bring your own meal.

If you can't get into a busy restaurant, consider breaking up your party. They may be able to fit in 2 people, whereas the larger party may get turned away.

Disney World Dining

Check Favorites	Planned Date of Visit	Name	Cuisine	Service Type	Cost	Dining Plan Option	Characters
		L'Artisan des Glaces	American, French	Counter Service	$	Snack*	
		Les Halles Boulangerie & Patisserie	French	Counter Service	$	QS	
		Les Vins des Chefs de France	French	Snack Kiosk	$	N/A	
		Monsieur Paul	French	Table Service	$$$	TS (2 Credits)	
		World Showcase, Germany					
		Biergarten Restaurant	German	Buffet	$$-L, $$$-D	TS	
		Sommerfest	German	Counter Service	$	QS	
		World Showcase, Italy					
		Gelateria Toscana	Italian	Snack Kiosk	$	N/A	
		Tutto Gusto Wine Cellar	Italian	Table Service, Lounge	$$	N/A	
		Tutto Italia Ristorante	Italian	Table Service	$$	TS	
		Via Napoli Ristorante e Pizzeria	Italian	Table Service	$$	TS	
		World Showcase, Japan					
		Kabuki Cafe	Japanese	Counter Service	$	Snack*	
		Katsura Grill	Japanese	Counter Service	$	QS	
		Takumi-Tei	Japanese	Signature Dining	$$$	TS (2 Credits)	
		Teppan Edo	Japanese	Table Service	$$	TS	
		Tokyo Dining	Japanese	Table Service	$$	TS	
		World Showcase, Mexico					
		La Cantina de San Angel	Mexican	Counter Service	$	QS	
		La Hacienda de San Angel	Mexican	Table Service	$$-$$$	TS	
		La Cava del Tequila	Mexican	Table Service, Lounge	$	N/A	
		San Angel Inn Restaurante	Mexican	Table Service	$$	TS	
		Choza de Margarita	Mexican	Counter Service, Lounge	$	N/A	

Dining Key

MEAL COST: $ = Low; $$ = Moderate; $$$ = High; $$$ = Premium

$ = $14.99 or less per adult entrée $$$ = $30 - $59.99 per adult entrée
$$ = $15 - $29.99 per adult entrée $$$$ = $60 or above per adult entrée
Characters are available only at the locations noted.
Insider's Tip! Any place that is counter service, you can bring your own meal.

If you can't get into a busy restaurant, consider breaking up your party. They may be able to fit in 2 people, whereas the larger party may get turned away.

Check Favorites	Planned Date of Visit	Name	Cuisine	Service Type	Cost	Dining Plan Option	Characters
		World Showcase, Morocco					
		Oasis Sweets & Sips	Mediterranean, Moroccan	Counter Service	$	Snack	
		Restaurant Marrakesh	Mediterranean, Moroccan	Table Service	$$	TS	
		Spice Road Table	Mediterranean, Moroccan	Table Service, Lounge	$-$$	TS	
		Tangierine Cafe	Mediterranean, Moroccan	Counter Service	$	QS	
		World Showcase, Norway					
		Akershus Royal Banquet Hall	American, Norwegian	Table Service (Family Style) for Breakfast; Buffet for Lunch & Dinner	$$$	TS	Y
		Kringla Bakeri Og Kafe	Norwegian	Counter Service	$	QS	
		World Showcase, Showcase Plaza					
		Frozen Ever After Dessert Party	Multiple Cuisines	Table Service, Special Event	$$$$	N/A	
		Refreshment Port	American	Counter Service	$	QS	
		Traveler's Cafe (Starbucks)	American	Counter Service	$	N/A	
		World Showcase, United Kingdom					
		Epcot Forever Dining Package	British	Table Service	$$$	N/A	
		Rose & Crown Dining Room	British	Table Service	$$	TS	
		Rose & Crown Pub	British	Table Service, Lounge	$-$$	N/A	
		Rose & Crown Pub & Dining Room Tea Experience	British	Table Service	$$$	N/A	
		UK Beer Cart	British	Snack Kiosk	$	N/A	
		Yorkshire County Fish Shop	British	Counter Service	$	QS	

Disney World Dining

Dining Key
MEAL COST: $ = Low; $$ = Moderate; $$$ = High; $$$ = Premium
$ = $14.99 or less per adult entrée $$$ = $30 - $59.99 per adult entrée
$$ = $15 - $29.99 per adult entrée $$$$ = $60 or above per adult entrée
Characters are available only at the locations noted.
Insider's Tip! Any place that is counter service, you can bring your own meal.

If you can't get into a busy restaurant, consider breaking up your party. They may be able to fit in 2 people, whereas the larger party may get turned away.

Hollywood Studios Restaurants & Snack Kiosks

Check Favorites	Planned Date of Visit	Name	Cuisine	Service Type	Cost	Dining Plan Option	Characters
		Commissary Lane					
		ABC Commissary	American	Counter Service	$	QS	
		Sci-Fi Dine-In Theater Restaurant	American	Table Service	$$-$$$	TS	
		Echo Lake					
		50's Prime Time Cafe	American	Table Service	$$	TS	
		Backlot Express	American	Counter Service	$	QS	
		Dockside Diner	American	Counter Service	$	QS	
		Epic Eats	American	Snack Kiosk	$	N/A	
		Hollywood & Vine	American	Buffet	$$-B; $$$-L, D	TS	Y
		Tune-In Lounge	American	Counter Service, Lounge	$	N/A	
		Hollywood Boulevard					
		Star Wars: A Galactic Spectacular Dessert Party	American	Table Service; Special Event	$$$$	N/A	
		The Hollywood Brown Derby	American	Signature Dining	$$	TS (2 Credits)	
		The Hollywood Brown Derby Lounge	American	Table Service, Lounge	$	N/A	
		The Trolley Car Café (Starbucks)	American	Counter Service	$	N/A	
		Grand Avenue					
		BaseLine Tap House	American	Table Service, Lounge	$	N/A	
		Mama Melrose's Ristorante Italiano	Italian	Table Service	$$	TS	
		PizzeRizzo	Italian	Counter Service	$	QS	
		Star Wars: Galaxy Edge					
		Docking Bay 7 Food and Cargo	American	Counter Service	$	QS	
		Kat Saka's Kettle	American	Counter Service	$	N/A	
		Milk Stand	American	Snack Kiosk, Lounge	$	N/A	
		Oga's Cantina	American	Table Service, Lounge	$	N/A	
		Ronto Roasters	American	Counter Service	$	QS	

Dining Key

MEAL COST: $** = Low; **$$** = Moderate; **$$$** = High; **$$$ = Premium

    $ = $14.99 or less per adult entrée   **$$$** = $30 - $59.99 per adult entrée

    $$ = $15 - $29.99 per adult entrée   **$$$$** = $60 or above per adult entrée

Characters are available only at the locations noted.

Insider's Tip! Any place that is counter service, you can bring your own meal.

If you can't get into a busy restaurant, consider breaking up your party. They may be able to fit in 2 people, whereas the larger party may get turned away.

Disney World Dining

Check Favorites	Planned Date of Visit	Name	Cuisine	Service Type	Cost	Dining Plan Option	Characters
		Sunset Boulevard					
		Anaheim Produce	American	Snack Kiosk	$	Snack*	
		Catalina Eddie's	American, Italian	Counter Service	$	QS	
		Fairfax Faire	American	Counter Service	$	QS	
		Fantasmic! Dessert & VIP Viewing Experience	American	Table Service, Special Event	$$	N/A	
		Fantasmic! Dining Package	Various	Table Service, Special Event	$$$-$$$$	N/A	
		Hollywood Scoops	American	Snack Kiosk	$	Snack*	
		KRNR The Rock Station	American	Snack Kiosk	$	QS	
		Rosie's All-American Café	American	Counter Service	$	QS	
		Toy Story Land/Pixar Place					
		Disney Early Morning Magic	American	Buffet	$$$$	N/A	Y
		Market Snack	American	Snack Kiosk	$	Snack*	
		Neighborhood Bakery	American	Snack Kiosk	$	Snack*	
		Woody's Lunch Box	American	Counter Service	$	QS	

Disney World Dining

Dining Key

MEAL COST: $** = Low; **$$** = Moderate; **$$$** = High; **$$$ = Premium

$ = $14.99 or less per adult entrée   **$$$** = $30 - $59.99 per adult entrée
$$ = $15 - $29.99 per adult entrée   **$$$$** = $60 or above per adult entrée
Characters are available only at the locations noted.
Insider's Tip! Any place that is counter service, you can bring your own meal.

If you can't get into a busy restaurant, consider breaking up your party. They may be able to fit in 2 people, whereas the larger party may get turned away.

Disney World Dining

Animal Kingdom Restaurants & Snack Kiosks

Check Favorites	Planned Date of Visit	Name	Cuisine	Service Type	Cost	Dining Plan Option	Characters
		Africa					
		Dawa Bar	African	Counter Service, Lounge	$	N/A	
		Famous Sausages	African	Counter Service	$	QS	
		Harambe Fruit Market	American	Snack Kiosk	$	Snack*	
		Harambe Market	African	Counter Service	$	QS	
		Kusafiri Coffee Shop & Bakery	American	Counter Service	$	Snack*	
		Mahindi	American	Snack Kiosk	$	Snack*	
		Tamu Tamu Refreshments	American, African	Counter Service	$	QS	
		Tusker House Restaurant	American, African	Buffet	$$-B; $$$-L, D	TS	Y-B, L; N-D
		Asia					
		Anandapur Ice Cream Truck	American	Snack Kiosk	$	Snack*	
		Caravan Road	Asian	Snack Kiosk	$	N/A	
		Drinkwallah	American	Counter Service, Lounge	$	N/A	
		Thirsty River Bar & Trek Snacks	American	Snack Kiosk, Lounge	$	Snack*	
		Warung Outpost	American, Mexican	Counter Service, Lounge	$	N/A	
		Yak & Yeti Local Food Cafes	American, Asian	Counter Service	$	QS	
		Yak & Yeti Quality Beverages	American	Counter Service, Lounge	$	N/A	
		Yak & Yeti Restaurant	American, Asian, Chinese	Table Service	$$	TS	
		DinoLand U.S.A.					
		Dino-Bite Snacks	American	Counter Service	$	QS	
		Dino Diner	American	Snack Kiosk	$	Snack*	
		Restaurantosaurus	American	Counter Service	$	QS	
		Trilo Bites	American	Counter Service	$	QS	

Dining Key

MEAL COST: $ = Low; $$ = Moderate; $$$ = High; $$$ = Premium

$ = $14.99 or less per adult entrée $$$ = $30 - $59.99 per adult entrée

$$ = $15 - $29.99 per adult entrée $$$$ = $60 or above per adult entrée

Characters are available only at the locations noted.

Insider's Tip! Any place that is counter service, you can bring your own meal.

If you can't get into a busy restaurant, consider breaking up your party. They may be able to fit in 2 people, whereas the larger party may get turned away.

Check Favorites	Planned Date of Visit	Name	Cuisine	Service Type	Cost	Dining Plan Option	Characters
		Discovery Island					
		Creature Comforts (Starbucks)	American	Counter Service	$	N/A	
		Eight Spoon Café	American	Counter Service	$	QS	
		Flame Tree Barbecue	American	Counter Service	$	QS	
		Isle of Java	American	Counter Service	$	Snack*	
		Nomad Lounge	African, Asian, Latin	Table Service, Lounge	$$	N/A	
		Pizzafari	American, Italian	Counter Service	$	QS	
		Pizzafari Family-Style Dining	American, Italian	Table Service, Family-Style	$$	TS	
		Terra Treats	American	Snack Kiosk	$	Snack*	
		The Smiling Crocodile	American	Counter Service	$	Snack*	
		Tiffins	African, Asian, Latin	Signature Dining	$$$	TS (2 Credits)	
		Main Entrance					
		Rainforest Cafe at Disney's Animal Kingdom	American	Table Service	$$	TS	
		Safari Bar at Rainforest Cafe	American	Table Service, Lounge	$$	N/A	
		Pandora					
		Pongu Pongu	American	Snack Kiosk, Lounge	$	Snack*	
		Satu'li Canteen	American	Counter Service	$$	TBD	

Disney World Dining

Dining Key

MEAL COST: $** = Low; **$$** = Moderate; **$$$** = High; **$$$ = Premium

   $ = $14.99 or less per adult entrée   **$$$** = $30 - $59.99 per adult entrée

   $$ = $15 - $29.99 per adult entrée   **$$$$** = $60 or above per adult entrée

Characters are available only at the locations noted.

Insider's Tip! Any place that is counter service, you can bring your own meal.

If you can't get into a busy restaurant, consider breaking up your party. They may be able to fit in 2 people, whereas the larger party may get turned away.

Disney World Dining

Disney Springs, Water Parks and Other Venues

Check Favorites	Planned Date of Visit	Name	Cuisine	Service Type	Cost	Dining Plan Option	Characters
		Disney Springs Restaurants & Snack Kiosks					
		AMC® Disney Springs 24 Dine-In Theatres	Multiple Cuisines	Table Service	$	N/A	
		Amorette's Patisserie	Multiple Cuisines	Counter Service	$	N/A	
		AristoCrêpes	French	Counter Service	$	QS	
		B.B. Wolf's Sausage Co.	American	Counter Service	$	QS	
		Blaze Fast-Fire'd Pizza	Italian	Counter Service	$	QS	
		Chef Art Smith's Homecomin'	American	Table Service	$$	TS	
		Chicken Guy!	American	Counter Service	$	QS	
		City Works Eatery & Pour House	American	Table Service	$$	N/A	
		Coca-Cola Store Rooftop Beverage Bar	American	Counter Service, Lounge	$		
		Cookes of Dublin	American, Irish	Counter Service	$	QS	
		D-Luxe Burger	American	Counter Service	$	QS	
		Disney Food Trucks	Multiple Cuisines	Snack Kiosk	$	Snack*	
		Dockside Margaritas	American	Snack Kiosk, Lounge	$	N/A	
		Earl Of Sandwich®	American	Counter Service	$	QS	
		Enzo's Hideaway	Italian	Table Service, Lounge	$$	TS	
		Erin McKenna's Bakery NYC	American	Counter Service	$	N/A	
		Everglazed Donuts & Cold Brew	American	Counter Service	$	N/A	
		Food Truck - 4 Rivers Cantina Barbacoa	Latin, Mexican	Snack Kiosk	$	Snack*	
		Food Truck - Hot Diggity Dogs	American	Snack Kiosk	$	Snack*	
		Food Truck - Mac & Cheese	American, Italian	Snack Kiosk	$	Snack*	
		Frontera Cocina	American, Mexican	Table Service	$$	TS	

Dining Key

MEAL COST: $** = Low; **$$** = Moderate; **$$$** = High; **$$$ = Premium

    $ = $14.99 or less per adult entrée   **$$$** = $30 - $59.99 per adult entrée

    $$ = $15 - $29.99 per adult entrée   **$$$$** = $60 or above per adult entrée

Characters are available only at the locations noted.

Insider's Tip! Any place that is counter service, you can bring your own meal.

If you can't get into a busy restaurant, consider breaking up your party. They may be able to fit in 2 people, whereas the larger party may get turned away.

Check Favorites	Planned Date of Visit	Name	Cuisine	Service Type	Cost	Dining Plan Option	Characters
		Ghirardelli Soda Fountain & Chocolate Shop	American	Counter Service	$	N/A	
		Gideon's Bakehouse	American	Counter Service	$	N/A	
		Häagen-Dazs® at Disney Springs West Side	American	Counter Service	$	N/A	
		House of Blues® Restaurant & Bar	American	Table Service	$$	TS	
		Jaleo by José Andrés	Spanish	Signature Dining	$$-L; $$$-D	TS (2 Credits)	
		Jock Lindsey's Hangar Bar	American	Table Service, Lounge	$	N/A	
		Joffrey's Coffe & Tea Company	American	Counter Service	$	N/A	
		Joffrey's Handcrafted Smoothies at Disney Springs Marketplace	American	Snack Kiosk	$	N/A	
		Lava Lounge at Rainforest Cafe®	American	Table Service, Lounge	$	N/A	
		MacGUFFINS	Multiple Cuisines	Table Service, Lounge	$	N/A	
		Maria and Enzo's	Italian	Table Service	$$	TS	
		Marketplace Snacks	American	Snack Kiosk	$	N/A	
		Morimoto Asia	Japanese	Signature Dining	$$$	TS (2 Credits)	
		Morimoto Asia Street Food	Japanese	Snack Kiosk	$	QS	
		Paddlefish	American, Seafood	Signature Dining	$$-L, $$$-D	TS (2 Credits)	
		Paradiso 37, Taste of the Americas	Multiple Cuisines	Table Service	$$	TS	
		Pepe by José Andrés	American, Spanish	Counter Service	$	N/A	
		Pizza Ponte	Italian	Counter Service	$	QS	
		Planet Hollywood	American	Table Service	$$	TS	
		Raglan Road™ Irish Pub and Restaurant	Irish	Table Service	$$	TS	
		Rainforest Cafe® at Disney Springs Marketplace	Multiple Cuisines	Table Service	$$	TS	
		Splitsville Dining Room™	Multiple Cuisines	Table Service	$$	TS	
		Sprinkles	American	Counter Service	$	N/A	

Disney World Dining

Dining Key

MEAL COST: $ = Low; $$ = Moderate; $$$ = High; $$$ = Premium

$ = $14.99 or less per adult entrée
$$$ = $30 - $59.99 per adult entrée
$$ = $15 - $29.99 per adult entrée
$$$$ = $60 or above per adult entrée

Characters are available only at the locations noted.
Insider's Tip! Any place that is counter service, you can bring your own meal.

If you can't get into a busy restaurant, consider breaking up your party. They may be able to fit in 2 people, whereas the larger party may get turned away.

Disney World Dining

Check Favorites	Planned Date of Visit	Name	Cuisine	Service Type	Cost	Dining Plan Option	Characters
		STARBUCKS® at Disney Springs Marketplace	American	Counter Service	$	N/A	
		STARBUCKS® at Disney Springs West Side	American	Counter Service	$	N/A	
		Stargazers Bar	American	Table Service, Lounge	$	N/A	
		STK Orlando	American, Steakhouse	Signature Dining	$$$	TS (2 Credits)	
		Sunshine Terrace at Disney Springs Marketplace	American	Snack Kiosk	$	Snack	
		Sunshine Terrace at Disney Springs West Side	American	Snack Kiosk	$	Snack	
		Terralina Crafted Italian	Italian	Table Service	$$$	TS	
		The Basket at Wine Bar George	American	Counter Service, Lounge	$	QS	
		The BOATHOUSE	Multiple Cuisines	Signature Dining	$$$-L, $$$$-D	TS (2 Credits)	
		The Daily Poutine	American	Counter Service	$	QS	
		The Edison	American	Table Service	$$$	TS	
		The Front Porch at House of Blues	American	Counter Service, Lounge	$	N/A	
		The Polite Pig	American	Counter Service	$		
		The Smokehouse	American	Counter Service	$	QS	
		T-REX ™	Multiple Cuisines	Table Service	$$	TS	
		Vivoli il Gelato	Italian	Counter Service	$	N/A	
		Wetzel's Pretzels® at Disney Springs Marketplace	American	Snack Kiosk	$	QS	
		Wetzel's Pretzels® at Disney Springs West Side	American	Counter Service	$	QS	
		Wine Bar George	American	Table Service	$$	TS	
		Wolfgang Puck® Bar & Grill	Multiple Cuisines	Signature Dining	$$$	TS (2 Credits)	
		YeSake	Asian, Japanese	Counter Service	$	N/A	

Dining Key

MEAL COST: $ = Low; $$ = Moderate; $$$ = High; $$$ = Premium

$ = $14.99 or less per adult entrée $$$ = $30 - $59.99 per adult entrée

$$ = $15 - $29.99 per adult entrée $$$$ = $60 or above per adult entrée

Characters are available only at the locations noted.

Insider's Tip! Any place that is counter service, you can bring your own meal.

If you can't get into a busy restaurant, consider breaking up your party. They may be able to fit in 2 people, whereas the larger party may get turned away.

Check Favorites	Planned Date of Visit	Name	Cuisine	Service Type	Cost	Dining Plan Option	Characters
		Typhoon Lagoon Restaurants & Snack Kiosks					
		Happy Landings Ice Cream	American	Snack Kiosk	$	Snack*	
		Leaning Palms	American	Counter Service	$	QS	
		Let's Go Slurpin'	American	Counter Service, Lounge	$	N/A	
		Lowtide Lou's	American	Counter Service, Lounge	$	QS	
		Snack Shack	American	Counter Service	$	QS	
		Typhoon Tilly's	American	Counter Service	$	QS	
		Blizzard Beach Restaurants & Snack Kiosks					
		Arctic Expeditions	American	Snack Kiosk	$	Snack*	
		Avalunch	American	Counter Service	$	QS	
		Cooling Hut	American	Counter Service	$	QS	
		Frostbite Freddy's Frozen Freshments	American	Counter Service, Lounge	$	N/A	
		I.C. Expeditions	American	Counter Service	$	Snack*	
		Lottawatta Lodge	American	Counter Service	$	QS	
		Mini Donuts at Blizzard Beach	American	Snack Kiosk	$	N/A	
		Polar Pub	American	Counter Service, Lounge	$	N/A	
		Warming Hut	American	Counter Service	$	QS	
		Disney's BoardWalk Restaurants & Snack Kiosks					
		AbracadaBar	American	Table Service, Lounge	$	N/A	
		BoardWalk Ice Cream	American	Counter Service	$	N/A	
		Big River Grille & Brewing Works	American	Table Service	$$	TS	
		BoardWalk Bakery	American	Counter Service	$	QS	
		BoardWalk Joe's Marvelous Margaritas	American, Mexican	Counter Service, Lounge	$	N/A	
		ESPN Club	American	Table Service	$	TS	

Dining Key

MEAL COST: $ = Low; $$ = Moderate; $$$ = High; $$$ = Premium

   $ = $14.99 or less per adult entrée $$$ = $30 - $59.99 per adult entrée

   $$ = $15 - $29.99 per adult entrée $$$$ = $60 or above per adult entrée

Characters are available only at the locations noted.

Insider's Tip! Any place that is counter service, you can bring your own meal.

If you can't get into a busy restaurant, consider breaking up your party. They may be able to fit in 2 people, whereas the larger party may get turned away.

Disney World Dining

Check Favorites	Planned Date of Visit	Name	Cuisine	Service Type	Cost	Dining Plan Option	Characters
		Flying Fish	American, Seafood	Signature Dining	$$$	TS (2 Credits)	
		Funnel Cake Cart	American	Snack Kiosk	$	N/A	
		Pizza Window	American, Italian	Counter Service	$	QS	
		The To-Go Cart	American	Snack Kiosk	$	N/A	
		Trattoria al Forno	Italian	Table Service	$$	TS	Y-B; N-D
ESPN Wide World of Sports Restaurant							
		ESPN Wide World of Sports Grill	Multiple Cuisines	Counter Service	$	QS	

Dining Key

MEAL COST: $ = Low; $$ = Moderate; $$$ = High; $$$ = Premium
   $ = $14.99 or less per adult entrée $$$ = $30 - $59.99 per adult entrée
   $$ = $15 - $29.99 per adult entrée $$$$ = $60 or above per adult entrée
Characters are available only at the locations noted.
Insider's Tip! Any place that is counter service, you can bring your own meal.

If you can't get into a busy restaurant, consider breaking up your party. They may be able to fit in 2 people, whereas the larger party may get turned away.

Disney Resort Hotels Restaurants & Snack Kiosks

Check Favorites	Planned Date of Visit	Name	Cuisine	Service Type	Cost	Dining Plan Option	Characters
		Contemporary Resort					
		California Grill	Multiple Cuisines	Signature Dining	$$$	TS (2 Credits)	
		California Grill Lounge	American	Table Service, Lounge	$	N/A	
		Chef Mickey's	American	Buffet	$$$	TS	Y
		Contempo Café	American	Counter Service	$	QS	
		Contemporary Grounds	American	Counter Service	$	N/A	
		Cove Bar	American	Counter Service, Lounge	$	QS	
		Outer Rim	American	Counter Service, Lounge	$	N/A	
		The Sand Bar	American	Counter Service, Lounge	$	QS	
		The Wave Lounge	American	Counter Service, Lounge	$	N/A	
		The Wave...Of American Flavors	American	Table Service	$-$$	TS	
		All-Star Movies Resort					
		Silver Screen Spirits Pool Bar	American	Counter Service, Lounge	$	N/A	
		World Premier Food Court	Multiple Cuisines	Counter Service	$	QS	
		All-Star Music Resort					
		Intermission Food Court	Multiple Cuisines	Counter Service	$	QS	
		Singing Spirits Pool Bar	American	Counter Service, Lounge	$	N/A	
		All-Star Sports Resort					
		End Zone Food Court	Multiple Cuisines	Counter Service	$	QS	
		Grandstand Spirits	American	Counter Service, Lounge	$	N/A	
		Animal Kingdom Lodge					
		Boma - Flavors of Africa	African, American	Buffet	$$-B, $$$-D	TS	
		Cape Town Lounge and Wine Bar	African	Table Service, Lounge	$	N/A	

Dining Key

MEAL COST: $ = Low; $$ = Moderate; $$$ = High; $$$ = Premium

$ = $14.99 or less per adult entrée $$$ = $30 - $59.99 per adult entrée
$$ = $15 - $29.99 per adult entrée $$$$ = $60 or above per adult entrée

Characters are available only at the locations noted.

Insider's Tip! Any place that is counter service, you can bring your own meal.

If you can't get into a busy restaurant, consider breaking up your party. They may be able to fit in 2 people, whereas the larger party may get turned away.

Disney World Dining

Check Favorites	Planned Date of Visit	Name	Cuisine	Service Type	Cost	Dining Plan Option	Characters
		Dine with an Animal Specialist at Sanaa	African, Indian	Table Service, Special Event	$$$	N/A	
		Jiko - The Cooking Place	African	Signature Dining	$$$	TS (2 Credits)	
		Jiko - Wanyama Safari	African	Table Service, Special Event	$$$$	N/A	
		Jiko Wine Tasting	African	Table Service, Special Event	$$$	N/A	
		Maji Pool Bar	African, American	Counter Service, Lounge	$	QS	
		Sanaa	African, Indian	Table Service	$$	TS	
		Sanaa Lounge	African, Indian	Table Service, Lounge	$	N/A	
		The Mara	African, American	Counter Service	$	QS	
		Uzima Springs Pool Bar	American	Counter Service, Lounge	$	N/A	
		Victoria Falls Lounge	American	Table Service, Lounge	$	N/A	
	Art of Animation Resort						
		Drop Off Pool Bar	American	Counter Service, Lounge	$	N/A	
		Landscape of Flavors	Multiple Cuisines	Counter Service	$	QS	
	Beach & Yacht Club Resorts						
		Ale & Compass Lounge	American	Counter Service, Lounge	$	QS (Breakfast)	
		Ale & Compass Restaurant	American	Table Service	$-$$	TS	
		Beach Club Marketplace	American	Counter Service	$	QS	
		Beaches & Cream Soda Shop	American	Table Service	$	TS	
		Cape May Cafe	American	Buffet	$$$	TS	Y-B; N-D
		Crew's Cup Lounge	American	Table Service, Lounge	$-$$	N/A	
		Hurricane Hanna's Waterside Bar and Grill	American	Counter Service, Lounge	$	QS	
		The Market at Ale & Compass	American	Counter Service	$	QS	
		Martha's Vineyard	American	Table Service, Lounge	$	N/A	

Dining Key

MEAL COST: $ = Low; $$ = Moderate; $$$ = High; $$$ = Premium

$ = $14.99 or less per adult entrée

$$ = $15 - $29.99 per adult entrée

$$$ = $30 - $59.99 per adult entrée

$$$$ = $60 or above per adult entrée

Characters are available only at the locations noted.

Insider's Tip! Any place that is counter service, you can bring your own meal.

If you can't get into a busy restaurant, consider breaking up your party. They may be able to fit in 2 people, whereas the larger party may get turned away.

Check Favorites	Planned Date of Visit	Name	Cuisine	Service Type	Cost	Dining Plan Option	Characters
		Yachtsman Steakhouse	American, Steakhouse	Signature Dining	$$$	TS (2 Credits)	
Boardwalk Inn							
		Belle Vue Lounge	American	Counter Service, Lounge	$	QS (Breakfast)	
		Leaping Horse Libations	American	Counter Service, Lounge	$	QS	
Caribbean Beach Resort							
		Banana Cabana Pool Bar	American	Counter Service, Lounge	$	N/A	
		Centertown Market Food Court	Multiple Cuisines	Counter Service	$	QS	
		Centertown Market Grab & Go	American	Counter Service	$	QS	
		Sebastian's Bistro	Latin, Seafood	Table Service	$$	TS	
		Spyglass Grill	American	Counter Service	$	QS	
Coronado Springs Resort							
		Barcelona Lounge	American	Table Service, Lounge	$	N/A	
		Cafe Rix	American	Counter Service	$	QS	
		Dahlia Lounge	American	Table Service, Lounge	$	N/A	
		El Mercado de Coronado	American, Mexican	Counter Service	$	QS	
		Laguna Bar	American	Counter Service, Lounge	$	QS	
		Maya Grill	American, Mexican	Table Service	$$	TS	
		Rix Sports Bar & Grill	American	Table Service, Lounge	$	N/A	
		Siestas Cantina	American	Counter Service, Lounge	$	QS	
		Three Bridges Bar and Grill	Latin	Table Service	$$	TS	
		Toledo - Tapas, Steak & Seafood	Multiple Cuisines	Table Service	$$$	TS	
Grand Floridian Resort							
		1900 Park Fare	American	Buffet	$$-B, $$$-D	TS	Y

Dining Key

MEAL COST: $ = Low; $$ = Moderate; $$$ = High; $$$ = Premium

    $ = $14.99 or less per adult entrée $$$ = $30 - $59.99 per adult entrée

    $$ = $15 - $29.99 per adult entrée $$$$ = $60 or above per adult entrée

Characters are available only at the locations noted.

Insider's Tip! Any place that is counter service, you can bring your own meal.

If you can't get into a busy restaurant, consider breaking up your party. They may be able to fit in 2 people, whereas the larger party may get turned away.

Disney World Dining

Disney World Dining

Check Favorites	Planned Date of Visit	Name	Cuisine	Service Type	Cost	Dining Plan Option	Characters
		Afternoon Tea at Garden View Room	British	Table Service, Special Event	$$$	N/A	
		Beaches Pool Bar & Grill	American	Counter Service, Lounge	$	QS	
		Citricos	American, Mediterranean	Signature Dining	$$$	TS (2 Credits)	
		Citricos Lounge	American, Mediterranean	Table Service, Lounge	$$	N/A	
		Courtyard Pool Bar	American	Counter Service, Lounge	$	N/A	
		Disney's Perfectly Princess Tea	British	Table Service, Special Event	$$$$	N/A	Y
		Enchanted Rose	American	Table Service, Lounge	$$	N/A	
		Gasparilla Island Grill	American	Counter Service	$	QS	
		Grand Floridian Cafe	American	Table Service	$-$$	TS	
		Narcoossee's	American, Seafood	Signature Dining	$$$	TS (2 Credits)	
		Victoria & Albert's	American	Signature Dining	$$$$	N/A	
		Victoria & Albert's Chef's Table Dinner	American	Signature Dining, Special Event	$$$$	N/A	
		Victoria & Albert's Queen Victoria Room	American	Signature Dining, Special Event	$$$$	N/A	
		Wonderland Tea Party	American	Table Service, Special Event	$$$	N/A	Y
Old Key West Resort							
		Good's Food to Go	American	Counter Service, Lounge	$	QS	
		Gurgling Suitcase	American	Counter Service, Lounge	$-$$	N/A	
		Olivia's Cafe	American	Table Service	$-$$	TS	
		Turtle Shack Poolside Snacks	American	Counter Service, Lounge	$	QS	
Polynesian Village Resort							
		Barefoot Pool Bar	American	Counter Service, Lounge	$	N/A	
		Captain Cook's	Multiple Cuisines	Counter Service	$	QS	

Dining Key

MEAL COST: $** = Low; **$$** = Moderate; **$$$** = High; **$$$ = Premium

   $ = $14.99 or less per adult entrée   **$$$** = $30 - $59.99 per adult entrée

   $$ = $15 - $29.99 per adult entrée   **$$$$** = $60 or above per adult entrée

Characters are available only at the locations noted.

Insider's Tip! Any place that is counter service, you can bring your own meal.

If you can't get into a busy restaurant, consider breaking up your party. They may be able to fit in 2 people, whereas the larger party may get turned away.

Check Favorites	Planned Date of Visit	Name	Cuisine	Service Type	Cost	Dining Plan Option	Characters
		Disney's Spirit of Aloha Dinner Show	American, Polynesian	Table Service, Dinner Show	$$$$	TS (2 Credits)	
		Kona Cafe	American, Polynesian	Table Service	$-B, L; $$-D	TS	
		Kona Island	American, Sushi	Counter Service	$	N/A	
		Oasis Bar & Grill	American	Counter Service	$	QS	
		Ohana	American, Polynesian	Table Service (Family Style)	$$-B; $$$-D	TS	Y-B; N-D
		Pineapple Lanai	American	Counter Service	$	Snack*	
		Tambu Lounge	American	Table Service, Lounge	$	N/A	
		Trader Sam's Grog Grotto	Polynesian	Table Service, Lounge	$	N/A	
		Trader Sam's Tiki Terrace	Polynesian	Table Service, Lounge	$	N/A	
		Pop Century Resort					
		Everything POP Shopping & Dining	Multiple Cuisines	Counter Service	$	QS	
		Petals Pool Bar	American	Counter Service, Lounge	$	N/A	
		Port Orleans Resort - French Quarter					
		Mardi Grogs	American	Counter Service, Lounge	$	N/A	
		Sassagoula Floatworks and Food Factory	American	Counter Service	$	QS	
		Scat Cat's Club	American	Counter Service, Lounge	$	N/A	
		Port Orleans Resort - Riverside					
		Boatwright's Dining Hall	American	Table Service	$$	TS	
		Muddy Rivers	American	Counter Service, Lounge	$	N/A	
		River Roost	American	Table Service, Lounge	$	N/A	
		Riverside Mill Food Court	Multiple Cuisines	Counter Service	$	QS	
		Riviera Resort					
		Bar Riva	American	Counter Service, Lounge	$	N/A	

Dining Key

MEAL COST: $ = Low; $$ = Moderate; $$$ = High; $$$ = Premium

   $ = $14.99 or less per adult entrée $$$ = $30 - $59.99 per adult entrée

   $$ = $15 - $29.99 per adult entrée $$$$ = $60 or above per adult entrée

Characters are available only at the locations noted.

Insider's Tip! Any place that is counter service, you can bring your own meal.

If you can't get into a busy restaurant, consider breaking up your party. They may be able to fit in 2 people, whereas the larger party may get turned away.

Disney World Dining

Disney World Dining

Check Favorites	Planned Date of Visit	Name	Cuisine	Service Type	Cost	Dining Plan Option	Characters
		Le Petit Cafe	American	Counter Service	$	N/A	
		Primo Piatto	American	Counter Service	$	QS	
		Topolino's Terrace	French, Italian	Signature Dining	$$$-$$$$	TS (2 Credits)	
Saratoga Springs Resort							
		Backstretch Pool Bar	American	Counter Service, Lounge	$	QS	
		Chip 'n' Dale's Cafe	American	Counter Service	$	N/A	
		On The Rocks	American	Counter Service, Lounge	$	QS	
		The Artist's Palette	Multiple Cuisines	Counter Service	$	QS	
		The Paddock Grill	American	Counter Service, Lounge	$	QS	
		The Turf Club Bar and Grill	American	Table Service	$$	TS	
		The Turf Club Lounge	American	Counter Service, Lounge	$	N/A	
Wilderness Lodge							
		Geyser Point Bar & Grill	American	Counter Service	$	QS	
		Roaring Fork	Multiple Cuisines	Counter Service	$	QS	
		Storybook Dining at Artist Point with Snow White	American	Signature Dining	$$$	TS (2 Credits)	Yes
		Territory Lounge	American	Table Service, Lounge	$	N/A	
		Whispering Canyon Cafe	American	Table Service	$-B; $$-L, D	TS	
Fort Wilderness Campground							
		Crockett's Tavern	American	Counter Service, Lounge	$	N/A	
		Meadow Snack Bar	American	Counter Service, Lounge	$	QS	
		P & J's Southern Takeout	American	Counter Service	$	QS	
		The Chuck Wagon	American	Counter Service	$	QS	

Dining Key

MEAL COST: $** = Low; **$$** = Moderate; **$$$** = High; **$$$ = Premium

   $ = $14.99 or less per adult entrée   **$$$** = $30 - $59.99 per adult entrée

   $$ = $15 - $29.99 per adult entrée   **$$$$** = $60 or above per adult entrée

Characters are available only at the locations noted.

Insider's Tip! Any place that is counter service, you can bring your own meal.

If you can't get into a busy restaurant, consider breaking up your party. They may be able to fit in 2 people, whereas the larger party may get turned away.

Check Favorites	Planned Date of Visit	Name	Cuisine	Service Type	Cost	Dining Plan Option	Characters
		Trail's End Restaurant	American	Buffet for Breakfast or Dinner; Table Service for Lunch	$$	TS	
Walt Disney World Swan & Dolphin Hotels							
		Cabana Bar and Beach Club	American	Table Service, Lounge	$-$$	N/A	
		Chill	American	Counter Service, Lounge	$	N/A	
		Fresh Mediterranean Market	American, Mediterranean	Table Service or Buffet	$$	N/A	
		Fuel	American	Counter Service	$	N/A	
		Garden Grove	American, Seafood	Table Service or Buffet	$$-$$$	N/A	Y-B (Sat & Sun Only); N-L; Y-D
		Il Mulino	Italian	Signature Dining	$$$	N/A	
		Il Mulino Lounge	American	Counter Service, Lounge	$$	N/A	
		Java	American	Counter Service	$	N/A	
		Kimonos	Multiple Cuisines	Table Service	$$	N/A	
		Kimonos Lounge	Multiple Cuisines	Table Service, Lounge	$-$$	N/A	
		Phins	American	Table Service, Lounge	$	N/A	
		Picabu	Multiple Cuisines	Counter Service	$	N/A	
		Shula's Lounge	American	Table Service, Lounge	$$$	N/A	
		Shula's Steak House	American	Signature Dining	$$$	N/A	
		Splash Pool Bar	American	Counter Service, Lounge	$	N/A	
		The Fountain	American	Table Service	$	N/A	
		Todd English's bluezoo	American, Seafood	Signature Dining	$$$	N/A	
		Todd English's bluezoo Lounge	American, Seafood	Table Service, Lounge	$	N/A	

Disney World Dining

Dining Key

MEAL COST: $** = Low; **$$** = Moderate; **$$$** = High; **$$$$ = Premium
    $ = $14.99 or less per adult entrée   **$$$** = $30 - $59.99 per adult entrée
    $$ = $15 - $29.99 per adult entrée   **$$$$** = $60 or above per adult entrée
Characters are available only at the locations noted.
Insider's Tip! Any place that is counter service, you can bring your own meal.

If you can't get into a busy restaurant, consider breaking up your party. They may be able to fit in 2 people, whereas the larger party may get turned away.

Parking on Disney Property

Parking at the Disney theme parks is currently $25 per day ($30 for RVs) for guests staying off-property. Visitors staying at a Disney Resort hotel get free parking at theme parks. Disney also offers preferred-parking spaces for $45-$50 per day at the Transportation and Ticket Center (for Magic Kingdom) and the other theme parks. These spaces are close to the park entrance, near disabled parking.

Insider's Tip!

Make note of where you parked. Use your phone or camera to take photos of your parking location. We see people searching for their car every day in the humongous parking lots. If you do get lost, contact a security patrol for help. They will drive you through the parking lot to help you find where you parked your automobile.

You pay to park once per day and your pass is good at all Disney's theme parks throughout the day.

Early Arrival. If you plan to arrive early in the morning, it may be quicker to walk to the park entrance than to take a parking lot tram due to the crowds waiting for a ride. If you notice many people walking to the entrance, you can assume it will save you time and is safe to do so.

If you leave the park for a midday break or go to your car to retrieve a change of clothes or snack, you may be able to move your car and score a parking spot nearer to the park entrance. If you encounter a

Insider's Tip!

If you are visiting Magic Kingdom for the day and have an evening dinner reservation at a nearby Disney hotel, move your car to the hotel location to avoid the exit rush from the TTC.

parking lot attendant trying to usher you into an undesirable space, simply tell them you're picking someone up at the disability drop-off and pickup near the front of the lot, then search for a closer space. You can also explain that you left a short time ago and want to go back to the great space you had earlier.

Parking Security

Each Disney Resort hotel and Disney's BoardWalk have security booths and traffic gates at the entrance to their parking lots. Guests with a valid reason to visit a resort hotel are welcome to park for free after showing a government-issued identification card and explaining the reason for visiting the hotel to the security guard. Valid reasons may include dining at the hotel or attending one of the hotel's special attractions (i.e. horse-drawn carriage rides at Port Orleans Riverside and night-vision viewing of animals at Animal Kingdom Lodge Resort).

Due to concerns about overcapacity, Disney's BoardWalk and certain resort hotels often limit parking only to hotel

Insider's Tip!

Disabled Parking. Valet parking is available to guests with a valid disabled parking placard at Deluxe Disney hotels for free if you cannot find an available spot in the designated parking area. Just let them know when you arrive that you were unable to find appropriate parking. Your government-issued parking placard is required.

guests or guests with valid dining reservations on busy days. Disney posts a sign outside of the security gate identifying when this restriction is in place. Be prepared to provide the restaurant name and guest name under which the reservation has been made, as the security guard may verify these details before directing you where to park. However, you can always choose valet parking at a Deluxe hotel or Disney's BoardWalk, even without a dining reservation. Simply let the guard know you plan to use that service.

Parking on Disney Property

Parking for Disabled Guests

Each parking lot on Disney property has designated parking for guests with valid disability parking placards. You don't have to have a placard issued by the state of Florida; any parking permit issued by your home state can be used if you remember to pack it in your luggage.

The advantage of these parking areas is they are close enough to the main entrances to walk without using the trams, which are not designed for guests with bad backs, wheelchairs, or scooters to name a few. Signs and a blue line lead the way to this parking area, and parking attendants are usually in the parking lots to check for valid parking placards and direct guests to the proper parking area.

Another parking option to note is for people with multiple small children requiring strollers. Ask the parking attendant if there is closer parking available if you are using multiple strollers for your children. The attendant will likely direct you to a parking area slightly further away from the entrance than the disability parking (but closer than standard parking).

Parking at the Theme Parks

Transportation and Ticket Center (TTC)

The Transportation and Ticket Center (TTC) is the primary transportation hub. From the TTC, you can use Disney's completely free transportation system to get anywhere on-property. Both guests staying at hotels on-property and off-property will benefit from getting to know the ins and outs of this location.

The TTC generally starts operating two (and sometimes three) hours before the Magic Kingdom park opens. This allows guests to make their way to the other theme parks in time to catch their opening.

If you are an off-property guest utilizing a shuttle system from your hotel, you will be dropped off and picked up by the shuttle at the TTC. If you plan to drive to the Magic Kingdom, you must park at the TTC or a nearby hotel and take transportation to the Magic Kingdom. There is no parking directly at the Magic Kingdom.

A tram or a walking tunnel provides access from the parking lot to the TTC, at which you can purchase park passes or souvenirs before heading to your final destination. There are three types of transportation found at the TTC: bus, boat, and monorail. We'll give you an overview of each shortly.

You can park at the TTC, catch a tram to the transportation hub and then hop aboard a bus, boat, or monorail to virtually any other location on Disney property. Be aware that the locations you can reach by boat or monorail are limited, though bus transfers are available to all hotels and other on-property locations. Disney buses do not offer access to off-property locations.

Guests visiting one of the other three amusement parks (Epcot, Animal

Insider's Note!

Buses travel to the TTC two-three hours after the last theme park closes. However, monorails only run for approximately one hour after parks close.

Kingdom, or Hollywood Studios) can catch a tram from the TTC directly to the entrance of those parks.

Any of the three forms of transportation typically run to/from the TTC for up to an hour after the close of the associated theme park/destination. However, always check with a Disney Cast Member to be sure you know that day's transportation schedule, so you don't miss your ride back to your car.

Security Booths

The TTC, Epcot, Hollywood Studios, and Animal Kingdom each have security booths at the entrance to their parking lots.

Guests must either show a valid parking pass or pay the daily fee to park before proceeding past the booths. The exception to this is that Disney often closes down the security booths one to two hours prior to park closing, and guests arriving after the booths have closed can proceed to the parking lot without paying a parking fee.

Insider's Tip!

Disney transportation is great if you have teens. They can travel by themselves; transportation is safe and easy to get around.

Free Parking Locations on Disney Property

You may have heard rumors about finding free parking for Disney's theme parks. It's a gray area, but we'll give you tips on how to navigate it without (hopefully!) angering the Disney gods.

There are a few places where parking is free to the visiting public and not regulated with a security gate. These include Disney Springs, Disney's water parks (Blizzard Beach and Typhoon Lagoon), and Disney's miniature Golf Courses (Winter Summerland and Fantasia Gardens).

Certain other places also provide free parking on-site. Parking at Disney Springs is free and openly available for customers, though preferred parking in the open-air grapefruit and lemon lots is available for a $20 fee. Parking is also free at Disney's BoardWalk, though often limited to guests with valid dining reservations. (This is usually enforced early in the day, but not in the evening, even if a sign is up.)

Disney also offers free buses from these parking locations to a Disney hotel or the Transportation and Ticket Center, from which you can hitch a ride to your favorite park. (You can actually walk to Hollywood Studios or Epcot from the BoardWalk Inn.) Alternatively, you can park for free at any Disney hotel if you plan to eat there or are visiting the hotel for one of its activities (such as walking the Wilderness Trail between Wilderness Lodge and Fort Wilderness Resorts).

You may be tempted to claim you're eating at a resort even if you're not just to take advantage of free parking. While you may be successful some times, during particularly busy days security at the parking gate may verify your reservation and turn you away if it cannot be confirmed. It's also possible Disney *could* have your vehicle towed if you're found out (though we aren't aware of that actually happening to anyone).

Check our hotel section to see which hotels are convenient to each park for eating and parking.

Using Disney's Free Transportation

Once you've parked or otherwise made your way onto Disney property, Disney

---

Disney properties with free parking:
- Disney Springs
- Disney's BoardWalk
- Blizzard Beach
- Typhoon Lagoon
- All Disney Golf and Miniature Golf Courses
- All Disney Hotels (Day Guests Only; Except for Swan and Dolphin)
- Disney's Wedding Pavilion

Disney properties with paid parking:
- Transportation and Ticket Center (for Magic Kingdom)
- Epcot
- Hollywood Studios
- Animal Kingdom
- All Disney Hotels (Overnight Guests)
- Walt Disney World Swan and Dolphin Hotels

Parking at Disney's Water Parks. Parking at Disney's two water parks or the two miniature golf courses is always free. Buses from these locations go to the Transportation and Ticket Center and Disney hotels, from which you can reach any Disney park.

Tables in Wonderland

Note: Disney is not currently selling memberships due to COVID-19.
We detail the benefits of *Tables in Wonderland* in our dining section and its many advantages available to Florida residents, seasonal passholders, and Disney Vacation Club members. The *Tables in Wonderland* card costs $100 to $150 (available at any Guest Relations location within each theme park and at Disney Springs). It gives you 20% discounts on food and beverages (including alcoholic) for up to 10 people at many table service restaurants, some lounges, and a few counter-service restaurants. Be sure to run the numbers to see if you'll be able to gain significant savings in your food budget.

In addition to the dining discounts, the program offers free valet parking service ($33 value) at each Deluxe Disney hotel and Disney's BoardWalk with a food purchase at participating locations at that property.

How does this help with theme park parking fees? You show up at the security gate of the hotel parking lot and tell the guard you have Tables in Wonderland and plan to valet-park. The guard will give you directions to the valet. Hand your keys to the valet, get your ticket, then head to the bus or monorail terminal to catch your ride to the park.

The key to this deal is you don't have any minimum food purchases. You can buy a beverage and use the receipt to validate your free parking. By making a nominal purchase, such as a $3 soda, you'll get curbside valet parking service and avoid the parking fee and hassles of parking at the theme park. Depending on the length of your stay, this approach might be beneficial.

provides free transportation to guests throughout its property. This means you can park at one location (or walk to Disney Springs if you're close enough) and get to anywhere else on Disney property. There is no identification required to use transportation, as the service is as much designed to encourage people to visit and spend money at the various on-property resort hotels as it is to be a convenience for on-property hotel guests.

Simply follow the signs wherever you are to the correct bus, boat, or monorail and walk on. You may need to take a roundabout route to get to a specific destination on-property, so plan for extra time if you need to use Disney transportation.

Note that some Disney hotels require multiple stops when traveling to/from the parks. Be sure to allow at least 30 minutes for travel time.

Bus Service: The TTC, each theme park, and Disney Springs are the primary hubs for bus transportation. Buses travel frequently (approximately every 15 minutes). You can reach the other theme and water parks (but not the Fantasia Gardens miniature golf course) directly from the TTC.

Buses from Disney Springs only provide transportation directly to the parks during afternoons and evenings, while Disney hotels are serviced all day. Cast Members are readily available to help direct you to your destination if you

Expect delays with Disney transportation during peak periods. Disney increases the number of buses running at those times, but you may find yourself waiting for a while with the crowd.

Some of the hotels have no queue for the buses. Start your own line near where the bus will be approaching if you wish to avoid clamoring for a space on the bus at the last minute. Other people will naturally line up behind you. This is particularly helpful during peak periods. When the bus arrives, wait until guests disembark and the driver gives you the go-ahead to climb aboard.

are unable to find a sign to the park or hotel of your choice.

From the TTC, you can catch a bus to the following locations:

- Magic Kingdom
- Epcot
- Hollywood Studios
- Animal Kingdom
- Blizzard Beach,
- Typhoon Lagoon
- Disney Springs

You can also find a shuttle for non-Disney on-property hotels, including Shades of Green and Good Neighbor Hotels. However, with the exception of Disney's Grand Floridian, Polynesian, and Contemporary resort hotels, if you plan to visit a Disney hotel or Disney's BoardWalk, you must first travel to the Magic Kingdom and make a transfer.

Generally speaking, you can't take a bus from one resort hotel directly to another. The exceptions to this rule are travel between: Disney's All-Star hotels; Disney's Wilderness Lodge and Fort Wilderness Campgrounds; and Disney's Port Orleans Riverside and French

Quarter hotels (each group of properties is connected).

Miniature Golf Courses. Disney's Fantasia Gardens and Winter Summerland miniature golf courses don't have direct bus transportation. However, properties with bus transportation are within easy walking distance from these two locations. Fantasia Gardens is just across the street from the Walt Disney World Swan hotel. Winter Summerland is next door to Blizzard Beach, and they share a bus stop/parking lot.

Late Night Service

Buses generally run to/from each of the theme parks until approximately one hour after the park closes. Buses typically run to Disney Springs until 2 a.m. However, it is important to ask a Disney Cast Member to verify the daily schedule if you plan to park at one location and use Disney's transportation, as special events or maintenance schedules may cause those hours to change.

Water Transportation (Boat Service):

Only select locations on-property offer water transportation. Again, it's completely free to use. While taking a boat can take a little longer than other forms of transportation, it is by far the most scenic option.

Disney Springs has three boat docks: two at either end of the property and one near the center. Boats run between the three docks, providing a great option if you don't wish to walk from one end of the sprawling property to the other.

You can also catch a boat from Disney Springs directly to the Port Orleans French Quarter hotel, which travels on to the Port Orleans Riverside hotel. Yet another boat stops at Saratoga Springs, Treehouse Villas, and Old Key West resort hotels.

BoardWalk – Epcot – Hollywood Studios area also offers boat transportation. The BoardWalk sits on a lake that is surrounded by five resort properties: BoardWalk Inn, Beach Club, Yacht Club, Swan, and Dolphin. On one side of the lake is a waterway that goes to Hollywood Studios. On the other side is a waterway that goes to Epcot. Boats run between Epcot and Hollywood Studios, stopping at each hotel on the way.

The final location with boats is the Magic Kingdom area. The Magic Kingdom sits on Seven Seas Lagoon, as does the TTC and five of Disney's deluxe resort properties: Contemporary, Polynesian, Grand Floridian, Wilderness Lodge, and Fort Wilderness. Boats run directly between the Contemporary, Wilderness Lodge, or Fort Wilderness to the Magic Kingdom entrance.

Disney provides large sternwheeler boats for access from the TTC directly to the Magic Kingdom. Though it is typically slower than other forms of transportation, these can be an enjoyable ride for boat enthusiasts and those wishing a scenic view across Disney's Seven Seas Lagoon.

Smaller vessels provide access from Grand Floridian, then to Polynesian before reaching the Magic Kingdom. They then return to Grand Floridian before going back to Polynesian.

Monorail Service: Perhaps the most iconic form of transportation at Disney is the monorail train. This is also typically the fastest and most efficient form of transportation.

The TTC is the main hub for the monorail, and there are only three monorail routes that run regularly. Service is limited to a few properties at Disney, including the Magic Kingdom and Epcot parks, as well as Contemporary, Polynesian, and Grand Floridian resorts.

There are two monorail routes to the Magic Kingdom. The express monorail provides direct service to the Magic Kingdom with no other stops. The resort monorail takes longer, as it stops at the Grand Floridian and Polynesian resort hotels before reaching the monorail station at the Magic Kingdom, then stops at the Contemporary resort hotel before returning again to the TTC station.

The trip to Epcot is interesting as the monorail actually goes inside parts of Epcot, giving an overhead view before pulling in at the monorail station at the park entrance.

Check the signs above the entrance to each monorail station to make sure you are boarding the correct monorail, or ask any Disney Cast Member if you

If the express monorail queue is backed up at either TTC or Magic Kingdom, check the queue for the resort monorail. It typically has a much shorter line than the express monorail. However, resort monorails don't run as often as the express monorails and, of course, they make stops at the hotels between the TTC and Magic Kingdom.

have questions about how to get to your destination.

If you are staying at a hotel served by the monorail, you'll be pleased to know that the resort monorails start 1.5 hours before the Magic Kingdom opens. It's a good idea to board the monorail one hour before the park opens to get in the queue before day guests begin to arrive.

Gondola (Skyliner): Take to the air with Disney's newest transportation system. Enclosed gondolas, called Disney Skyliners, take guests above the property for transportation routes that lead to Hollywood Studios and Epcot.

Hotel resorts offering the Skyliner service are: Art of Animation, Caribbean Beach, Pop Century, Riviera Resorts.

Walking: A lesser-known option is the ability to walk to both Disney's Polynesian and Grand Floridian Resort hotels from the TTC. There is a pathway at the far end of the transportation hub (the opposite side from the buses) that goes directly to the Polynesian Resort hotel. From there, you can continue on a walkway around the lake to the Grand Floridian. You can then take a monorail, boat, or bus from these resorts directly to the Magic Kingdom. You can also take a bus from these locations to the other theme parks and Disney Springs (but not to Disney's BoardWalk). This walk will also give you a chance to relax and get away from the noise and crowds.

Insider's Tip!

Day guests can board the express monorail at the TTC 45 minutes prior to opening. If you are parking at the TTC and arrive more than 45 minutes prior to Magic Kingdom park opening, walk to Disney's Polynesian Resort hotel and take the resort monorail from there.

Getting Creative with Disney Transportation

Here are some examples of how to use Disney's transportation:

Example 1:
Breakfast at the Contemporary Resort

You plan to eat a character breakfast at Chef Mickey's in Disney's Contemporary Resort hotel (reservations are strongly recommended), then spend the day at the Magic Kingdom park, followed by the Hoop-Dee-Doo Musical Review dinner show at Disney's Fort Wilderness resort campground.

Start your day by parking at the hotel. Simply tell the parking security guard that you're there to eat breakfast when you arrive. Security will likely verify your reservation details, as the Contemporary resort hotel is a very popular place for parking due to its proximity to the Magic Kingdom.

Onward to the Magic Kingdom

After eating breakfast, you have a couple of options to get to the Magic Kingdom. You can take the ten-minute stroll along a walking path to the Magic Kingdom. (Note: Disney's Contemporary resort hotel is the only hotel from which you can walk to the Magic Kingdom.) If you would like to save your legs, you can catch a bus, boat, or monorail to the Magic Kingdom park. The bus stop is outside of the lobby and the boat dock is found behind the hotel, beyond the pool. The monorail station is inside the hotel – just look up! Make your choice and travel to the Magic Kingdom park.

Onward to Fort Wilderness

To get to dinner at the Fort Wilderness resort, you have the option of either taking a bus or a boat. The boat is very easy to find just in front of the exit of the Magic Kingdom and drops you off very close to where you'll be eating dinner. The bus to the Fort Wilderness resort is to your left when you leave the Magic Kingdom.

Return to the Contemporary Resort

After your dinner show, take a boat directly from Fort Wilderness to the Contemporary. If boats are shut down for the evening, take a bus to get back to the Magic Kingdom, then walk or take one of the other two forms of transportation to get back to the Contemporary and your car.

Example 2:
Breakfast at the Boardwalk

You plan to eat breakfast at Disney's Boardwalk, then go to Hollywood Studios, after which you will park hop to Epcot for the remainder of the day (or vice versa).

Pick a restaurant that serves breakfast at one of the BoardWalk-area hotels or restaurants and make reservations. Go to Disney's BoardWalk (or Disney's Yacht or

Beach Club hotels if your reservation is at one of those properties) to park for free. The parking security guard may need to verify you have a dining reservation if it is a particularly busy day -- a sign will be posted if that's the case.

Onward to Hollywood Studios

After breakfast at the BoardWalk, you can walk or catch a boat on the lake to Hollywood Studios. The walk is approximately 15 to 20 minutes along a nice waterway.

Park-hop to Epcot

When it's time to park-hop to Epcot, you can catch the same boat you took to get to Hollywood Studios (it makes the rounds between the two parks and the hotels around the lake). Alternatively, you can catch a bus near the entrance of the BoardWalk walkway that takes you directly to Epcot. This is the quickest option to get between the two parks, though not the most scenic.

Of course, if you're feeling especially energetic, you can walk back to the BoardWalk, then past it all the way to Epcot's back entrance (about a 25 to 30 minute walk). The back entrance, also known as International Gateway, brings you into the park inside Epcot's World Showcase, between the England and France pavilions.

Back to the BoardWalk

At the end of the evening, you can exit the park at International Gateway, then make the short walk back to the BoardWalk or catch the boat at the "Friendship" dock just outside of the park.

Example 3:
Stay at an Off-Property Hotel and Start at the TTC

You are staying off-property at a hotel that provides a shuttle to/from the TTC. You plan to spend the day at the Animal Kingdom park, followed by dinner and night vision viewing of animals at the Animal Kingdom Lodge. Your bus will drop you off at the TTC in the morning.

Take a Bus Transfer to the Animal Kingdom

From there, follow the signs or ask the Disney Cast Member at the information booth where to catch the bus to the Animal Kingdom park.

Important Note: It's imperative that you keep track of the time to make sure you don't miss the shuttle back to your hotel that evening. This can result in a costly taxi cab ride. Explain to the Cast Member at the information booth that you plan to end your day at the Animal Kingdom Lodge and get approximate travel times to make sure you don't miss your shuttle.

Parking on Disney Property

Onward to the Animal Kingdom Lodge to See the Animals

After spending the day at the park, you can catch a bus outside the exit of the Animal Kingdom park directly to the Animal Kingdom Lodge. Since you are taking the bus, there is no need to explain to a security guard the reason for your visit. Just make your way to the restaurant at which you plan to eat and ask any Disney Cast Member where you can go for the free night vision viewing of the animals on the property.

Return to the TTC

Getting back to the TTC from the Animal Kingdom Lodge requires an indirect route. The easiest option is to take a bus to the Magic Kingdom, then either a bus or monorail back to the TTC. Remember, buses run about every 15 minutes, so you may need to wait that long to get the bus at the Animal Kingdom Lodge, followed by the 15-20 minute ride, followed by up to another 15 minutes to catch a bus or monorail back to the TTC.

Therefore, with travel and wait times, plus the time it takes you to walk to the shuttle pick-up location, plan to leave the Animal Kingdom Lodge about an hour before you need to catch your shuttle.

To make the dreams of Disney (World) come true took the companied skills and talents of hundreds of artisan's, carpenters, engineers, scientists, and craftsmen. The dreams that they built now become your heritage. It is you who will make Disney(land) truly a magic kingdom and a happy place for the millions of guests who will visit us now and in the future.

- Walt Disney

Park Security

You will find security guards outside the entrance to each of the parks, where they check your bags before entry (and randomly screen guests with metal detectors). They also have a visible presence at the Disney Springs shopping complex, particularly on weekend evenings.

But don't be surprised if you never see any security guards inside the actual parks. (They generally only show themselves at the beginning of parades and other events to help with crowd control.)

This doesn't mean security isn't everywhere, though. Disney has a sophisticated system that includes plain-clothes guards and cameras. Did we mention biometrics, such as fingerprint scanning at the gates, as well as facial-recognition and tracking technology? So, just because you're paranoid doesn't mean they aren't watching you!

In all seriousness, Disney has one of the most complete people tracking systems anywhere, designed to track your movements, figure out your buying habits, and determine how to get you to part with your money and feel like you're having the time of your life while doing it!

If you have something to hide, Disney is not the place to be. Recent news has reported that the US Department of Defense uses the Freedom of Information Act to regularly request the information that Disney gathers on its guests. Apparently nothing is sacred, not even quality time with your family.

The benefit to you of all this tracking technology is that thefts and assaults on Disney property are rare, and if something major happens, it's nearly impossible for the perpetrator to get away with it unpunished. That's why you see so many strollers lined up with backpacks and bags full of souvenirs left carelessly within them. Not only are nearby Cast Members keeping an eye on them, Big Brother is watching out, too!

Insider's Tip!

If you notice something missing during your visit, go immediately to the nearest Disney Cast Member. The Cast Member is likely to direct you to Guest Relations at the front of the park. However, if the item is something of great value or importance, request that they bring security out to you immediately. The quicker the investigation begins, the more likely you are to recover your possessions!

Insider's Tip!

One of the most common theft complaints in the parks is of blankets. Temperatures can drop quickly at night in Florida, and unprepared parents seem to have no compunction about stealing another child's blanket if their own child is cold. Keep your blankets and sweaters inside a bag or backpack when not using them, so they're not easy targets for thieves.

Disney Security & Bringing Extras to the Parks

Before you get to the entrance of each of the four main Disney theme parks, you'll have to go through a security checkpoint first. If you are bringing any sort of bag, purse, or backpack into the park, you'll need to open up that bag and allow a security guard to inspect what you have inside. People without bags get to walk directly past security using a "Guests without Bags" entrance.

Recently, Disney started conducting metal detector screenings for all guests, so you will be asked to remove any metal (keys, coins, etc.) from your pockets and walk through a detector after the initial bag inspection.

Security lines tend to move quickly, but you may find yourself waiting for several minutes during peak periods. On these days, you need to decide whether the convenience of bringing extra stuff with you is worth the extra wait time. You may want to travel light, if you can. Try to fit everything you need into your pockets or leave stuff behind in your car. (You also won't have to worry about carrying heavy items all day long or figuring out where to put your bags on rides.)

Passing Through the Entrance Gates

Once you make it through the security checkpoint, you will go to one of several gates with two small poles. Each pole is topped with a globe that sports a Mickey-shaped electronic pass and fingerprint scanner. Your fingerprint is scanned each time you use your pass.

Hold your pass or MagicBand in front of the Mickey silhouette where it will read the RFID chip wirelessly. When the blue lights start to flash, put your finger on the scanner until it turns solid green. Always use the same finger that you used initially. You will have to speak with a Cast Member to gain entry if it doesn't match what is stored in the system, in which case the light will stay blue.

Prohibited Items at the Parks

So, what are the security guards looking for in your bags? Most people mistakenly believe they're trying to keep you from bringing food in the parks. NOT TRUE! However, there are certain types of containers you can't use, and you need to limit the size of the bag or cooler in which you plan to bring your food or other items.

Here's the complete list of prohibited items published by Disney:

- Wagons
- Stroller Wagons
- Recreational devices, such as drones, remote-control toys, skateboards, scooters, inline skates, & shoes with built-in wheels
- Strollers larger than 31" x 52" (79 x 132 cm)
- Suitcases, bags, coolers, or backpacks with or without wheels larger than 24" (61 cm) long x 15" (38 cm) wide x 18" (46 cm) high. Coolers required for medication may be stored in a locker or at Guest Relations.

- Any trailer-like object that is pushed or towed by an ECV, wheelchair, or stroller
- Wheeled mobility devices with less than 3 wheels and devices that cannot maintain stability and balance when stopped, unpowered, or unoccupied. Training wheels or similar modifications are not permitted.
- Alcoholic beverages
- Loose or dry ice
- Medical or recreational marijuana
- Firearms, ammunition, knives, or weapons of any kind
- Objects or toys that appear to be firearms or weapons
- Self-defense or restraining devices (e.g., pepper spray, mace)
- Folding chairs
- Glass containers (excluding baby food jars and perfume bottles)
- Pets (service animals allowed)
- Balloons, plastic straws, and drink lids are not permitted in Disney's Animal Kingdom Park for the safety of the animals
- Tripod stands or monopod stands that cannot fit inside a standard backpack
- Selfie sticks
- Fireworks or other explosive and/or flammable objects, smoke machines, or fog machines
- Painted rocks (stones that people paint and find for others to find)

Carrying Your Items

It may seem convenient to bring a number of personal items, food, and/or a change of clothes. However, your backpack will feel heavier and heavier as the day goes on, and you may regret the decision to bring so much stuff to the park. In addition, you may find it difficult to carry bulky items on certain rides.

Insider's Tip!

If you want a convenient way to carry snacks, water, and souvenirs, bring a small stroller and place your bags and backpacks into it. You can take it with you and park it at each attraction, picking it up as you exit. You don't even need a child with you to take advantage of this convenience!

Strollers are never allowed on rides, and guests using wheelchairs or electric scooters must often transfer onto the rides and leave their transportation devices behind with a Disney Cast Member. If you're using a stroller, wheelchair, or electric scooter, try to bring bags you can hang off of these transportation devices or store within them. Just remember, you will be required to park your stroller in a common area that is accessible by everyone in the park, so NEVER leave valuables behind, especially if they're highly visible. (Remember, you don't have to carry around items you purchase at the park. You can have them sent to your Disney hotel or Package Pickup to retrieve later.)

Storing Your Items using Locker Rentals

You may find it most convenient to bring your personal items and store them in a locker that you and your family can access throughout the day. We mentioned lockers in a previous section, but the information is worth expounding on here.

Disney rents lockers inside each of its four main theme parks for $10, $12, or $15 per day, depending on size. Small lockers rented for $10 are 12.5" high x 10" wide x 17" deep. Large lockers rented for $15 are 15.5" high x 13" wide x 17" deep.

Park Security

Park Security

Jumbo lockers rented for $15 (available only at Magic Kingdom and Epcot) are 17" high x 22" wide x 26" deep.

If you're park-hopping, you must pay for a locker in each park.

The Animal Kingdom, Epcot, and Hollywood Studios parks also have large coin operated lockers outside of the main entrances that cost about $1 (4 quarters) each time you wish to open the locker. The Magic Kingdom, Epcot, and Hollywood Studios also have small lockers for rent outside the park for $.50 (2 quarters).

While this may seem like a cheaper option, consider how many times you may need to get into the locker throughout the day. Also, remember you must go back through security and the park entrance (and wait in line) each time you leave the park to get into the coin operated lockers.

Locker Rental Locations:

Magic Kingdom

- Inside the park entrance, go to your right. You will see locker rentals before the tunnel that takes you under the train station.
- You can find coin operated locker rentals near Guest Relations to the right of the park entrance.

Epcot

- Go through the right-hand walkway past Spaceship Earth (the big white ball). The locker rentals are near the Camera Center as you pass the attraction.
- If you enter the park through the back, International Gateway entrance, you will find locker rentals immediately to your left upon entering the park.

- You can find small coin operated locker rentals outside of the International Gateway entrance.
- You can find coin operated locker rentals large enough for luggage outside of the park by the Bus Stop booth.

Hollywood Studios

- Go immediately to your right upon entering the park. Locker rentals are at Crossroads of the World.
- You can find coin operated locker rentals directly outside of the park entrance by the Bus Stop booth.

Animal Kingdom

- You can rent lockers just inside the park entrance, to your left, at Expedition Storage Lockers.
- You can also find locker rentals near the back of the park in the Asian location of Kali River Rapids Expedition Storage Lockers (near the Kali River Rapids attraction).
- You can find coin operated locker rentals to your right just before you enter the park, near the restrooms.

Water Parks

Locker rentals at each of the water parks cost $10 to $15 per day, depending on size.

Disney Springs

Disney Springs also has coin operated lockers for rent near the marina.

Emergency Situations

You can rest assured that you and your family are in a safe place at Walt Disney World even if you experience any trouble. Security and medical professionals at Disney take their jobs extremely seriously. You won't find a better group of people to help.

They often deal with guests who accidentally overheat (or over-*eat*!) Other visitors might experience dizziness or fainting thanks to the hot Florida sun or intense rides. While rare, some people may also get minor sprains (or the very rare broken bone!)

It is not uncommon for children to get over stimulated, causing them to run or climb on things they shouldn't. Because of this, minor (but scary!) chin, knee, and hand scrapes are quite common.

Walt Disney World has First Aid Centers in each theme park to deal with these and other situations. Of course, if the situation warrants it, their attentive staff will ensure emergency personnel gets to you in a timely manner.

If any member of your party has any serious, pre-existing medical conditions that might put them at risk, create a form at home and print out a few copies. Have them put a copy in their purse or wallet and put another one in their pocket.

This form should include name, date of birth or approximate age, address, a description of any medical issues affecting them (such as diabetes, heart disease, or cancer), and a summary of their medical history including medications. It should include an emergency contact name, including the relationship between the patient and contact, as well as details of anyone who can make medical decisions for them.

Find a Cast Member

If you are afflicted by a medical issue while you are alone and cannot safely walk to the first aid office, ask another guest to help find a Cast Member. The Cast Member (or Disney management) will give instructions about what to do and will stay with you while security and Disney emergency services are contacted.

As with everything at Disney World, an emergency response is fast and efficient. Emergency personnel will take pertinent information, assess symptoms, and create a written accident report. If the symptoms are not severe, they will help stabilize you. If you need to lie down and rest, they will make sure you get to the first aid office to cool down and relax.

Disney folks will try to get these situations quickly under control and move you safely away from the rest of the crowd to provide you with some privacy and allow you to retain some dignity without the prying eyes of strangers. Disney has wheelchairs and gurneys that can transport you – behind the scenes! – as needed. They can also return you to the rest of your party once you are ready to join them.

If your issue is more serious, they can quickly get you to a hospital, and in extreme emergency situations, (AED) defibrillator machines are available throughout the park.

The nurses at the First Aid Center can provide minor first aid care, such as cleaning, disinfecting, and bandaging (minor) wounds, including skinned knees and blisters. They also have a way to safely dispose of needles (for diabetes testing or other health matters). The First Aid Center can also safely store refrigerated medicines if you need to keep some on-site for any member of your party.

If a member of your party realizes that they can't keep up with the pace due to medical issues, there is a place to rent wheelchairs, ECVs, and strollers located just inside the main entrance of each park.

Missing Family Members

Choose a meeting place that is easy to find. A good location may be the <u>Baby Care Center</u> located in each park. This is a particularly good location if there are young children in the group. The First Aid Station is always located nearby, along with Guest Relations and Lost Persons.

The Baby Care Center is a common location for missing children to be taken to be reunited with their family. Elsewhere we mentioned the importance of showing children how to identify a Cast Member's unique white name badge. Tell them to find one of these employees if they get separated from you, including any sales person at a shop or behind the counter of a food establishment. Most

Disney employees are very well trained (more so than you might expect!) when it comes to calming and helping children reunite with their families. Just educate your children to be calm and patient while the rest of the family is contacted.

As soon as you realize your child has wandered off, notify any Cast Member to get in touch with security. These professionals keep a low profile, but they are roaming around the park everywhere and can be quickly alerted.

Insider's Tip!

There is no way to keep Disney from tracking you inside the parks completely, but there are a few simple tips to reduce Disney's ability to keep tabs on you. The first is to leave the MagicBand at home. Every theme park ticket has a radio frequency identification (RFID) chip in it, but the ones inside of the credit card-style passes are short-range chips versus the long-range chips inside of the MagicBands. Long-range RFID chips allow Disney to easily track your movements within the parks, and as they're linked to your name and credit card information, they provide much more information about you to Disney than other bits of technology.

Insider's Tip!

Another thing you can do to help safeguard your privacy is turn the GPS feature off on your phone, especially if you're using the My Disney Experience app. You will lose a little bit of functionality, such as the ability to search for restaurants based on your current location, but you'll save on battery life. Better yet, Disney won't be able to profile you and your buying decisions so easily!

Buying Your Tickets & Choosing Options

Disney calls its ticket packages *Magic Your Way*, meaning you can customize the package to meet your needs. There are a number of options to consider when purchasing your pass, which include "Park Hopper" (visiting multiple parks in a single day), "Dining Plan" (on-property guests only), and "Water Park Fun and More" options in addition to the choice of where to buy and how many days to choose. The "No-Expiration" option was discontinued at Walt Disney World February 22, 2015. Existing no-expiration tickets are still honored, but are no longer sold.

You can even purchase one of several annual pass options, which may make sense for longer stays or if you plan to return to Disney within the year (see the Annual Passes section below for details).

If you're unsure of which options you need, go for less. With the exception of the Dining Plan, you can add whatever options you want to your pass at any time during your vacation (as long as you still have days left on your pass). Even annual passes can be upgraded during the year.

Two Ticket Categories

Disney separates its ticket offerings into two main categories: *Ages 3 to 9* and *Ages 10 and Up*. While Disney does not consider a 10-year old to be an adult, they

Insider's Tip!

When you decide which ticket options you want, don't delay, buy right away! Ticket prices increase each year in February, so lock in the current rate to ensure you don't pay more.

do assume a 10-year old child should be tall enough to experience all of the attractions and will therefore get full use out of the parks. There is no charge for children two and under to enter a park (or eat at a buffet with the purchase of an adult meal)!

To save money, some guests decide to lie about their children's ages if they're close to a cut-off. Disney doesn't check identification for children, since there is no such thing. We don't recommend or condone anybody doing this, as misuse of any system can lead to changes and hassles in the future (such as what surrounded relatively recent changes to Disney's Disabled Access system).

Insider's Tip!

Sign up for an account on the disneyworld.com website if you're considering a Disney vacation but haven't yet booked your stay. You will receive special offers delivered directly to your email that will notify you of upcoming deals to help plan your vacation.

Where to Buy

Let's start with where to get your tickets. The safest choice is to get them directly from Disney. Though you might pay a little more, the most choices are available directly from the source.

Check current specials offered by Disney, either on its website (disneyworld.disney.go.com/special-offers) or by calling (407) 939-5277. You may be able to save money by staying at certain properties or choosing to travel on certain dates. Occasional deals, such as free Dining Plan add-ons are sometimes offered!

Single and Multi-day Ticket Options

You have the option of a single-day ticket or multiple-day ticket (from two to 10 days). The two-day pass option is fairly new and was previously only offered to guests of Disney Fairytale Weddings or conventions.

Caution: Keep in mind, regardless of the length of your ticket, it is only valid for 14 days from initial use. Therefore, for example, don't expect to buy a 10-day pass and use it over a three-week vacation (unless you buy an annual pass instead)!

Variable Single-Day Ticket Pricing

Note that single-day ticket prices vary based on the season and day of the week that you plan to visit. (You will be asked to identify your expected travel date before purchasing.)

Insider's Tip!

If you plan to visit and don't know the exact date of your visit, choose the cheapest date available. Once your plans are confirmed, you can pay the difference if your actual visit date is a higher rate. However, Disney won't give you any money back if your actual date is cheaper than you initially purchased.

Tourist Trap!

<u>Online and roadside companies advertise discount tickets</u>. **Be careful if you find discounts that are extreme!** It is hard to be certain which companies are truly authorized by Disney as ticket resellers, and there are some shady operators. Always pay with a credit card that offers fraud protection!

Don't expect to get any real bargains at roadside stands or through sellers on Ebay (<u>ebay.com</u>) or Craigslist (<u>craigslist.com</u>).

Used Tickets Warning!

Used tickets cannot be transferred to another party for use. A number of ticket resellers have gotten into trouble selling used tickets which they claim still have days available on them. Sadly, people who fall for this story are regularly turned away at park gates with their worthless admission tickets.

There are news reports every year about individuals getting arrested in a law enforcement crackdown (working with Disney officials) to stop these fraudulent enterprises, but this practice continues.

Again, Disney tickets are *never transferable*. Ignore listings from anyone dealing in tickets that have "extra days that they didn't use." <u>Each ticket is assigned to a specific person</u> and Disney's advanced tracking system actually *uses each visitor's fingerprint* as an identifier every time a guest enters a park. *You simply can't use another person's ticket!* If you try, your identification will be checked at the gate.

Keep in mind that multi-day tickets also have this seasonal/daily fluctuation. However, they are always a better deal than a one-day pass.

Extended Daily Pricing Discount

The <u>per day</u> ticket price *decreases* with each added day. In other words, the more days you purchase on your pass, the lower the rate is for each day.

Insider's Tip!

Disney raises its ticket rates *without warning* once or twice per year, so if you're planning a vacation, don't wait to purchase. You can lock in the lower rate now for use any time in the future. Remember, the 14-day expiration doesn't start until the first time you *use* the ticket!

If you have any questions about purchasing tickets or what is included with the options, contact Disney via email (<u>wdw.ticket.inquiries@disneyworld.com</u>) or call (407) 939-5277.

Ticket Resellers

There are some legitimate <u>ticket resellers</u>. Authorized ticket resellers may offer discounted rates. Undercover Tourist (<u>undercovertourist.com</u>) is a highly-regarded Disney reseller. Taxes are included in their pricing, and unlike many companies, they will deliver your tickets to you in advance, allowing you to make your theme park reservations. Call (800) 846-1302 or visit their website to compare their ticket prices to Disney's. Remember to put your choices in a shopping cart to compare the total price, including all taxes and fees!

Buying Your Tickets & Choosing Options

Insider's Warning!

Timeshare Company Presentation "Freebies"

Many timeshare companies pose as discount ticket sellers or information booths to draw you into a timeshare presentation. You may find these folks at many locations including highly visible store fronts along the road. Westgate Lake Resorts, for example, has had a long-standing a relationship with many "along-the-side-or-the-road" information kiosks. These companies promise to give away admission tickets for free or at a discount if you only agree to sit through a (high pressure!) time share sales presentation.

While the offers of free or discounted tickets may be legitimate, don't believe the time commitment the salesperson claims you should expect. Instead, plan to spend at least two to three times longer at the presentation than promised! It is hard to be certain the savings are worth spending an *entire* morning or afternoon of your vacation.

The companies may offer a "free breakfast" and then start the sales pitch as you try to enjoy your meal. If you try to leave after your promised "two hour" time frame with your tickets, they will indicate that the presentation didn't begin until "after the meal was finished."

Few people actually value listening to a pressured pitch, and the meals are not noteworthy. The salesmen are extremely successful at convincing skeptical couples to sign an agreement.

We regularly hear of people who agree to a sale even though they attended just for the freebies. The easiest way to prevent becoming a victim to buyer's remorse is to say no to the presentation. Timeshare purchases rarely make good financial sense, no matter what you might be offered. (However, if you make a mistake and succumb to the sales, laws may allow you to cancel the contract within a very short time frame. Additionally, if you decide you want to make a purchase, look around at the many timeshare reseller companies for a 50% or greater reduction on the purchase price.)

Deposit Scams

Not only do we think that it is not worthwhile to agree to listen to a sales pitch, some of these folks actually require you to give them a "refundable" deposit that they promise will be returned to you at the presentation. Never agree to pay a deposit to these companies!

Some companies claim that they are saving you a limited seat, but they actually make money from people who never show up! Worse yet, they hold your pending refund over your head to keep you attentive and patient during their "dog-and-pony show."

If you're looking for deals on an annual pass, check with Auto Club South (autoclubsouth.aaa.com) to see if the savings they offer on annual passes is worth the membership fee.

Hidden Fees

Scrutinize hidden fees and sales taxes when purchasing your tickets, especially when purchasing from a non-Disney site. Even legitimate online travel companies may surprise you with additional fees. <u>Always</u> review the final price in your online checkout cart to accurately compare the total price of your tickets before accepting your transaction.

Upgrade Flexibility

If you pre-purchase your tickets and don't go directly through Disney, be aware that you won't have the option of *upgrading* your ticket options during your visit. Because itineraries can change, it might be worthwhile to buy direct and forego the cost savings you may be able to find by shopping around.

Discounts

You might reasonably expect to find 5 or 10% discounts. Remember, many listings that you will find on-line could be attempts at a scam, especially if the price sounds *too good to be true*.

Hotel Resellers

We continue to hear stories of legitimate hotels who have independent ticket sellers on-property (including at self-proclaimed but misleading "concierge" desks). They claim to sell tickets at a discount, only to have their customers find out later that they got hit with added fees and taxes which make the passes cost more than they would if purchased directly at the gate from Disney. Remember to get a total price, including taxes and fees, then do a price comparison before agreeing to buy.

Insider's Warning!

A s you consider whether or not to get the *park-hopper* add-on for your pass, keep in mind that trying to visit multiple parks in a single day can be exhausting and can also be very difficult to accomplish with young children and older folks.

Insider's Tip!

A long bus ride between parks can be an excellent way to sneak an air-conditioned nap for little ones. There's no requirement that you disembark at any stop, so you can stay on the bus until the tots are refreshed!

Discount for Convention Attendance

Convention organizers often receive cheaper group ticket rates for their attendees. AllConferences.com is a great resource for searching upcoming conferences within the Orlando area. Be sure to order your passes in advance and have them mailed to you, so you can make theme park reservations.

Discount Tickets Direct from Disney

When buying direct through Disney, discount tickets are available for Florida Residents, Disney Vacation Club Members, US Military Personnel, AAA members (and some other groups), large groups reserving 10 or more rooms, and certain convention guests.

Florida Residents

Insider's Tip!

B uy your tickets directly from Disney without the park hopper option directly from Disney if you're unsure about needing this feature. You can upgrade directly at the ticketing counter of any park if you decide you want to park hop later.

Florida residents with proper identification can purchase discounted tickets directly from Disney. While Disney periodically

Where are the crowds?

So, how can you tell which parks will be busy on a given day? As mentioned in our Rules to Avoid Crowds Section, holidays aside, a quick look at the park hours and events will tell you where the crowds will be.

If a Disney park has longer hours than usual, such as when the Magic Kingdom stays open until 3 a.m., expect it to be busy. The extra hours are designed to give visitors additional time to do even more than they would otherwise be able to during shorter days.

Also, when a special event is happening, such as a concert or celebrity autograph signing, expect not just vacationers, but also hoards of locals to come out for it.

offers a discounted three- or four-day pass, as well as resident discounts for hotel stays, it usually makes financial sense for residents to buy one of the many annual pass options. The annual passes don't cost much more than the price for a standard 10-day pass.

A couple of times a year (spring and fall), Florida residents are also offered complete resort packages at a discount.

Disney requires proof of state residency, which can be in the form of Florida-state ID; a utility bill with your name and address for your Florida residence; or a bank statement sent to you at your Florida residence. (See the Annual Passes section below for additional information.)

Park-Hop or Not?

The price of standard admission grants access to a specific park. Generally speaking, most people prefer to only visit one park in each day, feeling it takes too much time and energy to travel between parks.

Indeed, if you plan a longer vacation with, say, eight to 10 days spent in the parks, there is really no need to park hop. You should be able to see and do most of the attractions you want without tiring yourself out. More importantly, you'll save some valuable time and money.

Visiting more than one park in a day is referred to as *park-hopping* and there is a premium price to do so.

Consider the park-hopper upgrade only if you are certain you will be up for trying to pack as much in as possible in a short period of time. If you buy your tickets from Disney, you don't have to commit to a decision in advance and can add this option to your pass once you get settled at Disney World.

Park-hopping is a great idea for trips during which you'll only spend four days or fewer visiting the parks. This option may also be worthwhile if you plan to visit during peak periods.

Park-hopping is an excellent way to move with the flow of the crowds. If you'd rather avoid the masses, you can park-hop to *move away* from them.

Each transfer between parks can be expected to take 30 to 60 minutes when using Disney's transportation system. Going back and forth is only useful if you want to relax and enjoy the journey. Visitors to hotels around the Magic Kingdom or Epcot / Hollywood Studios might enjoy take relaxing, slow-paced boat rides back and forth across the lagoons and waterways. There are a lot of great photo and video opportunities along the way and it is a great time to stop and refresh during your long days.

When to Consider a Park-hopper Pass

Park hopping can be especially handy in the following instances:

1. You get to a park and discover it is too busy that day and want the freedom to change your mind in order to spend your time at a quieter park; or,
2. If a park is closing early, you may want to go to it in the morning and move to a different one for evening entertainment. For instance, Animal Kingdom often closes at 5 or 6 p.m. and you may want to go to the Magic Kingdom for fireworks and late-night rides.

Other Disney Adventures – Water Park Fun and Sports

The *Water Park Fun and Sports* is an optional add-on to your pass that gives alternative adventures. This option is beneficial if you have several free days allocated during your stay and wish to spend them on Disney property.

The number of days you get at these fun places will match the number of days for your theme park passes (e.g., you can spend five days at the water parks for every five-day theme park pass). The following venues are available:

- ESPN Wide World of Sport complex
- NBA Experience
- Water Parks
  - Blizzard Beach water park
  - Typhoon Lagoon water park
- Golf
  - Disney's Oak Trail Golf Course
  - Disney's Oak Trail FootGolf
  - Winter Summerland Miniature Golf Course
- Fantasia Gardens and Fairways Miniature Golf Courses

To get your money's worth, you will need to spend a few hours at your chosen venue. You wouldn't necessarily want to go to a theme park in the morning, for instance, then go to a water park in the afternoon, as you will have used a full day's pass at both (even if it is discounted).

Disney Water Parks

People of all ages enjoy playing at either of Disney World's two water parks, <u>Blizzard Beach</u> and <u>Typhoon Lagoon</u>. Both of these require either the Water Park Fun and More add-on to your theme park passes or a separate water park admission altogether.

They offer huge, fun pools that are great for children and families. There are also lounge chairs spread around sandy beaches for those who want to relax or soak up some sun.

Some of the inner-tube and raft-style water coasters are designed for families, while others are much more extreme. The most intense and exciting rides are the body water slides.

Both parks are encircled by self-propelling *lazy rivers* that flow around their perimeters. These act both as a comfortable way to keep cool and to provide a fun mode of transportation to get around the park. It also offers a great compromise between those wanting thrills and those wanting to relax.

Consistent to all Disney parks, the water parks are well-manicured, reflecting

Insider's Tip!

If it rains midday on your water park day, return to the park as soon as the rain stops. You will likely have the place to yourself!

Buying Your Tickets & Choosing Options

Insider's Tip!

Parental Warning: We would never recommend sending your (mature, older) children to the water parks without adult supervision. That's not just because even the best behaved children have a tendency to get a little wild in that environment.

The sad reality is water parks (and swimming pools) everywhere can be breeding grounds for sexual predators. Even though Disney has the strictest guidelines and a system in place to reduce the ability of these individuals to get into the parks, incidents occur. They most always happen to *tweens* and *teens* who are *out of their parent's view*. Another risk is the wave pools where predators can easily get within reach of young swimmers. Beware of environments where it is easy to "accidentally" brush up against somebody.

the customary attention-to-detail. Unlike the major theme parks, though, both water parks have unique themes and creation "back stories" on how they came to be. (We provide these details in a separate section.)

If you've been to water parks in the past, while uniquely-themed, these two don't really offer anything out of the ordinary.

Typhoon Lagoon opened in 1989 with a state-of-the-art wave pool that makes six-foot tall waves every 90 seconds. There is also a surfing lesson available for an added fee (before park opening on select days).

Blizzard Beach opened in 1995 with what are generally considered to be nicer water slides with more convenient features. Rather than having to carry your own inner tubes up a long flight of stairs, you can take a ski lift to the top of the park's highest peak while conveyor belts carry rafts to the top of the slide. The crowning jewel of this park is Summit Plummet, a nearly-vertical body slide that drops guests straight down 120 feet to the bottom.

Water Parks vs. Hotel Pools

You may decide to book one of the many area hotels that has a pool area. Many of these can offer nearly as much fun as a water park, especially for young children. They also have the added benefit of hot tubs for adults to rejuvenate after a long day walking around the theme parks (a feature which is sadly missing from water parks).

Many Orlando and Kissimmee hotels now have water slides and lazy rivers on their properties. Most resorts charge a daily resort fee to pay for the pool, so make good use of it. Disney hotels do not charge additional fees. The Moderate to Deluxe resorts also all have water slides and hot tubs.

Seasonal Variations at the Water Parks

Obviously, timing of your vacation is an important factor in determining whether or not to get a water park pass. We do not recommend it for a winter vacation. The weather is just too unpredictable and can get extremely cold, so unless you're from Canada (or a country with a similar cold climate), you may not want to spend a lot of time in the water. Not only that, Disney always closes one of the two parks during the winter for major refurbishment.

The parks are also shut down on particularly cool winter days. Bad weather can even affect your water park fun during the *summer months*, when it can rain nearly every day in Orlando (usually in the afternoons and evenings). That doesn't mean you can't go to the water park. Just plan to go early in the day and take care of your shopping or other fun errands when the rain begins. Spring and autumn vacations are usually safe with warm, sunny temperatures.

What to Wear

Women and girls should <u>always</u> wear one-piece suits or tankinis to the water parks, and men should not wear loose-fitting shorts. Many of the water slides move at a high-velocity, and both tops and bottoms do come off on occasion. You never know who's snapping a photo while you're trying to readjust and cover up!

Miniature Golf

Disney World has two on-property miniature golf courses. These are:

- Fantasia Gardens and Fairways
- Winter Summerland

Both charge only $14 per person for a single round (which is all you are allocated with the *Water Park Fun and Sports* premium add-on to your pass), so it is generally not cost-effective to pay for the water park fun and more option just to play miniature golf.

Fantasia Gardens and Fairways

Accessible by a short walk, these two, 18-hole miniature golf courses are located across from the Walt Disney World Swan hotel. Fantasia Gardens has holes with character themes from the movie *Fantasia*. It is complete with motion sensor reactions and the famous walking brooms at the final hole.

The second course, Fairways, is a miniature-scale, traditional golf course, complete with <u>real grass</u> and miniature

scenery (courtesy of Hollywood Studios). This is the most challenging miniature golf course Disney has to offer and is not as easy as you might think. Are you up for it?

Winter Summerland

Winter Summerland also has two courses and is located next door to Disney's Blizzard Beach water park. (They share the same parking lot.) There are no big challenges here. Each of the two 18-hole courses is built for pure Christmas fun.

Backstory

Like its related property (Blizzard Beach), Disney has created a fun back-story for this golf course.

> "Late one Christmas Eve, as Santa was flying back to the North Pole, he discovered snow in Florida. After surveying the strange sight, he decided to build a vacation destination for his off-duty elves - a Winter Summerland.
>
> Seeing that the only thing Winter Summerland lacked was a golf course, Santa and his elves divided into 2 camps, one that enjoyed the warm Florida sun and another that preferred the snow and cold of the North Pole. The elves then built two distinctly different 18-hole golf experiences: a sand course named 'Summer' and a snow course named 'Winter.'"

Miniature golf courses are open daily from 10 a.m. to 11 p.m. Parking is always free. Children ages three to nine cost $12 to play each 18-hole, while older children and adults (ages 10 and up) play for $14.

Disney's Oak Trail Golf Course

Disney has a variety of golf courses to entice even the most avid enthusiast. The Oak Trail Golf Course is included with the *Water Park Fun and Sports* pass. This

9-hole walking course is most basic of the on-property golf courses, perfect for beginners or those interested in a fun day out, rather than a major challenge.

The golf course is a good value to use with your *Water Park Fun and Sports* package, as tee times can cost as much as $36. Call (407) WDW-GOLF to reserve your tee time.

Disney's Oak Trail FootGolf Course

If you're not familiar with FootGolf, it's played on a golf course using a soccer ball and large holes.

Disney has a 9-hole footgolf course included with your *Water Park Fun and Sports* package. Call (407) WDW-GOLF to reserve your tee time.

ESPN Wide World of Sports

ESPN Wide World of Sports is a world-class sports training and exhibition center. It is by far the most elaborate athletics venue at any theme park anywhere on Earth, where professional and amateur teams play nearly every type of sport imaginable. It's famous for being home to the **Atlanta Braves** spring training center and is also the permanent home of the Amateur Athletic Union.

Playstation Pavilion

Your *Water Park Fun and Sports* package allows you use of the PlayStation Pavilion inside of the sports complex and provides you spectator-access to the entire venue. [This access is only for events that don't require separate tickets (at an additional cost).]

This is the place to be for sports nuts. It draws over a quarter million athletes and 1.2 million spectators every year.

The 220-acre state-of-the-art sporting complex holds events for over 50 sports each year. These include soccer, slow- and fast- pitch softball, basketball, martial arts, track and field events, marathons,

cheerleading, and competitions for USA Wrestling National Championships, USA Judo Championships, and Pop Warner Super Bowl.

Some of the features that draw spectators and visitors include:

- 4 major-league-sized fields
- 6 softball and youth baseball fields
- 12 collegiate basketball courts
- A 10-court tennis complex
- A complete track and field facility

The complex also features the **Milk House** facility, which is a 165,000 square-foot field house that seats 5,500 for basketball games.

The emphasis is on baseball at the 9,500-seat **Champion Stadium** ballpark, which hosts the spring training camp for the Atlanta Braves. At 100 feet high, this is Florida's tallest (and only) double-decker baseball stadium.

Multi-sport fields include the **Jostens Center** and **Hess Sports Fields**, which offer four fields for soccer, football, lacrosse, and other sports, along with four diamonds for baseball and softball.

Of course, no Disney destination would be complete without themed shopping and dining. There are sports-related Disney shops and an **ESPN Wide World of Sports Grill** counter-service restaurant.

Call (407) 939-4263 to find out what is scheduled during your vacation and to see what events will be covered with a *Water Park Fun and Sports* ticket. Note that parking is free at the complex.

Disney Dining Plans

If you're staying at a Walt Disney World Resort hotel, choose among six Dining Plan options with your package: (Some plans now include the option of alcoholic beverages for adults 21 years and older.)

- Disney Summer Quick-Service Dining Plan (available only during summer months)
- Disney Quick-Service Dining Plan
- Disney Dining Plan
- Disney Deluxe Dining Plan
- Disney Premium Dining Plan
- Disney Platinum Dining Plan

Dining Plans are strictly for convenience, not for saving money. Consider the convenience as though you're booking an all-inclusive vacation rather than *ala carte*. Restaurant options are all on-property, including Disney hotels and some locations at Disney Springs.

You may be able to save a (very) small amount of money through careful planning and scheduling. However, most people find the time it takes to realize maximum value out of a Dining Plan is not particularly worth it.

To determine if a Dining Plan is cost effective for you, try an online Dining Plan Calculator, such as the one found at: distripplanner.com.

Many guests also find that plan options are too limited, requiring them to spend extra money they hadn't planned on to get what they really want to eat each day! Still, if you wish to have the convenience of having pre-paid meals, particularly if people in your party tend to split up and eat separately, you may decide a Dining Plan is a good option for you.

Disney Quick-Service Dining Plan

This plan provides each member of your party with a refillable resort mug, two quick-service meals (meals from counter-service restaurants), and one snack per night of stay. The breakfast meals include an entree plus a non-alcoholic beverage, and the lunch and dinner meals include a dessert. Lunch and dinner prices are the same at quick-service restaurants (both higher than typical breakfast prices), so

you definitely get more value out of using your two meal options for lunch and dinner rather than breakfast.

This plan is **$55 per adult ($26 per child) per night** (based on double-occupancy) or **$330** for a **six-night stay**.

Cost: You may be able to find quick-service meals for $20, but most with desserts are about $15 each. A snack costs about $5, so you may actually lose approximately $15 per person per day.

Disney Dining Plan

This plan provides each member of your party a refillable resort mug, one quick-service meal, one table service meal, and one snack per night of stay. However, in order to use your table-service meal for a Signature restaurant, a dinner show, or Cinderella's Royal Table buffet, you must use two of your table-service meal credits.

Cost: This plan is **$78.01 per adult ($30.51 per child) per night** (based on double-occupancy) or **$468.06** for a **six-night stay**. Keep in mind that gratuities are not included for table service meals (except at dinner shows and at Cinderella's Royal Table).

Disney Deluxe Dining Plan

The next plan up is the Disney Deluxe Dining Plan. This plan allocates each person a refillable mug, two snacks, and three meals per person (your choice of quick or table service!) per night of stay. You can use your table service credits for character dining, Signature dining, and dinner shows on a one-for-one basis.

Cost: This plan runs **$119 per adult ($47.50 per child) per night** (based on double-occupancy) or **$714** for a **six-night stay**. That's a lot for food!

Other Dining Plans

Disney has two dining plans above the Deluxe. The Premium and Platinum

Dining Plans each include the same dining options as the Deluxe. The difference is with additional entertainment options included in the two higher plans. For instance, both the Premium and Platinum Dining Plans include guided park tours, with the Platinum option offering more of those tours than the Premium. The Platinum Dining Plan also includes a nighttime cruise at either Magic Kingdom or Epcot to view the fireworks from a private boat on the water.

There is also a seasonal dining plan offered only during the summer months. The Summer Quick-Service Dining Plan has the least options of any dining plan. Not only does it not include the refillable mug you find in every other plan, this plan only allocates a single quick-service meal and a single snack each night of your vacation.

How Many Park Days Do You Need

You can look at a hundred different resources and get a hundred different opinions on this matter. So much depends on your likes and dislikes, whether you have been to the parks before, and whether you plan to hit every ride, show, etc.

The considerations also have to do with your energy level and whether you

want to casually stroll and look about or aggressively move from one attraction to another. (We refer to these guests as "**Themepark Commandos**".)

On the other end of the spectrum are older folks who want to take it easy. They, along with people who are traveling with youngsters, should err conservatively and add as many additional days as possible to have a slow and peaceful vacation.

With the following discussion, we're going to make some assumptions to give you our overall take on how many days to book your vacation.

Assumptions

- First, we assume you are a first-timer who has never been to Disneyland either (as many of the rides are the same or similar).
- Second, we assume your family enjoys all types of rides and shows.

Dining Plans at a Glance (Per Person/Per Day)							
Plan Type	Snacks	Quick Service Meals	Table Service Meals	Specialty Meals/Dinner Shows	Admission to Extra Activities	Admission to Premium Activities	Length of Stay Refillable Mug
Summer Quick-Service	1	1	0	No	No	No	No
Quick-Service	1	2	0	No	No	No	Yes
Dining	1	1	1	Requires 2 TS Credits	No	No	Yes
Deluxe Dining	2	(May Use TS Credits)	3	Yes	No	No	Yes
Premium Dining	3	(May Use TS Credits)	3	Yes	Yes	No	Yes
Platinum Dining	3	(May Use TS Credits)	3	Yes	Yes	Yes	Yes

- Third, we assume your entire party prepares to spend entire days at each theme park, with limited breaks for dining.
- Fourth, we assume that no youngsters require additional rests.
- Fifth, we assume you plan to get to the parks each day when they open.
- Sixth, and finally, we assume you'll make full use of paid Lightning Lane reservations (individual and Genie+ options).

Using the above assumptions as your reference, read the rest of this section. Afterward, you should be able to adjust the required number of days up or down based on your family's specific circumstances.

If you plan to visit during the off-season, you should be able to enjoy all of the major attractions and most of the minor ones (if not all) at least once if you allocate two days for Magic Kingdom and one day for each of the other parks. That means you'll need a **five-day pass** if you plan to visit each park.

Add an additional day for the Magic Kingdom and one to use at one of the other parks (or park-hop) to pick up any attractions you may have missed due to excessive waiting if you plan to visit during peak periods, meaning three days at Magic Kingdom and four days for all of the other parks combined (**seven days total**).

In this case, a park-hopper pass is a good idea, as it will give you the option to travel between Hollywood Studios and Epcot to pick up any missed attractions there. It's unlikely you will ever need to use your extra day for Animal Kingdom.

You will probably be exhausted when you're finished with your visit, but you should feel like you had a full vacation.

For a more leisurely vacation that will allow you to do a little more exploration and a lot less running from ride to ride, come for the **full 10 days**. You will have time to do your favorite rides multiple times and enjoy leisurely breaks during the day.

If you have any children younger than about 12 or so, err on the higher side between these estimates. If you have multiple children and you want no headaches trying to see and do virtually everything, 10 days should be the minimum length for your once-in-a-lifetime family vacation. This will provide your family with plenty of time to enjoy both the parks, local attractions, and your hotel amenities. Importantly, it will give the kids plenty of time to play in the water while adults relax at the hotel (or go out for a quiet dinner if you have someone to watch the youngsters).

Of course, if you've been to Walt Disney World or Disneyland in the past, there may be a number of attractions you don't necessarily want or care to do. If that's the case, a shorter pass should work for you.

Insider's Tip!

Only one person in your party needs an annual pass to take advantage of some of its added benefits during your vacation. Just make sure that person will be the one reserving your hotel room and will always be present when parking or dining to get the discounts. For example, if you need parking, only one person would need to purchase a pass that includes parking. It will cover the entire party, assuming you all travel to the parks together and fit into a single vehicle.

Annual Passes

NOTE: Disney is not currently selling new annual passes due to COVID-19. You don't need to be a Florida resident to purchase an annual pass (although passes are cheaper for residents). Annual passes have definite advantages over regular ticket packages (not just the unlimited park-hopping) and may be more cost-effective when all the perks are evaluated.

Let's start with hotel discounts. Annual passholders often receive special pricing on Disney hotels that is nearly always cheaper than any other discounts that may be offered. This can save you hundreds, depending on the length of your stay. Another great perk is free parking. That's a savings of $20 per day!

Interested in saving even more? Annual passholders get discounts on merchandise and dining at select Disney restaurants. Having an annual pass also makes you eligible to purchase the Tables in Wonderland Card for $150. This card gets you 20% off at most table-service dining locations throughout Disney (including alcohol purchases!), limited free parking if dining at the parks, and free valet parking (normally $35 charge) if dining at the hotels.

Still not interested? Perhaps unlimited PhotoPass downloads is more your speed. For the three highest pass options, this is included for no additional cost - including attraction souvenir pictures and videos!

Annual Pass Options

There are several plans Florida residents can choose from. However, non-residents are limited to the two highest pass options. The cheapest of those two is the Platinum Pass, which provides 365-day park access. This option includes unlimited photo downloads, free parking, and access to the four main theme parks for 365 days at a cost for non-Florida residents (ages 10 and up) of about **$1,195 with tax**. The Platinum Plus Pass has the added benefit of admission to both water parks, ESPN Wide World of Sports (except for special events), and Disney's Oak Trail Golf Course. It will run you about **$1,295 with tax**.

In comparison, a 10-day pass with *Park Hopper Plus* (with the *Water Park Fun and Sports* feature) and *Memory Maker* (unlimited photo download) options costs about **$750 with tax (estimated). Add $250 to that for parking, and you're at $1,000**.

If you're planning to stay on-property, of course your parking would be free. In that case, find out what lodging specials are currently offered for annual passholders by contacting (407) 939-1936. If the savings are worth it, get an annual pass.

As *Disney doesn't offer a pass to US residents that's longer than 10 days*, an annual pass is your only option for longer visits.

Deluxe Annual Pass

The Disney Premier Passport is the most deluxe annual pass and can only be purchased at a Guest Relations booth. It costs **$2,199 plus tax** and gives you 365 day access to all four of Walt Disney World's theme parks, its two water parks, ESPN Wide World of Sports (except for special events), and Disney's Oak Trail Golf Course. It also includes annual admission to the company's Anaheim, California parks: **Disneyland** and **California Adventures**.

Shopping Venues

Insider's Tip!

Package Pickup. If you see something you like, there's no reason not to buy it then and there. This will make sure you don't have to try to hunt it down later. (Take a picture of anything you might want to ponder to help you find it later.) Use Disney's package-pickup service (available to all guests) to have your purchases sent to the park entrance within three hours of purchase, where you can pick it up when you leave the park.

Insider's Tip!

Merchandise Returns. If you change your mind about your purchase, you can **return it anywhere on Disney property.** If you buy a specialty glass ornament from the Germany pavilion in Epcot, for instance, you can return it when you go to Hollywood Studios later in your trip. Of course, you need to present your receipt to return an item, and Disney won't give refunds on used or customized merchandise (such as embroidered hats).

In past years, guests would need to visit a specific Disney park to find merchandise specific to each location. Disney has moved more towards homogenized merchandise and shopping lately, so that most Disney Park items are available (at the same prices) from many retail locations.

Many shoppers prefer to set aside time to browse the larger retail locations, rather than make small purchases throughout the day at a park. These include massive Disney-specific shopping locations such as the **Emporium** inside of Magic Kingdom, **Mouse Gear** inside of Epcot, and **World of Disney** at Disney Springs, which is, in fact, the largest Disney merchandise store in the world!

Be aware that you won't be able to find *everything* in these giant retail locations. Some Disney hotels continue to sell hotel-themed merchandise specific to each property. A few in-park attractions have specialty-themed merchandise, such as NASA action figures you can purchase at Mission:SPACE in Epcot. Additionally, World Showcase in Epcot has items, ranging from clothing to food, that are specific to the represented countries at Epcot.

Disney Springs

Disney Springs, formerly called Downtown Disney, is a giant shopping, dining, and entertainment complex within Walt Disney World. The outdoor mall sits along the shore of Village Lake, opposite Saratoga Springs Resort. There is no entrance or parking fee to gain access to Disney Springs

Disney Springs is not for everyone, as crowds can be intense. Guests who like large shopping malls love it. And, many people choose to spend an entire day of their vacation shopping, eating, and strolling about the property.

Insider's Tip!

Crowds are lightest at Disney Springs early in the day. Evenings, weekends, and holidays tend to be claustrophobic and overwhelming for many guests. Try to go before 5 p.m. on a weekday for the most pleasurable experience and shortest shopping lines.

Keep in mind that most of its merchandise can be found elsewhere on-property.

The complex comprises four main areas: Marketplace (located on the east side of the property); The Landing (along the central waterfront); Town Center (in the center of the property); and West Side (on the other end of the mall). Disney Springs recently underwent a major expansion, which resulted in a new theme, including new "neighborhoods" and a name change to Disney Springs (formerly Downtown Disney).

Disney Springs has two multi-story parking facilities on either end of Disney Springs (and one across the street) to relieve the traffic congestion problems guests have experienced in the past.

Most of the Marketplace remains the same as years past. West Side has many of the same shops and restaurants, along with a few new ones.

The former Pleasure Island has been renovated and turned into The Landing. The majority of new venues are found here and in Town Center, which is primarily large-chain stores.

The Theme

Disney Springs is a re-imagining of the complex. Rather than a "downtown" area, Disney Springs is meant to represent a city with distinct neighborhoods. In true Disney fashion, they have developed a backstory and theme to integrate the

Shopping Venues

sections/neighborhoods together. There are more bridges and water features with varying designs to tie into the "springs" theme.

According to Disney's backstory, Town Center is the "original" part of town, located in the center of the complex. From Town Center, the city of Disney Springs expanded to include three additional neighborhoods: The Landing, Marketplace, and West Side.

In other words, the current Marketplace and West Side stayed in place. As mentioned above, Pleasure Island converted to The Landing, which sits along the waterfront. Town Center replaced the central parking lot area.

The purpose of these changes was to improve the aesthetic appeal and shopping and dining options for guests. The complex now has more than 150 shopping, dining, and entertainment venues, more than double its old offerings. Additional bridges and walkways have somewhat improved pedestrian congestion. Disney kept the water taxis that run between areas of the complex, but they have moved the locations of some of the stops.

Marketplace

Generally speaking, Marketplace is the most child-friendly area of Disney Springs with most of its merchandise and décor still in keeping with Disney themes. This area contains the world's largest Disney merchandise store, World of Disney. (With the new construction, World of Disney grew even larger!) Next door is one of three Walt Disney World Bibbidi Bobbidi Boutiques (the others are inside of Magic Kingdom and Disney's Grand Floridian Resort & Spa).

Many of the retail merchandise locations in Marketplace sell the same Disney Parks merchandise you would find inside of the theme parks plus some that are more unique to Disney Springs, including a giant Christmas store and Mickey's Pantry, which sells only kitchen products. LittleMissMatched and The LEGO Store are other big shopping draws to Marketplace.

Expect a bottleneck outside of The LEGO Store. The LEGO Imagination Center is a fun play area outside of the store where kids can play with the little plastic building blocks, but the real draw is in the form of massive LEGO sculptures around the building. Check out some of your favorite characters in amazing detail, including Snow White and Buzz Lightyear. And there's no way to miss the giant LEGO sea serpent in the lake!

Where to Shop in the Marketplace

- The Art Corner by Artistic Talent Group carries some unique and collectible items, including colorful scarves and hand printed works.
- The Art of Disney showcases fine art for your walls and shelves – Disney style! Expect to spend fine art prices for many of the pieces here, but you can also find some more reasonably priced prints and trinkets.
- Basin is the place to pick up specialty soaps, bath salts, and lotions. You can choose from a wide variety of scents to match your mood.
- Bibbidi Bobbidi Boutique is a specialty boutique designed to transform your child into a knight or princess. Appointments are highly recommended.
- Build-A-Dino by Build-A-Bear Workshop is tucked away in the back of the gift shop for the T-Rex restaurant. Children can create their own stuffed dinosaur here and choose fun outfits for their creations.

Shopping Venues

- Crystal Arts by Arribas Brothers sells collectible goods and art, including customized crystal ware. This is an excellent place to find a truly unique souvenir, but be careful. You can spend hundreds or thousands here if you get carried away.
- Dino-Store is the gift shop attached to T-Rex restaurant. Get restaurant and dinosaur-themed merchandise here.
- Disney's Days of Christmas celebrates the holidays all year long with Disney-themed decorations and ornaments. You can even have your ornaments customized with hand-painted dates and names.
- Disney PhotoPass Studio is one of many locations on Disney property where you can view your Photo-Pass pictures, customize them with borders and text, and order prints or digital copies of your photos.
- Disney's Pin Traders is a large shop dedicated entirely to the sale of Disney's collectible pins. Remember to look for any Disney Cast Member wearing a pin lanyard to see if you can trade up your purchases!
- Disney's Wonderful World of Memories sells everything you need to memorialize your vacation, including scrapbooking supplies and camera accessories.
- Face Painting by Enjoy Your Face is a kiosk location for kids and adults to get fun designs painted on their faces.
- Ghirardelli Soda Fountain & Chocolate Shop doesn't just sell made-to-order goodies. You can purchase chocolate bars, cookbooks, and much more from the side entry to this shop. Plus, you get a free chocolate square just for walking in!
- Goofy's Candy Company has handmade sweets, including special Disney-shaped candy apples and chocolates, not to mention specialty fruity slushy drinks.
- Initial Rings is a kiosk that sells engraved jewelry.
- Lefty's - The Left Hand Store has fun items designed just for the south paw.
- The LEGO Store is a budding engineer's dream shop with one of the largest LEGO selections you will find anywhere. Keep in mind, though, they sell at retail price, and you can often find LEGO merchandise at other retailers for a discounted price that is much cheaper.
- Marketplace Co-Op is a fun and unique space with 6 separately themed boutiques, including clothing, technology, home décor, and kitchenware.
- Once Upon a Toy is a great place to find child-specific Disney toys and souvenirs.
- Pearl Factory is a kiosk that has high-end pearl jewelry for sale.
- Rainforest Café Retail Village is the gift shop inside Rainforest Café restaurant. You can purchase restaurant-themed and other rainforest-themed souvenirs at this location.
- Silhouette Portraits is a unique gift kiosk where an artist will create a silhouette of your face to frame and take home.
- Star Wars Trading Post is the best location for Star Wars clothing and souvenirs. You can even build your own droid and lightsaber there.
- Swings N' Things - The Hammock Experts is a kiosk with great hammocks and porch swings to fit any lifestyle.
- Tren-D has Disney's version of couture apparel and accessories for

women. This is a great place to get unique Disney clothing you won't feel embarrassed about wearing when you get back home.

- World of Disney, as mentioned before, is the world's largest Disney retail location. It includes most of what you can find in other on-property Disney stores, plus some extra items, such as Disney-themed fine jewelry.

Where to Dine in the Marketplace

- AristoCrêpes (S $) sells delicious counter-service crepes.
- B.B. Wolf's Sausage Co. (S $) is the counter-service kiosk for the sausage lover.
- Dockside Margaritas (S $) is a waterside, counter-service lounge that serves several varieties of margaritas.
- Earl of Sandwich (BLD $) is a tasty counter-service sandwich shop, which specializes in hot made-to-order sandwiches. This is arguably the best value in all of Disney with each sandwich made large enough to satisfy most appetites for only $6.99 each. You can also get tasty sides, smoothies, and desserts. We recommend you try the macaroni and cheese. You won't be sorry!
- Ghirardelli Ice Cream & Chocolate Shop (S $) has incredible chocolates and ice cream treats. We especially like the free chocolate square each guest gets when entering the side entrance to the chocolate store.
- Joffrey's Handcrafted Smoothies at Disney Springs Marketplace (S $) is a kiosk serving smoothies and specialty frozen beverages.
- Lava Lounge at Rainforest Cafe (S $) is an outdoor waterside lounge serving food and alcoholic beverages.

- Marketplace Snacks (S $) is a kiosk serving popcorn, hot dogs, and ice cream.
- Rainforest Café (LD $$) is famous for its animatronic, rainforest-themed atmosphere. Most people love the unique dining experience, but it is extremely noisy and frightens some children. The food is generally good, and you can get the best value by splitting an appetizer platter, rather than ordering entrees. The smoothies and blended drinks are especially good, as are the desserts.
- Starbucks at Disney Springs Marketplace (S $) is the Marketplace location for the world-famous coffee chain. This coffee shop has an outdoor window for walk-up traffic only.
- Sunshine Churros at Disney Springs Marketplace (S $) is a snack cart that sells the extremely popular dessert treat.
- T-REX (LD $$) is another animatronic restaurant owned by the same company as Rainforest Café (Landry's). The theme here is dinosaurs. Part of the fun of this restaurant is a sand play area for children to dig for "fossils" while you wait to be seated. Like Rainforest Café, it gets very noisy and can frighten children. The food is generally good, and you can get the best value by splitting an appetizer platter, rather than ordering entrees. The smoothies and blended drinks are especially good, as are the desserts.
- Wetzel's Pretzels (S $) sells pretzels out of a kiosk near World of Disney. The frozen lemonade is slightly tart and especially refreshing on a hot day.

Shopping Venues

Entertainment in the Marketplace

There are just a few entertainment options at the Marketplace. There are two children's rides (additional cost): Marketplace Train Express and Marketplace Carousel, each requiring tokens that cost $2 per ride. The engine and caboose cars on the train are especially popular with the little ones.

Also, just in front of World of Disney sits the Waterside Stage. There is a regular DJ who gets the crowd dancing on most days, as well as many live performances of dancing and music from schools around the country. It can get very loud near the stage, but there are nice tables on the waterfront in front of Ghirardelli Soda Fountain & Chocolate Shop that offer a great alternative to listen from a distance.

The Landing

The Landing incorporated the remaining Pleasure Island restaurants: Raglan Road and Paradiso 37. New retail shops and dining have since popped up in this Disney Springs neighborhood.

Where to Shop in The Landing

- The Art of Shaving is just for men, providing everything a man could need for grooming his facial hair. If you wish to pamper yourself a little more, get a beard trim or complete shave in the barber chair.
- The BOATHOUSE BOATIQUE is the gift store attached to The BOATHOUSE restaurant. The nautical-themed merchandise ranges anywhere from souvenir cups to high-end collectible boat engines.
- Chapel Hats has a broad selection of headgear to suit any purpose.
- eyCatchers is a small kiosk with uniqe spinning wind catchers.
- The Ganachery is a specialty chocolatier that sells high-end treats to take-away.
- Happy Hound is a kiosk for all things canine.
- Havaianas is a flip-flop shop where you can actually create your own sandals.
- Oakley offers golf apparel and accessories for the enthusiast.
- Pop Gallery goes to show you can never have too many shops selling high-end art work in a single shopping location.
- SANUK is a shoe store for those with a sense of flair.
- Savannah Bee Company has sweet honey-based products. Try a sample of multiple flavored honeys to choose your favorite to take home.
- Shop for Ireland is the gift shop attached to Raglan Road restaurant where you can buy authentic Irish merchandise.

Where to Dine in The Landing

- The Basket at Wine Bar George (S $) sells specialty wines with perfectly paired snacks to-go.
- The BOATHOUSE (LD $$$) provides waterfront dining with a twist. After your meal, you can pay to have a boat captain take you on the lake in

one of the unique vessels, including a floating car!

- Chef Art Smith's Homecoming (LD $$) serves fresh Florida entrees.
- The Edison (LD $$) is a 1920s electric company/steam punk-inspired restaurant serving American food. After 10 pm, the restaurant becomes an adults-only lounge.
- Enzo's Hideaway (LD $$) is a 1920s speakeasy-inspired restaurant serving Italian food. Guests must enter this fun restaurant through the basement entrance.
- Erin McKenna's Bakery NYC (S $) provides decadent vegan and gluten-free baked goods.
- Gideon's Bakehouse (S $) is a bakery with the most sought-after cookies at Disney Springs.
- Jock Lindsey's Hangar Bar may be the most interesting lounge at Disney Springs. The aviation-themed restaurant brings to life the fictional character's (from the Indiana Jones franchise) gathering place.
- Joffrey's Coffee & Tea Company (S $) serves specialty teas and coffees, including alcoholic options.
- Maria & Enzo's Ristorante (LD $$) is an Italian eatery set in a repurposed airplane hangar. The trattoria sits above Enzo's Hideaway.
- Morimoto Asia (LD $$) is a trendy Japanese restaurant, specializing in pan-Asian, dim sum, and sushi.
- Morimoto Asia Street Food (LD $) offers trendy Japanese street fare in a walk-up establishment.
- Paddlefish (LD $$$, Reservations Recommended) is a higher-end seafood restaurant, located on a permanently docked paddlewheel ship. This restaurant replaced the wildly-popular Fulton's Crab House.

- Paradiso 37 (LD $$) showcases food from all over the Americas. It has a Latin flare. The restaurant is an especially good choice for people who like to sit, eat, and have conversation while watching people walk by. There is a full bar area for adults.
- PIzza Ponte (LD $) serves tasty pizza in a casual diner.
- Raglan Road Irish Pub and Restaurant (LD $$) is the largest of the current Pleasure Island restaurants. It has a counter-service restaurant on one side, called Cookes of Dublin (LD $), which is very popular for its authentic fish and chips. The table-service restaurant has several full bars and hosts live Irish music bands each night. It gets loud and crowded with people drinking alcohol late into the evenings.
- STK Orlando (LD $$$) is a classic steakhouse.
- Terralina Crafted Italian (LD $$) is an Italian restaurant with a menu created by Chef Justin Park. It serves Italian favorites cooked in a wood-burning oven.
- Vivoli il Gelato (S $) specializes in seasonal gelato desserts, along with some sandwiches are drink options.
- Wine Bar George (LD $$$) is a local fan-favorite, serving small plates and more than 100 varieties of wine.

Entertainment in The Landing

- Vintage Amphicar & Italian Water Taxi Tours offers fun boat rides just outside of The BOATHOUSE restaurant. Choose from a variety of vessels, including vintage (and completely restored) floating cars.
- You can often catch live bands playing in front of (and inside!) Raglan Road.

- Live music plays at Waterview Park throughout the day.

Town Center

Town Center is where most people enter Disney Springs. It sits between Marketplace and The Landing, with one of the parking garages feeding into it. This neighborhood has shopping, a few eateries, and the primary Guest Relations building for Disney Springs.

Where to Shop in Town Center

- ALEX AND ANI - clothing and accessories.
- American Threads - clothing and accessories
- Anthropologie - clothing and accessories.
- Coach - high end purses and accessories.
- Coca-Cola Store has everything for the collector, including a meet-and-greet with the famous Coca-Cola bear!
- Columbia Sportswear - clothing and accessories.
- Edward Beiner Purveyor of Fine Eyewear's name says it all. Find some trendy shades here.
- Ever After Jewelry Co. & Accessories - jewelry and accessories.
- Everything But Water - clothing and accessories
- Fit2Run is a runner's paradise, selling athletic shoes and apparel.
- francesca's - clothing and accessories.
- Free People - shoes, clothing, and accessories.
- JOHNNY WAS - clothing and accessories.
- Johnston & Murphy - shoes, clothing, and accessories..
- Kate Spade New York - shoes, clothing, and accessories.

- LACOSTE - clothing and accessories.
- Levi's - clothing and accessories.
- Lily Pulitzer - clothing and accessories.
- L'Occitane en Provence has all natural beauty and spa essentials.
- Lovepop - a unique greeting card store featuring Kirigami art.
- lululemon - shoes, clothing, and accessories.
- Luxury of Time by Diamonds International sells fashionable watches and jewelry.
- MAC Cosmetics has a full selection of the popular cosmetics and beauty products.
- Melissa Shoes - shoes, clothing, and accessories.
- Na Hoku is the famous Hawaaian jewelry store where you can find island-inspired accessories.
- Origins sells high-end beauty and spa treatment products.
- Orlando Harley-Davidson is proof that Disney has something for everyone. You can pick up nearly anything Harley-related here – except a motorcycle. Feel free to sit on one of the prop motorcycles for a great photo op, though!
- Pandora Jewelry offers a full line of the popular jewelry and accessories.
- Ron Jon Surf Shop - clothing, gifts, and accessories for the avid surfing fan.
- Rustic Cuff - clothing and accessories.
- Sephora sells cosmetics and fragrances.
- Shore - clothing and accessories.
- Sound Lion offers audio-related electronics.
- Sperry - shoes, clothing, and accessories.

- Stance - trendy socks and accessories.
- The Store at Planet Hollywood - apparel and souvenirs.
- Sugarboo & Co. sells trinkets to delight any collector.
- Superdry - shoes, clothing, and accessories.
- Tommy Bahama - shoes, clothing, and accessories.
- UGG - shoes, clothing, and accessories.
- UNDER ARMOUR - shoes, clothing, and accessories.
- UNIQLO - clothing and accessories.
- UNOde50 sells unique, handcrafted jewelery.
- Vera Bradley - clothing and accessories.
- Volcom - clothing and accessories.
- ZARA - clothing and accessories.

Where to Dine in Town Center

- Amorette's Patisserie (S $) is a divine bakery and sweets shop.
- Blaze Fast-Fire'd Pizza (LD $) is a counter-service pizzaria.
- Chicken Guy! (LD $) is a very popular counter-service restaurant with chicken dishes created by Guy Fieri.
- Coca-Cola Store Rooftop Beverage Bar (S $) is a full-service lounge.
- The Daily Poutine (S $) is a counter-service French fry restaurant.
- D-Luxe Burger (LD $) is a counter-service burger joint with tasty barbecue options.
- Frontera Cocina (LD $$) serves American and Mexican-inspired dishes.
- Planet Hollywood (LD $$) serves American fare created by celebrity chef Guy Fieri in a planetorium setting. Come "dine amongst the stars."

- The Polite Pig (LD $) is the newest barbecue joint on the property. Get your favorite meats and sides in this fun counter-service environment.
- Sprinkles (S $) has creative cupcakes and ice cream desserts. Try the cupcake ATM for a quick treat!
- Stargazers Bar (S $) is an outdoor lounge attached to Planet Hollywood. Enjoy appetizers and adult beverages to live music entertainment.
- Wolfgang Puck Bar & Grill (L,D $$) is a popular signature dining restaurant by the famous chef.

Entertainment in Town Center

- Live music plays at Springs Overlook throughout the day.

West Side

Disney Springs West Side hosts most of the entertainment venues that Disney Springs has to offer. Flying high on one side of this neighborhood is the tethered Aerophile balloon, while the other end is capped with the giant circus tent-like structure that houses Cirque du Soleil's *Drawn to Life* show.

Between these locations are a number of Disney and non-Disney retail locations. These include:

Where to Shop in West Side

- Disney's Candy Cauldron is West Side's answer to Goofy's Candy Company, though it is much smaller. Stop by the outside window to watch candy makers creating candy apples and other confections.
- Disney Style sells trendy Disney apparel and accessories.
- House of Blues Gear Shop has unique folk art, music-themed souvenirs and clothing, as well as House of Blues merchandise.

Shopping Venues

Insider's Tip!

If you find the noise and congestion of Disney Springs overwhelming, relief is just a (free!) boat ride away. Take one of the water taxis to any of the five Disney hotels which are accessible along canals, past golf courses. There is no charge to take the boats between the hotels and Disney Springs along the scenic waterways. Each hotel has a unique theme, restaurants, lounges, and the two Port Orleans properties even boast free live entertainment on select evenings!

Shopping Venues

- M&M's™ is a kid favorite, selling everything from the signature candy to clothing and souvenirs.
- Memory Lanes is Splitsville Luxury Lanes' gift shop. You can advertise your love of bowling with any number of Splitsville-branded items here.
- NBA Store is the souvenir shop attached to the popular NBA Experience. It sells everything a basketball fan could want.
- Pelé Soccer will appeal to the hardcore soccer fanatic, providing everything from your favorite team's jersey to sports gear.
- Sosa Family Cigars is the place to go if you desperately need a few minutes away from the kids for a nicotine fix. They sell imports and hand-rolled cigars for the connoisseur.
- Star Wars Galactic Outpost is the single on-property location to find your favorite themed merchandise from one of the most popular franchises in movie history.
- Sunglass Icon is a specialty version of the Sunglass Hut stores found in many outlet malls. Unlike most Sunglass Huts, this store only has the most current models, sending last season's glasses to other Sunglass Huts to sell. Except on Black Friday, sunglasses here rarely go on sale.

- Super Hero Headquarters is the place for Marvel fans. Find clothing, toys, accessories, and other unique items.

Where to Dine in West Side

- AMC Disney Springs 24 Dine-In Theatres (LD $) offers a variety of meals and drinks to eat while you watch a movie. It's a great way to do dinner and a movie, while saving time.
- City Works Eatery & Pour House (LD $$) provides gourmet burgers and a great beer selection. Located with the NBA Experience, it's an upscale sports bar everyone will enjoy.
- Everglazed Donuts & Cold Brew (S $) is a shout-out to the classic donut shop experience.
- Food Trucks at Exposition Park (LD $) is a popular location with a variety of food trucks, each offering unique cuisine to pick up and go.
- The Front Porch (S $) is a lounge seated on the porch of House of Blues. You will often find a musician playing music to entertain the crowds here.
- Haagen-Dazs (S $) is an ice cream kiosk that sells specialty ice cream desserts from the famous maker.
- House of Blues Restaurant & Bar (LD $$) serves New Orlean's-based,

Insider's Tip!

If you really want to make an effort to get discounts, try befriending a Disney Cast Member on your vacation. Your new friend may be willing to use his/her discount for you or even get you into their exclusive on-property discount store reserved only for Cast Members and their families.

Insider's Tip!

Souvenir rain ponchos do a better job of keeping people dry than umbrellas and can be worn on water rides. Disney sells rain ponchos at the theme parks. For a fraction of the cost, you can purchase ponchos at Target and Walmart that are more durable and have all of your favorite characters on them, including Disney Princesses for the little ones! If you get a branded, quality poncho, your kids will be able to use them when it rains back home and remember the fun times from your trip.

Cajun-Creole foods, but it also has a number of American classics, such as hamburgers. We particularly enjoy the sweet potato fries and the live music played inside out and most nights.

- Jaleo by José Andrés (D $$) is an upscale signature restaurant with a Spanish flare.
- MacGUFFINS (LD $) is the restaurant and bar inside of the AMC movie theatre. However, you don't need a movie ticket to eat here. There is a restaurant and full bar located at the Dine-In Theatre entrance that's open to anyone, and the alcoholic drinks there are some of the cheapest on-property.
- Pepe by José Andrés (L,D $) serves Spanish influenced sandwiches from its to-go window.
- The Smokehouse (LD $) is a popular place to get smoked meats on Disney property. Enjoy all of your outdoor favorites from this counter-service to go restaurant located right in front of House of Blues.
- Splitsville Luxury Lanes isn't just bowling. You can get everything from sushi to burgers here, either while you bowl or at a separately seated table. No fewer than three bars also serve guests here, the

outdoor bar often featuring live musicians.

- Starbucks at Disney Springs West Side (BLDS $) is Disney Springs' indoor location for these world famous coffees. You can also sit down inside and enjoy small food portions and snacks from the coffee giant.
- Wetzel's Pretzels (S $) is the West Side's kiosk location for the delicious pretzels and snacks.
- YeSake (S $) has Japanese-inspired wraps.

Entertainment in West Side
Entertainment is what West Side is all about. From shows to music to bowling, there's enough here to keep guests busy for days. Here is a list of the featured venues:

- AMC Movies at Disney Springs 24 is a very large movie theatre with two sides, one a standard movie theatre, the other a dine-in location with reserved, extra-comfortable seating.
- Aerophile: The World Leader in Balloon Flight boasts that it is the world's largest tethered helium

balloon. You can pay $25 ($20 for children) to fly 400 feet above Disney Springs for eight to ten minutes, grabbing an amazing view of the parks in the distance. The 19 foot wide basket holds up to 29 people plus the pilot, though it often ascends with fewer guests. You can't bring strollers or motorized vehicles on board. Disabled guests need to transfer to a standard wheelchair. Operating hours for this attraction are 8:30 a.m. to 12 a.m., but it is completely dependent on the weather and often shuts down for high wind gusts of 22 mph or more. Check back later in the day if it's closed when you try to visit.

- House of Blues often has live entertainment for its restaurant guests. In addition, there is a separate concert venue (House of Blues Music Hall) that gets a wide variety of live bands. Separate tickets must be purchased for the concerts.
- Cirque du Soleil presents a Disney-themed show called Drawn to Life, shown only at Disney Springs. Adults and children alike love the acrobatics and fun theme.
- Splitsville Luxury Lanes is the premier bowling alley in Orlando. It has two stories of bowling lanes, and the upstairs also has a pool table. Add to that multiple bars and dining, plus live music often playing at its outdoor lounge, and you can spend a whole day here.

As we mentioned above, there is no fee to visit or park at Disney Springs, and only Cirque du Soleil, NBA Experience, Aerophile, and the music venue attached to the House of Blues have entry charges.

On-site hotel guests get free transportation to the complex via bus. There are also a few Disney hotels that offer free boat transportation to/from Disney Springs: Saratoga Springs and Treehouse Villas Resorts, Old Key West Resort, Port Orleans French Quarter Resort, and Port Orleans Riverside Resort.

Off-site guests can also use Disney's free bus system to travel to Disney Springs from the Transportation and Ticket Center or any of the Disney hotels. However, buses do not run directly between the theme parks and Disney Springs. If you plan to park at Disney Springs and go to one of the theme parks, you will need to take a bus to one of the Disney hotels or the Transportation and Ticket Center, and transfer from there.

Disney's BoardWalk

Disney's BoardWalk is a smaller dining, shopping, and entertainment location than Disney Springs. However, it offers Signature dining locations and street-type entertainment in a serene, waterfront setting, making this a favorite hangout for locals and Disney guests who are "in the know."

The BoardWalk is located between Epcot and Hollywood Studios and is accessible to each via boat, bus, or on foot. This shopping, restaurant, and hotel venue is best described as an idealized replication of a 1930s-circa East Coast waterfront resort. The area is anchored by the BoardWalk Inn & Villas, a Disney Vacation Club resort property, and the adjacent convention center.

Some of the more popular destinations here include the Wyland art gallery; a family-oriented ESPN sports bar; and an Italian restaurant. The Flying Fish Café is a favorite for seafood on Disney property.

There are also two adults-only nightclub venues (the only adults-only locations on Disney property!): Jellyrolls, a dueling piano bar, and Atlantic Dance

Hall, a DJ-emcee'd dancing club. You must be at least 21 years old to gain entry to these venues.

The BoardWalk is free to visit and has free parking for guests with valid dining reservations. Two adult-oriented bars have cover charges. To get there, you must park at The BoardWalk Inn hotel and either go through the hotel or use the stairs to the right of the hotel entryway.

Saving Money on Souvenirs

Generally speaking, Disney does not offer discounted merchandise at its retail stores in the parks or at the resort hotels. There are two nearby outlet malls (both called Orlando Premium Outlets) that have deeply discounted yet authentic Disney Parks merchandise. (Be aware that some items at these stores are still full price.) You will need transportation to get to these locations, and parking can be a challenge at peak times of the year. The selection is typically very similar at both malls, so most people choose to visit the store closest to Disney on Vineland Avenue.

Another great option for purchasing discounted souvenirs is online at the Disney Store (www.disneystore.com). They sell many of the exact same authentic Disney Parks items you would purchase at the parks, and if you sign up to receive emails, they often have sales promotions for those very items with free shipping. If you expect that you'll be simply holding on to the souvenirs for a Christmas or birthday gift, this can be an excellent money-saving option. This is also a good choice if you are planning ahead and can order merchandise *before* your trip. Don't forget that you can also have anything you purchase at a Walt Disney World store shipped directly to your residence to eliminate having to take them home in your luggage.

Other Options

Many people really don't care if their souvenirs or children's toys and T-shirts are stamped with the authentic Disney Parks logo. For those people, there are dozens of roadside souvenir stores all around Orlando. Surprisingly, some of the best deals can often be found at Target or Walmart stores, where you can find Disney and Florida branded merchandise.

Disney World's Four Major Theme Parks

The Magic Kingdom
Epcot
Hollywood Studios
Animal Kingdom

This is a unique guide book with an immense level of detail about Walt Disney World. Because we don't want to spoil the magic for anyone, we have divided our description into two separate volumes.

In this first volume, we share information about what to expect during your trip without the spoilers. You'll find a brief overview of each park and summaries of all the major shows and attractions. Details of each on-property restaurant are provided, including how much you can expect to spend and whether or not you can use Disney Dining Plan credits at that location. (Disney Dining Plans are optional add-ons to Disney vacation packages.)

Look for our top suggestions and tips to make your days as efficient as possible. You'll learn everything you absolutely <u>need</u> to know by reviewing these park summaries. These tips are where you'll get all the essentials you need to make your visit a great one.

The following few pages summarize important information you'll need to keep handy as you begin your trip.

Insider's Tip!

Walk-through and Back Story. If you wish to delve into more details about each attraction – including the backstory and walk-through description – you'll want to read our next volume (coming soon!)

Not everybody wants to know all the little details in advance. If you are someone who likes surprises, appreciate that we keep *spoilers* to a bare minimum in this part. But once you have visited, the details we share in our upcoming volume will help you re-live your experiences and also let you read about what you might have missed.

Insider's Tip!

Use your smart phone to take pictures of the pages and information you want to keep handy each day of your trip, so you can easily find it without thumbing through the entire book.

Disney World's Four Major Theme Parks

Park Primer

Base Admission Prices (February 2022 – One Day Pass)*

Adults	$109-159
Children (3-9 years old)	$104-154
Children under 3 years old	Free

*Price changes based on value, regular, peak season, or weekend dates. Disney increases prices every year in February.

How to Get Around the World

Magic Kingdom	Monorail; Bus (from resorts directly to the park); FriendShip boat from Magic Kingdom resorts to the park; or Ferry from TTC
Epcot	Monorail from TTC; FriendShip Boat or Syliner from Epcot resorts; or Bus

Note: Walking path connects Epcot, Epcot resorts, and Hollywood Studios

Hollywood Studios	Bus, Skyliner, or FriendShip Boat from Epcot Park and resorts
Animal Kingdom	Bus only

Parking

Except for the Magic Kingdom, parking is available at each park. After securing your vehicle, you can travel to the front of each park by tram or by foot. If you are traveling to the Magic Kingdom, parking is provided at the Transportation and Ticket Center (TTC).

Transportation and Ticket Center (TTC)

Many off-property hotel shuttles drop you off only at the Transportation and Ticket Center (TTC).

After arriving by shuttle, bus, or after parking your private car, you can travel to **Epcot** by monorail or bus. Catch a bus if you need to get to **Hollywood Studios** or **Animal Kingdom**.

After arriving at the TTC, you have a choice to reach the **Magic Kingdom**: Express monorail (5 minutes), Resort monorail (10 minutes), or Ferry boat (7 minutes).

Note: You can reach each park directly by bus from any Disney Resort. Buses are available from the TTC to take guests to any other park, to any Disney resort, and to Disney Springs.

Insider's Tip!

At peak periods, or when you see a long line at the monorail station, it may be faster to take the Ferry or the Resort monorail, as many people choose to wait in the Express monorail lines.

General Hours and When to Arrive

The following times are approximate. During peak periods and seasonal events, opening "rope drop" may occur (up to 30 or 60 minutes) before the official scheduled opening of each park, and the parks may be open later in the evening. When rope drop coincides with the official opening, guests are held at the entrance turnstiles. For details and daily schedules refer to the Times Guide, Disney's My Disney Experience app, Disneyworld.com, or call (407) 824-4321.

Magic Kingdom	9 a.m. to 9 p.m. Plan to show up 30 minutes early. If you can't arrive before 10 a.m., avoid the morning crush and arrive after lunch (1 p.m.) or later.
	Early Closures: The Hall of Presidents, The Country Bear Jamboree, and Tom Sawyer Island close at dusk.
Epcot	Future World hours: 9 a.m. to 9 p.m. Plan to arrive just before park opening.
	Early Closures: Close at 7 p.m.: Innoventions, Living with the Land, Imagination, Journey Into Imagination
	World Showcase hours: 11 a.m. to 9 p.m.
Hollywood Studios	9 a.m. to about 1 hour after sunset. Plan to arrive at least 30 minutes before opening to get boarding passes for Star Wars: Rise of the Resistance.
Animal Kingdom	9 a.m. to 7 p.m. Plan to arrive about 30 minutes early.
	Early Closures: Close at dusk: Rafiki's Planet Watch, Pangani Forest Trail, Maharajah Jungle Trek

Getting Around the Park

Lay of the Land: All parks have a Central Plaza (the "Hub"). Bridges over waterways or corridors between the main promenade serve to provide passage through each themed land. In addition to providing access, these sections also mark transitions and boundaries between lands. Most parks have a "hub and spoke" design where the lands are found along the "wheel rim" and passage is found via "spokes" and a promenade that gradually circles the hub.

Guest Relations and Information

Guest Relations is available at the front of each park. This is where you can pick up Guidemaps and Time Guides, make restaurant reservations, or get assistance with any other theme park or resort issues. This is also where you find Lost and Found.

Guidemaps and Times Guides

As soon as you arrive, you find *Guidemaps* and *Times Guides* available at distribution kiosks just inside each entrance. They are also found at Guest Relations and at many retail locations throughout the parks. These are updated weekly with entertainment listings and character greeting times and locations.

Location to Find Popular Attraction Listings & Estimated Standby Times

Magic Kingdom	At end of Mainstreet, U.S.A. at Hub entrance
Epcot	Innoventions Plaza near The Land; Mission:SPACE
Hollywood Studios	At junction of Hollywood and Sunset Boulevards
Animal Kingdom	Discovery Island near Wilderness Explorer Headquarters

Cast Member-Attended Lockers

Lockers are available at the TTC and inside each park: $7-$15 per day for unlimited use (within a single park). Pay directly at the lockers using cash or credit, or with the attendant if using a MagicBand or gift card.

Lost & Found

Same day: Report to Guest Relations or TTC

Claim recovered items: (407) 824-4245

Lost Children

Alert nearest Cast Member, then travel to City Hall (Magic Kingdom) or a Baby Care Center (Other Parks).

Medical Emergencies and First Aid

Call 911 or alert nearest Cast Member. First Aid Centers are located next to Baby Care Centers (listed below) for minor issues.

Camera Centers

Located near the entrance of each park.

Magic Kingdom	Box Office Gifts in Town Square Theater
Epcot	Camera Center in Entrance Plaza and World Traveler at International Gateway
Hollywood Studios	The Darkroom on Hollywood Boulevard
Animal Kingdom	Garden Gate Gifts; Disney Outfitters; Duka La Filimu; Mombasa Marketplace; Chester and Hester's Dinosaur Treasures

Baby Care Centers

Magic Kingdom	Next to Crystal Palace Restaurant
Epcot	Odyssey Center between Test Track and Mexico
Hollywood Studios	Next to Guest Relations at park entrance
Animal Kingdom	Discovery Island near Creature Comforts

Strollers (Pushchairs)

Stroller rental stations are available just as you enter each park. Rental rates are $15 per day for a single and $31 per day for doubles.

• • • • • • • •

Multiple Day Stroller Rentals: Obtain a "Length of Stay Ticket" for multi-day rentals to get $2-$4 per day discounts (i.e., $13 or $27 per day).

• • • • • • • •

Retain receipt to get same-day replacements at any park.

Special Children's Activities

Magic Kingdom	Sorcerers of the Magic Kingdom interactive card game; Pirates of the Caribbean treasure hunt game
Epcot	Duck Tales World Showcase Adventure; Kidcot arts and crafts
Hollywood Studios	Jedi Training: Trials of the Temple
Animal Kingdom	Wilderness Explorers

Insider's Tip!

Rely on Disney's strollers at your own peril. They are made with hard plastic shells that are not comfortable for children. If you must use these, bring along an extra blanket or two for your child to sit or lay on. Instead, bring a stroller from home or purchase an inexpensive (umbrella) stroller from a discount retailer after you arrive. If you don't want to take it home, you can easily leave it behind at a park or any resort. If you want a nicer model, very comfortable ones are available for rent from private companies.

Insider's Tip!

"Stroller Express" services may be available during peak times. This allows you to pre-pay and bypass lines.

Wheelchair and Electronic Conveyance Vehicle (ECV) Rentals

Wheelchair and ECV rental stations are available just as you enter each park. Rental rates are $12 per day for a wheelchair and $50 per day for ECV (with required $20 refundable deposit). "Quantities are limited."

• • • • • • • •

Multiple Day Wheelchair and ECV Rentals: Obtain a "Length of Stay Ticket" for multi-day wheelchair rentals for $2 per day discounts (i.e., $10 per day). Multi-day ECV rentals are not available (first come-first served each day).

• • • • • • • •

Retain receipt to get same-day replacements at any park.

Disabled Guests

Available services are detailed in each park's *Guide for Guests with Disabilities* (available at Guest Relations). Excellent parking is available for disabled guests with a placard issued by your home state, and most of the World's facilities are accessible to guests in wheelchairs. Deluxe Disney resorts also offer free valet parking to disabled guests if self-parking spaces are scarce.

Magic Kingdom: The disabled ramp to the monorail at the TTC is relatively steep. Disabled guests may prefer to take the ferry.

Package Pickup

You can arrange to have (most) of your merchandise purchases delivered to the front of the park for pickup when you leave. Allow three hours for this service.

Delivery Service: If you are staying on-property, you can also have packages delivered directly to your Disney resort for no charge.

Package Pickup Locations

Magic Kingdom	Main Street Chamber of Commerce, next to City Hall
Epcot	Gift Shop in Entrance Plaza or International Gateway in World Showcase
Hollywood Studios	Next to Oscar's Super Service at entrance
Animal Kingdom	Garden Gate Gifts

Park Rules

- All bags, backpacks, and purses are subject to inspection at the security checkpoint before getting to the park entrance. In late 2015, Disney added metal detectors after the initial bag check that all guests must pass through for screening.
- Proper attire is required.
- Smoking and vaping (use of E-cigarettes) are not permitted anywhere inside of theme parks. Guests must leave the park and use designated areas only, located outside the park entrance.
- Camera "selfie sticks" are not permitted.
- Weapons of any kind are not permitted.
- Glass bottles are not permitted.
- Oversized and "wagon"-style strollers are not permitted.
- To visit a park, children under 14 years old must be accompanied by a responsible person who is at least 14 years old.

For a complete listing of all rules: disney.com/ParkRules

- Same Day Re-entry: Keep your pass or MagicBand handy to gain re-entry.
- Purchases: Refer to the Guidemap for ATM locations. Cash, credit cards, Apple Pay, gift cards, and Disney Dollars can be used at retail and restaurant locations.

Download More Planning Checklists and View Our Complete Attractions & Entertainment Information Table At:

bit.ly/DisneyPlanners

Disney World's Four Major Theme Parks

Magic Kingdom Attraction Planner
Date of Visit: _____

Like To Do	Must-Do Priorities	Attraction Name	Min Height	Genie+/ Ala Carte LL
		A Pirates Adventure ~ Treasures of the Seven Seas		
		Astro Orbiter		
		Beacons of Magic		
		Big Thunder Mountain Railroad	40"	G+
		Buzz Lightyear Space Ranger Spin		G+
		Country Bear Jamboree		
		Disney Enchantment		
		Disney Festival of Fantasy Parade		
		Dumbo the Flying Elephant		G+
		Enchanted Tales with Belle		
		Festival of Fantasy Parade		
		Frontierland Shootin' Arcade		
		"it's a small world"		G+
		Jungle Cruise		G+
		Let the Magic Begin (Opening Ceremony)		
		Liberty Square Riverboat		
		Mad Tea Party		G+
		Mickey's PhilharMagic		G+
		Monsters, Inc. Laugh Floor		G+
		Peter Pan's Flight		G+
		Pirates of the Caribbean		G+
		Seven Dwarfs Mine Train	38"	Ala Carte LL
		Space Mountain	44"	G+
		Splash Mountain	40"	G+
		Swiss Family Treehouse		
		The Barnstormer	35"	G+
		The Hall of Presidents		
		The Haunted Mansion		G+
		The Magic Carpets of Aladdin		G+
		The Many Adventures of Winnie the Pooh		G+
		Tom Sawyer Island		
		Tomorrowland Speedway	32" or 54"	G+
		Tron Lightcycle Power Run	48"	Ala Carte LL
		Under the Sea ~ Journey of The Little Mermaid		G+
		Walt Disney's Carousel of Progress		
		Walt Disney's Enchanted Tiki Room		

Date of Visit: _____

Like To Do	Must-Do Priorities	Attraction Name	Min Height	Genie+/ Ala Carte LL
		Advanced Training Lab		
		American Heritage Gallery		
		Awesome Planet		
		Beacons of Magic		
		Beauty & The Beast Sing-Along		
		Bijutsu-kan Gallery		
		Buzz Lightyear Space Ranger Spin		
		Bruce's Shark World		
		Canada Far and Wide		
		Disney & Pixar Short Film Festival		G+
		Frozen Ever After		G+
		Gallery of Arts and History (Race Against the Sun)		
		Guardians of The Galaxy: Cosmic Rewind		Ala Carte LL
		Gran Fiesta Tour Starring The Three Caballeros		
		Harmonious		
		House of the Whispering Willows		
		ImageWorks - "The What If" Labs		
		Impressions de France		
		Journey Into Imagination w/Figment		G+
		Living with the Land		G+
		Mexico Folk Art Gallery		
		Mission: SPACE	40" or 44"	G+
		Project Tomorrow: Inventing the Wonders of the Future		
		Reflections of China		
		Remy's Ratatouille Adventure		G+
		SeaBase Aquarium		
		Soarin' Around the World	40"	G+
		Spaceship Earth		G+
		Stave Church Gallery		
		Test Track	40"	G+
		The American Adventure		
		The Seas with Nemo & Friends		G+
		Turtle Talk with Crush		G+

Hollywood Studios Attraction Planner
Date of Visit: _____

Like To Do	Must-Do Priorities	Attraction Name	Min Height	Genie+/ Ala Carte LL
		Alien Swirling Saucers	32"	G+
		Beacons of Magic		
		Beauty & The Beast - Live on Stage		G+
		Disney Junior Play and Dance!		G+
		Disney Movie Magic		
		Fantasmic!		G+
		For the First Time in Forever: Frozen Sing-Along		G+
		Indiana Jones™ Epic Stunt Spectacular!		G+
		Lightning McQueen's Racing Academy		
		Mickey & Minnie's Runaway Railway		G+
		Millenium Falcon: Smuggler's Run	38"	G+
		Muppet*Vision 3D		G+
		Rock 'n' Roller Coaster	48"	G+
		Slinky Dog Dash	38"	G+
		Star Tours - The Adventures Continue	40"	G+
		Star Wars Launch Bay		
		Star Wars: Rise of the Resistance	40"	Ala Carte LL
		The Twilight Zone Tower of Terror™	40"	G+
		Toy Story Mania!		G+
		Vacation Fun - An Original Animated Short		
		Voyage of The Little Mermaid		
		Walt Disney Presents		
		Wonderful World of Animation		

Animal Kingdom Attraction Planner
Date of Visit: _____

Like To Do	Must-Do Priorities	Attraction Name	Min Height	Genie+/ Ala Carte LL
		A Celebration of Festival of the Lion King		G+
		Affection Section		
		Avatar Flight of Passage	44"	Ala Carte LL
		Beacons of Magic		
		Conservation Station		
		DINOSAUR	40"	G+
		Discovery Island Trails		
		Disney KiteTails		
		Expedition Everest	44"	G+
		Feathered Friends in Flight!		G+
		Finding Nemo - The Big Blue...and Beyond!		
		Fossil Fun Games		
		Gorilla Falls Exploration Trail		
		Habitat Habit!		
		It's Tough to be a Bug!		G+
		Kali River Rapids	38"	G+
		Kilimanjaro Safaris		G+
		Maharajah Jungle Trek		
		Na'vi River Journey		G+
		The Animation Experience at Conservation Station		G+
		The Boneyard		
		The Oasis Exhibits		
		Tree of Life Awakenings		
		TriceraTop Spin		
		Wilderness Explorers		
		Wildlife Express Train		
		Winged Encounters - The Kingdom Takes Flight		

Disney World's Four Major Theme Parks

Download More Planning Checklists and View Our Complete Attractions & Entertainment Information Table At:

bit.ly/DisneyPlanners

Special Events and Tours

Magic Kingdom Events and Entertainment

Name	Type	Location
Bibbidi Bobbidi Boutique	Premium Experience	Cinderella's Castle
Casey's Corner Pianist	Street Performance	Casey's Corner, Main Street, U.S.A.
Citizens of Main Street	Street Performance	Main Street, U.S.A.
The Dapper Dans	Street Performance	Main Street, U.S.A.
Disney's Family Magic Tour	Tour ($39 per person)	Various
Disney Festival of Fantasy Parade	Parade	Main Street, U.S.A.
Disney's Keys to the Kingdom Tour	Tour ($99 per person)	Various
The Magic Behind Our Steam Trains Tour	Tour ($54 per person)	Various
Electrical Water Pageant	Floating Parade	Seven Seas Lagoon
Flag Retreat Ceremony	Street Performance	Town Square Flagpole
Harmony Barber Shop	Premium Experience	Main Street, U.S.A.
#INCREDIBLESSuperDanceParty	Music & Dance Party	Tomorrowland
Let the Magic Begin	Show (Park Opening)	Castle Courtyard
Main Street Philharmonic	Show	Main Street, U.S.A
Main Street Trolley Show	Street Performance	Main Street, U.S.A.
Mickey's Royal Friendship Faire	Stage Performance	Castle Courtyard
Move It! Shake It! Dance & Play It! Street Party	Parade	Main Street, U.S.A.
The Muppets Presents...Great Moments in American History	Street Performance	Liberty Square
The Notorious Banjo Brothers and Bob	Street Performance	Frontierland
Once Upon A Time	Show	Main Street, U.S.A.
The Royal Majesty Makers	Street Performance	Fantasyland
Taste of the Magic Kingdom	Tour (Price TBA)	TBA
Ultimate Day of Thrills	Tour ($299 per person)	Various
Ultimate Day for Young Families	Tour ($299 per person)	Various
Walt Disney: Marceline to Magic Kingdom Tour	Tour ($49 per person)	Various
Disney Enchantment Nighttime Spectacular	Fireworks	Main Street, U.S.A.

Note: Many tours and many special events are currently on-hold for Covid-19. However, we are listing the tours and events we expect to return soon.

Walt Disney: Marceline to Magic Kingdom Tour

This three-hour walking tour covers a lot of ground, both literally and figuratively, as it takes an in-depth look at the park through Walt's eyes. It focuses on Walt's boyhood in the small, railroad town of Marceline, Missouri, and how his childhood influenced his vision of the Magic Kingdom.

Interesting anecdotes are shared about his familial influences, as well as the huge impact of the 1964 New York World's Fair where his Abraham Lincoln Audio-Animatronic debuted and excited the public. While not an exact replica of Marceline, guests learn how Main Street, U.S.A. reflects Walt's idealized version of his Midwestern hometown and how he saw it with his heart. The tour covers Liberty Square, Fantasyland, Cinderella's Castle, and concludes in Tomorrowland.

With an exclusive "behind-the-scenes" glimpse of some attractions, the tour reviews their evolutions and the challenges of designing and implementing these world-class, magical experiences. Like Keys to the Kingdom, earpieces allow guests to stay in communication with the guide throughout rides and learn inside details about props, special effects, and attraction storylines.

Should you schedule a tour early in the morning, be sure to take advantage of the photo ops along a near empty Main Street, U.S.A. The tour is geared toward adults, but guests as young as 12 are welcome if accompanied by a paying adult. Please check in at the Town Square Theater within Main Street USA at least 15 minutes prior to the start of the tour. You will forfeit the tour price if you don't show or cancel within two days of your reservation.

Note that the only option for getting to the Magic Kingdom from the Transportation and Ticket Center at that time of day is the Ferry Boat, as the Monorails do not run that early. Late arrivals cannot join the tour so plan accordingly.

Bibbidi Bobbidi Boutique

Owned by Cinderella's Fairy Godmother and operated by her Godmothers-in-Training, *Bibbidi Bobbidi Boutique* is an "enchanted beauty salon" where young guests experience magical make-overs into fairytale princesses or knights. Located in Cinderella Castle, the royal spa offers a variety of differently priced packages for hair, nails, make-up, costuming, accessories, and photography. For example, the "Disney Frozen Package" includes your choice of the Anna or Elsa hairstyles and costumes, and the "Knight Package" includes hairstyling with gel, a mighty sword & shield, and confetti.

Enormously popular, appointments are recommended and can be made 180 days in advance. Plan to spend 30 minutes to an hour at the salon, and arrive at least 15 minutes prior to your appointment. To make reservations, call 407-WDW-STYLE (407-939-7895) and advise which costume your princess wants, as well as sizes for clothing and shoes. Guests are also welcome to wear previously purchased costumes.

A valid credit card number is requested at time of booking, and a cancelation fee will be applied for no-shows or cancelation within 24 hours of reservation.

Casey's Corner Pianist

Casey's Corner, the charming hot dog shop at the end of Main Street, U.S.A. also features live music: a talented pianist interacts with the crowd while performing Disney and ragtime songs.

The catchy and engaging tunes are a definite crowd pleaser, and many guests can't help but sing along. These songs from a bygone era will put a smile on your face, so stop by for some good old fashioned entertainment (and a foot-long hot dog).

Citizens of Main Street

A theatrical troupe attired in 19th-century costumes, the *Citizens of Main Street* mingle, sing, and talk with guests as they busily make their way through Main Street, U.S.A. Throughout the day, you can meet and take photos with a variety of citizens, such as Smokey Miller, the Fire Department Chief, Inga DaPointe (Fashion Editor of the Main Street Gazette), or even The Honorable Mayor Christopher George Weaver. Bringing smiles to all who pass by, the Citizens of Main Street appearances are unscheduled, so be on the lookout.

The Dapper Dans

This dapper, barbershop quartet has been entertaining guests on Main Street, U.S.A. since 1971. Bringing the past back to life with their four-part harmony and playful banter, *The Dapper Dans* entertain up and down Main Street with classic Disney numbers such as *Zip-a-Dee Doo Dah* and *Cruella de Vil*, as well American classics such as *Yankee Doodle Dandy*, *Mr. Sandman*, and even an occasional contemporary pop song.

In addition to singing a capella harmony, *The Dapper Dans* also tap dance and perform vaudeville comedic routines.

The group's schedule is sometimes in the Times Guide, and they can usually be found in the Main Street Trolley Parade as well as the daily Flag Retreat. (Side Note: On October 13, 2014, *The Dapper Dans* made a surprise performance on Southwest Airlines' first nonstop flight from Dallas to Orlando. Passengers were treated to songs like *Let It Go* and *A Dream Is a Wish Your Heart Makes*.) The shows are about 20 minutes long.

Disney's Family Magic Tour

This "high-energy interactive quest" is basically a guided scavenger hunt on behalf of Donald Duck who lost several of Mickey Mouse's items that are now scattered throughout the park. Your job is to solve the riddles, locate the items, and return them to Mickey.

The tour begins at the Town Square Theater where you and a few other families will decipher clues and embark on your hunt. As you journey from clue to clue, you are taken on an attraction, meet some surprise character guests, and stop for a break. At the conclusion of your quest, you return all of the lost items to a character.

All ages will enjoy this exciting adventure, however it's best for kids ages four through ten. Be sure to check the weather forecast and dress appropriately. Bring water, snacks, a camera, and remember to wear comfortable shoes for the two-hour tour. Guests check in at the Town Square Theater 15 minutes prior to your experience. Cancelations must be made two days in advance to avoid forfeiting the entire price of the tour.

Disney's Festival of Fantasy Parade

Typically starting at 2 p.m. in Frontierland near *Splash Mountain* and winding through Main Street, U.S.A., *Disney's*

Festival of Fantasy Parade presents "Mickey and his Fantasyland Friends" through a series of floats, music, and brightly costumed dancers.

Displaying a mix of classic and contemporary Disney characters, many of the floats' pieces are interactive and very tall, allowing optimal visibility for children. Rapunzel leads the *Tangled* float, a huge ship on which characters sway from side to side on pendulums. Maleficent, the villain from *Sleeping Beauty*, appears in dragon form and sporadically breathes fire (which may be scary to very young children).

Ariel sits high on a seashell throne, surrounded by adorable fish dancing the conga. Peter Pan and Wendy are in the front of a pirate ship with Captain Hook in the back, cowering as a menacing crocodile chases the float. Tinker Bell makes a delightful appearance from a special nook at the end of the ship. The grand finale features Pegasus horses, dancing hippos, and pink-haired Bubble Girls celebrating Storybook Circus. Mickey and Minnie Mouse float high above the crowd aboard a giant hot-air balloon called Mickey's Airship.

Since there is only one showing of this parade daily (weather permitting), be prepared to find a good viewing spot at least 45 minutes prior for front row viewing. Genie+ Lightning Lane is available for a reserved viewing area. Fast paced, colorful, and supported by a soaring soundtrack, *Disney's Festival of Fantasy Parade* is a definite crowd pleaser.

Disney's Keys to the Kingdom Tour

Keys to the Kingdom is a five-hour walking tour of the Magic Kingdom which includes some behind-the-scenes access, two rides, lunch, and a commemorative pin. Cast Members provide name tags and listening devices so guests can hear the tour guide even from several yards away.

The name derives from the four main "keys" on which Disney operates: Safety, Courtesy, Show, and Efficiency. The tour demonstrates how these keys of service work together to ensure that guests have a truly magical experience.

Little known secrets, such as how the color of the pavement changes to show a change in grade, are revealed. Water and restroom breaks are spaced throughout, and the tour ends with the Utilidors, the underground tunnel system which houses operations such as plumbing, electric, garbage removal, the computer system, and also allows Cast Members and characters to travel from one part of the park to another unseen by guests.

There is no photography allowed back stage, and children under 16 are not permitted as they may be exposed to characters without their full costumes. Discounts are available for annual pass holders, AAA members, and DVC members. Be sure to wear good walking shoes, and book a tour that begins close to 9 a.m. for the treat of seeing the guests take off running after Rope Drop.

Disney's The Magic Behind Our Steam Trains Tour

There are very few places in the world where you can get close to an antique locomotive, and the trains of the Magic Kingdom are some of the rarest.

This three hour tour is for early risers, allowing participants to peek behind the scenes as railroad engineers prepare the magnificent beasts before park opening. The guide, who is required to have completed basic engineering training, gives very interesting information about the equipment used on the Walt Disney World Railroad as well as the history of the trains, the necessary refurbishment, the operations, the safety protocols, and the way they communicate with the bells and whistles. You even receive a one-of-a-kind commemorative pin!

Much of this tour is outdoors, so don't forget hats, sunglasses and sunscreen, water, and perhaps a light snack. Guests must be 10 years of age or older. Check in at the Main Entrance of Magic Kingdom park 15 minutes prior to the start of the tour. Cancel at least two days in advance to avoid forfeiting the entire price of your tour if you can't make it.

Mickey's Royal Friendship Faire

Mickey's Royal Friendship Faire is a live stage show performed on the Forecourt Stage, in front of Cinderella Castle. The lovable Mickey Mouse is inviting friends over for a party, and the opening routine has him and Minnie, Daisy, Donald, and Goofy dressed in amazing Renaissance costumes.

Performed daily, the cast includes appearances by Anna, Elsa, Olaf, Rapunzel, Tiana, and others. Just under 23 minutes, the show combines dialogue with song-and-dance numbers involving the princesses, as well as fireworks and special effects.

Because the area in front of the Castle slopes upward as you move away from it, optimal viewing is toward the Partners statue. Closer to the stage the floor is flat, so tall people or children-on-shoulders may block your view, and you will be forced to swivel to see everything onstage. There is no shade in the viewing area, so a morning or evening performance may be cooler.

Show times are listed in the Daily Times Guide, and the performance may be delayed or canceled for inclement weather so be sure to check the weather report.

Electrical Water Pageant

Originally presented for the dedication of the Polynesian Luau in 1971, this short and simple electronic show takes place nightly on the Seven Seas Lagoon and around Bay Lake (weather permitting).

Barges transport 25-foot tall lighted screens with displays of King Neptune and sea creatures such as turtles, whales, seahorses, and flying fish. The delightful floating parade concludes with an inspirational salute to America, when the screens change to flashing American flags with twinkling stars set to a patriotic musical medley of *God Bless America*, *Yankee Doodle*, and *You're a Grand Old Flag*.

The parade can only be viewed from one of the three monorail hotels. Check with each Resort hotel front desk for show times. The *Electrical Water Pageant* remains one of the few original opening year shows to still be running at Walt Disney World.

When the Magic Kingdom Fireworks are scheduled for 9 p.m., the Electrical Water Pageant runs about seven to 20 minutes later.

Flag Retreat Ceremony

Modeled after a military ceremony called Evening Colors, the Magic Kingdom's *Flag Retreat Ceremony* pays tribute to the United States by honoring the American Flag. While Walt Disney himself was too young to join the Army during World War I, he did join the Red Cross so he could support the war effort. Walt was sent to France where he drove an ambulance for a year. Walt dedicated his parks "to the ideals, the dreams, and the hard facts that have created America… with hope that it will be a source of joy and inspiration to the world."

Since the Magic Kingdom opened, Disney has held this ceremony around the flagpole near the entrance where the American flag is solemnly lowered and folded for storage every day at 5 p.m. The Main Street Philharmonic and Dapper Dans begin the ceremony with a rendition of *God bless America* and other patriotic songs.

A few children are chosen to lead the crowd with a touching recital of the Pledge of Allegiance, and an honorary "veteran of the day" stands at attention and salutes as the Color Guard lower the flag. The flag, a certificate, and pin commemorating the event are then presented to the veteran while a history of his or her military service is read aloud.

The Band then falls into step and marches up Main Street followed by the Color Guard and the veteran carrying the flag close to his or her heart. The ceremony takes about 15 minutes.

Disney Enchantment

Magic Kingdom's fireworks show received a major overhaul for its 50th anniversary with multi-media evening spectacular.

Watch stories of friendship and love unfold in a fantasy world of projections, lasers, and lights that extend all the way from Cinderella Castle down Main Street, U.S.A. As you watch the incredible show, perfectly choreographed fireworks punctuate the night sky. This event is one you won't want to miss.

The Harmony Barber Shop

Unlike most of the quaint 1900s style buildings on Main Street, The Harmony Barber Shop is not a façade: it's a real barber shop with state-licensed cosmetologists who cut hair, trim facial hair, and dispense glitter pieces they call "Pixie Dust" (not to mention expertly manage the excited children in the barber chairs). You may even be treated to the

musical talents of *The Dapper Dans*, their resident barber shop quartet.

Though they cut hair for any age, the professional barbers specialize in first haircuts. For around $25, little ones can courageously endure their first haircut while inside the Magic Kingdom! To commemorate this special event, the child receives a certificate of bravery, a lock of their hair saved in a little pouch, Mickey stickers, and Mickey Ears that are embroidered with "My First Haircut."

For best results, come in with clean, dry hair as this is a high volume barber shop and not a salon.

Each appointment takes around 15 minutes, and (cash only) tips are welcome. The hours are typically 9 a.m. to 5 p.m., and advanced reservations are encouraged. Walk-ins are welcome, but not guaranteed as the small shop has only three barber chairs. Chances of being fit in are greatly improved during the 3 o'clock parade, and it is a good location for parade viewing.

#INCREDIBLESSuperDanceParty

The outdoor Rockettower Plaza Stage in Tomorrowland is transformed into the Agency Headquarters for a super-powered dance party to celebrate yet another successful mission of The Incredibles.

Join Mr. and Mrs. Incredible, Frozone, and their interactive DJ, Mr. Spin, as they tear up the dance floor to a body-shaking mix of current and classic tunes.

The costumes are incredibly real as the superheroes appear just like the actual cartoons, larger than life. The characters jump up and get down, but do not stop and pose or sign autographs.

This party starts nightly around 5 p.m. and runs continuously until close. Check the Daily Times Guide for the schedule.

Let the Magic Begin Opening Ceremony

Join one of the Royal Majest Makers as he welcomes guests each morning to the most magical place on Earth! "It is hereby decreed, that all are welcome in this happy place, where the young and young-at-heart can explore and laugh and play together. Here, where magic awaits you at every corner. Bursting with the joy and inspiration to make your dreams come true."

And so begins the opening show at the Magic Kingdom, typically five minutes before "rope drop" – that time when the ropes stretching across the entrance to each land are dropped, and the park is officially open to guests.

Performed on the castle forecourt stage inside the park, the Royal Herald introduces Mickey and several of his friends, including Chip, Dale, Merida, Jasmine, Aladdin, and even Cinderella's Stepsisters.

It is always a thrill to see a stage full of characters arrive to the park and welcome the guests, and they are soon joined by the Fairy Godmother who stands above in the castle balcony. The Fairy Godmother sprinkles her magic over the crowd and castle, ensuring there is enough magic to fill everyone's hearts as guests begin their day. She then leads the crowd to speak the magic words, "Bibbidi Bobbidi Boo" and "Let the Magic Begin!"

As the characters leave the stage, Mickey encourage everyone to enjoy the park before sharing a final, sweet kiss with Minnie. The gates officially open as the two leave the stage, allowing guests to flood the remaining lands.

Guaranteed to put you in a magical mood, the Welcome Show is a happy way to start your day at the Magic Kingdom. For optimal viewing, arrive at least 30 minutes prior to park opening and walk straight up Main Street, U.S.A. to the castle.

(To speed up the process of security checking your bags, open all compartments prior to reaching the security guard.)

Only about a third of guests make it to the park for rope drop, and this may be the only opportunity to walk Main Street with hardly anyone else around, providing for superb photo opps.

Once Upon A Time

Hosted by Mrs. Potts and Chip, *Once Upon A Time* is a truly magnificent nighttime projection show on Cinderella Castle. Beautifully set to Disney's most memorable music and stories, the special effects are simply breathtaking. Beloved Disney characters come together for a fantastical display that takes guests on a journey to the heart of Disney's most cherished stories.

Available for purchase are special "Made with Magic" items, such as Mickey ears that light up and glow in sync with the show. The best places to watch the show are on Main Street and the courtyard in front of the castle. Check the Times Guide each day for show times.

Disney World's Four Major Theme Parks

Disney World's Four Major Theme Parks

Epcot Events and Entertainment		
Name	**Type**	**Location**
Harmonious	Fireworks	World Showcase Lagoon
JAMMitors	Street Performance	Future World East
Jeweled Dragon Acrobats	Street Performance	China
Mariachi Cobre	Street Performance	Mexico
Matboukha Groove	Show	Morocco
Matsuriza	Show	Japan
Quickstep	Show	United Kingdom
Rose & Crown Pub Musician	Performance	Rose & Crown Pub, United Kingdom
Sergio	Street Performance	Italy
Voices of Liberty	Performance	American Adventure
British Revolution	Show	United Kingdom
Serveur Amusant	Street Performance	France
Wies N Baum	Show	Germany
Backstage Magic	Tour ($275 per person)	Various
Behind the Seeds	Tour ($20 per person)	The Land
Epcot Seas Adventure – Aqua Tour	Tour ($145 per person)	The Seas
Epcot Seas Adventure – DiveQuest	Tour ($179 per person)	The Seas
Epcot Seas Adventure – Dolphins in Depth	Tour ($199 per person)	The Seas
The UnDISCOVERed Future World	Tour ($69 per person)	Future World
World Showcase: DestiNations Discovered	Tour ($109 per person)	World Showcase
Holiday D-Lights Tour (Seasonal)	Tour ($199 per person)	Various
Yuletide Fantasy (Seasonal)	Tour ($79 per person)	Various

Backstage Magic Tour

Many people are fascinated with how Disney World operates, and this seven-hour tour is like the classic Disney short film Thru the Mirror where Mickey walks through a looking glass and enters a hidden world. Instead of traveling through a mirror, however, guests travel through a "Cast Members Only" door to a hidden world where workers diligently create Disney magic in a no-frills environment.

Exploring the inner workings of all four theme parks, plus two important areas outside the park, the tour is limited to groups of 20 and begins at Epcot promptly at 9 a.m. Though subject to change, guests can expect to go behind-the-scenes of "The American Adventure" show and see the huge structure located on a train-like track below the stage that mechanically delivers the Audio-Animatronics of the show. (This pavilion uses "forced perspective" in a manner opposite to Main Street U.S.A.: the American Adventure building appears to be three stories high, but is actually five stories. This was done so it blends in with the surrounding pavilions.)

The tour also visits the Creative Costuming Workroom in Hollywood Studios, where thousands of costumes are designed, created, and stored for characters, shows, and parades. One of the interesting facts revealed here is that the majority of fabrics and dyes used by Disney are trademarked. Next, the tour reviews the "Central Shops" warehouse, where, among other things, the ride vehicles are built, the carousel horses are refurbished, and the Audio-Animatronic workshop is located.

The tour of Animal Kingdom reveals how the lion's "Pride Rock" is cooled in the summer and heated in the winter to attract lions so they can be easily viewed from the safari vehicles. Lunch is usually held at Animal Kingdom's Wilderness Lodge, in a family-style barbecue that is abundant, delicious, and included in the tour price.

The Backstage Magic tour concludes at the Magic Kingdom, with a good portion spent in the "Utilidors," which are frequently referred to as tunnels as they are located underneath the park. Here guests learn that the Utilidors are actually the first floor of the Magic Kingdom, built to allow Cast Members and Land-themed Characters to move directly through the park unseen by guests and without clashing with other Land themes. Expect frequent security checks as you move from one off-limits area to another.

Comfortable bus transportation is provided as well as chilled, bottle water. For safety purposes, be sure to wear shoes with closed heels and toes, such as sneakers, as sandals, open-toe, or open-heel shoes are not permitted. Plan to arrive 15 minutes prior to the tour's scheduled start. No-shows forfeit the entire tour price unless reservations are canceled at least two days in advance. Photography of any kind is not permitted in the backstage area.

Behind the Seeds

Walt Disney's original vision of Epcot was for it to be a real city that would "never cease to be a blueprint of the future." Living with the Land is one of the few attractions to capture the spirit of classic Epcot, and its 90 minute walking tour, Behind the Seeds, offers terrific "edutainment" about the future of agricultural techniques, providing the opportunity to walk through the greenhouses seen from the boat attraction.

Guests are shown various methods for growing crops, such as "stacking" to save space and hydroponics for areas with poor soil. You also take part in a spice sensory challenge, a vegetable taste test, and a lady bug release (especially great for kids!) Children are given a handful of nutrition-filled pellets to feed a large tank of frenzied fish during the interactive element of the aquaculture area.

The tours are led by members of the botanical team at the Land, who are often graduate students in the agricultural sciences. Guests are encouraged to ask questions, and photography is encouraged. However, do not touch any plants – the greenhouses have exotic species from all over the world, providing the potential for unknown allergic reactions.

The tour is handicap accessible, but guests in ECVs must transfer to a wheelchair. The tour is not suitable for very small children. AAA, DVC members, annual passholders, as well as active military members are offered special discounts. Same day reservations are usually available. For reservations call 407-WDW-TOUR (407-939-868) or visit the reservation desk in Epcot, located in the lower level of the Land Pavilion right next to the Soarin' attraction. Tours start every 45 minutes between 10:30 a.m. - 4:30 p.m.

Epcot Seas Adventure – Aqua Tour

Swim with Nemo and 60,000 of his closest friends on an exciting snorkeling adventure through the magical coral reef habitat at Epcot's The Seas with Nemo & Friends Pavilion.

Presented by the National Association of Underwater Instructors (with profits going to conservation efforts), Epcot's Aqua Tour allows guests age eight and up to experience the other side of the glass inside the massive Epcot Aquarium. At 27 feet deep, all of Spaceship Earth could easily fit inside with plenty of room to spare. Including the filtration system, Epcot's inland salt water environment

is the largest of its kind (and the world's third larges aquarium!), holding 5.7 million gallons of saltwater and 65 species of marine life above a two feet deep floor of crushed seashells.

There are no waves and the visibility is optimized in the tank. The quantity and variety of creatures are spectacular. Guests begin the tour with an informational video about the sea and its creatures before being guided through the massive backstage infrastructure that filters and maintains the man-made coral reef habitat (which is so realistic that fish actually lay eggs on it).

The entire experience lasts 2.5 hours, 30 minutes of which are in the water. Snorkelers are outfitted with "Snuba" equipment, an easy-to-use scuba-assisted snorkel unit that keeps guests afloat and supplied with piped air. The swim is closely supervised and limited to the surface to comply with dive laws – another tour, DiveQuest, is available for SCUBA certified guests.

Tour groups are limited to 20, and the tank is large enough for participants to swim freely without intrusion from one another. Participants must wear their own swimsuits. No jewelry other than watches are allowed, and Disney provides hair ties that can be safely digested by the fish should they fall off inside the tank. Towels, shampoo, conditioner, body wash, and hair dryers are available in the shower stalls after the swim.

Since the tour is almost completely backstage, no pictures are allowed. Guests are given a complimentary photo as well as a souvenir, and Epcot admission is not required. Tours take place Tuesday - Saturday at 12:30 p.m. and can be booked by calling 407-WDW-TOUR (407-939-868) or online at Disneyworld.com. Be sure to ask if discounts are available.

Hollywood Studios Events and Entertainment		
Name	**Type**	**Location**
Citizens of Hollywood	Street Performance	Various
Disney Movie Magic	Show	Chinese Theater
Jedi Training: Trials of the Temple	Stage Performance	Echo Lake
March of the First Order	Parade/Show	Hollywood Boulevard
Mickey & Minnie Starring in Red Carpet Dreams	Show	Commissary Lane
Star Wars: A Galactic Spectacular	Fireworks	Hollywood Boulevard
Star Wars: A Galaxy Far, Far Away	Stage Show	Hollywood Boulevard

Disney Movie Magic

Each evening, watch the Chinese Theater transform to a giant movie screen in this 10-minute review of some of Disney's best movies.

Both live action and cartoon films are showcased with clips on the screen. Favorites include Pirates of the Caribbean and Indiana Jones.

Jedi Training — Trials of the Temple

Children between four and 12 years old can experience the excitement and danger of becoming a Jedi warrior. In this part show/part interactive adventure, children learn to confront their fears and battle the Dark Side.

FastPass+ is not available. However, children interested in being part of the show must register early in the day to attend.

Parents should take interested children to the *Indiana Jones Adventure Outpost* to sign-up immediately upon park opening to ensure a spot. (The child registering must be present.)

The experience takes about 45 minutes, including approximately 30 minutes of preparation. Kids are split into two

Insider's Tip!

Jedi Training - Trials of the Temple is held outdoors on an unshaded stage. Children who sign up to participate can choose from available times. Pick a time early in the morning or later in the evening to avoid standing in the intense heat with your child for up to 45 minutes.

groups: one that will face the Seventh Sister Inquisitor and one that will face the ultimate dark force, Darth Vader.

All park guests can watch the outdoor training/show several times daily, located on a stage next to the *Star Tours* attraction.

Star Wars: A Galactic Spectacular

Star Wars: A Galactic Spectacular is an intense blend of film projection, laser lighting effects, pyrotechnics, and dazzline fireworks. Watch as the Chinese Theater transforms each evening to display your favorite *Star Wars* film clips in an electifying production that will take your breath away.

Guests line the street in front of the Chinese Theater early for this performance. Plan to arrive at least 45 minutes early for an optimal viewing platform. FastPass+ is not availble. However, a reserved viewing area is available with a paid dessert party.

Star Wars: A Galaxy Far, Far Away

Star Wars: A Galaxy Far, Far Away is a stage show held several times daily. Favorite characters from the franchise entertain guests on-stage in front of the Chinese Theater.

Classic heroes and villains combine with those from the newest movies to the delight of fans from any generation.

Animal Kingdom Events and Entertainment		
Name	Type	Location
Burudika	Street Performance	Africa
Chakranadi	Street Performance	Asia
Discovery Island Carnivale	Street Performance	Discovery Island
Disney Kite Tails	Show	Discovery Island
DJ Anaan	Street Performance	Asia
Harambe Wildlife Parti	Street Performance	Africa
Tam Tam Drummers of Harambe	Street Performance	Africa
Viva Gaia Street Band!	Street Performance	Discovery Island
Winged Encounters – The Kingdom Takes Flight	Show	Discovery Island
Backstage Tales	Tour ($90 per person)	Various
Savor the Savanna: Evening Safari Experience	Tour ($169 per person)	Africa
Wild Africa Trek	Tour ($189-$249 per person)	Africa
Tree of Life Awakenings	Light Show	Discovery Island

Tree of Life Awakenings

Watch as the Tree of Life transforms, revealing the stories of animals multiple times each evening. Video and light project on the tree to display animals and nature's other creatures in this hypnotic visual extravaganza.

Disney KiteTails

Watch your favorite characters soar over the Discovery River Amphittheater in this enchanting show.

Your favorite Disney characters have been turned into extravagant kites and windcatchers, dancing to the tune of classic Disney songs. This is fun for all ages and backgrounds!

Hotel Resorts Specialty Tours		
Name	**Type**	**Location**
Sense of Africa	Tour ($249.99 per person)	Animal Kingdom Lodge
Starlight Safari	Tour ($74.17 per person)	Animal Kingdom Lodge
Wanyama Safari	Tour ($170 per person)	Animal Kingdom Lodge (Exclusive to Hotel Guests)
Wilderness Back Trail Adventure	Tour ($95.85 per person)	Fort Wilderness Campsites
Disney Family Culinary Adventure	Cooking/Dining Experience ($175 per person)	Contemporary Resort
Escape to Walt's Wilderness	Tour ($109 per person)	Contemporary Resort Marina
The Floral Experience	Tour ($50 per person)	Saratoga Springs, Beach Club Resort, or BoardWalk Inn

The Magic Kingdom

Park Overview

Opened in 1971, Magic Kingdom is the original Walt Disney World Park. It is physically centered in the heart of the 42-square mile property.

The park very closely mirrors the design of Disneyland, which opened its gates to visitors 16 years earlier (in 1955). Guests familiar with Disneyland almost immediately discover that even though the layout and rides of the Magic Kingdom are similar, the size is not: the Magic Kingdom is a full 57 acres larger than its Anaheim, California cousin!

Just as Sleeping Beauty's castle stands as the proud icon for Disneyland, Cinderella's Castle is what people envision when they think of Walt Disney World as a whole.

Towering over its prominent central location at the end of Main Street, U.S.A., the castle stands sentry over the park. The Magic Kingdom is the heart of Walt Disney World, and Cinderella's castle is the heart of the Magic Kingdom. The park itself is divided into six unique "lands," each of which is fully developed into its own unique theme.

Getting Around

Walking through the park lets you see everything, but your feet may need a rest at times. One of the best ways to get a unique vantage point of the park while taking a break is with a short trip aboard a real steam train.

The Walt Disney World Railroad takes you on a 20-minute loop around the entire park with three stops. The main station is at the front of the park, and the other two are equally-spaced around the perimeter.

Hub and Spoke Layout

Main Street, U.S.A. is the first land visitors see after entering the high-tech turnstiles at the front of the park and going under the railway tunnel. This is where the show begins.

Main Street, U.S.A. includes the central plaza – known as the Hub – where an iconic statue of Walt Disney and Mickey Mouse stands in the shadow of the castle.

Starting in the Hub, the other five lands span outward from this forecourt area, similar to spokes in a bicycle wheel with promenades that connect them all together. This layout is referred to as a "hub and spoke" system.

6 Magic Kingdom Lands (Clockwise Order)

- Main Street, U.S.A.
- Adventureland
- Frontierland
- Liberty Square
- Fantasyland
- Tomorrowland

The Magic Kingdom

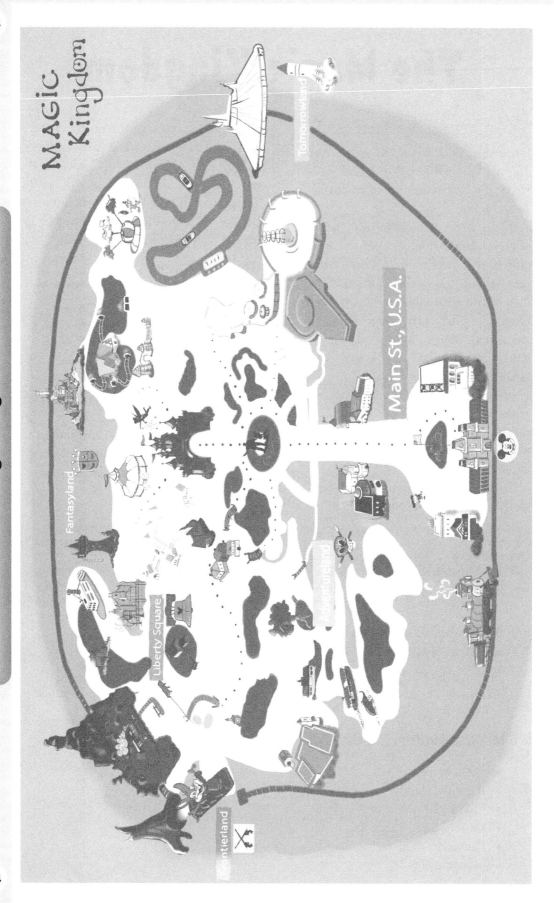

MAGIC Kingdom

Tomorrowland

Main St., U.S.A.

Fantasyland

Liberty Square

Adventureland

Frontierland

Insider's Tip!

If you arrive at a time when the front of the park (Town Square) is busy or there is a crowd waiting for a parade, hop on a train to one of the other two stops and start your tour there.

Fun Morning Transportation: A horseless carriage, a bright red fire engine, and horse-drawn trolleys take guests on one-way journeys from Town Square to the castle forecourt area early each day (before the park gets busy).

Magic Kingdom Resorts

For visitors who plan to spend a lot of time at the Magic Kingdom, six Disney hotels are accessible via monorail, buses, and boats (which travel along the main Bay Lake waterway that surrounds the park).

The Magic Kingdom hotels are:

1. Bay Lake Tower
2. The Contemporary
3. Polynesian Village
4. Polynesian Villas and Bungalows
5. Grand Floridian
6. The Villas at Grand Floridian

Insider's Hint!

You must have proper identification to get into the Utilidor area. However, tours are available that allow guests to see behind the scenes, including one that has an "underground" excursion. The Backstage Magic tour gives people a chance to go into these tunnels. (See Special Events and Tours section.)

Four additional Disney hotels are accessible via buses and boats:

- Wilderness Lodge
- Boulder Ridge Villas at Wilderness Lodge
- Fort Wilderness Campground
- The Cabins at Fort Wilderness

Note: Shades of Green is also a Magic Kingdom hotel. It is not *technically* a Disney hotel, as it was jointly established by Disney and the US Military exclusively for military personnel and their families. (It is accessible only via bus or auto.)

Utilidors (Cast Members Only)

A vast network of "underground" hallways called *Utilidors* (utility corridors) connects all sections of the Magic Kingdom, thus preventing guests from seeing "behind the scenes" operations. If you see a sign that says "Cast Members Only," chances are that it leads to these halls underneath the park which allow Cast Members to make the magic happen without interfering with guest experiences.

This is how equipment, merchandise, and even small vehicles all move about and then appear where they are needed in the park. There is nothing special about these well-lit industrial corridors (complete with conduit piping that runs along the ceilings); they are all about utility.

Utilidors were initially used by uniformed Cast Members who, dressed in costumes from one land, were not allowed to walk through a different land in front of guests. (While that was the original idea, recent changes to park policy now allow Cast Members to walk freely through the park in whatever outfit they happen to be wearing.)

The Magic Kingdom

Main Street Vehicles

Guests can take a romantic ride back in time when they climb aboard public transportation from yesteryear. There is nothing like giving your feet a break while taking a short ride on one of four nostalgic vehicles, including a classic horse-drawn street car, omnibus, open-air jitney (horseless carriage), or fire engine.

You don't have to plan this, as long as you leave time in your schedule to hop in line when you hear either the distinctive slow "clippity-clop" of the horse's hooves or the "clang-clang-clang" of the authentic automobile bells from a by-gone era.

The horse-drawn trolley is a treasure that is often overlooked, but is extremely popular with children and best friends. The trolley enters Main Street full of musical performers who put on a Trolley show (see Character Meet and Greets). When they are finished, the trolley stops at the firehouse location in Town Square for a short pause while it takes on passengers from among the crowd. It then transports the guests back up to the Hub (without performances). The guests disembark and the process repeats, returning new guests to Town Square. There are usually up to four trips each morning. This is a slow-moving, one-way journey up Main Street. Relax and enjoy crowd-watching as you gently rock around aboard the trolley while pedestrians *fly* past you on foot.

In addition to the horse-drawn trolley, guests can "travel back in time" while being driven down Main Street, U.S.A. aboard a 1903 vintage, open-air horseless carriage from the turn-of-the-century. During the leisure journey, there is plenty of time to appreciate Walt's idyllic town design, including the shop window displays and signs. Perhaps this is the first time you noticed how the street lights change from the "modern electrified" lights, replacing the old-style gas lamps. You will certainly be tempted as you slowly pass the Candy Kitchen shop and are forced to inhale the intoxicating sweet aromas.

The cars are driven by Disney Cast Members and travel the same route as the trolley, allowing you to jump aboard the classic vehicles to take a nostalgic ride from Town Square (near the Fire Station) to the central Plaza in front of Cinderella Castle or back.

In addition to the trolley, you can also cruise down Main Street, U.S.A. in a replica of the very first fire trucks or the 45 passenger Omnibus, a gas-powered, double-decker open-air bus. The Horse-Drawn Streetcars do not operate daily nor all day, due to the nature of using horses. The other Main Street Vehicles replace it. None of the vehicles operate during parades or after dark, for safety reasons. The different vehicles take from around seven to 10 minutes to travel approximately 500 yards each way.

The streetcars only run until the park starts to get pretty busy, when they have to shut down for safety reasons. Even more, they may only make two or three runs in a day. If you want to see them, get there early.

Background

It was Walt Disney's idea to use vehicles to transfer guests in Disneyland, and the concept was carried over to Disney World when it opened in 1971. The vehicles are perfect replicas of the various turn-of-the-century methods of transportation. All the vehicles are equipped with motors that replicate the realistic putting sounds natural to the turn-of-the-century engines.

The old-fashioned #71 red fire engine originates at the Fire Station in Town Square. It has a working siren and is painted with the words "Main Street." The engine number references the year the park opened.

There are two horseless carriages at the park. They are replicas of the 1915 jitney, and they allow guests to sit in the front seat or a back bench seat during transport. One has a yellow and black color scheme while the other is red and auburn. Young children particularly enjoy traveling up front in the fire engine and jitneys. The horn's well-known "aaa-OOH-gah" warns pedestrians of their arrival.

The omnibus is modeled after a 1920s New York City Omnibus that has two levels. Traveling on the upper deck gives a very unique view of the Main Street real estate and will provide photos that are very original. Used since 1971 to '82 at the Magic Kingdom, the Omnibus was then used at Epcot to transport guests around the World Showcase from 1982 until the late 1990s, when it returned to Main Street, U.S.A. In 2005, it was again used at Epcot as part of a moving character meet-and-greet. To honor Mickey's 60th birthday in 1988, it was decorated for a party and carried charters around the lagoon for a show.

Of course, the streetcar and horses get all decked out over the holidays. The horses are dressed with red, white, and blue ribbons braided into the tails and manes for the Fourth of July celebration. Similarly, red, white, and blue bunting adorn the street cars. Seasonal variations are introduced, such as using orange, brown, and yellow adorning the car and horse to reflect Autumn hues. During the Christmas holidays, pine garland wraps around the roof of the street car and sleigh bells are affixed to horse harnesses.

The trolleys and all carriages are pulled by horses who live comfortably at the **Tri-circle D Ranch** located on the grounds of Disney's Fort Wilderness Resort. Elsewhere, we explain how you can see them in their stalls and maybe even have a chance to see their keepers, who are also their controllers. The ranch is quiet and peaceful and worth considering for an *off-day excursion*.

The Magic Kingdom

Main Street, U.S.A. Attractions

Walt Disney World Railroad Station – Main Street Town Square (Not Currently Open)

This old-fashioned locomotive travels purely on steam power, making a twenty minute circuit around the park perimeter at a leisurely pace of 10-12 miles per hour. Guests are welcome to freely board and depart at any of the train's three stops at Main Street, Frontierland, and at Story Book Circus in Fantasyland. Departing every 10 minutes, each train holds about 100 guests.

Accessible by climbing a stairway to the station as you enter the tunnels leading into Town Square (or using a ramp near City Hall), the train opens daily at 9 a.m. and closes just before the nightly fireworks show. Beneath the train station, the ground floor of this building houses storage lockers and an ATM. This is where you can rent a wheelchair, ECV, or stroller.

Traveling the Magic Kingdom by steam train is a great way to save your feet and to avoid some crowds. The journey also gives you unique views of *Splash Mountain* and *Big Thunder Mountain*

Where did all that land come from?

The portion of the park guests see is actually the *second floor* of the Magic Kingdom. The entire underground tunnel network is not really "underground" but comprises the ground level of the original property. The park itself is built on top of the natural ground. The soil used for creating this enormous earthen framework was excavated from the surrounding land, and is the basis for the Seven Seas Lagoon.

Insider's Tip!

The second floor behind the Main Street train station is a popular viewing area for fireworks since it has a great, unobstructed view all the way down Main Street, U.S.A. to the castle. It is also a popular location from which to watch parades and the Flag Retreat ceremony (which happens each evening in Town Square).

Railroad, and it gives you the only vantage point to see interesting design features such as a Native American village, some Audio-Animatronic wild animals, and frontier structures from the Old West. None of these elements are visible from anywhere else in the park.

Travelers sit on wooden benches with wooden backs, with each bench comfortably seating four or five adults. Folding, non-rental strollers are permitted on the train, but those in ECVs must transfer to a standard wheelchair to board.

Note that Disney's rental strollers can not be taken aboard the train, because they are bulky and don't fold down or collapse. You'll have to empty your personal belongings from the rental stroller and leave it at the station, making sure to keep your stroller name card and rental receipt. With it, you'll be issued a replacement stroller at your destination train station when you disembark.

Town Square Theater (G+)

Two of the most iconic Disney characters wait inside the Town Square Theater for a "magical" meet-and-greet. This is where you can shrink down to pixie size for an encounter with Tinker Bell, the most famous fairy in the world! Of course, Walt's dream could not have come to life without a certain rodent. Meet the one-and-only Magician Mickey Mouse while he entertains you with a magic trick. Lightning Lane reservations are recommended, unless you go during a parade or late in the evening.

Adventureland Attractions

Swiss Family Treehouse

Based on the 1960 Disney movie about the shipwrecked Robinson family, this is the ultimate treehouse. The walk "up-and-through" attraction is one of Adventureland's original. At six stories tall, the amazing tree design offers unique vantage points high above the park, such as a great view of the Jungle Cruise river. Its summit provides fantastic aerial views perfect for photos, as well as for watching the evening firework show. Lightning Lane is not available.

The Magic Carpets of Aladdin (G+)

Disney's hit-animated feature *Aladdin* is brought to life with *The Magic Carpets of Aladdin*. This is a gentle, flying, midway-type ride that climbs high in the air as it spins around in circles. It even has its own "water-spitting" Arabian camel who sprays water on unsuspecting riders and passers-by. This is similar to Fanstasyland's Dumbo ride, although a flying carpet replaces the friendly cartoon elephant, and Aladdin's magic lamp sits atop rather than Timothy Mouse.

The up-and-down controls operate like *Dumbo's*, except those who sit in the front control the height and those in the back control the forward and backward tilt. Naturally, kids sitting up front try to fly at a level that gets everyone sprayed by the spitting camel.

This slow-loading ride takes about two minutes and the best time to experience it with little to no wait is typically before 11 a.m. or after dinnertime. Lightning Lane

is available, but not usually necessary due to generally short wait times.

Walt Disney's Enchanted Tiki Room

Housed in an air-conditioned, thatched-roof tiki hut, this classic "theater-in-the-round" attraction is a clever Audio-Animatronic show with a South Pacific-island theme. The musical-theater show is hosted by four wisecracking male parrots (Jose, Fritz, Michael, and Pierre) and features a cast of over 300 talking, singing, and dancing birds and flowers throughout a 20 minute performance.

Guests are seated on long, backless benches inside the tiki hut, surrounded by tropical foliage, tiki statues, and carvings.

Parts of the soundtrack date back to the original 1963 design when the technology was still brand new. Everyone is familiar with the Sherman Brothers' famous tune that starts the adventure, "In the Tiki Tiki Tiki Tiki Tiki Room." The entire room comes alive for the finale number. Guests are invited to clap and sing-along.

Some preschoolers may be frightened by the loud thunder and lightning effect that happens when the tiki gods "get angry," or by the loud, erupting volcano sequence. Visit before lunch or after 3:30

The Magic Kingdom

The Magic Kingdom

Insider's Trivia!

What appears to be an authentic tree is actually constructed with steel, concrete, and stucco. It is supported by a concrete "root system" that spans more than four stories (40 feet) underground. Its 300,000 plastic leaves were each attached by hand!

Insider's Warning!

Swiss Family Treehouse is a relaxed and pleasant attraction, but it may be frightening for children or adults who are afraid of heights. Additionally, the tree requires you to climb 116 steps and does not provide alternative methods for guests who have mobility issues. Nor is there a way to easily back out once entered, as you would be opposing on-coming traffic.

p.m. to find less than 15 minute wait times. Lightning Lane is not available.

Jungle Cruise (*G+*)

Another of the original Magic Kingdom attractions, *Jungle Cruise*, is an outdoor water ride that takes you back to the 1920s, which was a particularly-great era for exploration. During your deep-forest expedition, you float through a jungle waterway that is full of zany and humorous characters.

After boarding a covered boat that holds up to 32 people and getting underway, you pass by a large variety of Audio-Animatronic animals, including lions, elephants, zebras, and hippos. Watch out for the pygmy head hunter eagerly waiting for your boat to pass.

The tour is led by a trusty Jungle Cruise Skipper who delivers narration based on a memorized spiel interspersed with humorous ad-libs to tickle your funny bone.

During the tour, the canopied tramp steamer makes its way through sections of four rivers: the Amazon, the African Congo, the Nile, and finally the Mekong. It moves slowly along a concealed under water track. During the Christmas season (from early November through early January) Disney gives the Jungle Cruise a holiday makeover complete with Christmas lights and decorations added to the queue and throughout the

attraction. Holiday-themed jokes added to the skipper's shtick complete the transformation.

There has been a resurgence of popularity with this ride, due to the 2021 Jungle Cruise film release and a revamp of the attraction. The best time to see this 10-minute attraction is typically before 10 a.m. or in the last couple of hours before closing. Genie+ Lightning Lane reservations are usually available.

Pirates of the Caribbean (*G+*)

One of the most iconic of all Magic Kingdom attractions, this dark, indoor boat ride features an entertaining and realistic water voyage with colorful characters and a well-known theme song, "Yo Ho (A Pirates Life For Me)." This attraction was the basis for the blockbuster *Pirates of the Caribbean* movie series starring Johnny Depp, and it includes familiar scenes from the films. Be on the lookout for Captain Jack Sparrow as he makes *three* cameo appearances.

Housed inside a Spanish fort, the ride includes a Pirate's Cove, skeletons of dead pirates and Mermaids, a hurricane lagoon, and continuous, ominous echoes of "Dead men tell no tales!" Portions of this show may be somewhat scary for young children, as it includes simulated firefights with cannonballs that appear to shoot toward your boat and land nearby with a splash in the water. Additionally, the portrayal of the pillaging and burning of a town may be too intense for some children. There is also a gentle, but unexpected, flume drop.

The ride lasts fewer than 10 minutes, and the best time to go is generally before 11 a.m. or in the late afternoon, after dinner. This is considered one of the most efficient rides at Disney and can accommodate up to 2,000 guests per hour, so wait times are often 20 minutes or less. Genie+ Lightning Lane reservations are usually available.

A Pirate's Adventure ~ Treasures of the Seven Seas

Based on the Pirates of the Caribbean attraction and movies, this self-guided and interactive scavenger hunt challenges young pirates to find lost treasure hidden throughout Adventureland on behalf of Captain Jack Sparrow.

A "magic talisman," such as your MagicBand or a provided card, is used to activate a video screen that guides you to pirate maps to help you navigate the Seven Seas to raid treasures. Listen to the narration, see props pop to life and search symbols leading to the next raid.

Once each adventure is completed, guests receive Collector Cards as their reward for completing their tasks. The final reward is a card autographed by Captain Jack Sparrow.

The journey offers a fresh experience of Adventureland and is a great time filler before dinner and attraction reservations. Open every afternoon from 12 p.m. to 6 p.m., allow 20 minutes for each of the six tasks, which can be paused and resumed anytime.

Insider's Tip!

Wear a rain poncho to avoid getting too soaked on *Splash Mountain*. Even if you want the refreshing splash, you can use the poncho (or a plastic bag) to protect your camera and other electronics. Your poncho will also be useful for Walt Disney World's only other splash ride, *Kali River Rapids* in Animal Kingdom.

Frontierland Attractions

Splash Mountain (*G+*)
One of the largest thrill rides in both height and girth, *Splash Mountain* is an exciting dark ride set in the antebellum South. Based on the *Song of the South* Disney movie, this ride is a musical romp with colorful Audio-Animatronic displays.

Floating inside a log boat, you travel through the story of Br'er Rabbit, Br'er Fox, and Br'er Bear, passing their cave homes, swamp lands, and briar patches. The log ride uses flumes that seat people two across with four rows in each boat. You glide along the colorful bayou before reaching a climactic 40 miles per hour, 52-foot drop. As you begin the descent down the 47-degree waterfall, be sure to smile for the camera capturing your excited (or fearful!) expression.

The ride warns about getting you wet (Note the "Get Wet" sign featuring Br'er Rabbit!), and while there is definitely the potential for a *good drenching*, the threat is often worse than the reality. Expect to at least get damp, though. This can be particularly uncomfortable during cold and windy seasons. (Bring a towel to wipe off the damp seat before sitting down!)

The ride concludes with a rousing musical finale as you leisurely drift your way back to the unloading station.

Splash Mountain is one of the most popular rides in Magic Kingdom, making Genie+ Lightning Lane reservations highly recommended, especially during warmer months. There is a 40" minimum height requirement and each child younger than seven years old must ride with an adult. Please note that this attraction is closed for refurbishment annually starting in January for a few weeks (when it would otherwise be in low demand due to chilly winter weather).

Walt Disney World Railroad Station – Frontierland (Not Currently Open)

Seven minutes after leaving the Main Street station, the steam engine reaches the Frontierland Station, which is conveniently located next to *Splash Mountain*. This is the second of three stops, and it includes an insider's view of *Splash Mountain's* wondrous finale.

From this point, you'll head further into the American wilderness, and pass by the dusty desert town of Tumbleweed. Keep your eyes peeled for *Big Thunder Mountain Railroad's* runaway mine trains!

Continuing on to the Storybook Circus stop in Fantasyland takes about seven minutes more, and this leg of the train ride features hidden scenery of an Indian Village, frontier structures, and wildlife. Because of the popularity of both *Splash* and *Thunder Mountains*, the Frontierland station tends to be the most congested of the three train stops for rubber-neckers who want to see the unique vistas only available to train passengers. Lightning Lane is not available.

Insider's Trivia!

Tom Sawyer Island is the only Magic Kingdom attraction designed by Walt Disney himself.

Big Thunder Mountain Railroad (*G+*)

Big Thunder Mountain Railroad is one of the mainstay "mountain" attractions within Magic Kingdom. Walking through the queue, you will discover this facility was once the location for the successful Big Thunder Mining Company. However, through a series of bad luck, accidents, and possible supernatural interference, the company was shut down.

Now the mining business has been resurrected, but strange occurrences keep happening. Step inside your mine cart, which is pulled by a train engine on this wild and wacky roller coaster ride through the Big Thunder mountain and its ghost town. Will you make it back safely? You must be at least 40" to ride this attraction. Genie+ Lightning Lane reservations are highly recommended.

Tom Sawyer Island

You can only reach *Tom Sawyer Island* by floating on a raft across the *Rivers of America* waterway from Frontierland. Inspired by the writings of Mark Twain, Tom's island is a refreshingly low-tech, rustic playground for children of all ages to freely explore. The well-conceived island adventure is quite large and features a fort, swinging barrel bridges, waterfalls, caves, and tunnels. An old mine and bouncy rope bridge add to the fun for little ones.

Tom Sawyer Island allows you to "pick your own path" to explore several locations made famous by Samuel Clemens, including Harper's Mill, Injun Joe's Cave, Fort Langhorn, Potter's Mill, and the Tom Sawyer Scavage Fort. Easy-to-read maps are located throughout the pathways to ensure that you always know where you (and your children) are during your island adventure.

Journey to the island by log raft at the launch located across from *Big Thunder Mountain Railroad*, and arrive at Tom's Landing to embark on an expedition into the heart of early America. Lightning Lane is not available.

Liberty Square Attractions

Haunted Mansion (*G+*)
Liberty Square is a throwback to colonial America, in the era of the Revolutionary War. This is the smallest of all the lands, though it houses one of the most popular and elaborate of all the Magic Kingdom attractions: *Haunted Mansion*.

Enter the spooky home of 999 haunts in this creepy, yet fun adventure. Once you descend into the basement, the real fun begins. Step aboard your Doom Buggy to experience all the thrills and chills the "grim, grinning ghosts" can deliver.

The Haunted Mansion was the first ride constructed at Walt Disney World and is still a classic. Updated interior rooms and an interactive queue make the nine-minute attraction especially popular. Genie+ Lightning Lane reservations are recommended.

The Hall of Presidents
Enjoy a 22-minute respite from the heat in this air-conditioned theater. Watch as Audio-Animatronic versions of the nation's presidents tell the stories of their legacies.

Enjoy American history as told by George Washington and Abraham Lincoln. (Abraham Lincoln was Disney's first Audio-Animatronic figure, released for the 1965 World's Fair.) The attraction is updated each time a new President of the United States is elected. Lightning Lane reservations are not available or necessary for this attraction.

Liberty Square Riverboat (Liberty Belle)
Experience the Old South in an authentic riberboat. The Liberty Belle takes you on a journey around Tom Sawyer Island, as you relax on one of its enchanting decks.

Adults and children of all ages will enjoy the breeze, as you float past unique vistas, seen only from the boat. While the lack of air-conditioning makes this unpopular for extremely hot days, the

The Magic Kingdom

20-minute tour is an excellent way to rest your feet.

The riverboat seats 450 guests. Lightning Lane is not available.

Fantasyland Attractions

Peter Pan's Flight (*G+*)

One of the most popular rides in the park is this dark, indoor ride that runs along a suspended ceiling track to simulate a gentle moonlit flight over London.

Boarding a magical pirate ship, you follow the journey taken by Peter, Wendy, and the Darling brothers, as they travel through scenes in the story, from London, on to Never Land, and back again. Scenes include Old London Town, Big Ben, Never Land, Mermaid Lagoon, Skull Rock, and Peter's swashbuckling duel with Captain Hook. You even see Captain Hook standing precariously atop Tick-Tock the crocodile.

Superbly-designed with beautiful effects and charming music, *Peter Pan's Flight* is very popular and, therefore, typically has long lines. Genie+ Lightning Lane reservations are recommended, but the recently updated queue, which lets guests into the Darling home, is air-conditioned and includes interactive games to help pass the time. Other options include riding when the park first opens, during fireworks, or just before the park closes.

"it's a small world" (*G+*)

This is an original Magic Kingdom attraction and one that made history when Mary Blair and Alice Davis first designed it for the 1964-65 New York World's Fair. Small children especially love this boat ride and its catchy (perhaps too-catchy) tune. You will travel through various lands, singing along with Audio-Animatronic children from across the globe.

There is no height limitation to ride. This is our top choice for nervous children

to help them feel comfortable with Walt Disney World attractions. Genie+ Lightning Lane is available but generally not necessary early in the morning or in the evening.

Mickey's PhilharMagic (*G+*) (Not Currently Open)

Walt Disney's Feature Animation teamed up with Walt Disney Imagineering over the course of three years to faithfully bring Disney magic to life in 4-D (four dimensions) on the world's largest wrap-around projection screen.

Like most plots involving him, Donald Duck gets into mischief. While warming up the orchestra for an enchanted concert, Mickey must leave the conductor stand in order to solve a mystery. The hilarity ensues after Donald steals Mickey's Sorcerer's Hat. Coming to life on its own, the hat sneaks away from the duck. Donald frantically tries to find the hat so Mickey can conduct his symphony. Donald is then sent spiraling through several short clips of Disney's famous animated musicals, including *The Little Mermaid*, *Beauty and the Beast*, *Aladdin*, *Peter Pan*, and *The Lion King*.

The music is spectacular, and the addition of special 4-D effects to the long-beloved scenes enhances the sensory effects. The whimsical, fun storyline is based on the 1935 Mickey Mouse short film "The Band Concert." Running time is 12 minutes sitting on comfortable seats inside the cool and refreshing indoor theater. Genie+ Lightning Lane is available but not typically required.

Prince Charming Regal Carrousel

This very elaborate, antique merry-go-round has a few seating options, including either vertically-moving or stationary horses, or a (chariot) bench for those with mobility problems. The old-fashioned organ plays classic Disney tunes as you gently parade up and down atop a majestic, one-of-kind horse. Like most carrousels, parents can seat their younger children, secure them to a horse with a safety belt, and then stand with them during the ride.

Even longer lines for this ride tend to move quickly, since the carrousel can accommodate 90 people at a time on the 86 horses and one chariot, so the wait time is typically fewer than 15 minutes. The ride lasts about two minutes and should be ridden early (before 11 a.m.) or late (after 8 p.m.) to avoid waiting in the outdoor queue.

This attraction is especially nice at night when the colorful decorations are lit up. There are fantastic views, including Cinderella's Castle looming nearby, and photo and video opportunities are plentiful. Unless the park is particularly crowded, the wait time rarely exceeds five to 10 minutes. Lightning Lane is not available.

Enchanted Tales with Belle (*G+*) (Not Currently Open)

The most elaborate meet-and-greet offered at Walt Disney World, *Enchanted Tales with Belle* is truly enchanting: it's an interactive, storytelling attraction. Guests travel through a magic mirror into Beast's library to share a story with the real-life Belle. As she celebrates her birthday, she wants to act out her love story with Beast.

This is a favorite activity for children, because any who want to take part are invited to join in the play. After the play is finished, participants are given a souvenir bookmark, then get a very nice photo opportunity with Belle.

Each 20-minute show starts as guests first enter the wardrobe room, and the seating area accommodates approximately 45 people. The best times to enjoy this

attraction are before 10 a.m. or within the last two hours before park closing, especially on hot days. We recommend Genie+ Lightning Lane reservations, as the queue moves slowly and is not air conditioned.

The Many Adventures of Winnie the Pooh (*G+*)

This popular indoor ride runs along a continuous track – inside a giant honey pot – through Pooh's Hundred Acre Wood. It brings the pages of a huge picture book to life as you encounter Piglet, Eeyore, Owl, Rabbit, Kanga, and Roo grappling with a particularly blustery day. Tigger even joins the ride to teach you how to "bounce, bounce, bounce!"

A small portion of this four-minute attraction reflects a nightmare that Pooh is having, and a short period of dramatic lightening effects may frighten a small percentage of preschoolers. In short order, the ride mood quickly turns around, ending on a positive note with the entire gang partying together and Pooh finally getting his honey! This ride can get busy during the day, so the best time to see it is before 10 a.m. or within the last two hours prior to park closing. Genie+ Lightning Lane reservations are usually available.

Mad Tea Party

Take a ride in giant teacups on this spinning, midway attraction inspired by the Mad Hatter's loony antics during March Hare's nonsensical "unbirthday" party from Alice in Wonderland. Sitting inside the huge tea cups, you're sent

Insider's Warning!

The Mad Tea Party may induce motion-sickness in some people, so be careful and avoid eating immediately prior to taking part in the fun.

rotating around a giant tea pot, which itself spins in the opposite direction. You operate a round metal steering wheel that is located in the center of your cup. Gripping and turning the wheel causes the teacup to spin. Guests control the amount each individual cup spins, as the rest of the ride is rotating in motion. Working together with other people makes the cup spin faster and faster. Be on the lookout for the Dormouse to make a brief appearance from the top of the teapot.

The ride takes about 90 seconds and rarely has a long wait due to its propensity to induce motion-sickness. Lightning Lane is not available.

Seven Dwarfs Mine Train (LL)

The newest (and most popular) attraction in the Magic Kingdom, *The Seven Dwarfs Mine Train* is a very smooth roller coaster that uses innovative technology to take you on a journey through the dwarfs' gemstone mine. There are some quick turns and dips, made a bit more thrilling by the unique "multi-motion" technology incorporated into the mine cart that allows it to sway from side-to-side. Even if most adults consider this nothing more than a kiddy ride, smaller children definitely view this as a thrill ride. It is fast and fun by anyone's standards.

The coaster moves quickly up through the indoor mine shaft that has stunning visual props and a fun soundtrack. You see the Seven Dwarfs working in their jewel mine, and hear them break into song at the end of the work day when Doc calls the crew to head home. Outdoors, the ride

Insider's Tip!

Seven Dwarfs Mine Train feels more thrilling after dark.

Insider's Tip!

Seven Dwarfs Mine Train is the most popular attraction at the Magic Kingdom. If you can't obtain a FastPass+ reservation, get breakfast reservations before the park opens at Crystal Palace (or another Magic Kingdom restaurant) to be one of the first in line at park opening.

stays upright without the typical inversions and other roller coaster thrills.

Of course, no story about these dwarfs would be complete without cameo appearances by Snow White and the Evil Queen, and you'll be pleased to see each of them near the end of your journey. Snow White is dancing and singing with the little men as the old hag looms just outside their cottage door.

The ride features two on-ride cameras that provide videos and pictures for guests to purchase, and the queue has three interactive stations. Minimum height is 38." Purchase individual Lightning Lane reservations to avoid very long waits.

Under the Sea ~ Journey of The Little Mermaid (G+)

This gentle, dark ride tells the story based on the movie, using Audio-Animatronic figures, special effects, and music. Guests board a colorful clamshell that runs on a continuous indoor track. "Plunge beneath the waves," traveling past seaweed and coral and into the underwater caverns. Upon finally reaching Ariel's secret grotto, you get to hear Ariel sing "*Part of Your World.*"

Relive the movie's magic in this ride with more than 180 characters, from fish forming a conga line to an evil sea witch enticing wandering souls. You emerge from the depths of the ocean to watch as Prince Eric and Ariel celebrate their union with a fairytale wedding finale. Small children may find the loud music a bit overwhelming, and Ursula the sea witch is larger than life at more than seven feet tall and 12 feet wide.

The five-minute ride gets very busy during the day, but tends to slow down later in the evening. We recommend this attraction before 10 a.m. or within the last two hours prior to park closing. Genie+ Lightning Lane reservations are available, though they are generally not necessary later in the evening.

Walt Disney World Railroad Station – Fantasyland (Not Currently Open)

The Fantasyland Train Station is found next to *The Barnstormer* in Storybook Circus. This is the final stop before returning Town Square and is the gateway to the rest of Fantasyland and Tomorrowland. Board the train here to easily journey back to the entrance of the park in about seven minutes.

Built with wheelchair users in mind, this is easiest station to board and exit. The classic railroad roundhouse-themed station itself features signage for "Carolwood Park," a reference to Walt Disney's own backyard train, The Carolwood Pacific.

After leaving Fantasyland, the locomotive passes underneath the *Tomorrowland Transit Authority PeopleMover* before traveling between *Space Mountain* and the *Space Mountain* Gift Shop. Passing *Space Mountain*, guests get a look outside the park towards Bay Lake Tower and The Contemporary Resort. As you arrive back at the main station, enjoy the majestic view of Cinderella Castle down Main Street, U.S.A. Lightning Lane is not available.

Dumbo the Flying Elephant (*G+*)

Disney's iconic Dumbo the Flying Elephant ride received a recent makeover that included adding a duplicate ride to move the line fast. The twin rides spin in opposite directions! The addition of the Big Top Tent gives kids a place to run around and parents a place to cool down in an air-conditioned environment. This attraction uses pagers (akin to what is used in restaurants) so that kids can play while they wait for their turn on the ride. When the pager goes off, you go directly to the front of the line. Genie+ Lightning Lane is available for those who wish to bypass the indoor play area.

Casey Jr. Splash 'N'Soak Station

The *Casey Jr. Splash 'N' Soak Station* is just a few steps from the Fantasyland train station. This pit stop is a children's splash park with a theme based on the Casey Junior Circus Train from the *Dumbo* animated film.

Large restroom facilities are located across the square. These are especially nice and provide children an easy place to change out of soaked clothing after playing in the water.

The Barnstormer (*G+*)

This "junior-class" roller coaster is a small but fun airplane-themed ride, optimized for children who are at least 35" tall. Goofy is the Great Goofini, a stunt pilot whose stunts frequently go wrong to the delight of small children. Goofy's out-of-control path takes guests spiraling through the sky, eventually "crashing" through a giant billboard.

Zipping along at 25 miles per hour, this pint-sized ride lasts less than a minute, and much of that time is actually spent at the boarding and unloading stations. The cars are too small for most adults, and taller people may even feel "whiplashed."

The Magic Kingdom

Because *The Barnstormer* is over so quickly, it is a great introductory coaster for children and helps boost confidence in thrill rides for little ones. Wait times of 20 minutes or less are typical before 10 a.m., during parades, or after evening fireworks. Genie+ Lightning Lane reservations are usually available. Though benign and brief, expectant mothers are advised not to ride this attraction. Each child younger than seven years old must be accompanied by an adult.

Tomorrowland Attractions

Tomorrowland Speedway (*G+*)

These family-friendly, mini race cars travel around an outdoor raceway along multiple side-by-side lanes. Riders are seat belted into the gasoline powered go-carts covered in sleek race-car façades.

The winding track is comprised of a fixed-metal guide-rail so steering ability is not absolutely necessary, but children have some general directional control. The drivers operate floor pedals that actually accelerate and brake the vehicles. The carts can operate at "death-defying" speeds up to 7.5 miles per hour thanks to their nine horse power Briggs & Stratton engines.

Children must be 54" tall to drive unassisted, or 32" to be seated with an adult. The "race" duration is about four to five minutes, or the time it takes for children to finally figure out how to accelerate once around the $4/10^{th}$-mile track. Realistic sounds of race cars roaring along a speedway are piped into loudspeakers located around the attraction, along with "track-side announcements." A checkered flag is waved at every driver finishing a race.

Because it uses real go-carts, this ride is very popular and can have long standby wait times, which is not offset by the short ride duration. Sometimes exiting the ride can take some time, due to traffic congestion that backs up the go-carts at the finish line. Take a ride before 10 a.m. or after dinnertime to avoid the worst lines. Genie+ Lightning Lane reservations are usually available. Expectant mothers should not ride.

Tron Lightcycle Power Run (*LL*) (Opening in 2022)

Originally developed for Shanghai Disneyland, this roller coaster takes thrills to a whole new level. Just like the TRON movie series, this ride brings you into an electronic world of high speed adventure.

You mount a lightcycle (as seen in the move series), which is a vehicle that is similar to a motorcycle. Lean forward in the seat, hang onto the handlebars, and get ready to take off at speeds close to 60 miles per hour!

This coaster track zips you in and out of the building, along the *Grid*. You won't want to return to reality!

There is a 48" minimum height requirement and each child younger than seven years old must be accompanied by an adult.

When open, we expect Disney to offer individual Lightning Lane reservations for purchase and a virtual queue for this attraction, similar to Guardians of the Galaxy: Cosmic Rewind. This means no stand-by queue will likely be available, so advanced reservations will be necessary for any chance to experience this attraction.

Space Mountain (*G+*)

Disney's iconic *Space Mountain* roller coaster flies along at 28 miles per hour, making it the fastest and most intense ride at the Magic Kingdom. Adding to the thrill is its "remote darkness of deep outer space" which keeps you from seeing where you are going. Designed to emulate traveling through the dark recesses of the galaxy, *Space Mountain* has unique sound and lighting, and other special effects, including an animated galaxy filled with asteroids, stars, and planets projected across pitch-black walls and ceiling.

As your "rocket ship" leaves the space station (loading area), you'll go through a flashing "warp tube" that propels you into deep space. As you reach the end of the tube, note the bright strobe flash and smile: it's the on-ride camera taking your souvenir photograph.

There is a 44" minimum height requirement and each child younger than seven years old must be accompanied by an adult.

The dark indoor ride may frighten young children, but it only lasts three minutes. Like all rides at Disney, frightened children can exit when they reach the front of the queue and parents can rely on Rider Switch.

Due to its popularity, people without small children often race to Space Mountain as soon as the park opens. Go before 10 a.m., or later in the day when others are at dinner, or in the hour prior to closing. Purchase individual Lightning Lane reservations to avoid very long lines. For safety purposes, this thrill ride should be avoided by expectant mothers and guests with high blood pressure, heart, back or neck problems, motion sickness, or other health conditions that could be aggravated.

Astro Orbiter

Located high above the heart of Tomorrowland, *Astro Orbiter* gives children a chance to pilot their own fancy Buck Roger's-style jets.

This rotating midway-type ride rotates chrome-colored jets around its center, similar to *Dumbo*. Pushing or pulling the lever inside the spaceships lets you control how high you fly your rocket.

Although the experience is short-lived, this is a great place to be during a nightly fireworks show, since it provides an enchanting overhead glimpse of Cinderella's Castle. It also offers an excellent vantage point overlooking Tomorrowland and the Contemporary Resort.

Raised 20 feet and with 11 rotations per minute, *Astro Orbiter* goes much faster and higher than *Dumbo*, which may scare young children.

Unfortunately, the vehicles are much more cramped than *Dumbo* and guests are seated tandem (facing forward, with one sitting in the lap of the other) so it is also not as comfortable.

Though it's not really considered a thrill ride, because it flies high over the park, it is unsuitable for anyone with a fear of heights. (A small elevator carries guests to the 2nd-floor loading area.)

As with all such spinning rides, the fast centrifugal movement may also cause motion-sickness.

Fewer than two minutes in duration, *Astro Orbiter* generally has a long wait, both because it has no minimum height requirement and because it has a limited number of rockets. Standby lines are also impacted because Lightning Lane reservations are not available.

Tomorrowland Transit Authority PeopleMover

The *PeopleMover* is a slow-moving track-vehicle, which was envisioned as part of Walt's technological dream for an "emission-free mass-transit system of the future." The tram-like cars are powered magnetically, rather than by an emissions-laden engine. More than 500 electromagnets propel the vehicles using a technology called linear induction, which doesn't rely on any fuel, nor does it have any moving parts (other than the wheels under each carriage).

From its elevated vantage point, this quiet and relaxing "highway in the sky" takes approximately 10 minutes to make a one-mile journey around Tomorrowland. During the trip, you travel inside the dark recesses of *Space Mountain* and above *Tron Lightcycle Power Run*, a nicety for children not tall enough to experience those attractions. You also get a peek within *Buzz Lightyear's Space Ranger Spin*. One particularly special treat you view is an early architectural rendering of Walt Disney's model city. This diorama of his vision is what eventually became Epcot Center.

The *PeopleMover* is a continuous loader, so it loads quickly and moves up to 35 people per train. Even if the park is crowded the wait time should be fewer than five minutes, except at peak periods when it might take a little longer. You board and disembark from a circular moving walkway, and you must be ambulatory to ride. Lightning Lane is not available, nor is it needed.

Walt Disney's Carousel of Progress

This is an indoor theater that is unique in that the seated audience rotates around a stationary central stage as different scenes play out in a 20-minute production.

The attraction demonstrates how increasing automation has impacted our way of life over the past century. Changing home technologies and entertainment are revealed in four different settings, each reflecting a passage of time, inside the home of a typical American family. Whereas most carousels go around and around without getting anywhere, this one is said to "make progress at every turn."

Walt originally conceived this Audio-Animatronic theater production for the *1964–65 World's Fair*, and script changes

and updates have been minimal since then. The Carousel of Progress holds the record as the longest-running stage show in the history of American theater. Though adults may be amused by its references to ice boxes, car phones, and laser discs, children may be confused.

The attraction is only open seasonally (when the park is busiest). Lightning Lane is not available.

Buzz Lightyear's Space Ranger Spin (*G+*)

Fun for the whole family, *Buzz Lightyear's Space Ranger Spin* is an indoor, space-aged shooting gallery ride. Similar to the *Toy Story* ride at Hollywood Studios, space rangers cruise among the stars in an Omnimover spaceship to battle giant robots and explore strange planets.

Featuring the *Toy Story* film characters, you're "reduced to the size of an action figure" to defend the universe's crystollic fusion cell supply (batteries) from the Evil Emperor Zurg. Look through a giant View-Master® for mission instructions on how to save the world and rack up points!

Each car has two laser cannons and is controlled by a joystick that allows you to spin the car left and right to get the best shot. When the space cruiser's lasers zap a target, it triggers space-aged animation, galactic sounds, and neon light effects. A score board is located on the dash board to keep track of your success. Scoring is independent of your riding partner, allowing you to compete with each other.

Buzz Lightyear's Space Ranger Spin features 10 interactive scenes in about four minutes. The ride is extremely popular, in part because it has no height requirements. It includes a souvenir photo opportunity, which is sure to capture your enjoyment. Genie+ Lightning Lane reservations are usually available.

Monsters, Inc. Laugh Floor (*G+*)

This is a monstrous improvisation comedy stage show that uses state-of-the-art technology to let the on-screen monsters actually interact with the audience. Behind-the-scenes, live actors voice the characters using cutting-edge digital puppetry.

Audience members who have seen *Monsters, Inc.* will understand this show premise. The "Monster of Ceremonies" of the comedy show is the one-eyed Mike Wazowski of *Monsters, Inc.* fame. His goal is to generate and collect as many laughs as possible to convert into needed electricity. By doing so, he tries to save the city of Monstropolis by harnessing the "power of laughter" from the audience as jokes are told.

During the show, unsuspecting audience members get a few seconds of fame, as families suddenly pop up on-screen to be included in funny skits and used for added gags.

While waiting in line, pay attention to the overhead screens in the pre-show/queue area and be ready to send your favorite joke, as a text message, to the advertised number. You may be one of the lucky few whose jokes are used during the show!

This attraction may frighten some preschoolers if they don't understand that the *Monsters, Inc.* monsters are friendly. Queue times for the 15-minute show are typically short, even during peak periods, thanks to the venue's extra large capacity. The best time to see the show without much wait is before 11 a.m. or after 4 p.m. Genie+ Lightning Lane reservations are usually available, though often not necessary for this indoor, air-conditioned attraction.

The Magic Kingdom

I just want to leave you with this thought, that it's just been sort of a dress rehearsal and we're just getting started. So if any of you start resting on you laurels, I mean forget it, because...we are just getting started.

- Walt Disney

Sample Lightning Lane & Genie+ Magic Kingdom Itineraries

1 Day (non-Princess, no small children)

Approx Time		Approx Time	
7 AM	Make Lightning Lane reservations for Tron Lightcycle (2:35 PM-3:35 PM window recommended), Seven Dwarfs Mine Train (10-11 AM window recommended), and Space Mountain (12-1 PM window recommended).	3:40-4 PM	See the Monster's Inc. Laugh Floor.
		4-4:45 PM	Ride the Liberty Square Riverboat.
		4:55-5:30 PM	Visit Enchanted Tales with Belle.
7:15 AM	Arrive 45-60 minutes before park opening.	5:40-6 PM	Ride it's a small world.
		6:10-6:30 PM	Ride the Mad Tea Party.
8:10-8:30 AM	Ride Peter Pan's Flight	6:40-7 PM	Ride Buzz Lightyear's Space Ranger Spin.
8:40-9:00 AM	Ride Under the Sea: Journey of the Little Mermaid.	7:10-7:25 PM	Ride the Tomorrowland Transit Authority PeopleMover.
9:10-9:30 AM	Ride The Barnstormer		
9:40-10 AM	Ride the Many Adventures of Winnie the Pooh.	7:30-8:30 PM	Eat dinner.
		8:35-9 PM	Meet Mickey at Town Square Theater.
10:10-10:30 AM	Use Lightning Lane to ride Seven Dwarfs Mine Train.	9-9:30 PM	Watch fireworks show.
10:45-11:30 AM	Ride Splash Mountain.	9:40-10 PM	Ride the Jungle Cruise.
		10:05-10:30 PM	Ride Pirates of the Caribbean.
11:40-12 PM	Ride Big Thunder Mountain Railroad	10:35-10:50 PM	Ride the Magic Carpets of Aladdin.
12:10-12:30 PM	Ride the Haunted Mansion.	9:40-10 PM	Use Lightning Lane to ride the Jungle Cruise.
12:40-1:15 PM	Use Lightning Lane to ride Space Mountain.	10:05-10:30 PM	Ride Pirates of the Caribbean.
1:25-2:30 PM	Eat lunch at Pecos Bill & watch Festival of Fantasy Parade.	10:35-10:50 PM	Ride the Magic Carpets of Aladdin.
2:35-2:55 PM	Use Lightning Lane to ride Tron Lightcycle Power Run.		If longer hours, you can stay later to see Main Street Electrical Parade and visit more rides.
3:10-3:30 PM	See Mickey's Philharmagic.		

1 Day (non-Princess, w/small children)

Approx Time		Approx Time	
7 AM	Make Lightning Lane reservations for Peter Pan's Flight (8:10 AM-9:10 AM window recommended) and Seven Dwarfs Mine Train (10-11 AM window recommended).	8:40-9:00 AM	Ride Under the Sea: Journey of the Little Mermaid.
		9:10-9:30 AM	Ride the Barnstormer.
		9:40-10 AM	Ride Dumbo the Flying Elephant.
7:15 AM	Arrive 45-60 minutes before park opening	10:10-10:30 AM	Ride the Many Adventures of Winnie the Pooh.
8:10-8:30 AM	Ride Peter Pan's Flight	10:40-11 AM	Use Lightning Lane to ride Seven Dwarfs Mine Train.

The Magic Kingdom

Approx Time	
11:10-11:30 AM	Ride it's a small world.
11:40-12:15 PM	Visit Enchanted Tales with Belle.
12:25-12:40 PM	Ride the Tomorrowland Transit Authority PeopleMover.
12:45-1:10 PM	Ride Buzz Lightyear's Space Ranger Spin.
1:20-2 PM	See the Monster's Inc. Laugh Floor.
2-4:30 PM	Lunch and Break
4:40-5:30 PM	Visit Tom Sawyer Island.
5:40-6 PM	Ride Splash Mountain.
6:10-6:45 PM	See the Country Bear Jamboree.
6:55-7:30 PM	Ride the Haunted Mansion (could be frightening for some children).

Approx Time	
7:30-8:15 PM	Eat dinner.
8:20-8:50 PM	Ride the Jungle Cruise.
9-9:30 PM	Watch fireworks show.
9:40-10 PM	Ride Pirates of the Caribbean.
10:05-10:20 PM	Ride the Magic Carpets of Aladdin.
10:30-11 PM	Meet Mickey Mouse at Town Square Theater.
	If longer hours, you can stay later to visit more rides.
10:30-11 PM	Meet Mickey Mouse at Town Square Theater.
	If longer hours, you can stay later to see a parade and visit more rides.

1 Day (Princess, w/small children)

Approx Time	
7 AM	Make Lightning Lane reservations for Rapunzel (8:10-9:10 AM window recommended) and Seven Dwarfs Mine Train (11 AM-12 PM window recommended).
7:15 AM	Arrive 45-60 minutes before park opening
8:10-8:30 AM	Visit Rapunzel at Princess Fairytale Hall.
8:40-9:00 AM	Ride Peter Pan's Flight
9:10-9:30 AM	Ride Under the Sea: Journey of the Little Mermaid.
9:40-10 AM	Ride Dumbo the Flying Elephant.
10:10-10:30 AM	Meet Cinderella at Princess Fairytale Hall.
10:45-11:30 AM	Ride the Many Adventures of Winnie the Pooh.
11:40-12 PM	Use Lightning Lane to ride Seven Dwarfs Mine Train.
12:10-12:30 PM	Meet Minne & Daisy in Storybook Circus.
12:40-1:15 PM	Visit Enchanted Tales with Belle.
1:30-2:30 PM	Visit Tom Sawyer Island.
2:30-5 PM	Lunch and Break
5:10-5:30 PM	Ride Splash Mountain.

Approx Time	
5:40-6 PM	Ride the Magic Carpets of Aladdin.
6:05-6:35 PM	Ride Pirates of the Caribbean
6:40-7:10 PM	Ride the Jungle Cruise.
7:20-8:10 PM	Eat dinner.
8:20-8:50 PM	Ride the Haunted Mansion
9-9:30 PM	Watch fireworks show.
9:40-10 PM	Meet Mickey Mouse at Town Square Theater.
10:05-10:30 PM	Meet Tinker Bell at Town Square Theater.
10:40-11 PM	Ride Buzz Lightyear's Space Ranger Spin.
	If longer hours, you can stay later to visit more rides.
10:05-10:30 PM	Meet Tinker Bell at Town Square Theater.
10:40-11 PM	Use FastPass to ride Buzz Lightyear's Space Ranger Spin.
	If longer hours, you can stay later to see fireworks and visit more rides.

The Magic Kingdom

The Magic Kingdom

2 Day (non-Princess, no small children)

Approx. Time	Day 1	Approx. Time	Day 2
7 AM	Make Lightning Lane reservations for Tron (2:30-3:30 window recommended), Seven Dwarfs Mine Train (10-11 window recommended), and Space Mountain (3:40-4:40 window recommended).	7 AM	Make Lightning Lane reservations for Big Thunder Mountain Railroad. If you want to repeat any popular attractions from yesterday, make Lightning Lane reservations for them.
	Arrive 45-60 minutes before park opening.		Arrive 45-60 minutes before park opening.
8:10-8:30 AM	Ride the Peter Pan's Flight.	8:10-8:30 AM	Ride Big Thunder Mountain Railroad.
8:40-9 AM	Ride Under the Sea: Journey of the Little Mermaid.	8:40-9 AM	Ride Splash Mountain.
9:10-9:30 AM	Ride the Many Adventures of Winnie the Pooh.	9:15-9:35 AM	Ride Pirates of the Caribbean.
9:40-10 AM	Ride Dumbo the Flying Elephant.	9:45-10:15 AM	Ride the Jungle Cruise.
10:10-10:40 AM	Meet Minnie and Daisy or Donald and Goofy at Pete's Silly Sideshow.	10:30-11 AM	Ride the Haunted Mansion.
		11:15-12 PM	Ride the Liberty Belle Riverboat.
10:50-11:10 AM	Use Lightning Lane to ride Seven Dwarfs Mine Train (38" height requirement).	12:10-12:30 PM	See the Hall of Presidents.
11:20-11:40	Ride it's a small world.	12:30-1:30 PM	Eat lunch.
11:50-12:10	Ride the Mad Tea Party.	2-2:30 PM	Watch the Festival of Fantasy Parade
12:10-1:10	Eat lunch.	2:45-3:45 PM	Visit Tom Sawyer Island.
1:20-1:40	Ride Buzz Lightyear's Space Ranger Spin.	4-4:20	See the Country Bear Jamboree.
1:50-2:25	See the Monster's Inc. Laugh Floor.	4:30-5 PM	See the Enchanted Tiki Room.
2:30-2:50	Use Lightning Lane to ride Tron.	5:30-6 PM	See Enchanted Tales with Belle.
3-3:30	Visit the Carousel of Progress.	6:15-6:45 PM	Play A Pirate's Adventure: Treasures of the Seven Seas.
3:40-4:10	Use Lightning Lane to ride Space Mountain.	6:45-8:15 PM	Eat dinner.
4:10-5:30	Eat dinner.		See fireworks again, or revisit favorite attractions during these performances or late at night for shorter lines.
6-6:30	See Mickey's Philharmagic.		
7-7:30	Meet Mickey Mouse at Town Square Theater.		Want an afternoon break? Leave after visiting Tom Sawyer Island and come back in time for the parade, if you want to see it. See other afternoon attractions after visiting Enchanted Tales with Belle.
8-8:30	Watch fireworks show.		
8:30-10 PM	Shop & visit any rides with low wait times.		
	Want an afternoon break? Make your Buzz Lightyear LL reservation for later in the afternoon and Space Mountain for the evening. Leave after lunch and return around 3:30.		

2 Day (non-Princess, w/small children)

Approx. Time	Day 1	Approx. Time	Day 2
7 AM	Make Lightning Lane reservations for Peter Pan's Flight (8:10-9:10 window recommended) and Seven Dwarfs Mine Train (10:30-11:30 window recommended). If your child is too small for Splash Mountain or does not want to ride, use Rider Switch or select a Lightning Lane for a different ride.	7 AM	Make Lightning Lane reservations for Tomorrowland Speedway (8:10-9:10 window recommended) and Seven Dwarfs Mine Train if your group would like to repeat it.
		8:10-8:40 AM	Ride Tomorrowland Speedway.
		8:50-9:10 AM	Ride the Astro Orbiter.
8:10-8:30 AM	Ride Peter Pan's Flight.	9:20-9:40 AM	Ride Buzz Lightyear's Space Ranger Spin.
8:40-9 AM	Ride Under the Sea: Journey of the Little Mermaid.	10-10:30 AM	Ride the Jungle Cruise.
9:10-9:30 AM	Ride the Many Adventures of Winnie the Pooh.	10:40-11:15 AM	Ride Pirates of the Caribbean.
9:40-10 AM	Ride Dumbo the Flying Elephant.	11:25-11:45 AM	Ride the Magic Carpets of Aladdin.
10:10-10:30 AM	Ride the Barnstormer.	11:50-12 PM	Walk through the Swiss Family Robinson Treehouse.
10:40-11:10 AM	Use Lightning Lane to ride Seven Dwarfs Mine Train (38" height requirement).	12:15-12:45 PM	Watch a stage show at the castle courtyard.
11:20-11:50 AM	Ride it's a small world.	12:45-1:45 PM	Eat lunch.
12-12:20 PM	Ride Prince Charming's Regal Carrousel.	1:45-2:45 PM	Take an afternoon break.
12:20-1:30 PM	Eat lunch.	3-3:30 PM	Watch the Festival of Fantasy Parade.
1:30-3 PM	Take an afternoon break.	3:45-4:10 PM	See the Country Bear Jamboree
3:30-4:30 PM	Visit Tom Sawyer Island.	4:20-4:40 PM	Ride the Walt Disney World Railroad from Main Street or Frontierland to Fantasyland.
4:45-5:05 PM	Ride Splash Mountain (40" height requirement, may be too intense for some children).	4:45-5:15 PM	Meet Minnie and Daisy and/or Donald and Goofy at Pete's Silly Sideshow.
5:15-6 PM	Ride the Liberty Belle Riverboat.	5:15-6:45 PM	Eat Dinner
6-7:30 PM	Eat Dinner.	6:50-7:10 PM	Ride the Tomorrowland Transit Authority PeopleMover.
7:40-8:10 PM	See Enchanted Tales with Belle.	7:20-7:50 PM	See the Monster's Inc. Laugh Floor.
8:20-8:50 PM	See Mickey's Philharmagic.		Watch fireworks again. if you would like, repeat favorite attractions, or leave the park early.
9-9:20 PM	Ride Mad Tea Party.		
9:35-9:55 PM	Meet Mickey Mouse at Town Square Theater.		
10 PM	See fireworks show.		

The Magic Kingdom

2 Day (Princess, w/small children)

Approx. Time	Day 1	Approx. Time	Day 2
7 AM	Make Lightning Lane reservations for Peter Pan's Flight (8:10-9:10 window recommended) and Seven Dwarfs Mine Train (10:30-11:30 window recommended).	7 AM	Make Lightning Lane reservations for Tomorrowland Speedway (8:10-9:10 window recommended) and Seven Dwarfs Mine Train if your group would like to repeat it.
8:10-8:30 AM	Ride Peter Pan's Flight.	8:10-8:40 AM	Ride Tomorrowland Speedway.
8:40-9 AM	Ride Under the Sea: Journey of the Little Mermaid.	8:50-9:10 AM	Meet Merida at the Fairytale Garden.
9:10-9:30 AM	Ride the Many Adventures of Winnie the Pooh.	9:20-9:40 AM	Meet Rapunzel at Princess Fairytale Hall.
9:40-10 AM	Ride Dumbo the Flying Elephant.	9:50-10:15 AM	Ride the Astro Orbiter.
10:10-10:30 AM	Ride the Barnstormer.	10:25-10:45 AM	Ride Buzz Lightyear's Space Ranger Spin.
10:40-11:10 AM	Use Lightning Lane to ride Seven Dwarfs Mine Train (38" height requirement).	11-11:30 AM	Ride the Jungle Cruise.
		11:40-12:10 PM	Ride Pirates of the Caribbean.
		12:10-1:10 PM	Eat Lunch
11:20-11:50 AM	Ride it's a small world.	1:20-1:45 PM	Ride Splash Mountain
12-12:20 PM	Ride Prince Charming's Regal Carrousel.	2-2:30 PM	Watch the Festival of Fantasy Parade.
12:20-1:30 PM	Eat lunch.	2:30-3:40 PM	Take an afternoon break
1:30-3 PM	Take an afternoon break.	3:40-4 PM	Ride the Magic Carpets of Aladdin.
3:30-4:30 PM	Visit Tom Sawyer Island.		
4:45-5:05 PM	Meet Cinderella at Princess Fairytale Hall.	4:05-4:20 PM	Walk through the Swiss Family Robinson Treehouse.
5:15-6 PM	Ride the Liberty Belle Riverboat.	4:30-4:50 PM	Ride the Walt Disney World Railroad from Main Street or Frontierland to Fantasyland.
6-7:30 PM	Eat dinner.		
7:40-8:10 PM	See Enchanted Tales with Belle.	5-5:40 PM	Meet Minnie and Daisy and/or Donald and Goofy at Pete's Silly Sideshow.
8:20-8:50 PM	See Mickey's Philharmagic.		
9-9:20 PM	Ride Mad Tea Party.	5:40-7 PM	Eat Dinner
9:35-9:55 PM	Meet Tinker Bell at Town Square Theater.	7:10-7:30 PM	Ride the Tomorrowland Transit Authority PeopleMover.
10 PM	See fireworks show.	7:40-8:10 PM	See the Monster's Inc. Laugh Floor.
10:30-10:50 PM	Meet Mickey Mouse at Town Square Theater.		Watch the fireworks again. if you would like, repeat favorite attractions, or leave the park early.

Epcot

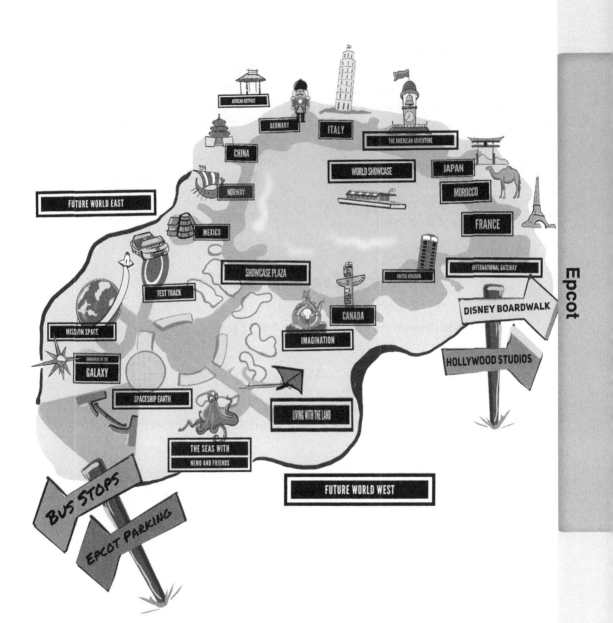

AFRICAN OUTPOST

GERMANY

ITALY

THE AMERICAN ADVENTURE

CHINA

WORLD SHOWCASE

JAPAN

MOROCCO

NORWAY

FUTURE WORLD EAST

FRANCE

MEXICO

SHOWCASE PLAZA

INTERNATIONAL GATEWAY

UNITED KINGDOM

TEST TRACK

CANADA

DISNEY BOARDWALK

MISSION SPACE

IMAGINATION

GUARDIANS OF THE
GALAXY

HOLLYWOOD STUDIOS

SPACESHIP EARTH

LIVING WITH THE LAND

THE SEAS WITH
NEMO AND FRIENDS

BUS STOPS

FUTURE WORLD WEST

EPCOT PARKING

Getting to the Park

Epcot is the only park with both a front and back entrance. At the front entrance, Epcot is directly accessible via monorail from the Transportation and Ticket Center (the Magic Kingdom parking lot). The park's International Gateway "back entrance" is accessible via either waterway or walking trail that run to both The BoardWalk and Hollywood Studios.

Just inside the back entrance, a short walkway connects to the main promenade between the France and United Kingdom pavilions.

Five Epcot resort hotels are located within a five to fifteen minute walk of the International Gateway. These hotel properties are also accessible via waterway on Disney-piloted ferry boats.

Epcot Resorts
- Boardwalk Inn and Villas
- Beach Club Resort and Villas
- Yacht Club Resort
- Walt Disney World Swan
- Walt Disney World Dolphin

Park Overview

Epcot opened in 1982 as a futuristic showplace and international showcase providing insight into 11 nations of the world. This atmosphere provides a backdrop of learning about technologies, along with international cultures and cuisines. This makes it a favorite among locals and adult visitors.

Walt Disney first envisioned the Experimental Prototype Community of Tomorrow (EPCOT) concept in which he

Epcot Center Dedication–

To all who come to this place of Joy, Hope and Friendship

~Welcome~

EPCOT Center was inspired by Walt Disney's creative vision.

Here, human achievements are celebrated through imagination, the wonders of enterprise and concepts of a future that promises new and exciting benefits for all.

May EPCOT Center entertain, inform and inspire.

And, above all, may it instill a new sense of belief and pride in man's ability to shape a world that offers hope in people everywhere.

– *Dedication Plaque dated October 24, 1982*
E. Cardon Walker, CEO of Walt Disney Productions

Insider's Trivia!

Disney executives opted to change the name from the original EPCOT acronym to a more proper name, "Epcot Center." It was later changed to just Epcot.

Insider's Trivia!

Introduced as a pavilion at the 1964 World's Fair in New York City, the original geodesic sphere dome was designed by Thomas C. Howard of Synergetics, Inc. That dome was taken apart, moved, and reassembled where it is currently used as an aviary by the Queens Zoo in Flushing Meadows Corona Park.

hoped to share his dream of a technologically-replete utopian "living community" and "world of the future."

Walt died before any part of his vision could come to fruition. His ultimate dream was modified and scaled down to amusement-park levels by Disney planners. However, Walt would have been honored that so many of his visionary ideals were somehow incorporated into what became of the functioning theme park.

Rather than being based on magic and fantasy like the Magic Kingdom, Epcot is more of a technological and educational facility: conceptually a type of permanent *World's Fair.*

The park has evolved over the years to add some thrills and excitement and is currently under a major renovation. Still, it remains more about ideas than heart-stopping action. There are very few attractions for adrenaline junkies. Epcot is about expanding visitors' minds by teaching about new and exciting cultures,

ecology, the environment, energy, communication, and more.

While children with inquiring minds enjoy most of what the park has to offer, some guests with small children experience disappointment. With careful planning, though, the entire family should find Epcot to be stimulating and entertaining. (See our section on Traveling with Small Children for tips on keeping children interested as they tour this park.)

Epcot's primary icon is the huge 18-story, silver geodesic sphere (or as visitors call it, the "giant golf-ball" based on its dimpled, up-close appearance). It houses one of the most popular attractions in Walt Disney World: *Spaceship Earth.*

Epcot

Insider's Note!

Spaceship Earth's spherical shape is comprised of many triangles that form an "omnitriangulated" surface. This geodesic dome design appealed to an engineer named Buckminster Fuller who championed it (initially as a post WWII home design) because, given its overall weight, it is an inherently stable structure, with extreme relative strength. While never popular for homes, these spheres can be found all over the world in the form of theaters, churches, exhibition halls, and museums. The design was a good fit for Disney's purposes – in which to conceal an attraction – because of the fact that spheres enclose the greatest volume with the least surface area.

Epcot

You may be surprised to find a high level of corporate branding throughout the park and its rides, as many of the exhibits and attractions are officially sponsored by major companies.

Thrill Rides are Limited

- Test Track
- Guardians of the Galaxy: Cosmic Rewind
- Mission:SPACE

Amusement rides are not prevalent here: you find only three thrill rides in the entire park. Of these rides, only Cosmic Rewind and Test Track are completely physical rides, while Mission: SPACE combines elements of 3D effects and movement to create a simulated ride effect. *Soarin'* is another extremely popular, wholly-simulated attraction, though not quite on the level of a thrill ride.

Park Layout and Design

Epcot's four themed pavilions are now called "neighborhoods" – World Celebration, World Discovery, World Nature, and World Showcase. Rather than the single hub design of other Disney parks, Epcot has two: CommuniCore Plaza for the front half of the park and World Showcase Lagoon for the back half (World Showcase). Think of the park as a giant figure eight or hourglass. Each park half is circular in shape and connected together by a long pathway that runs between them.

There are 11 world pavilions within World Showcase bordering the large World

"To the youngsters of today, I say believe in the future…"
- Walt Disney

In terms of overall size, this park is about twice as large as the Magic Kingdom or Hollywood Studios, although it is still much smaller than the Animal Kingdom. Physically, Epcot sits within a land area of about 300 acres. The promenade around World Showcase measures a whopping 1.2 miles long, encircling the 40-acre lagoon.

Showcase lagoon. The lagoon dominates the entire back portion of the park.

World Celebration

Located in the park's main entrance, World Celebration is the first neighborhood and features Epcot's landmark *Spaceship Earth*, an eighteen-story-tall geodesic sphere structure that houses a delightful ride through the history of communication. World Celebration also includes *Journey into Imagination with Figment*, *Disney & Pixar Short Film Festival*, and *Club Cool*.

World Discovery

Epcot's east side is the World Discovery neighborhood, home to science, technology, and intergalactic adventure. Attractions include *Guardians of the Galaxy: Cosmic Rewind*, *Mission: SPACE*, and *Test Track*, as well as the "Galaxarium," a planetarium that explores

Insider's Tip!

The World Showcase Lagoon sets the stage for the nightly fireworks presentation, *Harmonious*.

the galaxies of both Earth and Xandar, a war-torn planet in the Marvel Universe.

World Nature

Epcot's west side is the World Nature neighborhood, home to agriculture, ecology, and adventure both high above ground and deep under water. Attractions include *Soarin' Around the World*, a comfortable, indoor ride that simulates hang gliding over magnificent parts of the planet, and *The Seas with Nemo & Friends*, which is based on ocean exploration and features an aquarium.

World Showcase

World Showcase is a presentation of famous international landmarks, architectural styles, cultures, and art within its country pavilions. Found there are several cultural films, museum-style displays, and two low-key, water-ride attractions (in the Mexico and Norway pavilions).

Eleven World Showcase Pavilions

Surrounding the large World Showcase lagoon (which dominates the entire back portion of the park), the 11 national pavilions, moving clockwise from the Showcase Plaza, are:

- Mexico
- Norway
- China
- Germany
- Italy
- America (The American Adventure)
- Japan
- Morocco
- France
- United Kingdom
- Canada

The African Outpost, between China and Germany, is not counted as one of the nations that sponsored a formal pavilion.

Its theme provides a backdrop for a sales kiosk offering refreshments and souvenirs.

Getting Around the World Showcase Lagoon

Walking down the main promenade from World Celebration, you arrive at the Showcase Plaza. This is the main entrance to the World Showcase that circles around the lagoon. There are no attractions here, only a couple of stores and a character meet-and-greet.

Guests can get to the other side of the lagoon by walking around the promenade, or by traveling across it in one of two "FriendShip" boats. The vessels quickly take you between Showcase Plaza and the national pavilions that sit on the far side of the lagoon. (There is one lane of traffic between Canada and Morocco and another one between Mexico and Italy.)

If you get to a boat dock just as it is loading, it will save you a few minutes walking time. Otherwise, it takes about 15 minutes (strolling at a leisurely pace) to walk to the American Experience on the far side of the World Showcase.

Restaurants

Dining and libations are central to World Showcase. This park area features international cuisine, offering at least one restaurant in each country, though most have more than one dining (or drinking) option, making it the most diverse place to eat anywhere in Walt Disney World.

Restaurants open at lunchtime (11 a.m.), two to three hours after Future World opens in the front of the park (at 8 a.m. or 9 a.m.). The Norway and France pavilions are the only exceptions, as they host some popular rides and a Disney Princess character breakfast in Akershus Royal Banquet Hall each morning. Many guests shift to World Showcase during the evening hours to enjoy dinner and drinks.

World Celebration Attractions

Spaceship Earth (G+)

Spaceship Earth is found within the massive, 180-foot tall, 7,500 ton, shiny geosphere that is the iconic landmark of Epcot. The attraction itself is a "time-traveling" dark ride. Inside a continuous-moving vehicle, you get to comfortably journey back in time to witness many of mankind's most important advances in communication and other technologies, from the Stone Age to the current computer age.

Audio-Animatronic exhibits include the discovery of fire by prehistoric man, the Phoenician's creation of the alphabet, and the invention of Gutenberg's printing press. Cameo appearances include Michelangelo painting the ceiling of the Sistine Chapel and a famous computer enthusiast named Steve tinkering in his Silicon Valley garage with the first Apple Computer. (Disney intentionally left the question whether this is Steve Jobs or Steve Wozniak ambiguous, but many bloggers insist the physical appearance more closely resembles Wozniak.) The voiceover script was originally written by Ray Bradbury, and the current host narrator is Dame Judi Dench.

Devoted to technology and communication, *Spaceship Earth* also includes an in-car, interactive video which you can customize. As your vehicle initially climbs up the track, look to your right and smile or make a funny face. Your picture is taken and eventually incorporated into a fun video that is played back to you at the end of the ride.

The Omnimover safely returns you "back to the future" about 15 minutes after your initial departure. After disembarking, you'll even have the option of emailing an electronic postcard of your picture in the post-ride gaming area.

Don't go to this attraction first thing! Spaceship Earth is the very first attraction people see when they enter the park, so it fills up quickly. However, if you wait until early evening, you can often get on the ride with little to no wait. Genie+ Lightning Lane reservations are usually available.

Project Tomorrow: Inventing the Wonders of the Future

Spark your imagination with this series of hands-on exhibits in Spaceship Earth that bring the future to life. After a trip on Spaceship Earth, explore high-tech advances in energy, medicine, and transportation.

Exhibits allow you to scan the body to the molecular level, assemble a digitized human body for remote surgery, and hit the highway in a driving simulator game with an ace accident-avoidance system. Be sure to stop by the Project Tomorrow kiosk to send a "virtual postcard" to yourself from the future.

World Discovery Attractions

Guardians of the Galaxy: Cosmic Rewind (LL)

Help the Guardians travel back in time and save our planet during the formation of the universe in this innovative "storycoaster" that features movie scenes and character cameos from Guardians of the Galaxy!

Guests must be at least 42" or taller to ride. The first Disney ride to launch in reverse, Cosmic Rewind is a high-speed intergalactic chase back through time and space. The track is estimated to be about 5,000 feet long, making it one of the longest indoor roller coasters in the world. Designed to look like the Milano starship at a Xandarian outpost, its Omni Coaster car rotates 360 degrees, though it does not go upside-down.

SPECIAL NOTE: Guests must pay for an individual Lightning Lane reservation or reserve a spot in the virtual queue to ride this attraction. (There is no stand-by queue.) Keep in mind that Lightning Lane reservations are usually sold out immediately, so most guests, particularly those staying off-property, must vie for a spot in the very limited virtual queue for a chance to experience this ride.

To join the virtual queue, log into the My Disney Experience app at least ten minutes prior to 7 a.m. the morning of your visit (prior Epcot reservation required). On the main screen, follow the prompts to join a virtual queue and select your entire party.

The queue opens wxactly at 7 a.m. As the time nears, press the "Refresh" button, until the queue opens and a Boarding Group becomes available.

Once assigned a Boarding Group number, check the app frequently to see the approximate wait time. Head to the attraction as soon as your Boarding Group is called. From this point, there is about a 25-minute wait in line.

If you don't get into a Boarding Group at 7 a.m., you can try again at 1 p.m. However, you must already be in Epcot for a chance to join the 1 p.m. virtual queue. (Park hoppers who start their day in another park can't join a virtual queue for this attraction, so they are limited to the paid Lightning Lane.)

Mission: SPACE (*G+*)

Also found in Future World East, *Mission: SPACE* is a high-tech centrifugal force flight simulator attraction that goes far beyond normal 3-D effects, using high-speed spinning capsules to simulate the high-gravitational forces ("G-forces") of lift off and the sensation of being weightless. The Orange experience takes you through NASA-style training, culminating in a harrowing trip to Mars, complete with an accidental "crash landing" on the red planet. The Green experience takes you on a gentler ride around planet Earth. The duration of the simulated ride is about five minutes, not including the pre-show. Orange Team members must be 44" or taller to ride, while Green Team members must be 40" or taller. Lightning Lane reservations are recommended. However, you can usually get on this ride without much wait before 11 a.m. and after dinnertime.

Advanced Training Lab

Located in the post-show area of Mission: SPACE, this cosmic-themed indoor

Epcot

Insider's Tip!

*M*ission: *Space* has two experiences, each with different levels of intensity: Green and Orange. We suggest starting as a member of the tame Green Team, which omits the spinning motion, reducing the impact of the ride, to see how you fare with the 3-D effects. If you do well on Green Team, come back later to try the Orange Team for a more intense experience. Late evening is the best time to enjoy the Orange Team, as any motion sickness you may experience won't ruin your entire day.

Beware: Once the ride starts, there is no stopping it. Each guest is strapped inside a "space capsule" that has a magnified display of a video screen that looks like a window to space. The ride is not recommended for people with issues regarding claustrophobia.

playground is where young space cadets can crawl through worm holes and virtually "fly" above Mars with a jetpack. Ideal for children who want to visit Mars but not via rocket launch. Other activities include video games and a computer kiosk where you can email postcards of yourself from outer space.

Test Track (G+)

Right next to *Mission: SPACE*, *Test Track* takes you on an intense road trial where you test the performance of a (General Motors) race car of your very own design at speeds up to 65 miles per hour.

Using a touchscreen computer at a design kiosk, you get to create a prototype vehicle by choosing among body shapes, styles and colors, engine types, and wheels. Each change to the car's design updates on the screen along with performance data that is reflected in four metrics: fuel efficiency, handling capabilities, handling responsiveness, and engine power.

The design parameters of your prototype concept car are stored to your park pass or MagicBand account to become your "launch ticket." Just before entering the vehicle, scan your pass or MagicBand to transfer the design data to the ride vehicle's computer.

You begin the ride by going through simulated performance and handling tests inside a six-seat race car. These tests include braking maneuvers, testing the suspension up a bumpy hill, and testing traction and cornering ability on mild curves. Once these are complete, you get to test overall acceleration where you quickly pick up speed.

After your vehicle "crashes" through a wall and begins its grand finale around an outdoor track, smile and look to your right as a souvenir PhotoPass picture is taken of you. While the entire experience, including designing your vehicle, can take about 25 minutes on particularly busy days, the actual ride duration is less than five minutes. Lightning Lane reservations are highly recommended.

Insider's Tip!

Single rider lines are available at four Disney World attractions:

- Rock 'n' Roller Coaster in Hollywood Studios
- Millennium Falcon: Smugglers Run in Hollywood Studios
- Test Track in Epcot
- Expedition Everest in Animal Kingdom

These queues are intended for people who are riding alone and often have wait times that are much less than the regular stand-by queues. When you reach the front of the line, you will be paired with an odd-numbered party to fill an available space in the vehicle.

Keep in mind, if you have multiple people in your party and try to use the single rider line, you will not be allowed to sit together! Do not ask or pretend you did not understand when you reach the front of the queue, as Cast Members will not make an exception for you. You will simply hold up other guests waiting for their turn.

Future World West Attractions

The Seas with Nemo & Friends Pavilion and Aquarium

Located in Future World West, The Seas with Nemo & Friends pavilion contains a state-of-the-art 5.7 million gallon salt-water marine aquarium, the Nemo-themed ride (of the same name), an interactive animated film, and walk-through marine life exhibits.

The Seas with Nemo & Friends (*G+*)

Based on the hit movie *Finding Nemo*, the family-friendly ride runs along a continuously moving track along which "clam-mobiles" descend into the depths of the ocean in a playful search for the lost (or hiding) little clownfish, Nemo.

Revolving around the giant marine habitat, the ride employs puppetry, lighting, and animation for special effects. One such excellent effect projects videos of the film's characters onto the windows of the aquarium, so that they appear to be swimming together with the real, live fish. The clam-mobile glides past colorful tropical reefs, ancient shipwrecks, and dangerous jellyfish before it is gently swept up into the East Australian Current with Nemo, Crush, and Squirt. The joyful musical finale features the catchy song, "In the Big Blue World."

The ride lasts about four minutes and tends to be popular during the day. Some young children may be afraid of the shark scenes, but it's generally a safe bet for youngsters. Try to ride before 11 a.m. or after 3 p.m. If you wait until after 5 p.m. there is usually little or no wait. Genie+ Lightning Lane reservations are usually available.

Turtle Talk With Crush (*G+*)

Another headliner attraction in this pavilion is *Turtle Talk With Crush*. This 17-minute animated show stars the "most totally bodacious" 153 year-old turtle from the *Finding Nemo* film. When Crush appears on the screen, Disney magic allows him to see and speak directly to audience members. Cast Members are able to control the movement and voice of Crush to have real conversations with guests.

The resulting experience is incredibly realistic, and watching the children who actually believe they are speaking with the surfing turtle is truly magical. (The interactive technology for *Turtle Talk With Crush* is similar to that used in *Monsters, Inc. Laugh Floor* at Magic Kingdom.) This fun and engaging character puts on a thoroughly entertaining performance.

Though each show is unique, the format – essentially a question-and-answer session – remains the same.

This attraction can bring in very large crowds during the day. Try to visit before 11 a.m. or after 3 p.m. If you come back after 5 p.m. there is rarely a wait. Genie+ Lightning Lane reservations are usually available.

Bruce's Shark World

In a little corner of the aquarium at The Seas with Nemo and Friends Pavilion is a fantastic photo-op with Bruce, the nice shark from the Finding Nemo movie. Feel free to climb into his mouth and peer through his big, sharp teeth for a fun snapshot. This interactive exhibit challenges you to test your shark

Insider's Note!

Soarin' was revamped in 2016 with updated scenery and enhanced, digital film quality. The changes increased capacity with the addition of another theater, which reduced wait times.

knowledge and learn how to protect all of our undersea friends. Are the tiny three pearls inside the oyster depicted on the wall screen Bruce's Shark World actually a tiny, hidden Mickey?

SeaBase

The SeaBase is a world class aquarium, containing 5.7 million gallons of salt-water and more than 6,000 sea creatures. The second largest aquarium of its kind in the world, it provides a window to the magic and mystery of life underwater. Angelfish, dolphins, manatees, rays, sea turtles and sharks freely swim together within its 8-inch-thick tank walls. Feedings are daily at 10:00 a.m. and 3:30 p.m.

Visit the second floor for a prime view from the Observation Deck – a circular, windowed room that puts you in the center of the aquarium, surrounding you with aquatic life. Experienced scuba divers can dive into the aquarium as part of the Dive Quest experience.

Soarin' Around the World (*G+*)

One of the most sought-after attractions in all of Epcot, and maybe all of Walt Disney World, is located within the Land pavilion. Though not technically a thrill ride, the "flying" 3-D attraction is consistently given top reviews. From small children to senior citizens, everyone loves this attraction, despite the mild potential for motion-sickness.

Soarin' uses a hang gliding platform that resembles a giant Erector Set to lift you into the air in front of the super hi-definition IMAX-quality theater screen.

As the hang glider gently moves over several famous, international landmarks, soft winds and scents complete the realistic experience.

The places you'll glide over include Paris, Sydney, Tahiti, and Alaska before returning to Walt Disney World.

Soarin' has a 40" minimum height requirement. If you are in a wheelchair or scooter, you must be able to transfer into the ride vehicle. Many guests consider this to be Epcot's best attraction. The ride duration is just under six minutes, and standby wait times typically range from 45 minutes to two hours. However, thanks to a recent expansion of the attraction, evening wait times are often under 30 minutes. Genie+ Lightning Lane reservations are recommended.

Living with the Land (*G+*)

Also in The Land pavilion is *Living with the Land*, an educational boat-ride that explores the world's historical, current, and future food production techniques. Floating on a slow-moving current of water, your boat travels through artificial *biomes* (biological environments), working laboratories, and futuristic greenhouses. A variety of ecosystems are represented, from an African desert to a tropical rainforest.

Multimedia displays bring the historic scenery to life, integrating sound and lighting effects along with heat, wind, and mist that simulate real weather conditions. As you drift by, you'll learn about mankind's past successes and failures with farming techniques, as well as the hopeful future for living off the land. Live eels, catfish, tilapia, shrimp, and small alligators are also on display during your cruise through the aquatic fish farm. The boat floats through a theater that illustrates the struggles of the past and plans for the future including Aquaculture, Aeroponics, and Hydroponics.

The educational content on this 14-minute ride is geared mostly toward adults, but younger guests may enjoy the boat ride and spotting different kinds of fruits and vegetables they will recognize growing in ways not commonly seen.

Wait times rarely exceed 15 minutes. Genie+ Lightning Lane reservations are usually available.

Journey Into Imagination With Figment (*G+*)

Journey Into Imagination With Figment sits inside the Imagination pavilion. This is a lighthearted and upbeat fantasy-adventure where guests enter the zany Imagination Institute and travel with the purple dragon, Figment, through the senses of sight, smell, and sound.

There are a number of references to other Disney movies throughout the attraction, including *Flubber, The Absent Minded Profesor, Merlin Jones*, and *The Computer Who Wore Tennis Shoes*, giving movie-lovers an added thrill. This attraction also features 'One Little Spark,' an uplifting song written by legendary Disney composers, the Sherman Brothers.

While we don't recommend this as a high-priority ride, use it as a way to beat the heat and crowds when you need to schedule a short break. Because of its limited popularity and the relatively high capacity of the continuously-loading, six-minute long ride, it has low crowds and usually no more than 15 minute waits. Very young children particularly love Figment, but there are a few aspects that may be frightening, including a very loud "bang" near the end of the journey. Same-day Genie+ Lightning Lane reservations are usually available, though not typically necessary.

ImageWorks - The "What If" Labs

The Journey into Imagination with Figment ride exits into a continuation of the Imagination Institute's Sensory Laboratories with an interactive, creative playground called The "What If" Labs. What if you could lead an orchestra just by waving your hands in the air? What if you could jump on tones instead of stones, and compose a symphony? What

What has long been known as the adult theme park, Epcot is now a great destination for young children. Both the Norway and France pavilions have rides aimed at young children, while Norway also hosts a princess character breakfast each morning.

if you could record yourself in super-slow motion?

The "What If" Labs also let you design your own Figment dragon to send via email. Combined with the gift shop, this imaginary playground is about 5,000 square feet in size.

Disney and Pixar Short Film Festival (*G+*)

You will find this entertaining respite from the heat In the Imagination pavilion theater. The *Disney and Pixar Short Film Festival* includes three animated 3-D shorts showcasing both new and beloved characters.

This attraction is a must for fans of innovative film and animation techniques, as well as anyone needing a break from the heat in comfortable, air condition seating. Genie+ Lightning Lane reservations are available, though usually not necessary for this 18 minute show.

World Showcase

Country Pavilions

While you might think only of rides and shows when you hear the word "attraction," Disney has created an area within Epcot where the very buildings, people, and environment *are* the attraction. This is World Showcase with its country pavilions.

Mexico

Heading clockwise into World Showcase from Spaceship Earth, Mexico is the first pavilion you reach. It is dominated by its

Epcot

Epcot

iconic landmark, visible from across the lagoon: a beautiful replica of an ancient Aztec Pyramid.

There is a lot to do inside the pyramid. There's a folk art gallery, an "open air" marketplace, a high-end tequila bar, a traditional Mexican restaurant, and a whimsical boat ride on tour with Donald Duck and his band, "The Three Caballeros." The setting inside is always "dusk," marked by a cool and dark ambiance that is inviting and mysterious.

Outside the Mexico pavilion is a counter-service restaurant with covered outdoor seating along the lagoon as well retail kiosks along the promenade. A Mariachi Band performs hourly until early evening.

The Kidcot Fun Stop is located in the center of the pyramid's lobby.

Character Meet-and-Greet: Donald Duck

Norway

Designed to resemble a Norwegian town square, the Norway pavilion includes an authentic medieval wooden stave church building, as well as a replica of a 14th century fortress. Eateries include a delicious bakery with a deli counter and the very popular "Princess Storybook Dining" character buffet. A new "Frozen Ever After" ride opened in Norway in the spring of 2016.

Norway's impressive gift shops sell high-quality, imported Norwegian wares as well as the expected trolls, toys, Viking horns, and *Frozen*-related merchandise. A beer stand is located in a small kiosk on the promenade on the Mexico side of the pavilion.

The Kidcot Fun Stop is located across from the perfume section of The Puffin's Roost shop.

Character Meet-and-Greet: Princess Character Dining; Elsa and Anna

People of Germanic descent eagerly race to the Germany pavilion and are often disappointed to find the only real entertainment in the "land" is found inside a restaurant, which they must pay to experience.

China

Looming large overhead, a vibrant, triple-arched ceremonial gate welcomes visitors to China with its beautifully manicured gardens, ponds, a courtyard, and traditional pagodas. The courtyard is bordered by shops selling Chinese merchandise, as well as an art gallery and two Chinese restaurants. The *Lotus Blossom Café* provides counter-service meals, and the *Nine Dragons Restaurant* provides table-service.

Outside and across the promenade is *Joy of Tea*, a small tea stand with specialty teas, including uniquely-flavored alcoholic drinks. The *Yong Feng Shangdian Department Store* sells a wide selection of imported merchandise that represents classic Chinese art and culture, and live entertainment is provided by the Dragon Legend Acrobats. Aside from the museum, the primary attraction in the China pavilion is a 14-minute educational film located in a 360-degree Circle-Vision Theater.

The Kidcot Fun Stop is inside the large store past the restaurants.

Character Meet-and-Greet: Mulan

The African Outpost

African Outpost sits between China and Germany. While not an actual pavilion, this African-themed area is simply a snack bar and outdoor shopping venue with some outdoor seating.

A tarp covers a play area that includes several authentic African tribal drums. The drum circle entices children, both young and grown-up, to join in the fun.

This shaded spot extends over the waiting area of the snack bar. The food offered is limited to hot dogs, chips, soft-serve ice cream, cookies, frozen slushees, beer, and Coke products.

Each of the three African Outpost shops has unique African-themed gifts, including handmade beads, hand-carved wooden statues and walking sticks, and tribal masks.

Kidcot Fun Stop and Character Meet-and-Greet: None

Germany

The romantic Germany pavilion is designed to look like an authentic German town complete with cobblestone streets and central plaza with a fountain. It has numerous shops selling German goods, sweet treats, and hearty adult beverages.

Other than retail goods, food and libations is all this pavilion really has to offer.

Its main attraction is the German *Biergarten* buffet restaurant, featuring authentic German cuisine and imported beer along with live entertainment that consists of a 25-minute theatrical performance by an oompah band.

The quick-service counter restaurant, *Sommerfest*, offers bratwurst, potato salad, and house-made potato chips. Other kiosks serve pretzels and German libations, and you can also enjoy specialty caramel desserts.

Wine lovers will appreciate the wine tasting cellar where you can try several imported vintages or just a single glass. Opt for a "wine flight" to try different flavors. Purchase of these wine flights allows you to try samples in Germany, Italy, and/or France.

Take the time to catch the Glockenspiel as it plays on every hour and half hour. Kids especially enjoy seeing the characters move around the clock, located in the pavilion's plaza.

The classic and lovely Snow White can be found at her wishing well (on the African Outpost side of the pavilion), waiting to visit with families. On the opposite edge of Germany is a captivating, miniature German village with a working model train.

The Kidcot Fun Stop is inside the toy and souvenir store, Volkskunst.

Character Meet-and-Greet: Snow White

Italy

Venetian canals, bridges, and gondolas welcome you to Epcot's Italy pavilion. Designed after *Piazzetta di San Marco* in Venice, you immediately feel the romance of the city.

Purchase a glass of wine – or buy a bottle to take home – in Italy's counter-service wine shop to add to the ambiance.

If you're feeling more adventurous, request a "wine flight" to taste samples from any of the three wine tasting venues throughout World Showcase. Wine flights can also be redeemed in Germany and France.

Enjoy real Italian gelato, gourmet pizza, pastries, and high-end Italian dining at a selection of restaurants. Peruse clothing, fine leather goods, jewelry, and perfume amongst the Romanesque stone archways and columns. The center of the piazza offers theatrical performances throughout the day.

The Kidcot Fun Stop is in the plaza on the right before the center stage.

Epcot

Insider's Tip!

Take a moment to ask the friendly Kidcot Cast Member to write your child's name in Japanese on a paper fan. This makes an excellent (and free) souvenir that children find very unique, and your little ones will cherish theirs.

Character Meet-and-Greet: None

The American Adventure

The America pavilion is host to the surrounding countries. The American Adventure landmark is a massive three-story, Georgian mansion. Its primary stage attraction, "The American Adventure," is a 29-minute patriotic show including Audio-Animatronic historical characters, motion picture clips, lighting effects, and music.

Inside the mansion is *Regal Eagle Smokehouse*, a counter service restaurant that offers all-American barbecue fare. It has a bright, cool setting with ample indoor (and covered outdoor) seating. *Heritage Manor Gifts*, on the opposite side of the mansion from Liberty Inn, is a small gift shop with unique items made in America and representing American culture and history.

Along the promenade are several food-service kiosks, including the *Fife & Drum Tavern*, selling turkey legs, soft serve ice cream, and popcorn. Libations include ice cold, Samuel Adams draft beer. Across the promenade from the manor and food kiosks is a large amphitheater, the *American Gardens Theatre* which seasonally showcases various live entertainment pro-ductions. This venue roars to life during major festivals with many top-charting bands of previous decades.

The Kidcot Fun Stop is located to the right of the mansion in a shaded seating area under an awning.

Character Meet-and-Greet: None

Japan

Marking the boundary between the everyday and the sacred, the Japan pavilion welcomes visitors with a bright red torii gate. You'll find yourself surrounded by serene landscaping that features tranquil water gardens filled with koi, perfectly-sculptured shrubbery, and Zen rock gardens.

A five-story, blue-roofed pagoda includes an outdoor stage for regular performances of the incredible Matsuriza Taiko Drummers. Across the courtyard, the massive *Mitsukoshi Department Store* is housed within the Shishinden building.

Popular destinations within this pavilion include two highly-regarded Japanese restaurants, an art gallery, sake bar, walk-up snack kiosk, and candy store. The *Pick-A-Pearl* station is a particular favorite among children.

The Kidcot Fun Stop is just beyond the castle fortress entrance.

Character Meet-and-Greet: None

Morocco

The Kingdom of Morocco pavilion captures the country's romantic cultural history. Towering high above the land is the replica of the *Koutoubia Minaret of Marrakesh*, a 12th-century prayer tower. Exquisite attention to detail is credited to King Hassan II who dispatched his very own royal artisans to design authentic architecture and detailed mosaics.

Explore The *Fes House*, a recreation of a traditional Moroccan home, and *Gallery of Arts* and History, which regularly rotates exhibits of Moroccan art, artifacts, and costumes. A bustling market of six small stores sells a variety of popular clothing items and handmade crafts, such as belly dancing costumes, colorful robes, carpets, brassware, leather ware, jewelry,

Remy's Ratatouille Adventure attrac-tion opened in the France Pavilion late in 2021. It is a copy of *Remy's Totally Zane Adventure* in Disneyland Paris, allowing guests to shrink to Remy's size and go on a wild, high-speed chase throughout a restaurant in a trackless "ratmobile." Get ready to scurry along, dodging dangers in your mad dash to safety.

and more. Decorative Henna tattoos are available at the *Art of Henna* station. Across the promenade from a small shop and restaurant is a small stage for professional performances.

Authentic Mediterranean dishes are available at the *Restaurant Marrakesh*, which features belly dancing entertainment; *Spice Road Table*, which offers both inside and outside seating; and the counter-service *Tangierine Café*. The *Moorish Café* is a snack bar specializing in delicious pastries, coffee, and drinks.

The Kidcot Fun Stop is inside *The Brass Bazaar*.

Character Meet-and-Greet: Jasmine and Aladdin

France

It is always springtime in Paris in this beautifully landscaped pavilion. Walk the famous Seine River among flower carts, posters, easels, (caricature) artists, and boats with oars. A one-tenth scale replica of the Eiffel Tower looming high in the background further enhances the Parisian ambience. *Monsieur Paul* is a premier table-service restaurant, and *Les Chefs de France* is a brasserie-style table-service restaurant. *Les Vins des Chefs de France*, the third of three wine tasting venues in World Showcase, offers French wines and genuine Champagne.

Made-to-order French crepes, soft-serve ice cream, sorbets, and hand-scooped ice cream cones are all available in this pavilion. Everything you expect to find in

Disney's BoardWalk sits between the two theme parks, though it is much closer to Epcot than Hollywood Studios. The BoardWalk itself is designed to look much like Atlantic City around the turn of the century. Restaurants, shops, and nightclubs line the promenade.

a kitschy souvenir shop is located within *Souvenirs de France*, from miniature Eiffel Towers to authentic French berets. *Les Halles Boulangerie Patisserie* ("The Patisserie") in the back corner of the souvenir shop offers salads, soups, sandwiches, quiche, and arguably the best desserts in Walt Disney World.

Palais du Cinema, modeled after a theater in Fontainebleau, displays the *Impressions de France* film, a 200-degree viewing experience on five screens. A country-style store sells cookbooks, cooking utensils, and even some imported foods. A perfume store, designed to look like the flagship *La Maison Guerlain* shop in Paris, often carries extremely hard-to-find products directly from France. Belle (and sometimes Beast) greets guests on the Morocco side of the promenade.

The Kidcot Fun Stop is located inside of *Souvenirs de France*.

Character Meet-and-Greet: Belle

International Gateway

Tucked off on a side path between the France and United Kingdom pavilions is International Gateway, the "back entrance" providing access to Epcot-area hotels and Disney's BoardWalk. The *World Traveler* souvenir shop is located just inside this entrance and is one of the two package pickup locations for Epcot. Locker rentals, restrooms, and Guest Relations are found here as well.

Character Meet-and-Greet: Occasional Characters-in-Training

Water Transportation and Walking Paths

Disney's "FriendShip" boats navigate Crescent Lake between Epcot and Hollywood Studios, and make stops at Disney's BoardWalk, Yacht and Beach Club resorts, as well as Walt Disney World Swan and Dolphin hotels. A

Epcot

walking path also provides access to these areas, and it takes about 25 to 30 minutes to stroll all the way from Epcot to Hollywood Studios.

United Kingdom

Taking a "trip across the pond" to the United Kingdom pavilion, you find a British village with cobblestone streets, a courtyard, and an outdoor park. A charming pub sells imported lager by the pint, and the aroma of fresh fish and chips wafts from a roadside stand.

Central to the pavilion is *Britannia Square*, a mini-*Hyde Park* (outdoor theater) surrounded by perfectly manicured gardens, shrubbery, and topiaries. Architecture represents styles from the Victorian, 19th century London, Tudor, and Georgian eras. The shops sell imported toys, teas, clothes, and Beatles merchandise. The *Rose & Crown* building houses two eateries: a pub with counter-service, and a restaurant with table-service.

The *Sportsman's Shoppe* sells a plethora of merchandise related to rugby and soccer as well as some of Britain's most popular TV shows. The *Historical Research Center* is where you can look up the history of your last name and purchase a family "coat of arms" as a printed souvenir. Mary Poppins as well as Alice from Alice in Wonderland meet and greet visitors along the promenade next to the gardens.

The Kidcot Fun Spot is located at the very back of *The Toy Soldier*.

Character Meet-and-Greet: Mary Poppins; Alice (in Wonderland)

Canada

Totem poles and log cabins greet you as you enter the pavilion. You can purchase apparel and Canadian-themed souvenirs. Get a wide range of Native Indian (First Nation) and Inuit crafts, wine, and various edibles, including world-famous maple syrup.

The centerpiece of The Canada pavilion is the Victorian-style *Hotel du Canada*, which is patterned after a historic hotel found in Ottawa. The colorful grounds evoke the Canadian Rockies, complete with a refreshing 30-foot waterfall gorge. You even find a small-scale representation of Victoria's famous *Butchart Gardens*.

Canada's primary attraction is a nine-screen, 360° Circle-Vision film called *O Canada!* narrated by the Canadian-born comedian Martin Short. *Le Cellier Steakhouse* is an extremely popular signature restaurant that serves steaks, seafood, imported wines and beers, as well as delicious cheese soup.

The Kidcot Fun Spot is located near the *O Canada!* theater exit in a covered area along the canyon path.

Character Meet-and-Greet: None

World Showcase Attractions

Gran Fiesta Tour Starring The Three Caballeros (Mexico Pavilion)

The Gran Fiesta Tour Starring The Three Caballeros is a seven minute, indoor boat ride with joyful Mexican music. Based on the 1944 Disney film by the same name (and using similar colors and design elements) the stars of the show are

Insider's Trivia!

The spectacular videos and images for *Reflections of China* were captured using nine 35mm cameras that were fitted to a unique pod in order to create the 360-degree view.

the avian singing trio of Donald Duck, José Carioca (parrot), and Panchito, known together as the *Three Caballeros* (Gentlemen).

The attraction features lively traditional music combined with live action film sequences overlaid with animation. The video is high-definition, and the audio is spectacular for setting the mood. The ride showcases the people, scenery, and some history of Mexico.

Your leisurely Mexican boat tour floats throughout the back-most portion of Mexico pavilion's iconic pyramid. The best time to ride is before lunchtime or after dinner, as crowds may build in the early afternoon. However, there is usually very little wait for this attraction. Lightning Lane is not available.

Mexico Folk Art Gallery (Mexico Pavilion)

Exchange mourning for celebration in the Mexico Folk Art Gallery's current exhibit, "Remember Me! La Celebración del Dia de Muertos." Based on the Mexican holiday that honors the deceased, you will see papel picado, or elaborately cut paper flags, and calaveras, or decorative skulls made of sugar.

The Mirror de los Muertos reflects your own "Day of the Dead" skeleton in the Land of the Dead, as seen in the Disney Pixar movie Coco. A larger-than-life sculpture called the Bridal Couple, for whom death did not part, is prominently displayed in the center of the gallery.

Frozen Ever After (G+) (Norway Pavilion)

Frozen Ever After is an enchanting boat ride that takes you from Arendelle to visit Elsa in her ice castle. Of course, you visit all of your favorite *Frozen* characters along the way, each singing a rendition of the movie's popular songs.

The attraction features a unique overlay of digital imagery over character faces to emulate movement. The boat ride lasts five minutes, culminating when Elsa sends your boat backwards in a flurry of snow and ice. Unlike other World Showcase attractions, *Frozen Ever After* opens at 9 a.m. (before the rest of World Showcase opens at 11 a.m.). Use Genie+ Lightning

Duck Tales World Showcase Adventure

A new virtual experience is set to arrive in Epcot soon. Get ready to join your favorite adventurers, including Huey, Dewey, and Louie, as you travel the world solving mysteries, fighting villains, and maybe even picking up some treasure along the way!

The Disney Channel's Duck Tales show is brought to life in this special game, which is designed to keep children entertained and interested in exploring the World Showcase, since it otherwise has minimal activities.

Children can begin a mission using the Play Disney Parks app. This is a completely free app with various interactive elements in each park.

Each mission on this high-tech scavenger hunt takes about 30-45 minutes and can be played by small groups of up to four people.

Each game has between five and ten assignments. Tasks within the mission require you to go to specific locations or find certain objects within one of the pavilions.

Lane reservations to avoid long waits for this attraction.

Stave Church Gallery (Norway Pavilion)

A detailed reproduction of the wooden Gol Stave church located in Norway, this small museum is built with carved, corner-posts known as "staves," a technique that evolved from ancient Viking shipbuilding.

Currently on display are authentic Viking artifacts, some of which have not left Norway before, and many inspired by Norse mythology. Learn the legends that the medieval seafaring people shared around the family hearth together, such as myths about Thor, the hammer-wielding thunder god, and Loki, the shape-shifting trickster. Lightning Lane reservations are not available for this attraction.

Reflections of China (China Pavilion)

Viewers stand in the center of a 360-degree Circle-Vision Theater to watch this film about China's people, history, and culture. Narrated by an actor playing Li Bai, an ancient Chinese poet, it features a tour of many beautiful scenic attractions and historical structures across the Chinese countryside, including montages of The Great Wall of China, The Forbidden City in Beijing, Hong Kong, Tianamen Square, and Shanghai.

Shown continuously, expect few short delays to see the 13-minute film. There are no seats in this theater, and guests are welcome to remain in wheelchairs or ECVs. Lightning Lane reservations are not available for this attraction.

House of the Whispering Willows (China Pavilion)

This exhibit is an exclusive peek of Disney's groundbreaking new park, Shanghai Disney Resort. Artwork, costumes and models of the six lands

and two resort hotels located in China provide a fascinating depiction of how Imagineers built a culturally Chinese version of Disneyland. Imagineers used 3D modeling and advanced pre-visualization tools to develop rides such as the TRON Lightcycle Power Run in Shanghai's Tomorrowland.

Enchanted Storybook Castle is the largest and most complex castle built by Disney so far and is decorated with mosaic murals of Princesses of the Four Seasons. See how a winding staircase within the castle leads to a "Once Upon a Time" adventure where guests step through a mirror into the fairytale world of Snow White.

The American Adventure Show (American Adventure Pavilion)

Located at the very center of World Showcase, The American Adventure is the "host country" that is home to an elaborate 29-minute stage show (by the same name) featuring Benjamin Franklin and Mark Twain. This dignified centerpiece experience is a patriotic presentation that uses a series of elaborate moving sets, combining historical Audio-Animatronic figures, motion picture clips, lighting effects, and music.

Watch the Pilgrims arrive on the Mayflower; angry colonists stage the Boston Tea Party; and Americans declare their liberty with the Declaration of Independence, leading to The Revolutionary War (a.k.a. The War for Independence) and Valley Forge. See the struggles of our budding nation, including issues surrounding slavery, the Civil War, and the suffering of Native Americans. Other noteworthy historical moments include the Philadelphia Centennial Exposition, the founding of Yosemite National Park, and the trials and tribulations of the American citizenry as it coped through

World War I, the Great Depression, and then World War II. The presentation ends with a fast-moving 45-second film montage.

The huge theater assures that you won't have to wait long for a seat. At about a half-hour, the length of this show may be a bit much if you are traveling with small children, although the back of the darkened theater makes a good place for them to snooze in very comfortable seating. Many adults, including military veterans, find the show emotionally stirring. Lightning Lane reservations are not available for this attraction.

American Heritage Gallery (American Adventure Pavilion)

Housed within the American Adventure Attraction is an American Indian art gallery that showcases both historical Native artifacts and contemporary works from seven American regions. A wall sized map corresponds to the different regions featured in the exhibit. Browse the beautiful, handcrafted baskets, dolls, jewelry, outfits and musical instruments that are on display. Interactive elements include artists sharing their ancestral history, creative process and inspirations.

Bijutsu-kan Gallery (Japan Pavilion)

This adorable collection of everyday Japanese items explores the Japanese culture of cute, known as "kawaii," which is Japanese for "cute or loveable" and rhymes with "Hawaii." Included in the exhibit is Hello Kitty, one of Japan's most popular exports to the world.

Rooted in the ancient Shinto traditions of harmony and simplicity, modern kawaii culture took off as a stylish means of self-expression in the 1970s among Japan's schoolgirls. The exhibit demonstrates how precious kawaii is to all walks of Japanese life at home, work and play. A replica of a modern Tokyo apartment delightfully decorated in kawaii style features a refrigerator full of cute cuisine. Even "salarymen" in business suits are seen as superheroes in kawaii, for their dedication to the Japanese economy and marketplace.

Gallery of Arts and History: Race Against the Sun (Morocco Pavilion)

Morocco's "Race Against the Sun" showcases two intense sporting events that take place in the Sahara Desert: a six-day, 250km Ultra Run called Marathon des Sables (Marathon of the Sands), and a 2,500km, all-women motor race called Rallye Aïcha des Gazelles du Maroc (Rally of the Gazelles). A diorama sets the scene with displays of race gear, trophies and the nutrition and hydration required to fuel these incredible races.

Sit behind-the-wheel in the middle of the desert for a hot photo-op. Also explore how the ancient inhabitants of the Sahara, the Berbers, learned to thrive in one of the world's harshest climates.

Remy's Ratatouille Adventure (*G+*) (France Pavilion)

This attraction is based on the very popular Disney Paris ride, *L'Aventure Totalement Toquée de Rémy.*

Shrink to the size of a rat for a zany adventure, as you are chased through Gusteau's Restaurant with everyone's favorite chef and rat, Remy.

The 4D attraction uses the latest trackless ride technology, giving a smooth, yet exciting experience for riders. Don't miss it! Use Genie+ Lightning Lane reservations to avoid long waits for this attraction.

Beauty and the Beast Sing-Along

Located in the Palais du Cinema in the France pavilion, *Beauty and the Beast Sing-Along* is a 15-minute reimagining of the beloved story.

Mrs. Potts narrates a new version of the romance with a surprise behind-the-scenes hero. Of course, snippets from the movie's best songs are played for all to join in.

This is a favorite respite for adults and children to get out of the heat. It plays in the same theater as *Impressions de France*, so check for specific show times on the app the day of your visit. Lightning Lane reservations are not available for this attraction.

Impressions de France

Located in the Palais du Cinema in the France pavilion, *Impressions de France* is an 18-minute journey around 46 French locations, including the Eiffel Tower, Arc de Triomphe, and the French Alps. Delight in the view of majestic castles and chateaus, witness wine harvests, and even experience bicycling through Dordogne Valley.

Many regard this film to be the highlight of World Showcase, and it's easy to understand why. The film provides stunning aerial views mixed with intimate close-up views of guests touring the French countryside, major cities, and important structures. A medley of songs by famous composers (including Claude Debussy) blends beautifully with the scenery.

It plays in the same theater as *Beauty and the Beast Sing-Along*, so check for specific show times on the app the day of your visit. Five 21-foot high screens are spread across the room to form a continuous, 200-degree viewing experience. There is rarely a big wait to see the breathtaking film, since it has room for large audiences. Lightning Lane reservations are not available for this attraction.

O Canada!

Canada's primary attraction is a 360°, nine-screen, Circle-Vision film called *O Canada!* The theater itself is tucked inside the base of a Canadian mountainside. A truly immersive experience, this 18-minute panoramic show features the Canadian-born Martin Short as its narrator.

Your travels take you all the way from Prince Edward Island to the Toronto Film Festival and on to Vancouver, located in the farthest west province of British Columbia. You even experience the beauty of Victoria, famous for its enchanting Butchart Gardens.

Canada's favorite pastimes are highlighted, especially hockey, curling, and skiing. You also meet some familiar Canadians, including comedians Mike Myers and Jim Carrey. Sing along with Canadian Idol winner Eva Avila in her rendition of "Canada (You're a Lifetime Journey)."

During the show, you'll find yourself turning around to catch the film action as the whirlwind of events is projected all around you. The theater has a very large capacity and rarely fills up. However, Canada is one of the first pavilions people rush to each morning, so it's best to avoid the show until at least an hour or two after World Showcase opens. This is a standing-only show, though guests may use a wheelchair or ECV if necessary. Lightning Lane reservations are not available for this attraction.

Sample Lightning Lane & Genie+ Epcot Itineraries

1 Day (no small children)		1 Day (small children)	
Approx Time		Approx Time	
7 AM	Make Lightning Lane reservations for Test Track (9:10-10-10 window recommended), Remy's Ratatouille Adventure (early afternoon recommended), and Guardians of the Galaxy (late afternoon recommended).	7 AM	Make Lightning Lane reservations for Test Track (9:10-10-10 window recommended), Frozen Ever After (early afternoon recommended), and Remy's Ratatouille Adventure (late afternoon recommended).
8:30 AM	Arrive 30-45 minutes before park opening.	8:30 AM	Arrive 30-45 minutes before park opening.
9:10-9:30 AM	Ride Test Track.	9:10-9:30 AM	Ride Test Track.
9:45-10:30 AM	Ride Soarin' Around the World.	9:45-10:30 AM	Ride Soarin' Around the World.
10:40-11:10 AM	Ride Spaceship Earth.	10:40-11:30 AM	Ride The Seas with Nemo & Friends and visit aquarium.
11:20-11:45 AM	Ride Mission: SPACE.	11:30-12 PM	Visit Turtle Talk with Crush.
		12-12:30 PM	Visit Epcot Character Spot.
12-2 PM	Explore World Showcase and eat lunch.	12:30-1:30 PM	Eat Lunch.
2-2:30 PM	Use Lightning Lane to ride Remy's Ratatouille Adventure.	1:40-2:30 PM	Find a quiet place if child needs a nap/down time.
4-4:30 PM	Use Lightning Lane to ride Frozen Ever After	2:30-2:45 PM	Sign up for Duck Tales World Showcase Adventure
4:30-5 PM	Visit Mexico and ride The Three Caballeros.	2:45-3:45 PM	Visit Mexico and ride The Three Caballeros.
5-6 PM	Continue exploring World Showcase and eat dinner.	4-4:30 PM	Visit Norway and use Lightning Lane reservation to ride Frozen Ever After.
6:10-6:30 PM	View the Disney & Pixar Short Film Festival.	5-5:30 PM	Visit France and use Lightning Lane to ride Remy's Ratatouille Adventure
6:40-7 PM	Use Lightning Lane to ride Guardians of the Galaxy: Cosmic Rewind.	5:30-7:30 PM	Explore World Showcase and eat dinner.
7:10-8 PM	Ride The Seas with Nemo & Friends and visit aquarium.	7:40-8:10 PM	Ride Spaceship Earth.
8:10-8:30 PM	Find snacks and viewing location for Harmonious.	8:10-8:30 PM	Find snacks and viewing location for Harmonious.
9 PM	Watch Harmonious.	9 PM	Watch Harmonious.

Epcot

Hollywood Studios (formerly Disney-MGM Studios) changed its name in 2008 as a result of various legal disagreements between Disney and Metro-Goldwyn-Mayer, as well as Disney's decision to focus more on general entertainment, rather than just movies.

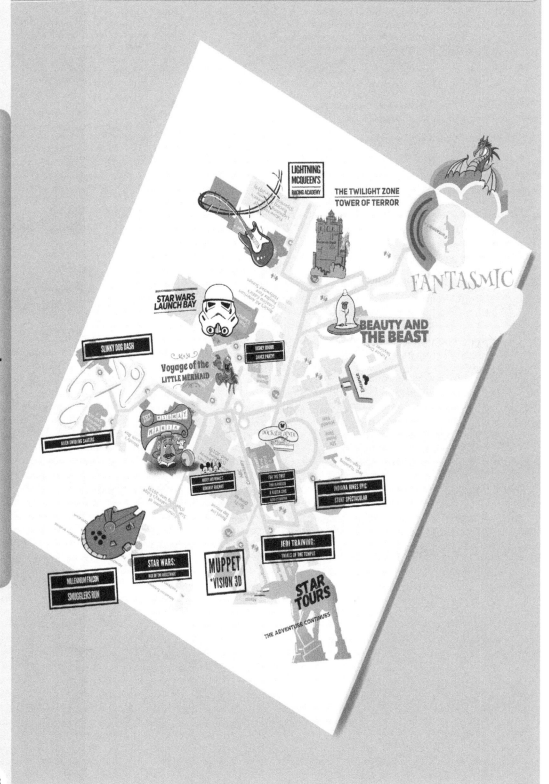

Hollywood Studios

Park Overview

Hollywood Studios (originally called Disney-MGM Studios) opened May 1, 1989. The park celebrates the glamour and glitz of Hollywood's big-screen productions and the small screen (television).

Hollywood Studios is somewhat larger than the Magic Kingdom and is divided into two areas, consisting of six themed sections.

The larger area makes up about 75 percent of the park and is based on motion pictures, music, and television entertainment. The highlights of this portion include a recreation of Hollywood and Sunset Boulevards set in the Golden Age of Hollywood. This area contains rides, musical shows, a movie stunt show, and Fantasmic!, the park's featured evening entertainment.

The second area, which used to be the "backlot," has been repurposed into the delightful Toy Story and Star Wars: Galaxy's Edge lands.

This re-imagining of the park included the removal of the iconic Earful Tower, as well as the closure of some popular attractions: *Lights, Motors, Action! Extreme Stunt Show* and *Honey, I Shrunk the Kids Movie Set Adventure.*

History

Hollywood Studios (then Disney-MGM Studios) was opened in 1989 to rival Universal Studios Orlando. Even though Universal Studios announced its project first, Disney made a mad dash to the finish line and completed its park a year earlier than its nemesis.

The centerpiece of the park was – and as of late 2015, is once again – an intricately-detailed replica of the historic Hollywood landmark, Grauman's Chinese Theatre, now formally known as TCL Chinese Theatre. Inside the theater, as we discuss later, is *The*, and you'll soon see what makes this ride so great!

This theater sits at the end of the road upon entering the park and was initially what guests saw as they entered the gates. However, that changed in 2001 when Disney executives decided to add a giant Sorcerer's hat directly in front of the theater. Their decision was made to celebrate the new millennium, but it had the effect of making the theater disappear from sight. Disney decided to right this wrong 14 years later, finally removing the hat during the summer of 2015, so that the theater again greets guests.

What's There to Do?

There are unique experiences at Hollywood Studios that are unlike what you can experience at any of Disney's other theme parks.

For instance, one popular event for a limited number of children (up to 12 years old) is to attend the *Jedi Training: Trials of the Temple*. This includes the opportunity to fight with Darth Vader or another *Dark Side* recruit.

A newer addition to the park is Star Wars: Galaxy's Edge, an entire land dedicated to all things Star Wars. This immersive land includes themed dining and attractions that delight even hard-core fans of the franchise.

Toy Story Land is a walkthrough wonderland for the children in all of us. Expierence what it's like to be one of Andy's toys as you shrink to the size of a toy and get to dash around on family-friendly rides.

Insider's Trivia!

Opened in 1927 by showman Sid Grauman, about four million tourists flock to the world's most famous Chinese Theater in Hollywood, California, each year. Over the years, it has changed its name, though it is still called "Grauman's Chinese Theatre" by most people.

In 1973, it was formally renamed Mann's Chinese Theatre. It went by this moniker until it was officially re-branded TCL Chinese Theatre in January, 2013 (after the Chinese manufacturer TCL paid more than $5 million for the naming rights to the 85-year old Hollywood establishment).

The park also hosts a museum dedicated to Walt Disney and the future of the parks, and there are even unique live-action shows to enjoy throughout Hollywood Studios.

Of course, some very popular and iconic rides draw visitors, including Walt Disney World's most extreme roller coaster and the iconic *Twighlight Zone Tower of Terror*.

Finally, entertainment troupes of varying styles wander the streets of the park and interact with guests. You may find yourself part of a fake movie production or witnessing a seemingly impromptu rock-and-roll concert during your visit.

Central Icon

With the removal of Mickey's humongous Sorcerer's Hat from the park in 2015, Hollywood Studios no longer has an easily identifiable main icon. The Earful Tower was initially given the role (which it previously held prior to the introduction of the Sorcerer's Hat). However, the tower was removed in April of 2016.

Many people associate Hollywood Studios with the nearly exact replica of

When Hollywood Studios initially opened, the park was an actual, working film and television studio. Not so long ago, Orlando was slated to be the "Hollywood of the Southeast," but the heat and humidity made it an unpopular choice. (Imagine having your stage makeup slide off between every outdoor take!)

As actual filming was scarce, using the backlot area of the park became problematic for the *Studio Backlot Tour*, where guests rode a tram through the functioning studios. Once production ceased on most of the shows, Disney then had to put "acting" Cast Members in unused rooms to make it appear as though they were still active.

Over the years, the *Backlot Tour* decreased in size and scope. Streets lined with trees and house façades – of such television hits as the Golden Girls – were demolished and replaced with the *Lights, Motors, Action! Extreme Stunt Show*, and the only working area guests were still brought through was the costume shop. Finally, near the end of 2014, Disney decided to close down the *Backlot Tour* for good. The decision came with very short notice and little fanfare.

Grauman's Chinese Theater. However, it cannot be the "official" icon because Disney has not been able to procure permission from the original building's owners to use it in such a prominent manner. In fact, Disney refers to the attraction building simply as the "Chinese Theater," since they lack official naming rights as well.

For now, the towering Hollywood Tower Hotel (home of *The Twilight Zone Tower of Terror* attraction) holds the coveted park icon crown.

Park Layout

The layout of this Disney World park is unlike the other three. Not only does Hollywood Studios not have a hub and spoke layout, it seems less clearly-defined. It does have a large, central courtyard and big lake, and some design elements blend seamlessly. However, transitions between areas can seem more abrupt than in other parks.

Some people feel it is more a hodge-podge of areas that don't flow together – each defined only by the streets that traverse them. This is, no doubt, due to expansions and thematic changes that have taken place over the almost 25 years that the park has been open.

Primary Lands/Streets of Hollywood Studio

- Hollywood Boulevard
- Echo Lake
- Commissary Lane
- Toy Story Land/Pixar Place
- Grand Avenue
- Mickey Avenue
- Animation Courtyard
- Sunset Boulevard

You enter the park on Hollywood Boulevard, which leads directly to the Chinese Theater (which formerly housed the *Great Movie Ride* attraction) that sits in a central courtyard.

This courtyard is the closest thing to a hub that Hollywood Studios has, and is where many of the streets come together. A couple of side streets intersect with Hollywood Boulevard before you get all the way to the Chinese Theater courtyard area.

Below we provide descriptions of the attractions in a clockwise fashion around the park, as you find yourself walking through each of the primary streets in the order listed above. (The exception to this is Commissary Lane, which runs between the promenade and the theater courtyard.)

Hollywood Studios

Disney's Purchase of the Star Wars Franchise

Disney fans had long-wondered why Disney did not capitalize on a mega-movie franchise the way Universal Studios has with Harry Potter. That finally changed when Disney paid $4 billion for the rights to Star Wars a few years ago. The Star Wars fan base has long proven to be devoted to the film series, and new generations of fans should add to the franchise's longevity with the introduction of three new movies in the series, beginning with *The Force Awakens*, released late in 2015. Capitalizing on this popularity, Disney constructed an entire Star Wars land (in both Walt Disney World and Disneyland). This is the largest ever single-themed land expansion, covering 14 acres at each park. Guests find themselves transported to a new world, viewing storm trooper battles and alien life. They even get a chance to pilot the iconic Millenium Falcon.

Insider's Trivia!

Hidden Mickey Courtyard The entire theater courtyard area was once in the shape of a giant Mickey Mouse head as part of the original park design. If you look at a map, you can still see partial remnants of that design. Echo Lake is the right ear, and planters form the shape of Mickey's eyes, however further construction on the park eliminated part of his silhouette.

Related Disney Resorts

This park does not have any associated hotels, but it is directly accessible by both boat and walkway to Epcot-area resorts, The BoardWalk, and Epcot. Aside from Epcot and its resorts, you can reach the other parks and hotels only via Disney buses. Hollywood Studios does not have monorail access.

What is Hollywood Studios About?
Is it a studio? Is it a theater? Is it an amusement park?

Disney fans have experienced much confusion over the years when it comes to Hollywood Studio's theme. Changes made to the park itself have not helped the confusion, including the name change from Disney-MGM Studios to Hollywood Studios.

The park has undergone vast modifications, leading to much excitement from fans everywhere.

Recent closures/replacements:

- The theme park's formerly iconic Sorcerer's Hat and center stage were removed during the Summer of 2015.
- After being reduced to a portion of its former grandeur over the years, the

Studio Backlot Tour and Streets of America were shut down.

- A small portion of Streets of America was replaced by Grand Avenue in late fall of 2017. This area features vintage office buildings and warehouses that represent the current Downtown Los Angeles.
- The working studios are no longer accessible to guests.
- Mainstay attractions, such as the American Idol Experience; Lights, Motors, Action!; and Animation Studio are now a thing of the past.

Changes brought speculation and rumors about the future of Hollywood Studios. Would it expand with a giant Frozen-themed land, owing to the enormous popularity of the film? Would a "Cars Land" finally make a Florida debut? Disney finally announced exciting changes for the park.

Expansions and Closures

In late fall of 2017, a minor addition opened called Grand Avenue. The highlight of what some consider the updated Streets of America (with a Downtown Los Angeles theme) is Baseline Tap House. This craft brew pub and tapas restaurant sits in the old Figueroa Printing Company building, which pays homage to a real print house with a connection to the Disney studios in Burbank.

The park's busiest attraction, *Toy Story Midway Mania*, recently expanded to add

Insider's Tip!

The front of the Chinese Theater makes a great place for families to meet if they get separated.

Hollywood Boulevard Entertainment

The courtyard in front of the Chinese Theater plays host to seasonal entertainment and events. Two Star Wars events are regularly scheduled at the courtyard stage: *A Galaxy Far, Far Away* and *March of the First Order*. Watch your favorite Star Wars characters (and villains) re-enact moments from the franchise in A Galaxy Far, Far Away, held multiple times daily. Parade lovers will enjoy watching Storm Troopers, led by Captain Phasma, march down Hollywood Boulevard throughout the day, ending in a show of strength in the courtyard.

another track. This was to reduce guest frustrations owing to massive congestion and wait times. Fans were even more thrilled when Toy Story Land opened in 2018. Toy Story Land replaces the former Backlot Tour area.

Guests shrink to toy size and enter Andy's backyard in this new land, which will includes Woody's Lunch Box, a counter-service restaurant serving meals and old-fashioned soda floats. The most exciting addition is a couple of brand new attractions, including a family coaster called *Slinky Dog Dash* and *Alien Swirling Saucers*, a spinning attraction which is much milder than *Mad Tea Party* at Magic Kingdom.

Toy Story Land was overshadowed by the park's most anticipated addition, though. An entire Star Wars: Galaxy's Edge land opened in 2019, giving fans the opportunity to experience exotic worlds from far, far away. This new land replaced the *Streets of America*.

Finally, *Mickey and Minnie's Runaway Railway*, a unique trackless ride, opened in 2020. This is the first Mickey-themed ride in a Disney park. It replaced *The Great Movie Ride*, which closed in 2017.

When to Go

Most of the park's live entertainment ends early in the evening, before sunset. The exception is *Fantasmic!*, which is typically shown once or twice per day, depending on park hours and the season, after dusk and near park closing.

Because of the popularity of certain attractions, such as *Star Wars: Rise of the Resistance* and *Rock 'n' Roller Coaster*, you absolutely must get to the park at or before opening. Otherwise, you may spend hours in line or miss the attractions altogether.

If your goal is to simply experience the thrill rides (*Rock 'n' Roller Coaster, Tower of Terror*, and *Star Tours*), evenings can be a great time for you to go to the park. Crowds tend to thin drastically after the primary shows shut down, particularly since dining choices at Hollywood Studios are very limited compared to nearby options at Disney's BoardWalk or Epcot (each a short walk or boat ride away).

Don't expect to be able to walk on to *Rise of the Resistance* or *Rock 'n' Roller Coaster* if you park hop in the evening, though. Both of these rides, especially *Rise of the Resistance*, tend to stay very busy all day long. Fortunately, *Rock 'n' Roller Coaster* has a single rider line that allows individuals in your party to bypass the worst of the wait times without a Lightning Lane reservation.

Hollywood Studios Shows and Attractions

Hollywood Studios has six distinct areas that are defined by streets. In total, there are only eight rides, six theater-style shows, and some alternative experiences. The result of this setup is a few very congested attractions with the rest of the day devoted to entertainment.

Hollywood Studios

Insider's Tip!

During slow seasons, *Fantasmic!* does not run every day. Be sure to verify the show is scheduled on the day you plan to visit.

The rides are:

- Alien Swirling Saucers
- Mickey & Minnie's Runaway Railway
- Millennium Falcon: Smugglers Run
- Rock 'n' Roller Coaster Starring Aerosmith
- Slinky Dog Dash
- Star Tours – The Adventures Continue
- Star Wars: Rise of the Resistance
- The Twilight Zone Tower of Terror
- Toy Story Midway Mania!

The shows are:

- Beauty and the Beast – Live on Stage
- Disney Junior Play and Dance
- Fantasmic!
- For the First Time in Forever: A Frozen Sing-Along Celebration
- Indiana Jones Epic Stunt Spectacular!
- Muppet*Vision 3D
- Voyage of the Little Mermaid

For the First Time in Forever - A Frozen Sing-Along Celebration (*G+*)

One of the most popular live productions, *For the First Time in Forever: A Frozen Sing-Along Celebration* has been delighting adults and children alike since the summer of 2014.

Queen Elsa is expected to welcome guests, but Princess Anna can't locate her at the moment. So Arrendale's recently-appointed "Royal Historians" must keep the guests occupied while Princess Anna searches for her older sister, their Queen. The historians do this by walking guests through the recent events that forever changed their land, stopping to play video of several key songs from the movie. While the songs play, the words are highlighted on three large screens, allowing everyone in the audience to sing along.

In a burst of snow flurries, Elsa finally appears during the show's last five minutes to take part in the finale. She bestows honorary Arrendale citizenship to everyone in the audience, and follows her pronouncement by making it snow throughout the theater. Elsa then leads the audience in a rendition of "Let It Go" to wrap up the performance.

The show takes place indoors, in typical (comfortable) theater seating. As with most theater presentations, strollers must be left outside. Lightning Lane reservations are not required, although they will ensure you have excellent seats for this 30-minute performance.

Disney Junior Play and Dance (*G+*)

This indoor dance party is especially fun for younger kids who need to burn off some energy.

Favorite stars from Disney Junior shows appear onstage, including Vampirina, Doc McStuffins, Timon, and Mickey Mouse himself!

A DJ emcees the performance,, which lasts about ten minutes, encouraging little ones to dance and wiggle to upbeat music, while characters do the same onstage.

There are no seats in the venue, so parents can either stand, sit on the floor, or join their preschoolers in the fun!

Lightning Lane reservations are available, but rarely needed.

Vacation Fun - An Original Animated Short with Mickey & Minnie

Large, comfortable, and cool, the newly reimagined Mickey Shorts Theater is now playing a ten-minute compilation of modern, animated shorts called "Vacation Fun." Exclusive to Hollywood Studios, the film highlights Mickey and Minnie's favorite vacation memories and foreshadows the fun to be had at the new Mickey and Minnie Runaway Railway ride that launched at the same time as the stylized theater.

The framed posters in the lobby are comical and animated, and each seat in the theater pays homage to Mickey's favorite shorts – his own! After viewing Mickey and Minnie's travel reel, pose for your own in the life-sized cartoon scenes as you exit the theater.

Indiana Jones Epic Stunt Spectacular! (*G+*) (Not Currently Showing)

This is a classic, live show designed to both entertain and instruct audiences about how professional movie stunts are performed and filmed. Directed by Jerry Rees and executively produced by George Lucas, stunts from the Raiders of the Lost Ark film are recreated by professional stunt actors.

Watch in awe as Indy negotiates perilous spikes and booby traps on his way to steal a prized golden idol statue from a Peruvian temple. The famous boulder scene is incredibly replicated to the amazement of onlookers. The final scene is a recreation of Indy and Marion attempting to stop a Nazi plane from leaving with the Ark of the Covenant.

Amid gunfire and explosions, and while fighting each other, these daring stunt actors must carefully dodge a moving plane and spinning propeller blades. The pyrotechnics and movement

Insider's Tip!

A few volunteer members of the audience are selected to go down onto the stage to play parts as "extras" in the production. Wear bright, distinctive clothes and show up early to make yourself more noticeable if you wish to be one of the several who are chosen.

must be precisely coordinated for the dangerous finale.

Bleacher seating for this 30-minute attraction is in a covered, open-air stadium. Seating for 2,085 guests is available on bench-style seats with no backs, which may be uncomfortable to some, given the long performance. Lightning Lane reservations are not required, but will get you into a prime seating location.

Luckily, this show plays several times each day and there is a huge crowd capacity, so there is never a real wait. Guests are permitted to enter the theater about 20 minutes prior to show time. If the loud explosions or gun fire noises might startle your children, sit near the top of the huge arena. This is where families can easily make a quick get-away if necessary.

Star Tours – The Adventures Continue (*G+*)

Based on the beloved Star Wars films created by George Lucas, this flight simulator ride – enhanced by ultra-high-definition 3-D – takes guests aboard the new *Starspeeder 1000* spaceship for a tour of a galaxy *far, far away...*

More than 50 different adventures are possible, giving "space tourists" the potential for a different ride experience each time.

Hollywood Studios

This is a simulated attraction with moving seats, so avoid it if you are prone to motion sickness. Use the Lightning Lane to avoid a wait, otherwise try to ride before 10 a.m., or within the last two hours before the park closes. If you have young children (or anyone) who is apprehensive about this attraction, ask the attendant about switching off using rider switch.

Insider's Tip!

While not technically attractions, Star Wars: Galaxy's Edge offers two very popular experiences, each of which typically requires reservations made a month or two in advance.

Design and build your own droid at the Droid Depot or your own lightsaber at Savi's Workshop.

Check for reservation availability for each at disneyworld.com.

Millennium Falcon: Smugglers Run (G+)

Have you ever wanted to pilot the fastest ship in the galaxy? Now's your chance!

Experience the ultimate adventure, as you take the reigns of Han Solo's famous Millennium Falcon. Can you outrun the Imperial forces?

Star Wars: Rise of the Resistance (LL)

This is a multi-part experience using the latest technology that the most ardent of Star Wars fans will appreciate.

The pre-show stars Rey and BB-8, who give you an important directive: don't let the location of the secret Resistance base fall into the wrong hands!

On your way to the base, your mission is compromised, as the First Order intercepts your spaceship and hauls you in for questioning by none other than Kylo Ren. Join with other freedom fighters to escape before it's too late!

This is one of the most popular attractions in all of Walt Disney World, so the standby queue is always long. Purchase individual Lightning Lane reservations to avoid extreme waits.

Celebrity Spotlight: Olaf Meet-and-Greet

There is only one place in Disney World where Frozen fans can meet their favorite snowman, and that's tucked away at the end of Commissary Lane. Olaf enjoys visiting all his friends in this sandy, summer retreat. Lightning Lane is not available.

Mickey and Minnie Starring in Red Carpet Dreams

Get dazzled by the world's most famous rodents in this fabulous meet-and-greet. Mickey reprises his role as The Scorcerer's Apprentice, while Minnie's dancing enchants her visitors. The celebrity duo is found on Commissary Lane, near the Sci-Fi Dine-in Theater Restaurant. Lightning Lane is not available.

Mickey and Minnie's Runaway Railway (*G+*)

Adventure awaits in the first and only ride to ever star Disney's famous duo. Of course, other favorite characters also appear throughout.

The story begins when you board a train with none other than Goofy as the conductor. As you might expect, things go hilariously wrong with the silly dog at the helm.

Don't worry, though. Mickey and Minnie quickly notice your plight and chase after the runaway train cars, helping to navigate your perilous journey through busy streets and even a dance class!

The ride uses trackless technology and screens, similar to Star Wars: Rise of the Resistance, giving it a smooth feel and allowing the cars to move in ways you wouldn't expect.

The queue on this attraction is often long, though it slows down later in the evening. Individual Lightning Lane reservations are available for purchase to avoid long waits.

Muppet*Vision 3D (*G+*)

This attraction is a 3-D film directed by Jim Henson. It features Kermit the Frog who guides tourists through the Muppet Studios, as they rehearse for an upcoming variety show starring Miss Piggy.

Things go hilariously wrong in Muppet Labs, however, when Dr. Bunsen Honey-dew's experimental 3-D invention, Waldo C. Graphic, escapes his control.

Combining Audio-Animatronics, special effects, and even Sweetums, a 9' tall full-bodied ogre, Muppet*Vision 3-D is a zany presentation and a total sensory experience great for all ages.

Hollywood Studios

The standing pre-show video lasts about 12 minutes and the theater show adds another 17 minutes. A delight for Muppet fans, the show itself has not been updated since its 1991 debut. This attraction provides an excellent way to get out of the sun and relax for about a half hour. Come back later if the wait is over 20 minutes. Lightning Lane is generally not required.

Toy Story Midway Mania! (G+)

This extremely-popular, interactive shooting game, based on Disney's hit *Toy Story* movie series, runs at its top capacity all day long, every day of the year. The premise of the high-tech, interactive ride is that Andy has received a carnival play set as a birthday gift, and while he is away eating his dinner, his older toys come to life and decide to play with the new toys.

You get to experience life at the "size of a toy" and play multiple midway-style games from the four-dimensional (4-D) carnival set. The ride moves on a real track through a simulated 3-D environment, so you must wear special glasses. Each car holds four people, and riders in your vehicle compete against each other for the highest score.

Due to its popularity, which is partially because it has no age or height limitations for children, wait times often reach as long as 90 minutes or more for this indoor ride. Because it only lasts five minutes, children can be disappointed after such a long wait. One way to increase the fun is to take time talking about all the classic games and other details that are showcased in the queue area. Due to the combination of movement and simulated effects, you may experience mild motion sickness on this attraction. Plan to arrive early or reserve Lightning Lane.

Slinky Dog Dash (G+)

Now smaller guests can experience the thrill of a roller coaster in Hollywood Studios. The coaster vehicles are shaped like its namesake character from the Toy Story franchise, making this fun attraction even more appealing.

Even adults love to zip around on this exciting coaster ride. The lack of inversions makes it a great beginner ride for budding thrill seekers.

Alien Swirling Saucers! (G+)

Find yourself shrunk down to toy size inside of a claw toy machine. The little green aliens from Toy Story twirl guests around and around on this fun ride.

An alien pulls you behind, as you zip around in circles. However, the wider turns makes this much more tame than the dizzying Mad Tea Party.

Genie+ Lightning Lane is available, though you can often find wait times of 20 minutes or less in the evening.

Walt Disney Presents

This former tribute museum to Walt Disney's life and the development of his cartoon characters, animation company, and eventual theme parks is now a preview center for upcoming attractions. It still holds some of its classic exhibits, but now guests can also view models of the soon-to-be-opened attractions, including Toy Story, Star Wars: Galaxy's Edge, and Mickey and Minnie's Runaway Railway.

Guardians of the Galaxy fans will be delighted to find a character meet-and-greet in this attraction. A theater showing previews of upcoming Disney films sits in the back of the attraction (and is a great place to get out of the heat and rest your heels).

Meet-and-Greet

Baby Groot and Star-Lord are on-hand in the preview center to take pictures and greet guests.

Voyage of The Little Mermaid (*G+*)

This 15-minute live-action and puppetry show is a stage production of *The Little Mermaid* film. It features the hit movie's Oscar-winning song "Under the Sea." Impressive special effects and sophisticated lighting techniques convincingly bring the audience into Ariel's beautiful underwater world.

The role of the evil sea witch, Ursula, is played by an enormous 12-foot tall puppet, and she performs a rendition of "Poor Unfortunate Souls." Scenes from the movie help tell the tale of the Little Mermaid, whose voice is stolen by Ursula.

Show Synopsis

Belle is a beautiful and bookish French girl who is aggressively pursued by Gaston, but she instead falls in love with the Beast. Audiences can't help but fall in love again with this classic "tale as old as time" as Belle and the Beast manage a fairy tale ending together. Favorite characters such as Mrs. Potts, Cogsworth, and Lumiere are in the show, and the romantic finale finishes with the release of white doves.

The story concludes with the ultimate defeat of Ursula's wicked plan in an extravagant musical finale. *Voyage of the Little Mermaid* appeals to all mermaid-lovers, young and old. You can usually get Lightning Lane reservations, but the attraction rarely has a wait in the evening.

Star Wars Launch Bay

Encounter the Force as you come face-to-face with your favorite *Star Wars* characters and memorabilia in the *Star Wars Launch Bay.* Enjoy a short film about the making of the latest *Star Wars* movies and TV shows. Following the show is an impressive museum-quality display area, complete with real and replica memorabilia from the popular franchise.

The highlights of this building are two character meet-and-greets: Chewbacca and Kylo Ren. Disney Chase credit card holders have their own special meet-and-greet with one of several characters in a separate STAR WARS™ Imperial Meet 'N' Greet area.

Enjoy experiencing life from a far away galaxy in The Cantina and be on the lookout for the robed Jawa for a photo opportunity. This is the only place you'll

The Twilight Zone Tower of Terror attraction takes place in the once famous but now creepy Hollywood Tower Hotel, which was abandoned long ago after guests mysteriously vanished from the elevator.

You are placed in a rickety "freight elevator," where you are greeted by Rod Serling's voice. Listen closely for the show's famous theme song, as it carries you into The Twilight Zone.

get to see the pint-sized, bright-eyed alien from Tatooine roaming around. The final sections of this building include a (free!) video game play area and a gift shop.

Beauty and the Beast – Live on Stage (*G+*)

This Broadway-quality theatrical production takes guests through reenactments of the most memorable scenes from the Disney movie, *Beauty and the Beast*, including a musical performance of "Be our Guest."

The 25-minute daytime performance takes place in a mostly-covered outdoor theater. With an enormous capacity of

Insider's Tip!

Tower of Terror usually has short wait times while guests are in the early evening Fantasmic! show. The moment the show lets out, guests rush to the *Tower of Terror* queue.

1,500 guests, it provides plenty of seating and good vantage points to see the large stage. Plan to arrive 20 minutes prior to the start of the show to get a seat under the canopy and out of the sun. An outstanding and popular show, Beauty and the Beast – Live on Stage is performed several times daily. Lightning Lane reservations are available to ensure great seats, though usually not necessary.

Rock 'n' Roller Coaster Starring Aerosmith (*G+*)

This wildly popular indoor roller coaster blasts guests to a speed of 60 miles per hour in only 2.8 seconds (!), making it Disney World's second fastest attraction.

Unlike any other thrill coaster in the Resort, this one features three inversions,

Insider's Tip!

Single rider lines are available at four Disney World attractions:
- Rock 'n' Roller Coaster in Hollywood Studios;
- Millennium Falcon: Smugglers Run in Hollywood Studios;
- Test Track in Epcot;
- Expedition Everest in Animal Kingdom

These queues are intended for people who are riding alone and often have wait times that are much less than the regular stand-by queues. When you reach the front of the line, you will be paired with an odd-numbered party to fill an available space in the vehicle.

Keep in mind, if you have multiple people in your party and try to use the single rider line, you will not be allowed to sit together! Do not ask or pretend you did not understand when you reach the front of the queue, as Cast Members will not make an exception for you. You will simply hold up other guests waiting for their turn.

Hollywood Studios

two rollover loops, and a corkscrew. Riders experience 5Gs (of gravity) as they enter the first inversion, which is more than what astronauts experience on a space shuttle launch.

Each "Super Stretch Limo" coaster train features different Aerosmith songs blasting out of five speakers per seat, creating an exhilarating ride that "rocks." The legendary rock band Aerosmith, which has sold over 80 million records worldwide, worked with Disney Imagineers to produce a custom soundtrack for their very smooth "metal coaster." Songs such as *Walk This Way*, *Back in the Saddle*, *Dude (Looks Like a Lady)*, *Love in an Elevator*, and *Sweet Emotion (live)*, blast guests as they accelerate into the Hollywood night.

The pre-show segment of this attraction lasts about two minutes, and the actual ride flies by in only about 1.5 minutes. The coaster uses black-lighting effects in complete darkness and has lots of unexpected twists and turns for added excitement. Each child under the age of seven must be accompanied by an adult. You must be 48" or taller to ride. We recommend Lightning Lane reservations,

though there is a single rider queue to help you bypass long lines.

The Twilight Zone Tower of Terror (*G+*)

Based on Rod Serling's classic TV series, *The Twilight Zone*, this accelerated tower-*drop* dark ride is considered by many to be Disney's best ever, due partly to its highly-detailed theme and complete backstory.

Even before you enter the creepy library for the short pre-show, the suspense starts building. What led guests to abandon food, drinks, games, and even their luggage in this neglected property? Moving into the even creepier cellar to the elevator loading bay is half the fun, and the suspense of just thinking about it can frighten children before they get on the ride. If this happens to your child, there is an easy exit from the basement before climbing aboard.

You never experience the exact same fear and panic twice, as each drop pattern is randomly selected by a computer that contains 50 different riding scenarios. Reaching a top speed of just over 30 miles per hour, the elevator plunges 13 stories down the haunted hotel's elevator shaft, abruptly rising again with a series of unpredictable short drops and climbs.

This ride is not advisable for people with claustrophobia, a fear of heights, or a fear of the dark. Also, pregnant women or others with medical concerns should not ride this attraction. You must be at least 40" tall to ride. We recommend Lightning Lane reservations, then return for a second ride within the last two hours before park closing.

Fantasmic! (G+)
(Not Currently Showing)

Fantasmic! is a 25-minute nighttime extravaganza that combines live actors, Audio-Animatronics, pyrotechnics, lasers, and famous Disney movie music. Surrounded by a moat of water, the 59-foot high outdoor stage is actually the tallest "mountain" on property. The water is cleverly used in a variety of ways, from providing a "water projection screen" on which film clips are played, to being set ablaze with fire, and even hosting a spectacular boat parade.

Designed after the famous Hollywood Bowl, the outdoor theater can accommodate a whopping 11,000 guests seated on backless benches, and there really isn't a bad vantage point.

Insider's Tip!

If there are two *Fantasmic!* shows scheduled on a day, the second is always less crowded. Since the second show also starts at park closing, you get the added benefit of more time to experience other attractions Hollywood Studios has to offer.

This show is enormously popular, and it's best to claim a seat early. Be aware that inclement weather may cancel the performance. Though visually fantastic, small children may be frightened by some of the darker scenes.

Use Genie+ to reserve excellent seats. The early show often fills to capacity during peak periods. If there are two shows on the day you visit, skip the first one and enjoy the generally less-crowded second showing.

In Fantasmic! guests are entertained by Mickey Mouse's imagination, which culminates in a dream battle against Disney Villains who threaten to take control. Mickey's dream becomes a nightmare when Jiminy Cricket is trapped in a large bubble, and is then pursued by Monstro the whale. The Evil Queen from Snow White and the Seven Dwarfs appears to invoke other Disney Villains such as Cruelle de Vil, Maleficent, Ursula, and Jafar. Maleficent transforms into a gigantic, 40-foot tall fire-breathing dragon, and her heat can be felt half-way through the audience!

Mickey ultimately reclaims control of his imagination, and a celebratory atmosphere prevails. Up to 26 beloved Disney characters, including Donald Duck, Minnie Mouse, Pinocchio, Mulan, Stitch, and the Toy Story gang celebrate Mickey's victory over evil as they float by the audience waving and singing aboard an 80-foot replica of the ship from Steamboat Willie.

Sample Lightning Lane & Genie+ Hollywood Studios Itineraries

1 Day (no small children)	
Approx Time	
7 AM	Make Lightning Lane reservations for Slinky Dog Dash (9:10-10:10 AM window recommended), Star Wars: Rise of the Resistance (late-morning recommended), and Mickey & Minnie's Runaway Railway (mid-afternoon recommended). Make reservations for lightsaber and robot building experiences, if desired.
8:30 AM	Arrive 30-45 minutes before park opening.
9:10-9:30 AM	Ride Slinky Dog Dash.
9:35-10:05 AM	Ride Toy Story Mania.
10:10-10:35 AM	Ride Alien Swirling Saucers.
10:50-11:25	Ride Millenium Falcon: Smugglers Run.
11:30-12:15	Ride Star Wars: Rise of the Resistance
12:30-1:30 PM	Eat Lunch
1:35-2:15 PM	Watch Indiana Jones Epic Stunt Spectacular show.
2:25-3 PM	Ride Mickey & Minnie's Runaway Railway
3:15-3:40 PM	Ride Tower of Terror.
3:45-4:05 PM	Ride Rock 'n' Roller Coaster.
4:15-5:15 PM	Visit Star Wars Launch Bay and meet characters.
5:30-6 PM	Ride Star Tours.
6:10-7:30 PM	Eat dinner.
7:30-8:30 PM	Watch Fantasmic.
9 PM	Watch fireworks show.

1 Day (small children)	
Approx Time	
7 AM	Make Lightning Lane reservations for Toy Story Mania (9:30-10:30 AM window recommended), Mickey & Minnie's Runaway Railway (early-afternoon recommended), and Star Wars: Rise of the Resistance (early evening recommended).
8:30 AM	Arrive 30-45 minutes before park opening.
9-9:30 AM	Sign up for Jedi Training: Trials of the Temple.
9:45-10:05 AM	Ride Toy Story Mania.
10:10-10:30 AM	Ride Slinky Dog Dash.
10:35-10:55 AM	Ride Alien Swirling Saucers.
11:15-11:30 AM	Watch Disney Junior Dance and Play
11:30-12 PM	Meet Disney Junior characters.
12:10-12:35 PM	Ride Mickey & Minnie's Runaway Railway
12:45-3:30 PM	Take boat to nearby hotel. Eat lunch and nap.
4-5 PM	Attend Jedi Training Academy.
5:15-5:45 PM	Ride Star Wars: Rise of the Resistance.
6-6:30 PM	Watch Muppets show.
6:35-7:15 PM	Eat dinner.
7:20-7:50 PM	Watch Voyage of the Little Mermaid.
8-8:30 PM	Watch Fantasmic.

GORILLA FALLS EXPEDITION TRAIL

RAFIKI'S PLANET WATCH

MAHARAJAH JUNGLE TREK

ASIA

KILIMANJARO SAFARIS

UP! A GREAT BIRD ADVENTURE

KALI RIVER RAPIDS

AFRICA

EXPEDITION EVEREST

FESTIVAL OF THE LION KING

RIVERS OF LIGHT

IT'S TOUGH TO BE A BUG

DISCOVERY ISLAND

FINDING NEMO MUSICAL

TRICERATOP SPIN

AVATAR FLIGHT OF PASSAGE

PRIMEVAL WHIRL

THE OASIS

PANDORA WORLD OF AVATAR

NA'VI RIVER JOURNEY

DINOLAND U.S.A.

BUSES AND PARKING

Animal Kingdom

Park Overview

The Animal Kingdom opened on Earth Day, April 22, 1998, and was the last magical theme park addition to Walt Disney World. Based on Walt Disney's own philosophy regarding animal welfare and conservation, the Animal Kingdom's predominant focus is to honor animals.

This is the largest Disney theme park in the world, with over 500 sprawling acres, including natural jungles and savannahs that feature exotic animals and birds. In keeping with Walt's passions, the park has a real steam train that transports guests to an exotic animal petting zoo; an actual safari ride aboard authentic safari buses; and several hiking trails through nature.

More a place to linger and learn, the park can be visited in a single day. Plan for a "slow" day, and plan to take your time. Kids, especially teenagers, should have the right expectations, or they'll be constantly asking where all the rides are and looking for more excitement than this park actually has to offer.

Insider's Tip!

The entire Animal Kingdom Park may close early (by 7 p.m.) during the short winter days.

Even though it is the largest in size, it has the fewest amusement rides of any Disney park. Instead, it has several shows and animal exhibits that make up for the lack of thrill rides.

Much of the park's space is off-limits to guests but instead is designated as homes to its many animal inhabitants. However, in recent years, certain areas have been opened up to paid guided tours to give small groups of tourists a behind-the-scenes look at the animals and their natural environment.

The animals are the focus of the show and, since they are put into the back area of the park at dusk each day, some attractions close early.

History

The Animal Kingdom was envisioned and designed to offer an alternative to the

Animal Kingdom is five times the size of the Magic Kingdom and more than twice the size of Epcot. In fact, Disney California Adventure, Hong Kong Disneyland, Walt Disney Studios Paris, Disneyland Park, and Tokyo DisneySea would **ALL** fit together inside Disney's Animal Kingdom Theme Park!

Busch Gardens theme park in Tampa, Florida, which had started siphoning off guests from Orlando. Disney decided it needed a similar animal-centric park to entertain guests. However, unlike Busch Gardens, which is dominated by thrill rides, Disney's animal park offers more of a wildlife experience without as much in the way of excitement.

While Disney likes to stress that the Animal Kingdom is a theme park and not a zoo, its work with animals is often at the forefront of zoological trends using progressive technology.

It is fully-accredited with The Association of Zoos & Aquariums (AZA, See aza.org) which required an initial, thorough review consisting of a multiple day, on-site inspection by a team of experts from around the country. To maintain its accreditation and to confirm that it remains current with evolving industry standards, the Animal Kingdom continues to undergo reviews every five years.

An early decision by Disney and its zoological experts was to obtain all the park's animals from existing zoos or reputable breeders rather than resorting to capturing wild animals. Disney determined that taking existing animals from their natural habitat would have made their company party to the depletion of natural wildlife populations. This was the problem on which they were attempting to focus. (This is in direct contrast to another, highly-visible Orlando-area theme park that is often criticized by Animal Rights activists for its animal purchasing practices.)

Species Survival Program

Disney's Animal Kingdom (along with The Seas at Epcot) works with other zoological facilities, wildlife organizations, and government agencies to promote species conservation

Sadly, even with Disney's careful preparations, several animals passed away during the transport and resettlement process when the park was being populated. Disney, being held to a high standard, made headline news. However, mandatory investigations cleared the company of negligence or wrongdoing. Though unfortunate, experts agreed that the large relocation of animals was a risky proposition, regardless of the precautions taken. They found that the animal handling was performed professionally and responsibly.

through recovery plans, rehabilitation, and reintroduction of endangered and threatened species.

As part of Disney's commitment to its role as an animal caretaker, the company takes an active role in 34 "Species Survival Plans" within AZA's Species Survival Program.

Species Survival Programs are designed to help endangered species through a range of activities, including research, public education, fundraising, and field conservation projects. A governing board keeps track of all the different species around the country and determines optimal population numbers for their management.

The national breeding program in which Disney participates includes the rhinoceros. They also transfer large cats and even manatees around the country for cooperative breeding and other purposes.

Realistic Natural Environments and Authentic Flora

The theme park is so stunningly detailed that you can easily believe you are walking through actual jungle paths and viewing animals in their native habitats. Lush,

Insider's Trivia!

Natural and authentic flora (vegetation) planted at the park is composed of over four million plants, ground coverings, shrubs, vines, epiphytes, and grasses from each continent on Earth, except Antarctica. Over 850 species of trees, 2,000 species of shrubs, and 260 different types of grasses are maintained throughout the park. Around 110 of the tree and shrub species had never before been cultivated in North America before Disney took on the challenge.

natural plants and trees blend seamlessly with rolling hills and toppling ruins in the incredibly immersive zoological environments. In the Kilimanjaro Safari attraction alone, Disney meticulously crafted three separate African ecosystems!

Meandering paths just inside the park lead you to placid lakes, flowing streams, and cascading waterfalls. Designers used authentic plants from around the globe to create realistic rain forests, flat grasslands, and tranquil, formal gardens. Add to that the intriguing architectural themes in both the Africa and Asia lands, and you have an immersive experience that rivals the intricately-styled pavilions in Epcot's World Showcase.

Focus on Fauna and Animal Safety

The Animal Kingdom incorporates both real and mythical animals into its rides, shows, and live entertainment. Unlike the other theme parks, which have an abundance of Audio-Animatronic characters, you may be surprised to find a lack of mechanical characters within the Animal Kingdom. Other than the figures in the *Dinosaur* attraction, a few stars of *It's Tough to be a Bug!*, and the Yeti in *Expedition Everest* (who sadly no longer moves due to a malfunction that can't be fixed), all of the moving animals in this park are real.

Disney chose realistic landscaping and natural habitat for its more than 1,700 real animals (comprising over 250 species) rather than try to create faux characters. Even the animated stage performances use puppetry with live puppeteers, rather than mechanical devices.

For the safety of the animals, the park does not allow fireworks or plastics of any kind, including straws and plastic bags. Security guards check your bags and ask you to throw away anything that poses a potential threat to the animals.

Keeping the park quiet is important for the animals' health. Due to concerns about noise and its impact on the living creatures, Animal Kingdom does not have a fireworks show, and all loud, outdoor

Insider's Trivia!

Unseen Animal Barriers. Whether you're traveling through the safari, walking through the Gorilla Falls Exploration Trail, or strolling among the other exotic habitats, Disney makes sure that barriers between humans and animals appear non-existent. The barriers are concealed with realistic-looking features. For example, the bamboo stand separating the gorillas from the guests is actually a set of steel rods placed in concrete. You also see what looks like simple ridges of earth that provide cover for large moats and barriers, keeping animals on one side of the path and you on the other.

performances are performed well-away from the animal exhibits.

To protect the animals and the natural environment, feeding the animals is forbidden. Also, unlike the other parks, where you find wishing wells seeking your donations to charity, throwing coins in the water ponds of the Animal Kingdom is strongly discouraged.

More Shows and Attractions than Thrill-rides

Size not withstanding, the park features a limited number of ride and show attractions. This is a walking park, designed for stimulating visual effects, rather than thrills. Because of this, some guests argue that the park is a glorified zoo. However, the shows and rides found here are top-notch compared to many other animal-related theme parks, and Disney has some additions currently in the works to add to the Animal Kingdom's overall appeal.

There are only eight rides (nine if you consider the Wildlife Express Train journey to Rafiki's Planet Watch). In addition, there are two outdoor amphitheaters and three indoor theaters, one of which is within the base of the Tree of Life.

There are plenty of things for young children to enjoy, including a large children's playground area, special scavenger hunt-style activities, a conservation exhibit, and a petting zoo.

The Festival of the Lion King and *Finding Nemo* are live performances that are especially well-developed and fun for everyone. Because of their popularity, they can get very crowded with long lines. Fortunately, the theater venues hold large numbers of guests, so you can usually get a seat if you arrive close to show time.

Winged Encounters – The Kingdom Takes Flight highlights the six different varieties

of macaws (hyacinth, green-winged, blue and gold, scarlet, blue-throated, and military) that reside at the Animal Kingdom. Several times a day, the birds fly through the air around the Tree of Life before settling into Discovery Island.

Be aware that animals vary in their activity levels throughout the day, just like at any zoo. Animals are usually more active early in the day, before the heat encourages them to find shade and sleep. Meal times are also great to catch their activity.

Recent Additions

The *Harambe* (opened in 2014) and *Pandora – The World of AVATAR* (opened in 2017) are Animal Kingdom's most recent lands. *Tree of Life Awakenings* is a stunning nighttime spectacular - projected onto the Tree of Life. It is a great draw for evening crowds. Disney KiteTails is a stunning visual display above the Discovery River Amphitheater. With these lands and attractions, the park is kept open much later during busy seasons than in past years.

Wildlife Express Train

Not all areas of the park are accessible by foot. *Rafiki's Planet Watch* can only be reached aboard a rustic African locomotive, *The Wildlife Express Train*, which departs from the Harambe area of Africa.

The open-air train is not air conditioned and is quite shaky, in keeping with its authentic feel and appearance. The abrupt train whistle blares loudly, much to the delight of kids, though the journey may not be suitable for napping children. Guests in wheelchairs or ECVs can board an accessible car with the help of a Cast Member.

Animal Kingdom

The trip itself is neither very exciting nor interesting. However, taking the train allows you a behind-the-scenes look at some animal housing and care areas of the theme park.

Dining

Disney's Animal Kingdom has only four full table-service restaurants, the Rainforest Cafe (Park Entrance), Tusker House Restaurant (Africa), Tiffins (Africa), and Yak & Yeti Restaurant (Asia).

Tiffins is the park's only Signature restaurant. It offers unique African and Asian-inspired fare.

The park's newest offering, Satu'li Canteen is a fast casual diner that serves healthy, international fare to the backdrop of Pandora's Valley of Mo'ara.

The Rainforest Café at the entrance of the park tends to be much less busy than its Disney Springs counterpart, with reservations needed only on very busy days and at peak periods. Park passes are not required to eat there, but those with passes get their own special entrance to the park from the back door of the restaurant.

Tusker House Restaurant features an all-you-care-to eat buffet with character dining where you get to meet Donald, Daisy, Pluto, and Mickey decked out in their safari gear. Later in the day, Tusker House offers a unique full-service, outside lounge.

Two counter-service restaurants are located on opposite sides of Discovery Island: Pizzafari and Flame Tree Barbecue. In addition, Yak & Yeti (Asia) offers counter-service and a walk-up alcoholic beverage stand just outside its full service (sit-down) restaurant.

Snack stands are also located through-out the other areas of the park, serving treats from ice cream to hot dogs. One very popular snack location, Tamu Tamu in Africa, serves the much-heralded Dole Whip pineapple concoction. (Previously, this treat was only available at Aloha Isle in Magic Kingdom, but at the Animal Kingdom you can get it with rum. Cheers!)

Animal Kingdom for Kids

Note: Only three rides at the park have no height restrictions: *Kilimanjaro Safari*, *Triceratops Spin*, and *Na'vi River Journey*. This makes them very popular with children and families.

Children who have first visited the Magic Kingdom may have wildly wrong expectations about what to expect at the Animal Kingdom. Give them advance warning that this park is slower and more about the experience itself.

While they'll get to go on a real safari excursion on the African plains of the Serengeti and take a real whitewater rafting trip on the Kali River Rapids, they'll get the most satisfaction if you have them take time to observe the interesting design features, like the intricate carvings in the Tree of Life. Make sure your children are prepared for long nature walks along trails where they'll see birds and bats in near-perfect recreations of jungles, as well as exotic animals in their natural African savannah habitat.

Turning the educational aspects of the park into a game is a great way to keep children engaged and having fun. Animal Kingdom once had a Discovery Club for children, where little ones could earn stickers at educational stations throughout the park. This has been replaced with Wilderness Explorers, an Up-movie-themed program that allows children to earn up to 30 badges by exploring the park.

You will find Cast Members standing near exhibits in colorful outfits. Encourage your kids to engage them by asking questions about the animals.

Animal Kingdom

(Remember to take pictures!) These Cast Members are there for the express purpose of sharing information with guests.

As you walk past the animal and trail-side exhibits, take your time looking around and feel free to open drawers where you see them. You and your children will delight when you find the drawer full of butterflies, hidden ostrich eggs, and lion skulls.

Getting There

The Animal Kingdom is somewhat isolated compared to the other three parks, located at the southwest quadrant of the Disney World property and about a mile from the Animal Kingdom Lodge. It is very close to Disney's Blizzard Beach water park.

It takes a bit longer to reach the park than the three other theme parks, unless you are staying at one of the Animal Kingdom resorts. Animal Kingdom is most readily accessible by taking Exit 64B off Interstate 4 and then traveling along US 192 (Irlo Bronson Memorial Highway) toward the main entrance on World Drive. There is ample signage pointing you in the right direction.

The park has a very large parking lot. Once you park, a Disney tram takes you to the entrance, or you may walk, depending on how far away you are. While the Animal Kingdom is not serviced via Disney's monorail or water routes, it is easily accessed via Disney's bus transportation system.

Disabled parking and taxi services are located very close to the park entrance.

Planning Your Day

Hours and Arrival

The Animal Kingdom opens around 9 a.m. most days, and about an hour earlier during peak periods and holidays.

The animals settle into their nighttime enclosures each evening shortly after dinner, making them unavailable to guests. Because of this, the park sometimes closes early. During the high season when the days are longer, it may stay open until 11 p.m., but during the shorter days of winter or during the off season, it may close as early as 5 p.m.

During the off season and when the weather is cold, some attractions may be delayed at opening. This includes the *Kali River Rapids* water ride in Asia, *The Boneyard* playground area, and the *Wildlife Express Train* that leads to Rafiki's Planet Watch and *Conservation Station*. Disney's Times Guide, Disneyworld.com, and My Disney Experience app specifies the hours for these attractions.

As with any of Disney's parks, the rope drop may occur before its official scheduled opening. At the Animal Kingdom, this allows guests early access to The Oasis and Discovery Island. The remaining park stays roped off until the official opening time. The timing of rope drop varies, and during peak attendance and holiday periods expect the park to open 30 to 60 minutes earlier than its published time.

Crowds and Attendance Levels

Each theme park has its major draws that guests rush to first thing in the morning.

Insider's Tip!

Without Lightning Lane reservations for the major attractions, plan to arrive 30 to 45 minutes before official opening in order to be in the first wave of people advancing towards the rides. On a good day, you might be able to walk right onto *Expedition Everest* twice!

Insider's Tip!

Generally speaking, crowds are thinner first thing in the morning. Therefore, Early Theme Park Entry is an especially great perk if you are an early morning person and don't need the extra rest. You're able to complete most of what the park has to offer within a few short hours, allowing you to park hop later in the day or just enjoy a quiet evening away from the parks.

For the Animal Kingdom, the biggest draw is the new Pandora land with its two rides: *Na'vi River Journey* and *Avatar Flight of Passage*, which quickly become mobbed with guests arriving early in the morning (a sizable number arrive prior to rope drop). Other popular attractions include *Expedition Everest* (Asia) and *Kilimanjaro Safaris* (Africa).

Starting around 10 a.m., wave upon wave of people arrive, and guests continue streaming in through the late morning and into the early afternoon. Popular attractions stay especially busy through early afternoon at the Animal Kingdom. This is because the park hosts large crowds while offering a relatively limited number of major offerings (including theater shows).

Expect particularly light attendance in later afternoons during non-peak seasons, as park crowds typically peak around 2 p.m. Most guests finish touring by 3 or 4 p.m.

Because of this, park hopping to the Animal Kingdom mid- to late-afternoon (depending on the park's scheduled closing time) is a great way to enjoy the park at a relaxed pace and to help you avoid long waits for some of the major attractions. (*Pandora* attractions are busy all day long.) Consider showing up after a late lunch on a couple of days to view some of the exhibits or to watch a show or two. By the time you are ready to get to the major attractions, there should be little wait.

The Attraction Commando versus The Easy Rider

The park takes at least two thirds of a day (or two full afternoons) for a reasonably-complete tour. An entire day is recommended to get through all the attractions without feeling especially

Insider's Tip!

To avoid the rush, obtain Lightning Lane reservations for *Avatar Flight of Passage* (the park's most popular ride) and *Na'vi River Journey* and enjoy other attractions first thing in the day. Alternatively, if you use Genie+ to schedule other events, join the crowds heading to these two favorites for an early morning ride.

Insider's Tip!

Rafiki's Planet Watch and the exploration trails usually close 30 to 60 minutes prior to sunset, so if they are on your must-do list, make sure you know when sunset is and verify closing time in advance with Guest Relations. The short winter days, coupled with daylight savings time, can push the closing time for the animal exhibits to 5 p.m. or slightly earlier.

Animal Kingdom

Insider's Tip!

You may see "Attraction Commandos" hurriedly rushing through the park seeking out only the major thrills and excitement. Not all tourists care about absorbing the details Disney designed into the park. However, you will miss much of what Animal Kingdom has to offer if you don't take the time to explore.

rushed. Guests interested in only the most popular attractions can complete a reasonably comprehensive tour in that time, given an early arrival.

Most guests want time to dawdle to see the unique merchandise in the shops; to take advantage of the myriad picture opportunities; and to see all the sights. Anything less than a full day will limit what you can fit into your schedule.

Similarly, park hoppers who plan to arrive at the Animal Kingdom in the early-to-late afternoon (to avoid the early crowds) should therefore plan on touring the park over two half-day periods.

Animal Kingdom Lands & Attractions

The Oasis

The first land you pass through as you enter the Animal Kingdom is The Oasis, a lush tropical rainforest designed to put visitors immediately in contact with wildlife in their natural environment. You are drawn to several live animal displays such as the Parma wallaby, tree-kangaroo, giant anteater, and sloth. The Oasis expands along walking paths where multiple animal exhibits are folded neatly within thick forest foliage.

This area is a "transitional experience" that prepares you for an exotic and wild

adventure without inundating your senses. It gives you a chance to get the look and feel of the rest of the park during the five minutes it takes to walk through The Oasis and reach Discovery Island, which is the hub of the park.

Guest Relations

There are no rides and minimal shopping opportunities within The Oasis, but near the front is where you find Guest Relations, which is where you can pick up Guidemaps, make restaurant reservations, or get assistance with any other theme park or resort issues. This is also the location for the Animal Kingdom's Lost and Found, missing persons (including lost children), rental storage lockers, and Wheelchair & Stroller Rentals. The Oasis stays open for 30 to 60 minutes after the rest of the park closes.

Wilderness Explorers

Similar to Epcot's Kidcot program (but much more interactive), Wilderness Explorers was created as an interactive way to engage kids and teach them about the environment and natural world. When they join, players are given self-paced "directed activities" that are fun and educational. Each task connects them with natural beauty and animals while learning about international cultures.

There is no fee to participate in this experience. Much like the games targeted to children that are available in other parks, Wilderness Explorers also greatly interests kids, but this one is neither high-tech nor uses special effects.

How to Join the Elite Club

Becoming a member of the club is easy, just show up at the headquarters in The Oasis (located on the bridge between the Oasis and Discovery Island) or one of four other stations: Rafiki's Planet Watch, Africa, Asia, and DinoLand U.S.A.

After learning the special pledge, children become official members of the Wilderness Explorers troop. Your friendly Cast Member will give each child a free official Wilderness Explorers field guide to begin their adventure. This includes a map and instructions to learn about the different challenges to be completed. Completing each challenge earns a badge, while working on the ultimate quest to complete all the challenges across the park.

Important Note! Some of the badges require going on rides, so be sure to read through the tasks in the booklet before going on any rides for the day. Plan for the rides in advance to make sure you have the necessary Lightning Lane reservations.

Discovery Island

Discovery Island is the central hub of the park that connects to each of the other lands. The Tree of Life is located at its center.

Discovery Island Trails

Discovery Island is filled with a series of unmarked, self-guided walking trails that provide views of wildlife in their natural habitat. The tranquil paths are found under the canopy of the Tree of Life, encircling the base of the tree, and giving up-close views of hundreds of beautiful animal carvings.

Insider's Tip!

Wilderness Explorers are given their own "scout handbook" in which children collect their stickers. This makes a great souvenir even if they don't do many of the challenges.

Meander along the paths, cross over streams on wooden foot bridges, and pass through cave-like tunnels in your search for lemurs, porcupines, Macaws, kangaroo, the giant Galapagos tortoise, and the world's largest living rodent, the capybara.

As the name of the island implies, its trails are meant to be semi-hidden and "discovered" similar to real worldwide hikers coming across the unknown. You're bound to find a few shaded rest areas with colorful benches to take a break. There are also many observation stations ideal for photo opportunities. These serene trails are truly an oasis away from the crowds and noise typically associated with Disney parks.

It's Tough to be a Bug! (G+)

Based on the Disney-Pixar hit, *A Bug's Life*, this nine-minute performance is designed to humorously demonstrate the challenges of being a tiny insect.

The four-dimensional (4-D) attraction combines high-definition 3-D film with Audio-Animatronic characters, scent, and misting effects. It is considered by many

Animal Kingdom

Go on *Kilimanjaro Safaris* to earn your Safari Badge. Two badges, the Mount Everest and Yeti, require a visit to *Expedition Everest*, though you may be able to get the badges without riding the runaway coaster. A fun train trip to *Rafiki's Planet Watch* and *Conservation Station* will allow you to earn even more Wilderness Explorers badges. Be sure to plan in advance for these attractions, including Lightning Lane reservations!

The World of Pandora

Prepare to enter an alien landscape with your tour directors, Alpha Centauri Expeditions (ACE). On your eco-tour, discover the Valley of Mo'ara, the fictional world within Pandora made famous in the movie *Avatar*. Become immersed in the lush scenery and floating mountains of this 12-acre land. Cast Members speak Na'vi, the language of the native people of Pandora, adding to the inclusive atmosphere. At nighttime, the world becomes awash in a dazzling spectacle of bioluminescent glow. (Look down as you walk. The pathway glows with an "organic" internal light!)

With the opening of Pandora in 2017, Animal Kingdom's healthy dining options increased. Satu'li Canteen offers out-of-this-world options of wholesome grains, fresh vegetables, and hearty proteins, including selections for vegans. Meals are served fast-casual within the Quonset-hut. Guests can relax with some specialty drinks and desserts before stepping out on their adventure within the moon of Pandora.

The land includes two attractions: *Avatar Flight of Passage* and the *Na'vi River Journey*. Experience the wonder and magic of all Pandora has to offer from the unique vantage points offered by these rides. It is truly a transformative experience.

Avatar Flight of Passage (*LL*)

Board a mountain banshee to bond with your winged creature as you take flight over the moon's landscape. The winged animal seats a single person, straddled on it like a motorcycle. Soar and whoosh high over incredible landscapes while experiencing the Na'vi hunter right of passage. The experience is so real, you can easily believe the vehicle is a living, breathing creature flying beneath you.

Using 3-D technology, Flight of Passage is limited to guests 44" and taller. Gentle restraints around your calves ensure a safe flight. With the unusual seat design, guests with large calves or very long legs should ask to try the ride vehicle before waiting in line.

Purchase Lightning Lane reservations to avoid very long wait times.

Na'vi River Journey (*G+*)

Settle into a reed boat and glide down a river within the Valley of Mo'ara. The gentle ride takes you deep in to the valley's mysterious foliage, where you'll explore dark caves and the lush rainforest, including fantastical creatures and exotic, glowing scenery. The Na'vi Shaman of Songs is the most realistic Audio-Animatronic on-propery with incredible facial expressions and fluid movments. She joins you, showcasing her deep-rooted connection to all living things within the forest. There is no height limit, so all ages are welcome to join this excursion. Purchase Genie+ for Lightning Lane reservations to avoid very long wait times.

Insider's Tip!

Flight of Passage is the most popular attraction at Disney's Animal Kingdom and usually has very long wait times. As a Tier 1 attraction, Lightning Lane reservations are not available through the Genie+ system. You can purchase an individual Lightning Lane reservation the morning of your visit.

Na'vi River Journey is also quite popular and often has long wait times, though it tends to slow down late in the evening. You can reserve a Lightning Lane return time for Na'vi River Journey if you are using Genie+.

Environmental crusaders with the My Disney Experience App will enjoy being guided through Pandora on an interactive exploration by Fitsimti "Fits" Buckley, one of the moon's ecological experts. Upon entering Pandora, Fits will message you to find out if you want to participate in the *Connect to Protect* adventure. With the completion of missions in this interactive game, you can unlock donations for the Disney Conservation Fund.

Animal Kingdom

to be one of the finest shows throughout Walt Disney World.

Hosted by the loveable ant Flik, the "Off-Off-Bugway" (a play on the expression "Off-Broadway") show features his bug friends (and enemies!) along with many other characters from the animated film. After putting on special "bug eye" glasses and becoming an "Honorary Bug" for the day, you're educated about bug survival techniques from their perspective.

This depiction of the world of insects uses our natural fears to keep us on the edges of our seats, but the show integrates humor in order to keep the performance light-hearted for children.

The show is located in the 430-seat Tree of Life Repertory Theatre, which is found in the base of the gigantic park icon, the Tree of Life.

Rarely crowded even on busy days, the show may be too intense for anyone with a fear of insects (or spiders!). The dark underground theater (designed to represent the hollow of the tree) might frighten young children. You can usually obtain Lightning Lane reservations for this attraction, although they are rarely needed past mid-afternoon.

Disney KiteTails (G+)
Watch your favorite characters soar over the Discovery River Amphitheater in this enchanting show.

Your favorite Disney characters have been turned into extravagant kites and windcatchers, dancing to the tune of classic Disney songs. This is fun for all ages and backgrounds!

Tree of Life Awakenings
At over 14 stories high, this giant sculpture of a baobab tree is home to more than 300 animal species carved in its trunk and surrounding roots. At night, these animals magnificently stir to life

through state-of-the-art media projections and cutting-edge special effects.

Using the same technology as Celebrate the Magic, Tree of Life Awakenings rotates delightful shows every ten minutes after dark until closing. Music signals the start of each presentation, and the best viewing spot is from the Island Mercantile in Discovery Island.

Africa

Kilimanjaro Safaris (G+)
This safari attraction takes you into the fictional *Harambe Wildlife Reserve* aboard authentic, open-air safari trucks driven by a professional and entertaining tour guide. Hang on tight as you make the 18-minute journey across rugged terrain, along winding pathways, and past washed-out roads. Along the way, you get to see a plethora of free-roaming animals and encounter sweeping photogenic vistas across wide-open spaces.

Some highlights of the trip include warthog burrows and a lion den complete with a pride of lions! From Addax screwhorn antelopes to zebras, more than 34 species of exotic animals live across the expansive 100-acres. You will even see tall giraffes foraging for leaves high in the trees, as well as rhinos lazily wallowing in their mud pit.

While it appears some of the more dangerous animals such as lions can easily reach your vehicle, Disney has cleverly hidden barriers to keep them away from guests and other animals.

Lightning Lane reservations are strongly recommended, as this is one of the most popular attractions in Animal Kingdom.

Gorilla Falls Exploration Trail
The *Gorilla Falls Exploration Trail* is an ultra-modern zoo with incredible wildlife encounters. It's former name, Pangani

(pronounced "Pawn-Gahw'nee"), means "place of enchantment" and is an apt word to describe this five-acre habitat for exotic animals. Your self-guided journey takes you along winding paths through rich green, verdant landscapes, and through a world of fast-rushing streams and splashing waterfalls.

The trail is just under 1/2-mile long, so expect your excursion to take anywhere from 20 to 30 minutes. The entertaining hike takes you through the heart of a lush African tropical forest and sprawling savannah, featuring a Gorilla Sanctuary, a Hippo Pool, and a Bird Forest.

Two groups of gorillas give this trail its name: a bachelor and family group. The family group consists of a silverback male leader, three adult females, and their offspring, which often play in full view of guests.

The trail is mostly shaded, either under the lush jungle canopy or under thatched roofs. However, it can still get hot and muggy during the day. There are no places along the trail to purchase water or other beverages. Since there are no restrooms along the trail, you'd need to return to Harambe Village for the nearest facilities. Be sure to hydrate well and take care of any personal needs before embarking on your trek. As this is a self-paced hike, no Lightning Lane is offered or required.

Wildlife Express Train to Rafiki's Planet Watch (from Africa)

Board the rustic *Wildlife Express Train* at the station in Harambe for a pleasant seven-minute ride bound for *Rafiki's Planet Watch*. A forest trail with a petting zoo called "Affection Section" awaits at your destination.

The 1.2-mile, round-trip journey takes you behind-the-scenes on a recreated African train. (The trains are similar in design to those used by Magic Kingdom's *Walt Disney World Railroad*.)

Paying attention to the signs around the station, you can actually believe the backstory that these rustic steam engines are part of the Eastern Star Railway (a fictional company) that takes guests between Lusaka, Nairobi, and Kisangani.

You pass through backstage areas of the park, where most of the safari animals are cared for, listening to the ring of the train signals and the short blasts of a blaring steam whistle. While it is unlikely you'll see any animals being moved about, the tracks run along the backside of their housing facilities. Lucky travelers might catch a glimpse of the nighttime homes of lions, warthogs, and elephants.

When you're ready to depart *Rafiki's Planet Watch*, hop aboard the train for the slightly shorter five-minute return trip to Harambe. The train runs non-stop until about dusk. The line can get long by midday after guests have experienced the nearby popular attractions, Kilimanjaro Safaris and Pangani Forest Exploration Trail.

Each trains holds 250 people, so guests usually do not have to wait to get a seat. Unlike the front-facing seats at the trains in the Magic Kingdom, these cars have seats that face to the side to make the journey more fun. Guests are welcome to remain in their wheelchairs or ECVs to board the train. Lightning Lane reservations are not available.

A Celebration of Festival of the Lion King (*G+*)

You can feel the love in this high-quality 40-minute live show based on Disney's classic movie, The Lion King. Reminiscent of the original Broadway production, this popular revue dazzles with dance, puppetry, special effects, and award-winning music to recreate

Animal Kingdom

an African savanna of birds, elephants, gazelles, giraffes, lions, and zebras.

More than 100 costumes make their way into the tribal festival that includes animatronic floats, flame dancers, and stilt-walkers. Each seat has a good view of the action, and audience members are encouraged to clap and sing along. The line for Animal Kingdom's longest running show often stretches to Pandora.

Rafiki's Planet Watch

Habitat Habit!

Habitat Habit! is a shaded walking trail between the *Rafiki's Planet Watch* train station and the *Conservation Station.* Signs with characters from Disney's Lion King, including Rafiki, are placed along the path to increase awareness about ways each of us can conserve the environment.

Children and adults alike delight in the centerpiece of the exhibit: playful cotton-top and golden lion tamarins. These adorable, furry monkeys could easily fit in the palm of your hand, and you will be fascinated watching them swing about their habitats.

Habitat Habit! gives an up-close look at the inner workings of Disney's Animal Kingdom theme park and lets you take part in fun, educational activities that increase awareness of global animal issues.

Conservation Station

The end of the *Habitat Habit!* trail brings you to the *Conservation Station.* This area is devoted to the preservation and care of animals. The large, air-conditioned building is filled with several small animal displays and exhibits, a working veterinarian hospital, a nutrition center, an animal tracking center, and a character meet-and-greet.

Insider's Trivia!

The cotton-top tamarin is one of the most endangered primates in the world, and the Disney Conservation Fund has partnered with a conservation group located in Colombia to save them and their habitats.

Inside the animal exhibits you can view tarantulas, snakes, and poisonous dart frogs in their glass habitats. Educational videos and entertaining interactions for children are found throughout the building. These diversions are great for a short break from the outdoor heat, but they generally do not keep childrens' attention for long.

Character Meet-and-Greet: The characters on hand are usually Rafiki, who is the monkey that holds Simba up in the Lion King, and Chip'N Dale. However, other characters, such as Jiminy Cricket and Flik, are also known to greet guests inside the station building.

The Animation Experience at Conservation Station (*G+*)

Learn to draw a favorite character in this fun experience for all ages. An experienced Disney artist takes you through the drawing process, step-by-step. When you're finished, walk away with a great souvenir drawing!

Affection Section

A favorite area that children discover just outside *Conservation Station's* rear exit is a small petting zoo known as *Affection Section.* You can physically interact with some of the animals in a partially-shaded, outdoor petting yard.

A handy washbasin located near the entrance to the petting zoo encourages you to cleanse your hands before and after making contact with the animals.

Animal Kingdom

Insider's Tip!

*A*ffection Section is the only animal meet-and-greet (petting zoo) area within any of the parks, featuring goats, sheep, donkeys, cows, and pigs. In addition to petting, fur brushes are lying around the enclosure for you to use on the goats. These are popular (for both children and the animals!) and available on a first-come, first-served basis, so you're free to grab any one you see lying around.

Asia

Feathered Friends in Flight

This entertaining and educational outdoor stage show presents different species of free-flying, exotic birds, including hawks, macaws, cockatoos, and – what is known as the best singing parrot in the world – the Yellow-napped Amazon parrot. These amazing winged creatures are trained to demonstrate activities in ways that emulate how they get about in their natural environment.

Watch them take flight around the stage and above the crowd. Some of the birds are trained to fly unexpectedly low, and whisk by while barely grazing your head.

The show takes place on the Caravan Stage in the Asia area of Animal

Insider's Trivia!

A maharaja is a king or prince in India (who ranks higher than a rajah). In the Kingdom of Anandpur (pronounced "ah-NAHN-dah-poor"), Bengal tigers are the royalty who live within the ruins of the maharaja's palace at the Animal Kingdom.

Kingdom. It lasts about 25 minutes and is performed several times a day, so check the current Times Guide when you arrive. The theater is under a canopy and has bench-style seating with no backs. Guests may remain in their wheelchairs or ECVs to experience the attraction.

Lightning Lane reservations are not available for this attraction.

Maharajah Jungle Trek

Similar to the *Gorilla Falls Exploration Trail*, the *Maharajah Jungle Trek* is a self-guided, wildlife excursion along a half-mile long trail showcasing Asian animals in a realistic setting. Wildlife is the main attraction...but the surroundings are also wondrous! The lush home of these fascinating creatures is reminiscent of the rainforests found in Thailand, Indonesia, and India.

Insider's Tip!

B rochures that describe the wildlife and provide viewing tips are provided near the entrance, and Cast Members are available along the trail to answer questions and provide information.

The trail features a Komodo dragon, one of the world's largest lizards. Inside a bat cave along the trek are two species of the flying mammals: Rodrigues Fruit and Malaysian Flying Fox. You'll also get to encounter crumbling ruins and gold-trimmed murals that depict ancestral royal hunts. The trail concludes with an aviary habitat that houses over 50 species of exotic birds.

A typical tour duration is only 20 minutes or so. Guests may remain in their wheelchairs or ECVs.

Insider's Tip!

A hike through *Maharajah Jungle Trek* is a great way to end the day, as the tigers are usually alert and moving about as they wait to be fed about an hour before park closing.

As this is a self-paced hike, no Lightning Lane is offered or required.

Kali River Rapids (*G+*)

This thrill ride is a very wet, free-floating whitewater rafting adventure. Randomly traveling along the trackless design ensures that each ride down the river is unique as you float through a rainforest and alongside temple ruins.

The proprietors of "Kali Rapids Expeditions" host guided tours that support conservation efforts in the village. The exciting expedition along the Chakranadi River (meaning "river in a circle") encounters mild to intense drops over – and under! – waterfalls.

You're strapped securely into tall seats inside a 12-person, circular river raft that looks like a giant inflated bicycle inner tube. Once you're under way, the peaceful setting is quickly interrupted by the sounds of chainsaws and scents of burning timber. A message of conservation and the dangers of deforestation plays throughout your ride.

The 4½-minute ride has a height restriction of 38", and guests using wheelchairs or ECVs must be able to transfer from their chair to board the raft. It is not recommended for expectant mothers, or guests with neck or back problems or motion sickness.

Lightning Lane reservations are strongly encouraged during warmer months, but are generally not necessary on cool days. (You will get soaked on this ride! Do this ride during the hottest part of the day to gain the most heat relief from this soggy experience and to ensure your clothes dry quickly!)

Insider's Tip!

W ear a rain poncho to avoid getting too soaked on *Kali River Rapids*. Even if you want the refreshing splash, you can use the poncho (otherwise, take a plastic bag) to protect your camera and other electronics. The poncho will also be useful for Walt Disney World's only other splash ride, *Splash Mountain* in Magic Kingdom.

Insider's Warning!

P repare to get thoroughly soaked on *Kali River Rapids*. No water ride would be complete without a plunge or two down falls, and almost nobody makes it out of the attraction dry. Heed the warnings that are posted on signs everywhere: "The Proprietors of Kali River Rapids Expeditions wish to inform you: You WILL get wet! YOU MAY GET SOAKED!"

The water splashes high at many places around the river, as the tube-raft bounces around eddies and tumultuous currents. This results in some level of soaking for each passenger. While it may be refreshing to some park-goers on a hot day, beware of colder days.

Warning: Children love it … until they get soaked. Be prepared with a change of clothes or you'll succumb to having to head back to the hotel or buy a new outfit at a nearby shop.

Expedition Everest – Legend of the Forbidden Mountain (*G+*)

Located in the Himalayan village of Serka Zong, two entrepreneurs (an Australian named Bob and a native Himalayan Sherpa named Norbu) have figured out how to use an old tea plantation train to get you to the base of Mount Everest. Unfortunately, your trek will take you through the mystical mountain territory guarded by the dreaded *yeti*, which is known to those in the West as the "Abominable Snowman."

This is considered by many to be the greatest roller coaster in the "world"...Walt Disney World! There may be no inversions, nor any 90-degree drops; and it doesn't take you from zero to sixty at the speed of light. What this attraction <u>does</u> offer is a high-speed, backwards sensation of floating in complete darkness. And it incorporates some of the most incredible theming of any attraction in the world.

To top it all off, Expedition Everest boasts one of the most terrifying monsters found in any theme park, based on the legend of the yeti.

This is the most extreme of all Disney's roller coasters, providing an exciting and fast, yet relatively smooth ride, with sharp turns and thrilling drops. Rider switch is allowed, and guests using wheelchairs must be able to transfer.

Lightning Lane reservations are recommended, and the minimum height requirement is 44". A single rider queue is also available.

DinoLand USA

Finding Nemo – The Big Blue... and Beyond! (*G+*)

DinoLand's "Theater in the Wild" is home to *Finding Nemo: The Big Blue...and Beyond*. The storyline was refreshed in

2022. This spectacular live-action musical stage show brings to life a 40-minute, abridged version of the *Finding Nemo* movie. Animated backdrops, innovative lighting, and vibrant special effects simulate the undersea world of Nemo, Marlin, Dori, and all your favorite characters.

The production is set to an original music soundtrack written especially for this show. It dazzles audiences with colorful costumes, elegant dance routines, and aerialists performing alongside sophisticated puppetry.

While you may have to wait outside before the show, getting a seat in the stadium-style theater – with its enormous capacity of 1,500 guests – is virtually assured even if you encounter a large line. Seating inside the dark, cool theater begins 10-15 minutes before the start of each of five daily performances.

Bleacher-style seating (without back rests) can be a problem for some people during the 40-minute show. Lightning Lane reservations are available to ensure great seats.

The Boneyard

The Boneyard is a fantastic outdoor children's playground designed so little paleontologists can explore a prehistoric dinosaur fossil dig site. The sand pits contain skeletal remains of a Triceratops, a Tyrannosaurus Rex, and a gigantic Wooly Mammoth which need children's help to be discovered and unearthed.

Uncovering bones from beneath the sand, kids learn about the extraordinary world of dinosaurs and how fossils are recovered by scientists. They also gain hands-on (or feet-on!) experience composing their own melodies on giant musical footprints or a set of dino bones they can play like a xylophone!

Insider's Tip!

If there are no paying guests playing these midway games, you can request to play for free. Most Cast Members will allow you a turn, but you won't be eligible for a prize.

The Boneyard is more than just a paleontology dig site, it is also a giant, fenced-in playground area, complete with rope bridges and slides. The little ones can roam through mysterious caves, climb atop ancient rock formations, and traverse a giant, multi-level maze of dinosaur bones, while parents relax comfortably in the shade.

Chester and Hester's DinoRama

This section of the park is themed to be like a roadside "tourist trap" for guests as they make their way to the Dino Institute. Similar to any respectable carnival, it comes complete with rides and silly games.

Fossil Fun Games

Enjoy five authentic carnival midway games, typically found at state fairs and country carnivals everywhere. *Fossil Fun Games* require actual money (about $3 each) if you want to play to win a prize.

You can show the dinosaurs that you're the boss with the *Whac-A-Packycephalosaur* mallet game (familiar as "Whack-a-Mole"). In this game, small dinosaur heads peak up and beckon you to smack them back down.

Fossil Fueler is a water-gun game where you use a water pistol and take aim at a target to beat your opponents with the quickest fill time. *Mammoth Marathon* is a wooly mammoth take on the classic horse race carnival game, where you roll balls into scored holes to move your mammoth toward the finish line.

Animal Kingdom

Comet Crasher is an end-of-the-world-themed version of another old carnival game where you toss your "comet" (Frisbee) onto a table filled with prizes that float on water. If your comet lands on one of these moving prizes, you win it! Lastly, the *Bronto-Score* is a basketball game where you shoot for a great score to win a prize.

TriceraTop Spin

Similar to *Dumbo* at the Magic Kingdom, each four-person, flying vehicle is shaped as a friendly Triceratops cartoon dinosaur. Your family is seated two in front and two in the backseat, using on-board joystick levers to control the up/down (rear seat) and forward/backward (front seat) tilt movements during flight.

The Triceratops vehicles circle around a gigantic "spinning top" while comets and other dinosaurs pop up around you. During the flight, a secret dinosaur pops out from the top's center. This is a very popular ride for small children, as it is one of only two in the park without any height restrictions. (The other is the safari.) The duration is just two minutes, and it is necessary to transfer from wheelchairs and ECVs into the ride vehicles. Lightning Lane is not offered for this attraction.

DINOSAUR (G+)

DINOSAUR is a unique track ride utilizing Disney-patented "enhanced motor vehicles" (EMV), which are intense motion simulators that independently move around as they travel along a track. While not technically a roller coaster, this very fast and dark ride offers great thrills for children and adults.

The trip takes place in the Dino Institute, a state-of-the-art paleontology research facility and fossil museum where "the future is truly in the past." You board a 12-seat super high-tech Time Rover

and are taken on a turbulent journey 65 million years back in time. Your mission is to rescue a living dinosaur before the species is wiped out by meteor strikes.

The Time Rovers bounce, bump, and careen through dark prehistoric forests populated with large and loud Audio-Animatronic dinosaurs that emerge seemingly out of nowhere. The visual effects are brilliant and synchronized to the Time Rover's non-stop, exciting, and dramatic 3½-minute journey.

Because the ride intensely bucks, spins, and pitches, DINOSAUR is not recommended for anyone with back, neck, heart, or motion sickness issues. Expectant mothers should also skip this ride.

Try not to look too terrified as your souvenir photo is snapped near the end of the journey when you encounter a great beast towering overhead.

Minimum height requirement is 40" and children under the age of seven must be accompanied by an adult. The rider switch option is available for children who get cold feet at the last minute. Guests must transfer

Insider's Trivia!

DINOSAUR may seem oddly familiar to those who have been on the Indiana Jones ride in Disneyland. That's because Disney used the exact same track layout and ride design for both attractions! They simply overlaid DINOSAUR with a different theme than its California counterpart.

from their wheelchairs or ECVs to board the EMV. Lightning Lane reservations are recommended, though you can often get on this ride with little wait from early evening to park close.

Sample Lightning Lane & Genie+ Animal Kingdom Itineraries

Animal Kingdom

1 Day (no small children)	
Approx Time	
7 AM	Purchase Lightning Lane and Genie+. Make reservations for Avatar Flight of Passage (mid-morning), Expedition Everest (late-morning), and Kilimanjaro Safaris (9:15-10:15 AM window recommended).
8:30 AM	Arrive 30-45 minutes before park opening.
9:15-9:40 AM	Use Genie+ to ride Kilimanjaro Safaris. (Make next reservation for Na'vi River Journey.)
9:45-10:15 AM	Walk through Gorilla Falls Exploration Trail.
10:25-10:45 AM	Use Genie+ to ride Na'vi River Journey. (Make next reservation for Kali River Rapids.)
10:50-11:15 AM	Use Lightning Lane to ride Avatar Flight of Passage.
11:30-11:50 AM	Use Lightning Lane to ride Expedition Everest. (Prepare Mobile Order lunch while waiting in line.)
11:50-1 PM	Eat lunch.
1:10-1:30 PM	Walk through Maharajah Jungle Trek
1:30-1:50 PM	Use Genie+ to ride Kali River Rapids. (Make next reservation for Festival of the Lion King.)
2-2:30 PM	Watch Feathered Friends in Flight.
3-3:30 PM	Use Genie+ to watch Festival of the Lion King show. (Make next reservation for DINOSAUR.)
3:45-4:05 PM	Use Genie+ to ride DINOSAUR. (Make next reservation for It's Tough to be a Bug.
4:15-4:45 PM	Use Genie+ to watch It's Tough to be a Bug show.
5-6:30 PM	Eat dinner.
6:30-7 PM	Watch Tree of Life Awakenings show.
7-9 PM	Catch any rides or shows you may have missed.
7 AM	Purchase Genie+. Make reservations for DINOSAUR (9:45-10:45 AM window recommended).

1 Day (small children)	
Approx Time	
8:30 AM	Arrive 30-45 minutes before park opening.
9:15-9:35 AM	Ride TriceraTop Spin.
9:45-10:05 AM	Use Genie+ to ride DINOSAUR. (Skip if your child is easily frightened!) (Make next reservation for Kilimanjaro Safaris.)
10:15-10:35 AM	Use Genie+ to ride Kilimanjaro Safaris. (Make next reservation for The Animation Experience at Conservation Station.)
10:40-12 PM	Visit Conservation Station. Use Genie+ to attend The Animation Experience. (Make next reservation for Kali River Rapids.)
12:05-12:30 PM	Walk through Gorilla Falls Exploration Trail.
12:45-1 PM	Use Genie+ to ride Kali River Rapids. (Make next reservation for Na'vi River Journey.)
1:05-1:35 PM	Walk through Maharajah Jungle Trek. (Prepare Mobile Order lunch while walking through the exhibit.)
1:45-3:30 PM	Eat lunch & nap time!
3:45-4:15 PM	Use Genie+ reservation to ride Na'vi River Journey. (Make next reservation for Festival of the Lion King.)
4:30-5 PM	Use Genie+ reservation to watch Festival of the Lion King show. (Make next reservation for It's Tough to be a Bug.)
5:30-6 PM	Use Genie+ to watch It's Tough to be a Bug show.
6-7:30 PM	Eat dinner.
7:30-7:45 PM	Watch Tree of Life Awakenings show.
8-9 PM	Catch any rides or shows you may have missed.

Disney World Resort Hotels

Whether you've decided that staying on-property at a Disney resort is right for you or you need some additional information, we have incorporated the most important factors in this section to let you know exactly what to expect at the various resorts.

We won't throw unimportant details at you or a bunch of confusing and meaningless charts. We have boiled the information down to exactly what you need and want to know.

The sections below detail how resorts are categorized and how to determine which location and resort type works best for your needs.

Categories and Themes: What They Mean

Disney Resort hotels are separated into five categories: Value, Moderate, Deluxe, Deluxe Villas, and Campground. Additionally, each resort has its own theme. For instance, Port Orleans French Quarter is themed to look like the French Quarter in New Orleans (albeit a clean, Disney version of the Quarter), along with decorations and activities specific to that theme.

Think of the hotels as miniature theme parks. While they don't have rides, the attention to detail and immersive atmosphere make many of the properties destinations unto themselves.

Value resorts are the most basic of the Disney lodgings (aside from the Campground). The standard size rooms in these hotels are the smallest on Disney property, though you can pay extra for a suite in certain Value resorts.

Expect to get two double beds per room with basic comforts, including

Disney World Resort Hotels

decent, frequently changed mattresses, sheets with 180-thread-counts, and standard poly-filled pillows. Additionally, all the rooms have exterior entrances.

There are fewer amenities in the Value resorts than in other categories. Mini-fridges are now standard in the rooms (a recent change), as they are with the higher categories. However, you won't find any hot tubs, gyms, room service (unless you count pizza delivery!), or table service restaurants at these properties.

What you will find are fun themes and child-friendly pools and grounds. In fact, these resorts are the most child-friendly on Disney property. Even the landscaping is designed to allow the little ones to run freely and climb on the yard-art.

For food, guests can enjoy counter-service meals from the single food court located at each hotel. Each Value resort also offers a pool-side lounge for thirsty parents.

Value Resorts						
Amenities & Standard Features	Food Courts	Pizza Delivery	Luggage Service (Hourly)	Swimming Pools	Bus Transportation	Free Disney Merchandise Delivery
	2 Double Beds	260 Sq Ft Min	Outdoor Lounge	No Hot Tubs	No Waterslides	Mini-Fridge In-Room

So, what are the themes at the Value resorts? The original hotels built in this category were the <u>three All-Star Resorts</u>: **Music, Movies, and Sports**.

The **All-Star Music Resort**, with its massive guitar-shaped main pool, is decorated to celebrate music in all its forms, while **All-Star Movies Resort** showcases classic Disney movies, incorporating giant decorations from such classics as 101 Dalmations, Fantasia, and many more.

All-Star Sports Resort has buildings and decorations of oversized sports memorabilia, such as surfboards and tennis racquets. Your little football player will especially enjoy running off some extra energy on the faux football field.

Pop Century Resort is another hotel in the Value category. It highlights retro favorites from decades past. From the giant Rubik's cubes to the flower-power pool, this resort is a favorite for people who love to reminisce about their childhoods.

The newest Value resort is often called "<u>Value Plus</u>": **Art of Animation Resort**. The Value Plus designation is based on the fact that the majority of the rooms at this hotel are suites with kitchenettes. The other "plus" for this resort is that the rooms have completely immersive themes. You can choose from The Little Mermaid (standard-sized rooms), Finding Nemo, Cars, or Lion King rooms. This resort is the only on property with a uniquely designed main pool that plays underwater music!

Moderate Resorts						
Amenities & Standard Features	Food Courts & Table Service	Pizza Delivery & Limited Room Service	Luggage Service	Swimming Pools with Hot Tubs & Waterslides	Bus Transportation & Limited Boat Transportation	Free Disney Merchandise Delivery
	2 Double or Queen Beds	314 Sq Ft Min	Indoor & Outdoor Lounge	On-Site Recreation	Limited Story Rooms	Mini-Fridge In-Room

Moderate resorts have slightly better amenities (for a higher cost) than Value resorts. You will get similar sheets and pillows, and room doors are also exterior. However, you will find at least one hot tub and water slide at each Moderate resort, and most offer at least one table service restaurant. These resorts also have indoor lounges themed to match the resort.

Additionally, while Caribbean Beach Resort only has two double beds standard in each room, the other Moderate resorts offer two queen beds standard. Port Orleans Riverside even has an added pull-down bed in many rooms!

Most Moderate resorts have very expansive grounds with some rooms far away from central pool and dining areas. The landscaping and layout of these properties are generally great for people who like to walk or run on a daily basis.

When it comes to "theming," Moderate resorts tend to have more relaxed atmospheres than Value resorts, appealing more to adults than small children. Of course, Disney still provides enough whimsical appeal to please children, but the environments don't encourage running off energy and being silly the way the Value resort themes do.

Caribbean Beach Resort has colorful buildings set on white sand beaches, designed to evoke several of the Caribbean islands. **Coronado Springs**, the only Moderate resort with conference facilities, brings to mind the Spanish colonies of old Mexico, including a spectacular main pool area complete with Mayan pyramid.

The two **Port Orleans Resorts**, set along a river and within walking distance to one another, represent the Southern United States. **Port Orleans French Quarter**, as noted above, is designed to look like the French Quarter in New Orleans with decorations that remind guests to celebrate each day like it's Mardi Gras. **Port Orleans Riverside** is much larger than its counterpart and comes complete with old mansions, sprawling estates, and bayous.

The final Moderate resort is the **Cabins at Fort Wilderness Resort**. Set in a rustic campground setting, these cabins feel very remote and have full kitchens, making them ideal for families. Perhaps the biggest draw to this resort is the live animals, from wild deer roaming the paths to stately horses and ponies at the on-site ranch.

Disney World Resort Hotels

Deluxe & Deluxe Villas Resorts

Amenities & Standard Features	Signature and/or Character Dining	Room Service	Interior Rooms	Swimming Pools with Hot Tubs & Waterslides	Bus, Limited Boat and/ or Monorail Transportation	Free Disney Merchandise Delivery
	2 Queen Beds	340 Sq Ft Min	Mini-Fridge In-Room	Indoor & Outdoor Lounge	On-Site Recreation	Luggage Service
	Limited On-Site Childcare	Fitness Equipment	Limited Spas & Salons	Valet Parking for Fee	Limited Beach Access	250 Thread-Count Sheets & Deluxe Pillows

Deluxe resorts add to the amenities you can expect. They also add to the cost. What you'll get at one of these pricey establishments is larger rooms off of interior hallways, room service, and

valet parking (for an additional fee). The comforts extend to the bedding and bathrooms with higher thread-count sheets and feather/down pillows, as well as luxury soaps and better toilet paper. (Yes, that's important!) Many of the Deluxe resorts also offer character dining and/or signature dining.

When it comes to the Deluxe resorts, there's theming, and then there's *theming*. That's where the Animal Kingdom Lodge and Wilderness Lodge shine. Both designed by the same architect, Peter Dominick, these two resorts are so incredible, locals make excuses just to go to one and hang out for the day.

Animal Kingdom Lodge is an African safari-themed land, complete with live animals out on the savannah. The theme is further enhanced by available safaris and signature dining.

Based on the Northwest region of the United States, **Wilderness Lodge** calls forth the Northwest's National Park Lodges built in the early twentieth century. Native American designs are artfully incorporated into the building design, and the landscape is so realistic, you will be hard-pressed not to believe you're walking along natural springs and viewing the real Old Faithful spout every few minutes.

Disney World's **Star Wars: Galactic Starcruiser** sits adjacent to Hollywood Studios, but is in a world all its own. The resort allows guests the opportunity to experience living aboard a space ship in the most immersive Star Wars experience a fan can have.

The other truly immersive theme in the Deluxe category is the **Polynesian Resort**. Here you will find music, decorations, and even a volcano-themed pool that bring to life many of the South Pacific islands, including the Hawaiian Islands.

Other Deluxe resorts tend to take a more subtle approach to themes. Contemporary Resort, for instance, is designed to be a past and present look at the future of hotels with its unique A-frame, open-atrium design. The rooms and décor here are understated and elegant.

Grand Floridian Resort & Spa provides a stately look at Victorian-era grandeur with its lovely white buildings and red roofs. The interior design is more ornate, in keeping with the theme, and the Alice in Wonderland children's water play area is one of the few whimsical reminders that this is a Disney resort.

Beach Club Resort has very little architectural theming, though it is decorated with some beach designs. It's most obvious nod to the beach theme is the incredibly popular sand-bottom pool complete with shipwreck waterslide feature.

Next door, **Yacht Club Resort** is very similar architecturally, but its interior is full of dark woods and nautical decorations in keeping with its sailing theme.

The BoardWalk Inn is a slightly more immersive experience, mostly because the hotel sits on a replica 1930s wooden pier that recalls the Eastern Coast resort towns of that era.

The **Walt Disney World Swan** and **Dolphin** hotels are the final Deluxe resorts. Each has its namesake animal in statue form on the top of the respective hotels, though that is really the only nod to each hotel's "theme" you will see. (On a side note, the dolphin refers to the dolphin fish, not the mammal. Many people outside of Florida get confused by the apparent discrepancy.)

Disney's newest category is the *Deluxe Villas*. The term is used for Disney Vacation Club (DVC) properties. DVC members use a certain number of their "vacation ownership" points to stay on these properties. You don't need to be a DVC member to rent one of these units, though. Disney rents them for a nightly rate, just like any other property, or there are places where you can purchase DVC points directly from members.

With the exception of Saratoga Springs and Old Key West resorts, each of the Deluxe Villas resorts sits on a regular Deluxe resort property, so the amenities available and theming are exactly the same. The primary differences are that most units are designed to accommodate larger families, and any villa room larger than a studio has a *complete* kitchen.

The Deluxe Villas properties are:

- Bay Lake Tower at Disney's Contemporary Resort
- The Villas at Disney's Grand Floridian Resort
- Boulder Ridge Villas at Disney's Wilderness Lodge
- Copper Creek Villas & Cabins at Disney's Wilderness Lodge
- Disney's Beach Club Villas
- Disney's BoardWalk Villas
- Disney's Animal Kingdom Villas (Jambo House & Kidani Village)
- Disney's Old Key West Resort
- Disney's Polynesian Villas and Bungalows
- Disney's Riviera Resort
- Disney's Saratoga Springs Resort & Spa

Old Key West Resort, which was Disney's first DVC property, has the laid-back feel of its namesake island, though the theme isn't necessarily obvious with its generic Victorian-style buildings surrounding a golf course. However, the central pool and dining area have a wonderful seaside feel, complete with dockside dining.

Riviera Resort brings to mind the luxury and style of the Mediterranean Riviera. Eat atop a rooftop restaurant with amazing views, or stroll through the parklike setting. Either way, expect to be treated like royalty.

Saratoga Springs Resort & Spa also has Victoria buildings, styled to be a lakeside retreat from upstate New York. Horse lovers will especially appreciate the equestrian touches from the resort's namesake town. However, this is not the only theme to this sprawling resort situated along another golf course. Saratoga Springs' second themed area is the **Treehouse Villas**, which are circular apartments built high on stilts within a forested area.

Campgrounds

The final resort type at Disney is the Campground resort, which includes a single property, **The Campsites at Disney's Fort Wilderness Resort**. This is the same property that houses the Moderate resort, The Cabins at Disney's Fort Wilderness Resort. The property theming and amenities are the same, except centralized shower facilities are provided to all guests. Additionally, those paying for an RV space will receive electrical and sewer hook-ups, something you don't find at other Disney resorts!

Noise at the Resort Hotels

Chances are, you're looking for a resort where you can rest peacefully and get away from the excessive stimulation of the parks each evening. Because of this, it's important to choose your hotel, and even your actual room placement, wisely.

If you're an extra-sensitive sleeper, consider whether a convenient location, nice view, or sleep is most important to you. That's because a room above a pool is likely to be noisy until late at night, since pools may not close until 11 p.m. (though that is not always enforced) and children commonly scream and shriek when playing in the water. A courtyard view is likely to have increased foot traffic when compared to a room that sits on a back

Disney World Resort Hotels

Insider's Tip!

The quietest Value resort rooms are at All-Star Music (west facing rooms in Buildings 5 and 6 and northwest facing rooms in Building 4) and All-Star Sports (west facing rooms in Building 3 and north facing rooms in Building 2).

pathway facing undeveloped green space. Want that theme park view? Well, you're going to hear each and every firework as it explodes in the distance.

An interesting fact is that the Value and Moderate resorts, with their *exterior* doors, have better noise insulation than the Deluxe resorts. This is because of the additional weather-proofing necessary to keep the elements out and energy costs down.

However, that doesn't necessarily mean you'll get a more peaceful night's sleep at one of these resorts.

The Value resorts often host large groups of children and teens, particularly for sporting events at the ESPN Wide World of Sports. We're sorry to say that we have heard numerous complaints from visitors about the lack of supervision and extreme noise levels from these kids.

It seems many chaperones would rather hang out at the lounge than supervise the children. Many guests tell us that Disney employees also do a terrible job of enforcing late-night noise regulations at

the Value resorts, claiming there's simply nothing they can do about it. Imagine having a group of teenagers practicing cheers right outside your bedroom at midnight and nobody telling them to stop. It really happens.

That's not to say you shouldn't stay at a Value resort. We have a couple of suggestions to make sure your stay is a pleasant one: 1) Call the resort directly and ask if there are any groups being hosted during your planned stay, and 2) Be very specific about your room request to make sure you are in a quiet area.

At least two weeks before your vacation, review your reservation online to ensure your request is still in place. You can call the resort three or four days in advance of your arrival to verify the request is in their computer and being considered. When you check into your resort, before the process starts, reiterate your desired location to the front desk employee. You can even ask the Cast Member to show you on a map where the available rooms are to make sure you get one to your liking.

Moderate resorts tend to be quiet due to their sprawling designs. For these properties, noise issues are all about the foot traffic. Rooms at these hotels don't commonly sit directly over the pools, as with Value resorts, but guests heading to/from any central area can lead to noise issues. Also, the Port Orleans resorts host their campfires and Movies Under the

Insider's Tip!

Disney does NOT assign you a specific room until you actually check in, so it's useless to ask for a specific room number at the time of your reservation. Rather, you should identify the area and view you want. For instance, at a Value resort, request a room that does not open up to the pool (Pool areas are always noisier until about 11 PM.) or an open courtyard. Also request that the windows not look onto a parking lot. What you should end up with, if available, is a room on a side path that faces the bushes.

Insider's Tip!

The quietest Moderate resort rooms are at Caribbean Beach (lake facing rooms in Buildings 35 and 38 of Trinidad South), Port Orleans Riverside (east facing rooms in Buildings 26 and 28 of Alligator Bayou and west facing rooms in the north wings of Acadian House), and Port Orleans French Quarter (water facing rooms in Building 1 and water facing rooms in the north wings of Buildings 6 and 7).

Insider's Tip!

The quietest Deluxe Villas resort rooms are at Bay Lake Tower (any room), Beach Club Villas (north-northwest facing rooms in southern wings), Treehouse Villas (any room not directly on the water), and Wilderness Lodge Villas (east facing water-view rooms in southern building).

Stars in open courtyards, which increases noise levels slightly.

Generally speaking, the same request we recommend for Value resorts should work for Moderate resorts, as well.

Deluxe resorts all have rooms that open onto an atrium. This is where you're most likely to have noise issues. However, rooms near an elevator or a door leading out to the pool are also subject to lots of people walking by. Request a room away from the atrium and elevators.

Deluxe Villas properties vary widely. Many have sprawling designs like the Moderate resorts and follow the same noise patterns. The Deluxe and Deluxe Villas properties along Disney's BoardWalk offer balcony rooms. If those balconies face the water, you may be kept

awake by fireworks from both Epcot and Hollywood Studios.

For any Disney Springs resort, keep in mind that boats run up and down the waterway until 11 p.m. at night. Rooms situated right on the water, especially the Treehouse Villas that are close to the water, are subject to constant blowing horns from the watercrafts.

Resort Lighting

Lighting can be an issue if you need to spend time working during your vacation. Reading in bed and getting ready for the day make the lighting in the bathroom and bed areas a concern for many people, as well.

As with all other amenities, expect your lighting to correspond with the amount of money you're spending on a room. Most Deluxe and Deluxe Villas resorts have excellent lighting (with the exception of BoardWalk Inn, Yacht Club, and Swan Hotel). Moderate resorts have acceptable lighting, and Value resorts have poor lighting.

In other words, if you're staying in anything but a Deluxe room, plan to bring a makeup mirror with lighting and a reading lamp.

Insider's Tip!

The quietest Deluxe resort rooms are at Beach Club (east facing rooms in the east buildings), BoardWalk Inn (courtyard facing rooms east of the main lobby), and Wilderness Lodge (northwest facing rooms in the northern wing).

Hotel Differences within Categories

Most people choose a category (Value, Moderate, etc.), then determine which resort they like best in that category based on theme. However, there may be some other factors you want to consider when making a choice. For instance, if you want luxury, not all Deluxe resorts offer the same level of luxury.

Starting with Value resorts, the actual design and layout of those resorts are surprisingly similar, as are the room rates (starting at $118 per night during value season). Aside from decorations and pool areas, it would be difficult to differentiate between the properties.

The exception in the Value resorts category is Art of Animation. While the buildings and room layouts are nearly identical to the other Value resorts, rates are higher there. In part, this is because it is a newer property with an abundance of color and theming everywhere you look. In addition, most of the rooms are larger suites (except for the Little Mermaid area).

In the Moderate category, resorts vary widely, although rates are comparable at all Moderate properties (with the exception of The Cabins at Fort Wilderness). Value season nightly rates start at $232 ($360 for The Cabins). Why the difference in price? The Cabins at Fort Wilderness are all stand-alone suites with full kitchens, while the other rates are for standard studio rooms.

There are other differences you will find among Moderate resorts. The Cabins at Fort Wilderness and Caribbean Beach Resorts typically have two double beds, while the other Moderate categories have two queen beds in most rooms. Also, the two Port Orleans Resorts share amenities, so staying at either property gets you two themed pool areas, two excellent food courts (some of the best counter-service food on property), plus boat transportation to Disney Springs.

Caribbean Beach and Port Orleans Riverside Resorts both offer upgrade options to specialty-themed story rooms, something even the Deluxe resorts don't have.

Coronado Springs and both Port Orleans Resorts have excellent lounges for adults to enjoy. The Rix Lounge at Coronado Springs Resort is by far the hippest hotel lounge on property, while the two Port Orleans Resorts lounges offer live entertainment on select days of the week.

And don't forget that Coronado Springs is the only Moderate resort that has conference facilities – the largest on Disney property, in fact! You can rent out one of these locations for your special event, or try to talk your bosses into having the company retreat there.

The Deluxe resorts have the most variation in the category, as well as the widest price range. Nightly rates range from about $434 (Animal Kingdom) to $737 (Grand Floridian) per night for the most basic rooms during value season. If that seems too cheap, feel free to spend upwards of $4,000 per night during value season for one of the larger concierge suites at Grand Floridian. (Animal Kingdom will set you back about $5,200 for a concierge suite of similar size.)

The actual differences you will find at these resorts are somewhat apparent based on the hotel theme. For instance, Animal Kingdom and Wilderness Lodge are highly imaginative and immersive in design, clearly appealing to families. Contemporary and Grand Floridian are more stately and have a more classically luxurious "feel" to the properties. (This can read boring and stifling to smaller children.)

There are also wide variations in standard room sizes for the Deluxe properties, ranging from about 340 square feet at Animal Kingdom and Wilderness Lodge to about 440 square feet at Grand Floridian.

You will even find large differences in the restaurant offerings at these hotels. While many of the Deluxe resorts offer signature dining, which appeals primarily to adults, only a handful of these properties also have character dining to appeal to the children. Polynesian, Contemporary, Grand Floridian, and Beach Club are the only Deluxe resorts with character dining options (although children love the unique dining experience at Wilderness Lodge's Whispering Canyon Café, and two Dinner shows can be found at the neighboring Fort Wilderness Resort).

Of special note in the Deluxe resorts category are the Walt Disney World Swan and Dolphin Hotels. Though they're on-property, these aren't technically Disney hotels. That means they only offer some of the benefits of Disney resorts (including Early Theme Park Entry and free on-site transportation). However, the comfort level of the beds is better than the Disney Deluxe resorts, often for a fraction of the price.

Deluxe Villas resorts also vary widely with starting nightly rates from about $416 at Animal Kingdom Villas to $737 at The Villas at Grand Floridian. Bay Lake Tower tends to have a very exclusive feel, and it's the only Deluxe Villas property that has a lounge reserved only for DVC members.

Saratoga Springs and Old Key West are golf resorts, and the layouts are not conducive to allowing children to run around the properties. On the other hand, BoardWalk and Beach Club Villas, with the nearby BoardWalk entertainment and beachfront walkways, are excellent choices for younger families who have children with extra energy to spare.

Couples celebrating a romantic occasion also have an incredible Deluxe Villas option. Disney's Polynesian Villas & Bungalows offer suites built on stilts in the lagoon! You get all of the ambiance of a Tahitian resort plus an unobstructed view of Cinderella's castle and nightly fireworks. We're swooning already!

Resort Locations & Convenience

In this section, we address the ease of getting from place to place from either your chosen resort or from within the resort property to help you make an informed decision about the resort differences.

In addition to categories and themes, Disney resorts are further classified by their location on Disney property. The general areas are: Magic Kingdom, Epcot (& Hollywood Studios), Animal Kingdom, Disney Springs, and Wide World of Sports.

When choosing which resort at which you plan to stay, it's important to know where it's located on Disney's property and how convenient it will be to the parks you wish to visit. This is particularly important if you don't have your own vehicle and are relying on Disney transportation.

Generally, the most convenient resorts to the four main parks are the Deluxe properties, some of which are within walking distance to the parks and offer multiple forms of transportation. The least convenient are the Value resorts, which only offer bus transportation and are situated on the outskirts of the property.

You will also need to consider your dining options during your vacation and how you're going to get to restaurants that aren't at your resort. We address that below.

Finally, we discuss the actual resort layouts and the convenience of getting to main areas within your resort.

Convenience to Resorts

It's important to consider how often you plan to visit each theme park. If you plan to spend several days at Magic Kingdom and visit the other parks only once, for instance, you may become frustrated with the long commute back to your Value resort each day.

Before we discuss the distance from each resort to the parks, let's first consider how you're getting to each park from your resort.

Each Disney resort offers bus transportation to the theme parks, water parks, and Disney Springs. Some hotels also provide boat and/or monorail transportation to the theme park or parks in its vicinity (or Disney Springs in the case of those area resorts). However, many people prefer to drive and park.

Aside from getting to the Magic Kingdom, driving your own vehicle is generally as quick and efficient as using bus or boat transportation. If you're an early riser and find a parking spot close to the park entrance, driving is usually a faster option. However, if you show up to the parks after 10 or 11 a.m., expect to park farther out in the lot. The farther out you park, the longer it will take you to use the parking lot trams to/from your vehicle, losing you any time savings you may have gained from driving in the first place.

There is no parking lot for the Magic Kingdom entrance. Drivers must park at the TTC and take a bus, boat, or monorail to the park. Because of this, driving is never the quickest or most efficient way to get to Magic Kingdom. Disney buses (as well as boats and monorails for Magic Kingdom resorts) drop resort guests off directly at the Magic Kingdom entrance, saving a lot of time and hassle.

Magic Kingdom: If you plan to visit Magic Kingdom several times throughout your stay, you may want to consider staying at one of the Magic Kingdom monorail resorts (Contemporary, Polynesian, Grand Floridian, and their Deluxe Villas counterparts).

Of these, Contemporary and Bay Lake Tower are by far the most convenient to Magic Kingdom. These two resorts have bus and monorail service, plus there is a walking path that gets you to the front gate in about 10 minutes. Walking is typically faster than waiting for any form of Disney transportation.

Grand Floridian, The Villas at Grand Floridian, Polynesian, and The Polynesian Villas & Bungalows are all nearly as convenient to Magic Kingdom as Contemporary and Bay Lake Tower. Grand Floridian is the last stop on the monorail line before you reach Magic Kingdom, and Polynesian is the last stop on the boat line before you reach the park, making both a good option.

However, Polynesian and The Polynesian Villas & Bungalows have an advantage over their Grand Floridian counterparts. The TTC with its monorail to Epcot is a very short (less than five minute) walk from Polynesian, making it the most convenient Magic Kingdom resort to Epcot.

Fort Wilderness (and The Cabins at Fort Wilderness), Wilderness Lodge, Boulder Ridge Villas at Wilderness Lodge, and Cabin Creek Villas & Cabins at Wilderness Lodge are slightly less convenient to Magic Kingdom. The sprawling layout of Fort Wilderness in particular means it can take you 20-30 minutes just to get to the final bus stop on property before heading over to the park.

Keep in mind, these "Wilderness" resorts share buses, so depending on the park you're visiting, you will end up having an extra stop either in the morning or evening. Because of this, most people choose to use the boat transportation to Magic Kingdom, which is a direct route from each property.

As with buses, boats are supposed to take off around every 20 minutes. However, Disney speeds up service during the busy times of the day, so the wait is often 10 minutes or less for a boat. Considering it takes just under 10 minutes to reach Magic Kingdom once the boat leaves, you can plan on a 20-30 minute commute each way (plus the time it takes you to get to your camping location if you're staying at Fort Wilderness).

Epcot (& Hollywood Studios): The Epcot resorts (BoardWalk Inn, Beach Club, Yacht Club, Swan and Dolphin Hotels, BoardWalk Villas, Beach Club Villas, Riviera, and Caribbean Beach) are the most centrally located on-property. With the exception of Caribbean Beach, boats take you from each location to either Epcot or Hollywood Studios approximately every 15 minutes, and you can walk to both Epcot and Hollywood Studios from any of these hotels (except Caribbean Beach) within 5-25 minutes. Also, both Magic Kingdom and Disney Springs are a very short drive or bus ride away.

Star Wars: Galactic Starcruiser is the only official Hollywood Studios resort. This intensely themed space hotel sits adjacent to Hollywood Studios. Disney offers special Star Wars: Galaxy's Edge access packages with stays at this Deluxe property.

BoardWalk Inn and BoardWalk Villas are our top picks for overall on-property convenience. These are the closest in distance to both Epcot and Hollywood Studios, as well as all of the dining and entertainment Disney's BoardWalk has to offer.

Caribbean Beach is actually located between Hollywood Studios and Disney Springs. While the resort itself is conveniently located, much like Fort Wilderness, your location on the property can have a big effect on the time it takes to use the offered bus transportation. The resort is extensive and sprawling, and buses stop at several locations on the property. Unless you're located very close to the main bus terminal, it can take 20-30 minutes just to get off the property, and then you need to wait through all of those stops again in the evening.

Animal Kingdom: Animal Kingdom theme park and its resorts (Animal Kingdom Lodge, Animal Kingdom Villas, Coronado Springs, and the All-Star Resorts) are all located on the far edge of Disney's property, away from the other parks. This makes them among the least convenient to any property other than Animal Kingdom theme park.

Each hotel only has bus transportation, and the three All-Star Resorts all share buses, meaning you have to wait for a few stops either in the morning or evening.

Animal Kingdom Lodge and Villas are slightly closer to Animal Kingdom theme park than the other resorts, but Coronado Springs is also quite close to it and even closer to Blizzard Beach. Still, any of these resorts will leave you with a lengthy commute to the other parks.

Disney Springs: Saratoga Springs, Old Key West, and the two Port Orleans resorts are Disney Springs resorts. All offer both boat and bus transportation to the shopping and entertainment district. Saratoga Springs and Old Key West each have walking paths that lead directly to Disney Springs, but Old Key West is a long walk away (especially in the heat). Saratoga Springs sits directly across the waterway from Disney Springs, making it the most convenient resort to the area.

The Disney Springs area, while on the edge of Disney property, is situated close to Hollywood Studios and Epcot. Magic Kingdom is a bit farther away, and Animal Kingdom is the farthest park away on Disney property.

The two Port Orleans resorts share buses. Port Orleans French Quarter is a small resort with only one bus stop. However, Port Orleans Riverside is quite large and has multiple bus stops, though not as many as Caribbean Beach or Fort Wilderness. Depending on the resort you're visiting, you will need to wait through several stops either in the morning or evening.

Similarly, they share boat transportation. However, Port Orleans French Quarter is closer to Disney Springs, so it is always the last stop on the way to Disney Springs and the first stop on the way back, making it slightly more convenient to the dining and shopping district.

ESPN Wide World of Sports: ESPN Wide World of Sports has two resorts in its vicinity: Pop Century Resort and Art of Animation Resort. Both of these hotels are in the Value category and only offer bus transportation.

As the ESPN Wide World of Sports is on the outer edge of Disney property, close to Animal Kingdom, these two resorts are only convenient to Animal Kingdom. Similar to the Animal Kingdom properties, they take quite a bit of time to get to any other theme parks on-property.

Convenience to Restaurants

Dining might be an important consideration for you during vacations,

or it could be more of an afterthought. Whichever is the case for you, you should be aware of what dining options will be available to you at your resort and how easy it will be to get to restaurants outside of your resort.

Aside from the Value resorts, each Disney hotel property has uniquely themed dining options. Value resorts *only* have food courts, which provide a decent variety for those who don't want specialty dining. However, you might be interested in attending a dinner show at Fort Wilderness or eating Southern fare at Port Orleans Riverside. If you're celebrating a special occasion, you may even plan to eat at one of Orlando's premier restaurants, Victoria and Albert's, found at Grand Floridian. If that's the case, it's important that you plan your accommodations to reduce the hassle of getting to other properties.

Driving your own vehicle is nearly always the most convenient way to eat at a non-theme park location away from your resort. Driving from one hotel to another will take you no more than 20 minutes to get from one end of Disney's property to the other. In most cases, you can expect about 15 minutes of travel time between your resort and the on-property dining destination of your choice.

You may want to use Disney's free transportation to get to your dining location, though, particularly if you only wish to eat away from your hotel once or twice during your visit. In most cases, to get to another Disney resort to eat or enjoy its unique activities you will need to first go to one of the theme parks, Disney Springs, or the TTC from your resort, then take another bus from there to get to the resort of your choice. That means you can expect 45-90 minutes of travel *each way* if you're using Disney transportation.

Insider's Tip!

Don't take a bus or monorail to Epcot if you plan to transfer to an Epcot area hotel. Buses don't run between Epcot's parking lot and its resorts (with the exception of Caribbean Beach). Instead, take a bus to Hollywood Studios and walk or take a boat to the hotel of your choice.

As we mentioned in the previous section, the most centralized hotels are the Epcot area resorts. One major advantage to staying at any of these properties (other than Caribbean Beach) is that it's so quick and easy to get to the bus depot at Hollywood Studios. A quick walk or boat ride there will have you on a bus to the resort of your choice within a few minutes.

The other advantage to these Epcot area resorts is that they're within close walking distance to each other and Disney's BoardWalk, so a wide variety of dining options is extremely convenient.

Of course, the Disney Springs area resorts also have excellent dining options nearby via a boat or bus ride. Saratoga Springs is by far the most convenient resort to Disney Springs' restaurants, as it is a short walk away.

The two Port Orleans resorts share a single table service restaurant, but each has unique Southern and Cajun food options at its respective food court, including beignets for dessert (a local favorite) at Port Orleans French Quarter.

The three monorail hotels and their Deluxe Villas counterparts (Grand Floridian, Contemporary, and Polynesian) have excellent, albeit expensive, dining options that are easy to get to on the monorail.

Also, Fort Wilderness, Wilderness Lodge, and Contemporary have direct boats between each other, making it easy to share restaurants if you're staying at any of the above.

For the remainder of the hotels, we suggest you plan to go to the nearest theme park, either to your resort or to the resort you plan to dine at, for a transfer bus. For instance, if you're staying at Pop Century and want to eat at Sanaa, take a bus to Animal Kingdom theme park, then another bus to Animal Kingdom Lodge. If you're staying at Art of Animation and plan to eat at Boatwright's Dining Hall, take a bus to Disney Springs, then another bus to Port Orleans Riverside. (Or take a leisurely boat ride to the resort from Disney Springs if you have extra time. It takes about 35 minutes each way.)

Resort Layouts

Each Disney resort has a centralized area where you can find lounges, food courts, table service restaurants (though Animal Kingdom Lodge has an additional table service restaurant and lounge at Kidani Village), a themed pool area, and transportation. In some cases, such as Fort Wilderness, this is a separate area from the resort check-in desk. Certain resorts also have multiple transportation pick-up locations. In these cases, buses still travel to the centralized area before leaving the hotel for the theme park.

Regardless of the resort or its layout, this centralized area is considered the prime location for guests...and you will be charged extra for a guaranteed room near there.

The trade-off is that these areas are higher traffic, so a room near the resort's hub tends to be noisier than those tucked away in the far corner of the hotel property.

Whether or not the convenience of being near dining and transportation is worth the additional cost is most dependant on the layout of the particular resort you're considering.

For Deluxe and Deluxe Villas properties that share a property and theme (such as Grand Floridian and The Villas at Grand Floridian), the most centralized location will be in one of the regular Deluxe buildings, so Deluxe Villas at these resorts are generally a little less convenient.

At Deluxe or Deluxe Villas resorts, request a room in the main building near whichever convenience is most important to you. For instance, transportation is often on one side of the main building, whereas the pool is usually on the other side.

Each of the Moderate and Value resorts has a widely spread-out design. The most sprawling designs are at Coronado Springs, Port Orleans Riverside, and Caribbean Beach. Expect to walk long distances at any of these resorts to get to the hub if you haven't reserved a preferred location room. Port Orleans Riverside and Caribbean Beach have multiple bus pick-up locations, though we've heard complaints from guests at Port Orleans Riverside that buses often bypass these locations and drop off only at the main bus depot.

Port Orleans French Quarter, while a small resort, does not have its own table service restaurant. Its lounge, food court, and themed pool are all fairly convenient, regardless of your room location. However, you will need to walk about 10 minutes or take a boat to Port Orleans Riverside if you wish to dine at their shared table service restaurant, Boatwright's Dining Hall.

The other property of note is Fort Wilderness. It is by far the most expansive of the Disney resort properties, and being in a non-preferred location can mean a lot of walking and waiting a very long time for bus service from one of the multiple pick-up locations. It's so expansive, there are two main bus depots, one on either end

Insider's Tip!

Consider staying at a Value resort for most of your vacation, then at a Deluxe property for the one or two days you don't plan to spend at the park. This can actually be cheaper than staying at a Moderate resort for your entire trip, and you get to enjoy the best amenities Disney has to offer!

of the property. Also, the property's main pool is tucked away closer to the center of the resort than near the bus terminals. You should determine which convenience is most important to you before booking to ensure you have the best experience at this property.

Luxury Versus Value

You may look at all of the amenities offered at the higher-end Disney resorts and be tempted to pay the extra money. Before you do, let's take a realistic look at how much time you'll be at the resort and how many of those luxuries you will be able to use.

Time Spent at the Resort

If you are planning your first visit to Walt Disney World, it is likely you will spend much of your time touring the parks or the Orlando area. If you've been to Disney before, you may be planning a more relaxed vacation. Look at your itinerary. Is each day filled with activities? Will you be spending enough time at the pool to care about its theme? Will you get back to the resort early in the evenings, or will the restaurants and pools be closed by the time you come back from the parks?

Pool and hot tub hours are from 7 a.m. to 11 p.m. If you plan to take midday breaks from the parks or if you have non-activity days planned into your vacation, the resort pool is likely something you will need to consider. Value resorts don't have waterslides. Moderate and above do, though you shouldn't expect the level of thrills you get from water slides at a water park.

Value resorts also don't offer indoor lounges or table service restaurants, but they do have poolside lounges and counter-service restaurants. Disney lounges and counter-service restaurants close at 12 a.m., while table service restaurants typically stop taking new diners at 9:30 or 10 p.m. Unless you plan to take afternoon breaks from the theme parks or have days you won't spend at the parks, it's unlikely you'll eat dinner at your resort's table service restaurant.

Of course, there are other niceties and services you can expect at the higher-end resorts. The real question you must ask yourself is whether or not you will spend enough time at the hotel to take advantage of the offerings. If the answer is no, go cheap.

Special Celebrations

There may be other reasons you wish to stay at one of the Deluxe properties. Perhaps you're celebrating a birthday or planning to ask someone to marry you. There are times when it just makes sense to splurge.

In these cases, consider a club/concierge level room at one of the Deluxe resorts. These rooms are on an exclusive, lock-out floor that only club level guests can access. They come complete with a dedicated concierge for the floor, as well as a private lounge that serves snacks all day long. The concierge is especially adept at preparing special occasion settings while you play at the park. Imagine coming back from the Magic Kingdom to find a path of rose petals leading to your private dinner table for two!

Insider's Tip!

Disney sometimes runs specials on their room rates with a sliding scale. Greater discounts are given to Moderate and Deluxe resort reservations than to Value resort pricing. This means your per person cost during one of these specials could be less if you upgrade to a nicer room! Look for special offers during your planned vacation here: disneyworld.disney.go.com/special-offers

Disney World Resort Hotels

Family Size	4	5	6	7
Suggested Hotel	Any Value Resort (Non-Suite)	Port Orleans Riverside (Alligator Bayou Section)	Art of Animation (Suite) or The Cabins at Fort Wilderness	2 Rooms at a Value Resort or Rent DVC Points for a DVC Suite

Determining Best Value for Your Family Size

Four People: Disney room rates are for four people, either two adults and two children or four adults. (There is a per person surcharge for more than two adults in a room.) For families of four, Value resorts are typically the cheapest option for Disney hotels. However, on rare occasions you may find specials directly on the Walt Disney World Swan and Dolphin website (https://swandolphin.com/) that are less expensive.

Five People: Surprisingly, families of five or more may find better values at the higher-end Disney resorts. Typically, the best value for families of five is the Alligator Bayou section of Port Orleans Riverside. Rooms here house up to five people and can be as little as $34 per person per night. Compare that to a suite at Art of Animation which starts at $53 per person per night (prices are based on value season rack rates, excluding tax).

Six People: Art of Animation comes in as the best value for families of six. Expect to spend $44 per person per night. However, you may wish to consider an upgrade to The Cabins at Fort Wilderness for $49 per person per night. The Cabins gives you a full kitchen, rather than the small kitchenette at Art of Animation, allowing you to save a bundle on meals (prices are based on value season rack rates, excluding tax).

Seven People or Above: There aren't great, inexpensive options for groups this size. The least expensive option normally is to rent multiple rooms at a Value resort. However, you may consider renting DVC points (directly from an owner). You may find a great deal for enough points to rent a two-bedroom suite for less than the cost of two studios at a Value resort.

Hotel Restaurants & Lounges

Counter-Service Restaurants

Each Disney resort has a counter-service/food court type restaurant. These restaurants are generally much less expensive than table service restaurants. They stay open from 6 a.m. to 12 a.m. each day and serve breakfast, lunch, and dinner, as well as desserts.

The food courts have offerings that vary slightly, though you can nearly always find pasta, hamburgers, and standard breakfast items.

The counter-service restaurants at Polynesian Village and the two Port Orleans hotels have really unique food offerings that match the hotel themes, and locals often frequent these locations for reasonably-priced food. For instance, you can get stir fry and pineapple ice cream at the Polynesian, or enjoy gumbo at Port Orleans French Quarter and muffuletta flatbread at Port Orleans Riverside.

The hotel food courts are also where you pick up your all-you-can-drink refillable beverage containers. These mugs have embedded RFID chips that activate the soda machines, giving you unlimited refills of soda across all Disney resorts during your stay. In addition, you can get unlimited refills of coffee, tea, and hot cocoa during this timeframe (although the machines for the hot drinks are not activated by RFID, so you can theoretically get unlimited refills of hot drinks past the timeframe you've purchased).

The cost for your mug is $18.99, which is good for the entire length of your stay if you're staying at a Disney resort. You can still purchase one of these mugs if you're staying off-site. (It will be good for two weeks.)

Character Meals & Dinner Shows

NOTE: Character meals and dinner shows may not be available at every restaurant listed due to COVID-19 concerns.

Some of the Deluxe resorts have character dining or dinner shows, which allow you to treat yourself and your children to certain characters and entertainment outside of the theme parks. If you plan on having a character meal, consider one at a resort instead of inside the theme parks. Depending on the day you do the character meal, you can get one of two great benefits: 1) you can park at the resort in which you're dining and take a bus to a theme park to avoid paying for parking at the theme park that day, or 2) you can eat at a hotel and meet the characters during a non-theme park day, freeing up your paid theme park days to do other activities.

The biggest deciding factor for choosing a character meal has to be the characters you can expect to meet. Breakfast is the most popular meal for character dining, so many restaurants only have characters available then. Here is a list of some characters you can expect to meet:

Resort Hotel Character Breakfasts

Disney Resort	Restaurant	Characters
Beach Club	Cape May Café	Goofy, Donald, Minnie
BoardWalk	Trattoria al Forno	Royal Couples (Varying Princes and Princesses)
Contemporary	Chef Mickey's	Mickey, Minnie, Pluto, Donald, Goofy (The Fab Five)
Four Seasons	Ravello	Mickey, Minnie, Goofy

Grand Floridian	1900 Park Fare	Mary Poppins, Alice in Wonderland, Mad Hatter, Pooh, Eeyore
Polynesian	'Ohana	Stitch, Lilo, Mickey, Pluto
Riviera	Topolino's Terrace	Mickey, Minnie, Donald, Daisy
Wilderness Lodge (Dinner Only)	Storybook Dining at Artist Point	Snow White, Evil Queen, Seven Dwarfs

Dinner Shows

There is only one dinner show currently available at Walt Disney World: Hoop-Dee-Doo Musical Review at Disney's Fort Wilderness. This experience, which includes all-you-care-to-eat dining, comedy, and singing is great for younger children and adults.

Expect to pay a bundle for it. Dinner shows typically cost $60-$78 per person.

Casual Table Service Restaurants

Value resorts do not have table service restaurants. With the exception of Port Orleans French Quarter (which is a short walk or boat ride from Port Orleans Riverside), all Disney resorts in the Moderate and above categories have at least one casual table service restaurant.

These restaurants are always themed to fit the hotel in some way. For instance, The Wave has contemporary, Californian food, inside the Contemporary Resort; Beaches and Cream is an adorable seaside soda shop to match the Beach Club Resort atmosphere; and Whispering Canyon Café is a Wild Western experience at Wilderness Lodge.

Signature Dining

Fine dining restaurants, known as "Signature Dining" at Disney, can be found at several of the Deluxe resorts, in addition to the few found inside theme parks. There are definitely levels among the Signature restaurants. Victoria & Albert's at Grand Floridian is the most elite, while Flying Fish Café at Disney's BoardWalk has a more relaxed feel to it.

Keep in mind that none of the Signature restaurants are very child friendly. They lack the whimsical appeal that many Disney restaurants offer, opting instead for classical elegance that's lost on most children. In fact, some of the highest-end Signature restaurants don't even allow children under the age of 10, and most have a dress code.

However, if you're tired of "theme park" food, or if you want to have a romantic evening, any of the Signature restaurants at the Disney resorts are excellent choices. In fact, if you're celebrating an extra-special event, consider reserving the chef's table at Cítricos or Victoria & Albert's.

Disney World Resort Hotels

Here is a complete listing of the Signature restaurants found at the Disney resort hotels:

Disney Resort	Restaurant	Primary Cuisine
Animal Kingdom Lodge	Jiko – The Cooking Place	African
BoardWalk Inn	Flying Fish Café	Seafood
Contemporary	California Grill	Californian
Dolphin Hotel	Shula's Steak House	Steak
Dolphin Hotel	Todd English's bluezoo	Seafood
Grand Floridian	Cítricos	Mediterranean
Grand Floridian	Narcoossee's	Seafood
Grand Floridian	Victoria & Albert's	American
Riviera	Topolino's Terrace	French, Italian
Swan Hotel	Il Mulino	Italian
Yacht Club	Yachtsman Steakhouse	Steak

Nightlife

Nightlife? At Disney? Okay, it may not be the wild scene that Pleasure Island was in the past, but the hotels do have some great options to relax and enjoy good company after the parks.

While each resort has at least one lounge, keep in mind that the pool lounges at Moderate and above category resorts always close early (most by 7 p.m.), so the real nightlife is found at the indoor lounge locations, which are all open until 12 a.m. Value resorts only have poolside lounges, so they keep those open until 12 a.m., as well.

Very few of the lounges serve more than snacks. One notable exception to this is Crew's Cup Lounge at Yacht Club Resort. This lounge has a full food menu with excellent burger options. In fact, it's a favorite among men as a great hangout location.

Each resort has free transportation to/from Disney Springs, allowing you to enjoy their restaurants and lounges late into the evening. Of course, the Disney Springs resorts, especially Saratoga Springs, are the most convenient to Disney Springs. Locals know the hotels provide great options if your goal is just to relax, though.

Disney Springs Resort Lounges

Resort	Lounge	Notes
PO Riverside	River Roost	Free Live Entertainment on Select Nights
PO French Quarter	Scat Cat's Club	Free Live Entertainment on Select Nights
Saratoga Springs	Turf Club Lounge	Restaurant Waiting Area, Lots of Kids, Free Pool Table
Old Key West	Gurgling Suitcase	Outdoor, Limited Seating Near Bar

Disney Springs Lounges & Evening Entertainment

Name	Notes
AMC Movie Theatre	Full Bar, Dine-In Theater Option
The BOATHOUSE	Full Bar, Waterfront
Bongos Cuban Café	Full Bar
Aerophile: The World Leader in Balloon Flight	Tethered Balloon, Weather Dependant
Cirque du Soleil	Extra Admission Required, Acrobatic Show
House of Blues	Full Bar, Free Live Music, Paid Music Venue
Dockside Margaritas	Outdoor, Free Live Music
Jock Lindsey's Hangar Bar	Full Bar
Lava Lounge	Outdoor, No Large Group Seating
MacGUFFINS	Located on Side of AMC Move Theatre, No Ticket Required
Paradiso 37	Full Bar
Raglan Road	Full Bar, Free Live Music
Splitsville Luxury Lanes	Multiple Bars, Bowling Alley
Various Dining Locations	Quick-Service or Table-Service, Most Serve Alcohol
Various Shopping Locations	Disney & Non-Disney Retailers

If you're interested in exploring different options each evening without waiting for bus service, stay in a Magic Kingdom monorail resort or a Deluxe Epcot resort.

The Magic Kingdom monorail resorts are simple and convenient for exploring the lounges at the three hotels. Locals sometimes do a "monorail crawl," where you start at the lounge of one of the monorail resorts and take the monorail around the loop until you've experienced all of the resort lounges. The lounges will even give you a to-go cup for your drink, which you are welcome to take on the monorail with you.

Monorail Resort Lounges

Disney Resort	Lounge	Notes
Grand Floridian	Cítricos Lounge	
Polynesian	Tambu Lounge	Limited Seating, Lots of Kids
Polynesian	Trader Sam's Tiki Lounge	Outdoor
Contemporary	The Wave Lounge	Seating for Large Groups
Contemporary	Outer Rim	Next to Chef Mickey's, Lots of Kids
Contemporary	California Grill Lounge	Fireworks View

Deluxe Epcot Resort Lounges

Disney Resort	Lounge	Notes
BoardWalk Inn	Belle Vue Lounge	Board Games Available
Beach Club	Martha's Vineyard	
Dolphin Hotel	Lobby Lounge	Off Lobby
Dolphin Hotel	Shula's Lounge	Full Shula's Steakhouse Menu Avail
Dolphin Hotel	bluezoo Lounge	Full bluezoo Menu Avail
Swan Hotel	Il Mulino Lounge	
Swan Hotel	Kimonos Lounge	Nightly Karaoke
Yacht Club	Ale and Compass Lounge	Off Lobby, Limited Seating
Yacht Club	Crew's Cup Lounge	Full Food Menu

Deluxe BoardWalk Lounges

Lounge	Notes
Abracadabar	Small Lounge, Indoor & Outdoor Seating
Atlantic Dance Hall	Ages 21+, Cover Charge, Open to 2 a.m., Large Dance Floor
Big River Grille & Brewing Works	Restaurant & Lounge, Open to 11 p.m.
BoardWalk Joe's Marvelous Margaritas	Walk-up Bar
ESPN Club	Restaurant & Lounge, Open to 1 a.m.
Jellyrolls	Ages 21+, Cover Charge, Open to 2 a.m., Dueling Pianos Entertainment Nightly

Disney World Resort Hotels

The best variety and convenience can be found at the Deluxe Epcot resorts. You can explore the very relaxed lounges within each of the hotels on foot, or walk to the more lively BoardWalk options, two of which are adults-only.

Jellyrolls is a very popular entertainment venue with its dueling pianos-style entertainment. The feedback from guests is that it's fun and lively. However, some guests complain that the show changes little, making this a one-time-only destination.

Atlantic Dance Hall has a very nice dance floor, complete with giant screen to showcase the songs being played (mostly from the 90s and 00s). Unfortunately, the venue is pretty hit-or-miss. It tends to be more lively on the weekend. Ask what the crowd is like before paying the cover charge.

Not everybody is going to want to pay Deluxe resort prices for the added convenience of being able to walk to dining and nightlife. Other Disney resorts have themed lounges that make them popular destinations for locals. They are all very easy to get to if you have your own vehicle. Using Disney transportation to get to another resort from where you're staying can be a bit time-consuming, as you must first take transportation to a central bus location (any theme park or Disney Springs). You should also be careful to ask how late buses, boats, or the monorail are running to make sure you can get back to your hotel without having to pay for a taxi.

There are some other great options. The two Port Orleans resorts are within easy walking distance to one another, and boat transportation takes guests between the two resorts. Similarly, Wilderness Lodge and Fort Wilderness are connected with a wilderness trail. Boat transportation will not only take you between these two resorts, but there are also boats that take you between them and Contemporary.

Keep in mind that relying on boat transportation can be tricky. Boats typically stop running before lounges close, and heavy rain or lightning will put a stop to all boat traffic.

Local favorites for the harder-to-get-to lounges include **Victoria Falls Lounge** inside <u>Animal Kingdom Lodge</u> and **Territory Lounge** inside <u>Wilderness Lodge</u>. However, the hippest resort lounge is considered to be **Rix Lounge** at <u>Coronado Springs</u>. Aside from Disney Springs locations, Rix Lounge is where you're most likely to find the 20- 30-something crowd at Disney.

Insider's Tip!

Most Disney lounges allow children inside. This is not necessarily a good environment for the little ones, as people can and do drink heavily. Consider hiring a babysitter for the evening, or leave your children at one of Disney's on-site daycare centers if you plan to experience Disney's nightlife (See our Traveling with Small Children section).

Other Resort Lounges

Disney Resort	Lounge	Comment
All-Star Movies	Silver Screen Spirits Pool Bar	Outdoor
All-Star Music	Singing Spirits Pool Bar	Outdoor
All-Star Sports	Grandstand Spirits	Outdoor
Animal Kingdom	Cape Town Lounge & Wine Bar	Full Jiko Menu Avail, Limited Seating
Animal Kingdom	Maji Pool Bar	Outdoor, Open to 11 p.m.
Animal Kingdom	Sanaa Lounge	Limited Seating
Animal Kingdom	Victoria Falls Lounge	Overlooking Boma Restaurant
Art of Animation	Drop Off Pool Bar	Oudoor
Caribbean Beach	Banana Cabana Pool Bar	Outdoor
Coronado Springs	Laguna Beach	Outdoor, Open to 11 p.m.
Coronado Springs	Rix Lounge	Dress Code
Fort Wilderness	Crockett's Tavern	Walk-up, Limited Seating, Open to 10 p.m.
Pop Century	Petals Pool Bar	Outdoor
Wilderness Lodge	Territory Lounge	

As mentioned before, each Moderate and above resort also has poolside lounges that close earlier in the evening. We have only included those poolside lounges in our list that stay open late enough to enjoy after the theme parks.

Exclusive Lounges

Deluxe properties also have exclusive, club-level lounges available only to guests paying to stay on a club-level floor. While service is excellent in these lounges, their exclusivity makes them more appropriate for quiet contemplation than socializing. Of the club-level lounges, we suggest the one at Polynesian. It has incredible views of the fireworks.

In addition, Bay Lake Towers has **Top of the World Lounge**, which is only accessible to DVC members. Unlike club-level lounges, this one seems to be plagued by service issues. Guests consistently complain about long waits and poor quality for snacks and drinks. However, the view from this lounge that sits at the top of the hotel overlooking Magic Kingdom is amazing. If you know someone with a DVC membership, we highly recommend a visit to enjoy the view, but you'll likely only want to stay for one drink.

Disney World Resort Hotels

Resort Check-in & Check-out

Remember the days when you had to stand in a lobby queue, all of your luggage stacked behind you, while trying to keep the kids corralled until it was your turn to check into your room? Well, Disney has worked to vastly improve the efficiency of the process with the on-line check-in system. The result is that you will get you into your room quicker.

What is on-line check-in, and how can you use it? If you've pre-reserved a room at any of the Disney resorts (not including Walt Disney World Swan & Dolphin), you can go online or use the My Disney Experience app up to 60 days in advance and begin the check-in process. This includes identifying each member of your party and tying a credit card to the reservation for incidental expenses. You can also make special room requests during this process. Remember to create a four-digit PIN for members of your party to use when making charges to your account during your vacation.

In other words, you can save the time it normally takes to go through all of these details at the front desk, so your normal check-in procedure of around 15 minutes should be much less. Better yet, you won't need to wait the 15 minutes for each person in line before you!

Keep in mind, you need to complete your on-line check-in at least 24 hours in advance, or the system won't be updated with your details. If you forget, you'll still need to complete the normal check-in process.

When you arrive at the hotel, there is no need to go to the regular check-in desk. If you have already linked your MagicBand(s), simply wait for the notification that your room is ready in your My Disney Experience app. Once ready, you can go straight to your room and use the MagicBand or enabled smart device to unlock it.

If you do not have a MagicBand or enabled smart device, head straight for the "Online Check-In Service" desk when you arrive at the hotel (unless there's a shorter line for the other desk, of course). You will still need to show valid government-issued ID, but the rest of your information will already be tied to your reservation. The Cast Member can assign MagicBands you have purchased to your party at this time.

Note: your room is assigned during the check-in process, not before. If you receive a room assignment you do not like through the My Disney Experience app, go to the check-in desk to request an alternative assignment.

So, when can you actually get into your room? Rooms at most resorts are available for check-in after 3 p.m. The campsites are available after 1 p.m., while guests at Deluxe Villas resorts need to wait until 4 p.m. (Those kitchens take time to clean!)

You may get lucky and get into your room before this time, but don't count on it. Fortunately, if you haven't used Disney's Magic Express luggage service, you can check your bags with a luggage concierge and spend the time waiting however you want (including at the pool).

Insider's Tip!

You are allowed full access to resort amenities on the days of check-in and check-out, even if you don't have access to your room. Pack your swim wear in your carry-on bags. You can change clothes in the bathroom and head straight for the pool. Moderate and above resorts have towels by the pool, but you'll need to ask for towels at the front desk if you're staying at a Value resort.

Disney will call or text you when your room is ready, and your luggage will be waiting for you in the room (or will arrive soon thereafter).

If you haven't checked-in online before you arrive, just head to the regular check-in line. Fortunately, Disney has also improved its procedures for standard check-in, so wait times aren't usually as long as they were in the past.

The biggest recent improvement to the check-in process is that there are special lines just for group check-in. There are also employees that come out with handheld devices during busier times to help check-in guests waiting in the queue. You may still experience a wait at peak times, but these newer procedures have really made the process faster.

When it's time to leave, check-out is very simple. Check-out time is 11 a.m. at all Disney resorts. This doesn't mean you need to leave the resort at this time, but you must be out of your room by then.

If you're using Disney's Magical Express, you will provide your flight information to the hotel when you check in. At that time, you will be told when you need to check into your flight and give your luggage to the flight check-in concierge at the resort. You may need to give your luggage to them the night before your flight for an early take-off. However, you have the option of keeping your luggage with you and checking in once you reach the airport if Disney's flight check-in option doesn't work for you.

Remember to keep your carry-on baggage with you, along with swimsuits or other changes of clothes you might need to stay occupied until it's time to head to the airport.

The night before you check out of your room, the hotel staff will leave a detailed list of your charges on your room door. Review it carefully to make sure all of the charges are accurate. If so, that's it. You don't need to do anything more (not even return keys to the front desk). You will automatically be checked out of your room at 11 a.m. the next morning.

If there are any issues with the charges to your account, be sure to go down to the front desk and address them immediately. This process can be time-consuming, but Disney's hotel staff is trained to handle it courteously and professionally, just like everything else. However, handling any billing issues before check-out is generally much less of a hassle than trying to deal with them when you get back home.

Disney World Resort Hotels

Traveling with Small Children

Disney seems like an ideal destination for families with small children. However, you should be aware that there are <u>height restrictions</u> for some of the attractions and <u>age restrictions</u> for children riding alone. Spending all day in the Florida heat can also bring its own challenges for which you'll want to plan in order to have a successful vacation. We've prepared some advice to avoid the most common pitfalls for families.

Parking

If you have multiple children needing strollers, getting on and off parking trams is a nightmare. This is **not** something Disney advertises, but if you are using strollers, follow the blue line in the theme park parking lot toward disabled parking.

Once you see the parking lot attendant who is directing traffic and checking for disabled parking placards, ask him/her if there is closer parking for people with strollers. Unless the lot is full, you will usually be directed to a parking lot just outside of disabled parking that is close enough for you to walk to the park entrance without needing to use the tram.

Set Realistic Expectations in Advance

Walt Disney World is full of magic and wonder, especially for small children. However, it's important to prepare your child and set expectations to ensure your day doesn't end in heartbreak.

The discussion should include meeting characters. Most of the characters are larger than expected and the ones in full costume do not speak, which may come as a shock to your children. Let them know that Mickey is really a lot larger than he appears on television and doesn't talk. You can use a fun excuse, such as he doesn't like the children who can't hear to feel left out, so he uses hand gestures for everyone.

Fortunately, princesses, fairies, and a few other characters who do not wear full head-covering costumes (face characters) do speak and are trained to make your children feel like little princes and princesses themselves. But remember, your child might expect to find a Tinker Bell who fits inside her hand and be surprised to see she has used magic to make herself big!

Your child might see Goofy walking through the park and want to rush up to meet him only to be turned away by someone. Let your children know there are set locations to meet the characters, and they can't stop on the way, or they'll be late! We have also witnessed parents try to cut the lines and send their children ahead of others who have been waiting for a while. Don't do this. Not only will your child be ignored or turned away, but you will be the one who gets to deal with the crying and disappointment.

Speaking of lines or queues, they can be long. <u>Very long</u>. Make sure your children expect this and understand how

Traveling with Small Children

Insider's Tip!

All of Disney's resorts are unique and fun, but there is one that we think is absolutely the best for families with pre-teen children: Disney's Art of Animation Resort. Every room is a family-sized suite with kitchenette. Each section is uniquely themed, including an incredible Cars Movie area and Lion King area, complete with unique play areas. Add to that a swimming pool with underwater music, and you have a complete children's fantasy land.

Insider's Note!

A quick note about dining for children. There are many special events that are designed to specifically appeal to children, such as the options of two different tea parties at Grand Floridian. Pirate cruises originating from the Contemporary Resort offer desserts and refreshments.

to wait in line without pushing or fighting or otherwise making a nuisance of themselves. Some queues have interactive items to keep people from getting bored, but others will require you to come up with creative ways to keep your children entertained.

If you have more than one adult in your party, and if the queue allows, it's a good idea to let one person wait while the other takes the children around the park. Only do this in outside queues where you can easily get back in line without pushing through the crowd and where you can keep an eye on the person you left behind, though, or you will risk not being able to get back in time for the ride!

NEVER talk about an amazing ride with your child if there is any possibility your child won't get to ride on it. Check the height requirements in advance for each ride. If your child is not clearly above that height, there is the possibility he/she could get turned away, leading to major heartbreak.

Fireworks

This may seem strange, but you also need to prepare your children for fireworks. They're loud – extremely loud! Young children often get frightened by the noise and start crying, so be sure they know what to expect and that it won't hurt them.

Insider's Note!

While most restaurants have children's menus, certain signature restaurants do not. Some even have age limitations where only children over 10 are permitted.

Also, be aware that Epcot's fireworks send a haze of smoke into the crowd, and ashes sometimes end up in the eyes of onlookers. Be sure to gauge the wind and keep your child upwind of any fireworks.

Insider's Tip!

Consider an alternative viewing location, such as the beach at Polynesian Resort for Magic Kingdom fireworks or The BoardWalk for Epcot fireworks, as you can enjoy the fireworks there without the loud bangs.

Suggested Trip Itinerary

There is no doubt that the Magic Kingdom is the favorite destination for small children. It has everything that embodies the Disney experience, as well as the most attractions designed especially to appeal to the little ones.

Many families start out their vacation at the Magic Kingdom, which can make the other parks seem bland and boring in comparison, particularly Epcot. For that reason, we recommend you save the Magic Kingdom for last, building your children's expectations up as you go.

Start your visit with Epcot. Future World is where children can find the most entertainment in this park. Be sure to explore everything, as it's often the Innoventions stations, aquariums, and after-ride games that keep children amused.

Epcot is **THE #1** place for princess meet-and-greets. While there are a few princesses you can't meet here, there are many you will find throughout World Showcase. They typically have shorter lines than at the Magic Kingdom, and the activity offers a great way to keep children entertained while you explore the countries.

Each country also has a Kidcot Fun Stop, where the little ones can create a custom fan featuring favorite Disney characters or special animals from that country.

Our final small-child advice for Epcot is to stop into a kiosk to start the Duck Tales World Showcase Adventure. There are Future World and World Showcase variations of this scavenger-hunt/mystery-solving attraction for kids that will have you running to keep up with them, as they race from clue to clue.

Make your second day Hollywood Studios. Slinky Dog Dash is one of the most popular attractions in Walt Disney World, and you definitely need a Lightning lane reservation to enjoy it with your younger children. Afterwards, you can spend the day enjoying entertaining shows and meeting fun characters from Toy Story, Disney Junior, and Star Wars. Meet the "Fab Five" characters here or at the Animal Kingdom on your third day to minimize the number of characters you need to meet when you make it to the Magic Kingdom on your fourth day.

Fantasmic is a must-see show for adults and children, so plan to stay late to attend. You won't be sorry!

Your third day should be Animal Kingdom. This park often closes earlier than the others, and you're likely to be tired on that third day. You can take it easy and rest in the evening, preparing for your marathon day at the Magic Kingdom the following day.

By the time you get to the Magic Kingdom on the fourth day of your vacation, you will have met most of the characters, leaving your day open to enjoy the rides and magical atmosphere.

Keeping Children Safe at Disney

The number one risk at any theme park is losing track of your kids or other members getting separated from the group. The next highest concern is for medical emergencies. There is very little in the way of fights or other violence (or even serious arguments) among guests. Seeing someone get drunk is even pretty rare. The best thing to do to abate security risks like these is to maintain situational awareness. If you can spot potential trouble from a distance, you can take your family quickly on a safe detour away from any threat.

Always track where your kids are. They're small and adorable, so I'm sure you think your children stand out in a crowd. Unfortunately, at Disney they'll be surrounded by other small and adorable children, making them easy to lose!

Both children (and adults) are easily distracted by the many sights and sounds of Disney. Between the costumed characters and sparkly lights, it is easy to see how kids can become distracted and get lost. You wouldn't believe how often children latch onto the hands of complete strangers, thinking it is their own parent that is right beside them.

Keeping Track of Children

What can you do? Aside from the "don't go with strangers" talk we're sure you've had with your children many times, we have a few Disney-specific suggestions:

- The most important tool is to use the <u>buddy system</u>. Assign each younger kid to a responsible sibling or adult.
- If you have a relatively large group, take roll before moving on from one

attraction to another. Use this opportunity to train the older "buddy" to make sure he knows where his younger buddy is.

- Take a picture on your cellphone of your kid after he is fully dressed each morning (and after any changes throughout the day) for help identifying him if he wanders away. Disney staff can easily text the image to all their staff.

- Take a Sharpee pen and write your phone number on his arm if he is too young to remember it. Use silver or gold rather than black so it is not ugly. Young girls will especially appreciate the thought!

- Dress alike in a bright color. If everyone in the family is wearing a bright green shirt, it will be easy to spot each other in a crowd. Plus, your kids might have fun preparing special Disney shirts at the craft store to get ready for the trip.

- If your children are old enough, pick a meeting location to go to in case of separation. Make sure it's a very specific location at a centralized place that can easily be seen throughout the park, such as the Bibbity Bobbity Boutique in Cinderella's Castle at the Magic Kingdom.

- For younger children, show them how to find and identify a Disney Cast Member if they should get separated from you.

- When you arrive at the park, show them what the Disney staff look like and how they dress. Show them the unique white name tags. Then quiz young kids a couple of times early during the day to stop and look around and tell you who the child would go to if they got separated from you. The employee will take your child to the First Aid Center to wait for you.

- Once children realize they are separated, you may want to tell them to stay PUT for the first three to five minutes before attempting to find help. This is so you will be able to locate them as soon as they have been separated from you. If your children remember exactly where they last saw their parent, that should be the first place they ask the Cast Member to look, unless the staff member is within direct line of sight from that location.

- Even better, give your child a pre-printed (handwritten) business card with your contact information on it, so Disney can easily contact you to let you know your child has been found.

- Disney has highly-trained, competent, and friendly private security personnel. They are probably the best you will find anywhere. They have also been trained to maintain the Disney fantasy experience, so children will not be scared if they have to intervene. Even their uniforms are designed to evoke a feeling of friendliness.

- We love walkie-talkies, and so do children! They're much easier for small children to use than phones, not to mention cheaper. Get a set of walkie-talkies and give one to your child. You'll be able to reach your child within moments of getting separated, plus it will be a fun way for you to communicate with each other if your family intentionally splits up within the park.

What to Bring for Children

Comfortable shoes and clothes are a requirement that should go without

Insider's Tip!

You can write your phone number on your small child's arm in case you get separated. Cover it with liquid bandage to make sure sweat doesn't melt the number away throughout the day. Be careful not to write the number where it's too obvious, though. You don't want creepy strangers able to contact your child later, and fashion-sensitive children won't want their outfits ruined by hastily scrawled writing on their arms!

saying. See the section above on When to Travel & What to Wear regarding the different seasons to make sure your child is kept comfortable.

It's important to stop your child frequently throughout the day to check his or her feet for blisters. Children get excited in Disney and will keep going even with painful feet. Don't forget to bring **blister bandages** just in case there is a problem.

For younger kids, giving them lanyards with their name and contact information will help if they can't easily communicate with strangers. Older children will also appreciate lanyards for trading pins.

You may want to consider bringing **pirate and princess costumes** for your children from home or purchase them from a department store after arriving in town. Disney dresses children up – for a hefty price – like pirates, knights, or princesses, so your children will see them in all their finery – every day throughout every park. You can buy costumes for a fraction of the cost at home and bring them along. There are even tutorials online to fix your princess' hair to look just like they do at Disney.

A **stroller** should be at the top of your list for any child still able to fit in one (even if your child no longer uses a stroller at home). If you can, bring a larger stroller you can use to store your cooler and snacks. The little ones may seem like they have unlimited amounts of energy, but thinking their smaller legs will keep up with yours all day long without tiring out is probably too much to ask. See our section below on Stroller Rentals if you prefer not to bring one from home. However, you may find it is much more cost-effective to purchase an inexpensive stroller at Walmart to use just for the trip.

There are many advantages to bringing a stroller. Children can sit back and nap when they get tired, plus you can use it to carry all of your bags when your child isn't using it. Stroller parking is available outside each attraction, so you can park it until you need it. Add a bow or bright name tag to the stroller to allow you to find it easily, though!

Bring a **blanket** to use for shade during the day and warmth at night. If you don't have a stroller with a rain cover, make sure to bring along a **plastic sheet or rain poncho** to use to cover the stroller during inclement weather. You can store all of your goodies under it to keep them dry, as well!

Sunblock, hats, and dark sunglasses are absolute musts for your children (and for yourself!). Never leave your child's delicate skin and eyes unprotected in the Florida sun, even if the day is overcast. Sunburns are painful and can ruin a vacation. Just in case, though, pack some aloe vera gel to treat burned skin.

Children tend to get overstimulated easily, and many attractions, such as live concerts, get very loud. It's a great idea to bring **earplugs** for your children. (Waterproof earplugs are also great for protecting your child's ears in swimming pools.) You can also bring **eye masks** to block out light. Use them with the earplugs for easy napping in the parks (see suggested nap locations below).

Traveling with Small Children

Snacks are another must-have. Sure, you can buy food and snacks at Disney, but why pay their prices when you can pack a cooler and store it under the stroller you were so smart to bring along? Remember, you can go to any counter-service restaurant that serves fountain beverages and get a free cup of ice water, so it's up to you whether or not you wish to bring your own beverages or flavor packs to mix with the water.

Cooling down by getting wet feels great on a hot day, but wearing soggy clothes can be miserable for children. With a swimsuit under their clothes, children can remove their regular clothes and keep them dry for after the ride. Swimsuits, designed to quickly dry out, allow your children to cool down in the water without worrying about them getting too uncomfortable. Alternatively, you can bring a **change of clothes**.

Why is this so important for children? Here's an example of a true story. It was a sunny December day, around 80 degrees Fahrenheit. Some guests decided to go on Splash Mountain to cool off. Shortly after they got on the ride, an unexpected downpour started and the temperature dropped drastically, soaking and chilling them thoroughly by the time the ride ended. They quickly headed for shelter,

Insider's Tip!

Involve your child in choosing and packing their own personal box of snacks and juices. Freezing the juice boxes will keep everything else cool in the sweltering heat, and giving your child ownership of choosing and packing treats will make it easier to steer your child toward the snack box and away from the expensive snack stands at Disney.

Insider's Tip!

It's a great idea to let your children wear **swimsuits** under their clothes at the parks. Both the Magic Kingdom and Animal Kingdom have water rides designed to get you wet. Epcot has a nice water feature on the main path between Future World and World Showcase where children enjoy playing in the cool water on a warm day.

but the rain and wind made it impossible to dry off. Their child was so cold and miserable, he started crying. They were forced to purchase new clothes for him at the store to dry him off, costing them about $50 more than they had planned to spend that day. Had he been wearing a swimsuit or had they brought a change of clothes, this expensive mistake could have been avoided.

As we mentioned before, get a set of **walkie-talkies**. Let your child carry one to allow for easy communication if you get separated.

Don't forget **natural insect repellant**. This is Florida, after all. (Disney offers free insect repellant due to Zika virus concerns. However, the brands offered are chemical-laden and do not include natural ingredients.) Some people attract bugs and their bites much worse than others, and keeping insect repellant on-hand can save you and your child much misery.

The final item we suggest you bring for children is a **first aid kit** that includes blister bandages. It's simply a fact that children get distracted at Disney and often fall or bump into things. Additionally, the wrong shoes can and will cause painful blisters. Disney has First Aid Centers, where they will help you with injuries, but do you really want to carry a crying child across the park just to get a bandage? Keeping a small kit handy can help you kiss those booboos away quickly to carry on with your fun.

Dining with Children

This may be a touchy subject, but it is important to be considerate of other Disney guests when dining out. When children are overstimulated or tired, they tend to act out. Because of this, we do not recommend taking small children to the especially nicer (and expensive) restaurants on-property.

If you do take your child to a sit down restaurant, be mindful of his or her behavior. If he starts to get noisy or can't stay in his seat, take your child to the restroom or outside to calm down before returning. Remember, diners are paying a premium to enjoy Disney restaurant atmospheres, and they can't do that if your child is creating too large a distraction.

Keep in mind that you won't even be allowed to take your small child (under the age of 10) to Victoria & Albert's at Disney's Grand Floridian. Similarly, many of the Signature restaurants do not have children's menus, so if you plan to take your child to one of these pricey restaurants, expect to pay quite a bit of money for the experience.

If you do wish to have a premium dining experience, try one that is designed specifically for the little ones. The Grand Floridian offers two tea party experiences, one with princesses and the other with none other than Alice and the Mad Hatter!

Stroller Rentals

Disney provides single or double strollers for rent at each park and Disney Springs (only singles available at Disney Springs). These are hard plastic, upright strollers. They don't fold or allow children to lay down flat, making them unsuitable for infants. In addition, the hard plastic can really heat up in the harsh sun.

Single strollers rent for $15 per day or $13 per day if you rent for multiple days. Double strollers, which are side-by-side, rent for $31 per day or $27 per day for a multi-day rental.

You only need to pay once per day if you're park-hopping. Just keep your receipt and present it at the next park to get another stroller.

You don't need to return your stroller to the rental counter each day when you're done using it. Security guards make sure you don't take them outside of the parks, so you can leave the rental stroller anywhere you want. The exception to this is Disney Springs, where you must provide a $100 credit card deposit, which is removed once you return the stroller at the end of the day.

Strollers aren't allowed on any attractions. Disney provides a stroller parking area outside of each attraction, which is attended by a Cast Member. These parking locations are out in the open and not heavily guarded, so be sure to leave valuables out of sight and cover your stroller with plastic if the weather is spotty.

Rental strollers are not collapsible, so they are not allowed on the train in the Magic Kingdom. Disney allows you to leave your stroller at one train station in the Magic Kingdom and pick up another where you get off the train. Remember to keep your receipt to prove you've rented a stroller for the day!

Other Area Stroller Rental Companies

There are many companies within the Orlando area that rent high-quality (much nicer than Disney), collapsible strollers that have been cleaned and sanitized between uses. Most will deliver to your hotel for no additional charge, meaning

Insider's Tip!

Be forewarned, all Disney strollers are identical. They issue a nametag to put on the back of the stroller, but it's very common for families to walk away with the wrong stroller. Even if you bring your own stroller, this mistake can happen.

Make sure you put something bright and obvious on your stroller (rented or otherwise) to make sure someone doesn't accidentally take it. Otherwise, you'll find yourself trudging all the way to the front of the park to pick up a new stroller.

To avoid having a stroller stolen from you, lock the wheels with a bike lock. (You can't lock attach the lock to a gate or post, but you are allowed to lock the wheels.) Fortunately, if your personal stroller is taken, Disney will find a way to replace it -- though don't expect anything fancy. Head directly to Guest Relations if this happens to you!

Don't presume your stroller is missing if you don't see it right away, though. Disney Cast Members often rearrange strollers while guests are on rides. Always check with a nearby Cast Member to help you look for your stroller first if it isn't where you left it.

you can use them throughout your vacation and save the hassle of renting each day. Here's a short list of some of the area's top providers:

- Orlando Stroller Rentals offers single and double strollers plus rain covers. Call (800) 281-0884 or go to orlandostrollerrentals.com to get a quote and reserve.
- Magic Strollers offers single and double strollers. Call (866) 866-6177 or go to magicstrollers.com to get a quote and reserve.
- Kingdom Strollers offers single and double strollers, as well as special needs strollers. You can also rent a crib for your hotel from this

company. Call (407) 674-1866 or go to kingdomstrollers.com to get a quote and reserve.

- Simple Stroller Rental advertises itself as the only area provider to offer triple strollers in addition to its single and double offerings. They also offer a stroller base if you have your own infant car seat. Call (407) 374-2029 or go to simplestrollerrental.com to get a quote and reserve.

Smoking

No, we're certainly <u>not</u> giving advice on where to take your child for a cigarette. Rather, we want to make sure you know how to avoid smokers in the park, particularly if your child is asthmatic.

Disney has banned smoking and vaping in the parks. However, smokers often try to sneak a cigarette inside the park, rather than go to a designated zone outside of the park entrance.

Disney takes their guests' health seriously, particularly since they have so many guests with lung problems who can't be around cigarettes at all. If you see anybody smoking outside of a designated

Insider's Tip!

You may want to leave the park for a short break during the day. To save yourself the hassle of returning and re-renting a stroller (at no cost with your receipt), park your stroller in a location convenient to the park entrance. You can easily pick it up when you return!

area, feel free to speak up to a nearby Disney Cast Member, so they can direct the person to the appropriate area.

Baby Care Centers

Each of the four main theme parks has a Baby Care Center in it, but they're not just for infants. These locations are excellent places to meet up if people from your group get separated. These are also great locations to give toddlers a break from the heat and noise of the parks.

These centers have everything you might need for a baby or toddler, including baby food, diapers, and medicine. There is also a little kitchenette with a water cooler (with both hot and cold water) and a microwave oven for warming food. There is a TV room with rocking chairs, high chairs, and a little table for siblings to sit and color or have a snack. The environment also has a private room, dimly lit, with a rocking chair for nursing mommies. Consider this a priceless refuge for hot, wet, cranky children who need a quiet place to cool down. It is very peaceful and for some reason, seldom used.

Many women choose to breastfeed their babies out in the open. Unfortunately, with the number of adolescent boys in the park, doing so can garner much unwanted attention (not to mention the concern of having pictures of your breasts posted on various websites). Additionally, many mothers complain their babies are too over-stimulated or hot to nurse.

Baby Care Centers provide a quiet and private place for both breastfeeding and diaper changing. There are private rooms within the Baby Care Centers for you to be alone with your baby.

The main room of each Baby Care Center provides chairs and activities for toddlers. Your children can read books,

play, or even watch a video, all in a quiet, air-conditioned building.

There are no time limits to using the Baby Care Centers. They only ask that you keep noise to a minimum, so don't take your kids there for raucous play time. Go ahead and take them there for short naps, though.

Baby Care Centers are found at the following locations:

Magic Kingdom
Turn left at Casey's Corner, a restaurant near the end of Main Street. Walk past the outdoor tables. There's a small courtyard on the left where you will find the Baby Care Center.

Epcot
The Baby Care Center is in the World Showcase side of the Odyssey Center building. This building is located on a side path that runs along the water between Test Track and the Mexico Pavilion in World Showcase. (It is not inside the main part of the Odyssey Center but along the arm of the building closest to World Showcase, near the restrooms.) This may be one of the best-kept secrets (for families with small children) at Epcot. It's always nice and cool and you will find the attendant to be kind and helpful.

Hollywood Studios
You will find the Baby Care Center immediately to your left upon entering the park, near Guest Relations and First Aid.

Animal Kingdom
From the entrance, take the left pathway toward the Africa section of the park. Just before you cross the bridge to Africa, you will see the Creature Comforts shop on your left. Follow the path to your left, just as you pass Creature Comforts. The Baby Care Center is located next to First Aid on the back side of the building.

Traveling with Small Children

Family Restrooms

You may not feel comfortable letting your small child use a restroom alone. For this reason, Disney provides family restrooms at the entrance of most of the restrooms throughout the parks, water parks, and at Disney Springs.

Please use <u>family restrooms</u> if your child of the opposite sex needs to accompany you to use the toilet. That is what they are available for.

Many mothers choose to bring their sons into the women's restrooms. Know your child. If your son is the type to look through the door cracks or under the doors at other women who are using the toilet, he should not be taken into the women's restroom. Women have the right to privacy and should not have to worry about little boys invading that privacy.

Similarly, fathers should NEVER take their young daughters into a men's restroom. Men use urinals that do not have enclosed stalls, and they should not have to worry about little girls seeing them unclothed. You must pass by the urinals to reach bathroom stalls, so it is impossible to take your child to the toilet without bypassing them.

Please remember, Disney has visitors from all over the world who have varying belief systems. Just because you don't mind your child seeing nudity doesn't mean another person doesn't have the right to not be seen going to the bathroom by a youngster of the opposite gender.

On a final note, you may want to consider whether or not you feel comfortable having your little boy use a urinal. Little boys will be happy that most Disney restrooms have low-to-the-ground urinals just for their use. However, many Disney urinals do not have privacy dividers. Amusement parks attract children. Therefore, they attract people who are attracted to children. Consider having your child use a bathroom stall or the family restroom if you notice anybody strange in the restroom.

Naps

Long days at Disney can be exhausting. Most parks stay open late, and with the heat and crowds, they can be most enjoyable in the earliest and latest hours of the days. The parks don't fill up until mid-morning, so you'll want to be there when they open to make the most of your day. The Magic Kingdom also tends to empty out after fireworks, so staying until closing is a great way to make sure you get to do everything on your list.

However, it's important to pace yourself and any children with you to get the most enjoyment out of your visit. You don't want to be one of the many families who stopped enjoying themselves around mid-afternoon when their hot and cranky children began acting out, pushing through the rest of the day in misery.

Hot afternoon hours, when the parks are full and the lines are at their worst, are perfect for the whole family to take a break from the parks.

Relaxing without Leaving Disney

If you are staying off-property, it might not be easy or cost-effective to get back to your hotel for a couple of hours. Possibly the best way to plan for these breaks is to combine them with your lunch breaks, so the rest of your family members don't feel like they're missing out.

A relatively easy way to do this is to head to a nearby Moderate or Deluxe Disney hotel. Each of these properties has an indoor lounge that is closed for business until 4 p.m. or 4:30 p.m., depending on the lounge, and a counter-service restaurant with value-priced meals you can take to go. (Value resorts,

Insider Tidbits to Slow Down Children

When your children are getting hot and tired, they may still be reluctant to leave all the fun. It is important to plan diversions. Obviously, most children will be eager to take a pool break, but how do you get them to slow down so they will be ready to hit the evening shows with vim and vigor. As you start to put them down for a nap, you will have a great time making the entertainment educational.

During meals or during rest breaks when you want to slow down your children, talk about what you have just seen. Have a few thought-provoking questions about the encounters they are having with other people or characters. Ask them what they like the most about each attraction or area of the park. It gets the children to remember what they saw and to ask questions about what they may not have understood.

Ask them to draw out what inspired them. If you brought along a coloring book, find a picture that reflects what they want to talk about to let them color. For older children, have them write a few sentences in a journal. Your autograph book could be used as a catch-all for notes and journal entries. As you review your photographs, you can ask them to help create captions for the photographs.

These tips provide an excellent excuse to take a break any time you want to get children to settle down.

such as All-Star, Art of Animation, and Pop Century don't have indoor lounges.) You can pick up a meal and eat inside the closed and quiet lounge, while your younger children rest and the older children explore.

If you don't want to leave the park but still need a quiet place for your children to nap, there are limited options within the parks. Other than the The Baby Care Centers we have already outlined, we've come up with some suggested venues for naps on-property at or near the parks below. We also provide suggestions of nearby Disney resorts that offer food and quiet nap locations.

Magic Kingdom

- Walt Disney's Carousel of Progress is a seated, indoor show that lasts about 22 minutes. While it's a nice, cool location for a nap, you will need to take your child and leave once the show lets out.

- Catch the Walt Disney World Railroad at one of three train stations located near the park entrance, by Splash Mountain in Frontierland, or by The Barnstormer in Fantasyland. The train ride is 1.5 miles long and takes 20 minutes to complete a loop. However, you are not required to get off the train at any stop, so you can stay on as long as the little ones need to rest. Don't use this option if your child is a light sleeper, unless you've brought earplugs to wear.

- The Monorail is a quieter option to the Walt Disney World Railroad. The Resort Monorail stops at the three surrounding resorts plus the TTC. It only takes a few minutes to make a revolution around the resort properties, but you are welcome to stay on the train for as long as you need.

- A wonderful (and quiet!) option for naps near the Magic Kingdom is at the Contemporary Resort, especially if the rest of your party would like to eat or explore while the younger children are napping. The first stop of the Resort Monorail takes you directly to the Contemporary Resort. Take the escalator or elevator down one floor to the 3rd Floor. Here you will find the counter-service restaurant, where you can purchase refreshments. Go one more floor down to the 2nd Floor. Here you will find several couches in quiet areas that are perfect for relaxing and taking a quiet nap (even for adults!).

Epcot

- Epcot has a monorail that runs between the front of the park and the TTC. This is a longer ride than the Magic Kingdom monorails. Be forewarned, though, that the Epcot monorail doesn't run as often as the Magic Kingdom trains, so you may need to wait 10 minutes to get on a train.
- Epcot has nearby hotels that are even more convenient than the Magic Kingdom options. The best option for a quiet nap is to take your child to Disney's Beach Club Resort. Exit Epcot through the International Gateway exit between the France and England Pavilions. Head straight toward the large pirate ship. Just before you reach the pirate ship (which is a water slide for the pool), you will see the hotel lobby on your right. Enter the lobby and take the hallway to your right. You will see a sign for the Solarium on your left.

The counter-service restaurant is just past it on your right. The Solarium has seating and chairs for a nice nap. There is also a television and games to keep the rest of the family occupied while the little one naps.

- Just outside of the International Gateway exit is the FriendShips boat dock. You can catch a covered boat here that will take you on a round trip boat ride throughout the Epcot resort area. Stay on the boat as long as you need. It will eventually come back around to Epcot when your child is well rested.

Hollywood Studios

- As you exit the park, go left to the boat dock. Here you can catch the same boat that goes down the canal to the Epcot resorts and to the back entrance of Epcot. This is a nice, long roundtrip to give yourself a rest and your child a chance to nap. If you want, you can stop at Disney's Beach Club Resort to get a counter-service meal and rest in the Solarium, as mentioned above.
- Unfortunately, there aren't a lot of quiet places within the park for naps. However, you can try the *Star Wars Launch Bay*. It's nice and cool with a few places to sit. You may be able to find a quiet spot to rest during the day, while the rest of your family plays video games, meets a character, or looks at interesting *Star Wars* memorabilia.

Animal Kingdom

- Hop aboard the Wildlife Express Train, which you can find near the exit of Kilimanjaro Safaris. This will take you to Rafiki's Planet Watch and the Conservation Station. People constantly come and go in this building, but it's not hugely popular, particularly after 11 a.m., when most veterinary procedures you can witness stop. We like this area, as it is indoors and there are usually quiet corners to rest and nap.

- The nice thing about the Animal Kingdom is there are little trails all over the park. Many of them have benches, so if it is not too hot outside, it is relatively easy to find a quiet corner where your children can rest. Do a little exploration of the trails when you first get to the park, so you know where to look when it's time to get away for a few minutes.

- You can easily get to the Animal Kingdom Lodge by catching a free bus outside the exit of the park. There are some nice outdoor balconies where families can rest, but our favorite spot for napping during the day is Victoria Falls Lounge. The lounge opens for business at 4:30 p.m., but its comfortable seating area is available for anyone to use before then, providing a quiet place to get away right next to the hotel lobby. The rest of the family will love exploring the hotel property, viewing its live animals, and catching a bite to eat at the counter-service restaurant near the pool, while the little ones are resting upstairs.

Height Restrictions on Attractions

Okay, now that we've got the boring stuff out of the way, let's talk about getting your small children on the exciting rides!

Some attractions have height limitations, meaning your children must be at least a certain height to ride. As we mentioned earlier, if your child is close to that height, he/she may not be allowed to ride. It's also possible that one Disney Cast Member may allow your child into the line, while another turns your child away. This can be especially distressing, as there are two checkpoints for each ride. We've seen many children make it through the first checkpoint only to get turned away after waiting a long time in the queue.

Before you leave home, please measure your child while wearing the shoes he/she plans to wear in the parks. If necessary, buy shoes with thick soles. This may help push your child over the limit. Also, work with your child on standing up straight and good posture.

Most importantly, don't tell your child how amazing the bigger rides are, unless you know for sure he's tall enough to ride!

It's not all bad news, though. The two water parks each have attractions designed only for children, so the height requirements keep adults away!

Here are rides with the height limitations for each park:

Magic Kingdom
- The Barnstormer: 35in (89cm)
- Big Thunder Mountain Railroad: 40in (102cm)
- Tron Lightcycle Power Run: 48in (122cm)
- Seven Dwarfs Mine Train: 38in (95cm)
- Space Mountain: 44in (113cm)
- Splash Mountain: 40in (102cm)
- Tomorrowland Speedway: 32in (82cm)

Epcot
- Guardians of the Galaxy: Cosmic Rewind: 42in (107cm)
- Mission: SPACE: 44in (113cm) for Orange or 40in (102cm) for Green
- Soarin': 40in (102cm)
- Test Track: 40in (102cm)

Hollywood Studios
- Rock 'n' Roller Coaster: 48in (122cm)
- Star Tours: 40in (102cm)
- Star Wars: Rise of the Resistance: 40in (102cm)
- Slinky Dog Dash: 38in (95cm)
- The Twilight Zone Tower of Terror: 40in (102cm)
- Millenium Falcon: Smugglers Run: 38in (95cm)

Animal Kingdom
- Avatar Flight of Passage: 44in (113cm)
- DINOSAUR: 40in (102cm)
- Expedition Everest: 44in (113cm)
- Kali River Rapids: 38in (95cm)

Typhoon Lagoon
- Bay Slides: 60in (152cm) or shorter. That's right! This limitation benefits the kids.
- Crush 'n' Gusher: 48in (122cm)
- Humunga Kowabunga: 48in (122cm)
- Ketchakiddee Creek: 48in (122cm) or shorter. One just for the kids!

Blizzard Beach
- Chairlift: 32in (82cm)
- Downhill Double Dipper: 48in (122cm)
- Slush Gusher: 48in (122cm)
- Summit Plummet: 48in (122cm)
- Tike's Peak: 48in (122cm) or shorter. Another kids only attraction!

Age Restrictions on Attractions

One of the most heartbreaking scenes we have ever witnessed was a young mother trying to console her three young children at the Magic Kingdom after being turned away from The Barnstormer. It wasn't that the little ones didn't meet the height requirement; two of them did. The problem was the child who didn't meet the requirement needed to stay behind with his mother.

That's where Disney's age restriction came in: Children under the age of seven are not allowed to go an attraction unless they are with someone who is at least 14 years old. Of course, this also means Disney won't allow you to leave two children waiting unsupervised while you go on the ride with each child that meets the height requirement.

In other words, if you are the only person in your party who is 14 years or older and you plan to take multiple children with you, you will be limited to only those attractions all of the children can go on.

This can severely limit your vacation if you are a single parent, so you might consider a way to make friends with another family early on during your vacation. It may seem strange, but you could also ask another family to take your child on a ride with them.

Another option is the Meetup website (meetup.com). This is a website that allows you to join different groups of people who have similar interests. There are several Walt Disney World groups in the Orlando area, so you may be able to sign up before your vacation and meet others who want to take their children to the parks.

Attraction Height Requirements

Minimum Height	Magic Kingdom	Epcot	Disney's Hollywood Studios	Animal Kingdom
54"	Tomorrowland Speedway	*Note:* Must be 32" to ride with an older driver.		54"
48"	Tron Lightcycle Power Run		Rock 'n' Roller Coaster Starring Aerosmith	48"
44"	Space Mountain	Mission: SPACE (Orange Team)		Expedition Everest · 44"
				Avatar Flight of Passage
42"		GOTG: Cosmic Rewind		
40"	Splash Mountain	Soarin'	The Twilight Zone Tower of Terror	DINOSAUR · 40"
	Big Thunder Mountain Railroad	Test Track	Star Tours - The Adventures Continue	
		Mission: SPACE (Green Team)	Star Wars: Rise of the Resistance	
38"	Seven Dwarfs Mine Train		Slinky Dog Dash	Kali River Rapids · 38"
			Millenium Falcon: Smugglers Run	
35"	The Barnstormer			35"
32"	Tomorrowland Speedway	*Note:* Must be 54" to ride alone.	Alien Swirling Saucers	32"

Traveling with Small Children

Insider's Tip!

There is an advantage to waiting in line if you have a child who is too timid to go on the ride. While you never want to force a child to go on a ride that he finds too scary, using rider switch gets your child close to the action. It gives your child a chance to see other children his/her own age braving the ride, and you can strike up conversation with those other children to show your own child there is nothing to worry about. Often times, your child might decide that it is not so scary and hopefully will decide to try the ride, after all!

Attraction & Ride Suggestions

Be sure to schedule your Lightning Lane reservations early in the morning. It's just as important to get to the park as soon as it opens, so you can do the other rides you weren't able to reserve. You'll find that many of the rides for small children get very busy during the day, so if you don't get to them first thing, you may find yourself waiting in line all day.

A newer phenomenon at Disney is extremely long wait times for character meet-and-greets. This is due to the system of housing characters in specific locations with specific times for their character greetings, rather than the older, more informal system.

Insider's Tip!

If your child just wants to see a character and doesn't really care about meeting him or her, consider going through the exit line to take a quick peek at the character while they are interacting with other children. If the attendant gives you a hard time, tell them other members of your party are near the front of the line, and you simply want to get photos.

You won't be able to get Lightning Lane reservations for each attraction or character meet-and-greet, so it's important that you get into the park as soon as it opens. Most visitors forego the early morning hours, choosing to have breakfast and get to the parks around 10:30 a.m. or 11 a.m. This leaves most rides open and available for anyone there earlier in the morning.

Here are our suggestions for early-morning rides with small children (See the section below if you think your child might be timid, though):

Magic Kingdom

- Head to Fantasyland first thing, straight to Seven Dwarfs Mine Train if your children meet the height requirement. It's the most popular attraction and sure to fill up fast.
- Peter Pan's Flight has consistently been one of the busiest rides since the Magic Kingdom opened. Make this your next stop.
- We recommend finishing up the rest of the Fantasyland rides as quickly as you can (in no particular order), then moving on to other areas of the park.

Epcot

- Take your children to Frozen Ever After in the Norway Pavilion first thing. When World Showcase "officially" opens at 11 a.m., head back to the Mexico Pavilion to experience The Gran Fiesta Tour.
- Very small children won't be able to go on Future World's most popular attractions, Test Track and Soarin'. Fortunately, the other rides for smaller children in Future World don't typically have long waits. We recommend heading to the Sea Pavilion for Turtle Talk with Crush and The Seas with Nemo & Friends.
- After the Sea Pavilion, make your way around Future World, exploring everything it has to offer.

Hollywood Studios

- Star Wars: Rise of the Resistance and Slinky Dog Dash are the rides you should race for. Go on them as many times as you can before the park gets too busy.
- If your child meets the height requirements for the Twilight Zone Tower of Terror and Rock 'n' Roller Coaster, go to Rock 'n' Roller Coaster first, then Tower of Terror.

Insider's Tip!

Try to get to the park entrance 30-45 minutes before park opening. Disney opens the gates a bit early to allow guests to shop on Main Street and view the Opening Ceremony in front of the castle before the rides open. Being there early will ensure you are near the front of the line to gain access to the park as soon as the rope drops. This will give you the best head-start to make sure you do every ride on your list!

- The remainder of the rides generally have quicker wait times. However, get into line early for Fantasmic at the end of the day. These shows often fill up quickly, and your child will not want to miss it (nor will you)!

Animal Kingdom
- Flight of Passage should be your first stop. It is the busiest ride at the park and offers some of the best technology anywhere.
- Kilimanjaro Safaris should be on your early morning list. The animals are most active early in the morning, and the lines get unbearably long as the day goes on.
- If your child is tall enough for Expedition Everest, go there next. It's amazing!
- It's Tough to be a Bug! is another favorite for children, though you can often get into the show without much of a wait.
- The shows at Animal Kingdom can't be beat. Be sure to get in line early for Finding Nemo - The Musical. The best seats are taken quickly.

Use these suggestions only as a guide. If your child exhibits any sort of hesitation about the rides or characters, ignore this list and read the *Scary Side of Disney* section below. Also, if your child has a favorite character or movie, don't hesitate to go to the corresponding attraction or character meet-and-greet first. After all, what makes Disney magical is different for each person.

Special Experiences
There are many special experiences designed specifically for small children. This includes a nighttime Pirate Cruise, princess tea parties, pony rides, and many others. In fact, most special events and entertainment are very family-friendly. However, it is a good idea not to take small children to entertainment inside of a lounge, as adult guests will be drinking.

Of the special experiences, the most popular (by far!) is the Bibbidi Bobbidi Boutique.

The Scary Side of Disney!
If your child has never been to an amusement park, you may be surprised to find out how intimidating these places can be for small children. Everything from larger-than-life characters to loud fireworks to dark rides can seem like a new and scary event for little ones.

When discussing character meetings below, we offer suggestions about preparing your child for certain things, such as the large and intimidating characters. Here we detail specifics about what other things may be a cause for concern and some potential ways to deal with your child's fears.

Rides & Shows: From fear of the dark to fear of heights, not to mention loud noises and scary monsters, there are a lot of reasons why a child might be frightened during a ride or show at Disney.

Take your children on some of the very tame rides first. This will help set an expectation for your child that most of

Bibbidi Bobbidi Boutique

NOTE: This experience is currently closed due to COVID-19.
Cinderella's Fairy Godmother owns this magical beauty salon that is a favorite place for kids to get all dolled-up for their special days at Disney.

The Bibbidi Bobbidi Boutique is "where any little girl can make her dream of becoming a princess come true"...with a wave of Fairy Godmother's magic wand and help from her skilled "Fairy Godmother-in-training" apprentices. Young knights-in-training also have a great option here.

There are two locations for this experience:

- Cinderella Castle at Magic Kingdom theme park;
- Grand Floridian Resort,
- Next to World of Disney store in Disney Springs Marketplace.

Price for each child is from $69.95 - $199.95.
Girls get to first choose their hairstyle before considering the options:

- Adding make-up to the up-do
- New nail color
- Disney princess costume, if your heart desires, and all the commemorate accessories (including tiara

As a keepsake for the magical memories, the experiences include a picture of the new princess in all her splendor in a themed photo holder.

To appeal to little boys (and girls!) who want in on the fun, the Fairy Godmothers-in-training can expertly <u>transform them into heroic knights</u>!

Of course, no dress-up adventure would be complete without some role-play. Watch your new little royal get introduced to her adoring subjects in a delightful parade of princesses and knights!

> ## Insider's Tip!
>
> Fairy Godmother may make an appearance at the Castle location.

---

the rides are safe and fun. Wait until later to build up to the more extreme rides, like Splash Mountain. A tame ride might be different for each child. Dumbo the Flying Elephant or Peter Pan are usually safe bets at the Magic Kingdom, but if your child is afraid of heights, these might be terrible starting points.

"it's a small world" is probably the safest choice of any ride in the Magic Kingdom, and small children love it (although teens and adults often find it akin to torture). Peter Pan is just across from "it's a small world" and is *usually* a safe choice. Peter

Pan takes you flying over London and Never Land in a very dark environment, though, so prepare your child for what to expect.

The Seas with Nemo & Friends and Turtle Talk with Crush are good starting attractions at Epcot. Toy Story Midway Mania! and Muppet*Vision 3D are generally safe starting attractions at Hollywood Studios. TriceraTop Spin and the Wildlife Express Train over to the Affection Section are the top choices to get kids started at Animal Kingdom.

Sometimes the names of rides are frightening. There's an easy fix for this if your child doesn't read yet. Give the ride a different name! For instance, The Haunted Mansion can be changed to Mickey's Magic House. There's a magician version of Mickey Mouse at the meet-and-greet in the park, after all, and you can explain all the strange things are magic tricks Mickey performs. Be prepared to make light of the screams and scary narration, especially in the stretching room at the beginning of the ride, though.

Other rides may frighten children just from an intimidating exterior. The Twilight Zone Tower of Terror is intentionally frightening, and even the bravest of children (and some adults!) get nervous when they see it. Roller coasters or other thrill rides, such as Splash Mountain, can be visually frightening for even grown-ups.

Try to distract your children from the visual spectacles. This is pretty easy to do in a place like Disney. It's also not always obvious that a queue you're entering into is for a particular ride, so a little bait-and-switch deception may coax your otherwise unwilling child onto a ride.

However, your child might not forgive you if the ride itself ends up being traumatizing. Always give your child an idea of what to expect and how you will keep him or her safe. For instance, there's a big elevator drop on the Twilight Zone Tower of Terror. Let your child know it's a flying elevator, just like the airplane you took to get to Orlando, and that you'll both be wearing seat belts to keep you safe.

You can also download nightlight apps on your smartphone to give your child to hold during darker rides. This personal nightlight might be enough to keep the fear at bay.

Of course, if you've never been to Walt Disney World yourself, you may not know which rides or attractions could be frightening for your child. We've included a list of potential frights in our Attractions & Entertainment section for you to use as a guide to prepare your child and know which you should avoid completely. See the section below on Rider Switch (aka Child Swap) on how you and the rest of your family can still enjoy rides even if your little one refuses to go.

Rider Switch

Parents often split up, allowing one to take the older children on bigger attractions, while the other waits it out with the child who either can't *or won't* go on the ride. Don't despair or think you'll be unable to go on the bigger rides if you have a smaller child with you. Disney offers a rider switch or child swap program that allows one person to wait with the child while the rest of the party goes on the ride.

At the entrance of the attraction queue, tell the attendant you need to do Rider Switch. The attendant will give the waiting parent a return pass good for him and the other kids in the party, while the rest of the family goes on the ride. After the ride, the adults swap using the return pass to enter the Lightning Lane queue, allowing everyone a turn on the ride.

The best part? If you have other children who are tall enough to go on the ride, they get to go back on it with the other adult who had to wait. They get to ride twice with no waiting in line a second time!

Of course, waiting while everyone else goes on the ride can be disappointing for kids who don't meet height requirements. Coach the others in your party to minimize talk about how much fun the ride is and what your little one is missing to avoid tears and resentment for the rest of your trip.

Traveling with Small Children

Disney Area Childcare Services

Let's face it, even though you love your children and would do anything for them, spending days of uninterrupted time with them can get a bit overwhelming. Since Disney is also about romance for couples, you may want to hire a babysitter for an evening to give yourselves a break.

No matter whether you are staying on or off Disney property, there are services that will come to your hotel and watch the little ones, allowing you to enjoy a nice evening out. Here are some of the area babysitting providers that are licensed and bonded:

- **Kid's Nite Out** is the primary Walt Disney World childcare provider, but they also provide babysitting services to all Orlando area hotels. They charge standard rates of $20 per hour for the first child, $3 per hour for each additional child (4 hour minimum), plus a $12 transportation fee. Holidays cost extra. You can reserve your in-room babysitter by calling (800) 696-8105, or local (407) 828-0920 or by completing the form at kidsniteout.com/reservations.aspx.
- **Super Sitters** has been in business in the Orlando area for more than 25 years. They provide training and background checks for all of their sitters. There is a 4-hour minimum. Contact (407) 382-2558 or info@super-sitters.com to get a firm price and reserve a babysitter.
- **Sunshine Babysitting** is another babysitting option in Orlando. Their standard rates are $16 per hour for the first child, $2 per hour for each additional child, plus a $10 transportation fee. They also have a 4-hour minimum and charge extra for holidays. However, they also offer babysitting services within the theme parks, a nice option if you're feeling guilty about leaving the kids in a hotel during their Disney vacation! Call (407) 421-6505 or email resortchildcare@gmail.com to reserve this service.

Activity Center

A babysitting service is a great option, especially if your child is still an infant, but you may not want to leave your children in a hotel room.

Camp Dolphin is a fun, activity-filled childcare center located at the Walt Disney World Dolphin hotel.

Drop off your child to play with other children, while you relax and have some alone time. You receive a pager upon dropping off your child in case of emergency (refundable deposit required).

The center opens at 5 p.m. and stays open until midnight. The location features movies, video and board games, as well as arts and crafts uniquely themed to fit the hotel environment. Dinner for your child is even included in the fee!

Your child must be between the ages of 4 and 12 and completely potty-trained (no pull-ups allowed!). Reservations are required.

Here are the details for this activity center:

Camp Dolphin at Walt Disney World Dolphin Hotel

- Hours: 5 p.m. – 12 a.m.
- Rates: $15 per hour per child (minimum 2 hours)
- Reservations Required, Cancellation Policy Applies

Special Travel Considerations

Senior Guests

For seniors, Disney is generally more about the entertainment and experience than the rides. This often means you, as a senior, get to experience Disney in a much more profound way, taking the time to view and explore all of the hidden gems throughout the property. Unfortunately, this style of travel often means you'll be at odds with younger members of your traveling party who wish to race from ride to ride all day long.

It's important that you set limits for yourself and don't try to keep up with children all day long. This can ruin your vacation and potentially lead to health risks, depending on how much you push yourself. Remember, visitors typically end up walking about five or six miles per day in severe Florida heat. We've seen paramedics taking seniors to the hospital on many occasions due to these conditions.

Consider reserving a wheelchair for family members to push you around when you need it (and leave it parked when you don't!) It's free if you stay on-property and reserve it through your Disney hotel. Even better, rent a scooter for your vacation. Seniors have a blast zipping through the parks, and you can even get them with a sun shade to stay cool while the rest of your family melts in the heat. See our section on Guests with Mobility Disabilities for information on renting wheelchairs or scooters (also known as Electric

Conveyance Vehicles or ECVs on Disney property).

Definitely rent a scooter, rather than a wheelchair, if you don't have multiple people in your party who can push you around in it to make sure no single person is tasked with the job. Wheelchairs get heavy, and many people are simply not up to the task for several hours a day, particularly other seniors.

We've seen countless seniors put in this position and barely able to walk themselves by the end of the day, much less push someone else around. In fact, the bridge leading from the France Pavilion to the United Kingdom Pavilion at Epcot seems to be a particularly troublesome spot after a long day of pushing someone in a wheelchair, as is the bridge leading from the International Gateway exit at Epcot to the Epcot resorts.

Most seniors prefer to get away from the crowds and noise during the hottest part of the day. Eating lunch before noon is your best bet for having a quiet and leisurely meal. Plan to also make your dinner reservations for early meals. A reservation at 4:30 p.m. (which is when most restaurants at Disney open for dinner) often means you'll have the run of the restaurant and the undivided attention of your waitstaff!

When it comes to attractions, Disney has a lot to offer seniors. In fact, even Disney's "thrill" rides are pretty tame compared to most amusement parks, so unless you have a specific disability, such as a bad back, most should be fine for you to ride.

The exception to this may be simulated ride experiences. For instance, Mission:SPACE in Epcot's Future World is a claustrophobic simulated thrill ride that can cause extreme issues ranging from motion sickness to seizures.

Pay attention to Disney's warnings for specific attractions (found in the park guide or at the attraction) if you have any health concerns. In general, attractions we recommend caution riding due to excessive shaking or speed are as follows:

Magic Kingdom
- Space Mountain
- Seven Dwarfs Mine Train
- Tron Lightcycle Power Run
- The Barnstormer
- Big Thunder Mountain Railroad

Epcot
- Test Track
- Mission:SPACE
- Guardians of the Galaxy: Cosmic Rewind

Hollywood Studios
- Rock 'n' Roller Coaster Starring Aerosmith
- Slinky Dog Dash
- The Twilight Zone Tower of Terror

Animal Kingdom
- Expedition Everest – Legend of the Forbidden Mountain
- DINOSAUR

You may find the most enjoyment out of your vacation by staying at a Disney on-property hotel. You'll be able to use their transportation to easily get back to your room for a rest during the hottest part of the day, while others remain at the parks. You can request a room that's close to hotel restaurants or buses if you need to limit your walking, and your family will think you're a hero for getting them more convenient lodgings!

Disney can provide other amenities to seniors staying on-property. One such perk is that you can request a golf cart ride to and from your room to avoid walking long distances. On especially busy days, you may need to wait 30-45 minutes for a ride, though. If you have other disabilities, take a look at our section for Guests with Disabilities to see the many amenities you can request during your stay.

Many of the Disney resort properties are also uniquely themed. Some of our favorite Disney resort properties for seniors are as follows:

Magic Kingdom Resort Area

Contemporary Resort provides monorail access with little walking.

Epcot & Hollywood Studios Resort Area

Yacht Club Resort is close to the boat dock that runs between the parks.

Animal Kingdom Resort Area

Animal Kingdom Lodge requires little walking to buses.

Disney Springs Resort Area

Port Orleans Riverside is scenic and quiet, though there is a lot of walking.

KOA Campground

Seniors traveling to Disney by RV have choices both on and off Disney property. KOA has a campground that's very close to Disney, located at 2644 Happy Camper Place in Kissimmee. Call (407) 396-2400 or (800) 562-7791, or go to koa.com/campgrounds/kissimmee for reservation information.

The Campsites at Disney's Fort Wilderness Resort

One of Disney's best kept secrets is its very own campground, The Campsites at Disney's Fort Wilderness Resort, located a short boat ride away from the Magic Kingdom. This is a beautiful, natural setting nestled within the Disney property where deer and other wildlife roam free. In addition to pools and beaches, horseback riding, carriage rides, and even

sing-alongs with Chip and Dale add to the experience. Call (407) 939-2744, or go to disneyworld.disney.go.com for reservation information.

Disney provides excellent entertainment choices for couples and senior citizens. Each Moderate and Deluxe resort has its own unique lounge, some with live entertainment. For a quiet evening, enjoy Territory Lounge at the Wilderness Lodge. For a lively and fun evening, enjoy the cabaret performer Yehaa Bob at River Roost Lounge in the Port Orleans Riverside Resort. For an upscale opportunity to watch fireworks away from the crowds, try the lounge at California Grill inside the Contemporary Resort.

Each lounge has its own unique personality for you to enjoy, so explore and have fun. You may want to steer clear of Rix Lounge at Coronado Springs Resort, though, as it has more of a nightclub atmosphere.

Guests with Disabilities

Visitors to Walt Disney World have varying needs, and there is no single system to accommodate all. However, Disney has programs and devices many guests are unaware of to make their visits magical.

Generally speaking, Disney gets high marks from disabled guests. Of course, any time you're dealing with a large organization – even one with a strict training program like Disney – you may hit a snag or two. Don't be afraid to speak up if you have specific needs or a Cast Member is ignoring proper protocol.

Whether a guest is visually-impaired, suffers from hearing loss, or even is recovering from an injury, Disney has ways to help.

Special Travel Considerations

At the Hotel

Whether you're staying on-property or off, it's important to make sure your hotel will meet your needs. Each of the larger chain resort companies should have special accommodations for guests with disabilities. However, many rentals around Orlando are timeshare or condo properties that may not provide the amenities you need.

Before booking a hotel, call and verify that a room with the specific accommodations you need will be available during your stay, as these rooms tend to be very limited. Also, get confirmation of your reservation for a room with special accommodations in writing in case there are any difficulties when you check in.

If you're staying at a Disney resort, you can request the following special accommodations (based on limited availability) at its resorts:

- Wheelchair Accessible Rooms (Request Specific Items Below)
  - Lowered Vanities
  - Double Peepholes in Doors
  - Handheld Showerheads
  - Lowered Beds
  - Portable Commodes
  - Roll-in Showers
  - Rubber Bed Padding
  - Shower Benches
  - Widened Bathroom Doors
- Hearing Accessible Rooms (Request Specific Items Below)
  - Braille on Signs (Also on Elevators)
  - Strobe-Light Smoke Detectors
  - TTY Equipment
- Knock and Phone Alerts
- Refrigerators for Medications
- Closed Caption Televisions
- Wheelchair and Scooter Accessible Paths
- Disabled Parking

- Service Animals Allowed

Call the Disney Reservation Number (407) 939-7807 or (407) 939-7670 TTY. Press 1 to discuss disability accommodations.

Parking

The first thing you'll notice upon entering a theme park parking lot is a blue line painted on the ground. If you have a disability that prevents you from riding the standard tram, follow this line to park in a lot that's close enough to walk to the park entrance.

A parking lot attendant will check to verify that you have a disabled parking placard, so be sure to bring that with you from home.

However, in some cases you may have a need for disabled parking but don't have a placard. For instance, if your child has broken her leg, it's not viable for her to get on and off the parking tram. If staying on-property, request a parking placard from your hotel. Otherwise, explain the situation to the parking attendant. If your reason is valid, Disney will allow you to park in the disabled parking lot.

Limited Mobility at the Parks

Pick up a specially-marked map at the entrance of each park, called the Guide For Guests With Disabilities. It's a customized version of Disney's free park map that explains most of the options available for disabled guests. Symbols on the map identify wheelchair-friendly attractions.

The first stop is Guest Relations if you or someone in your party has a disability or medical condition that somehow impairs your ability to get on rides or understand attractions. Go there immediately upon entering a park on the first day of your Disney visit. This is where Disney keeps the tools and passes to make your visit more enjoyable.

Disability Access Service

You may have heard about recent changes (made in October of 2021) to the way Disney accommodates guests with disabilities. The old "skip the lines" system for anybody sporting a scooter or leg brace is gone. Disney uses a system that's much closer to that used by other theme parks, such as Universal Studios.

Disney Guest Relations will issue Disability Access Service (DAS) to guests who are unable to wait in the regular queue. This is different from the old "Red Card" Disney used to pass out that allowed disabled guests to use any Lightning Lane line, or alternative entrance, rather than use the standby line.

First, Disney will only issue you DAS if your disability somehow keeps you from being able to wait in line. Be prepared to explain to the Disney Cast Member at Guest Relations why standing in line for long periods of time is a hardship for you. You don't need to identify the exact nature of your illness or disability.

If you need to use a wheelchair, you don't necessarily qualify for DAS. In fact, this system is specifically designed to change the procedure that previously allowed people in wheelchairs and scooters who were perfectly capable of waiting in line to bypass any wait times.

People in wheelchairs or scooters won't have to wait in line at ALL the rides. Some of the queues are simply not designed to allow access for wheeled vehicles. In these instances, if you are in a wheelchair or scooter, the attendant will either direct you to an alternative entrance or give you an assigned time to return, just like you would get with DAS.

Here's how DAS works. If you can, contact Disney's online chat at least 48

hours prior to the first day of your visit. (If you don't do this ahead of time, simply go to Guest Relations when you arrive at your first theme park.) The Guest Relations Cast Member will take your photo and link the DAS (with the photo) to your MagicBand or pass for the length of your stay (up to 60 days for annual passholders).

Have the park ticket for each member of your party available, so they can include the correct people able to join you on rides.

The Cast Member will then go over the process to make sure you understand how to use DAS and agree to the terms of use.

If you complete this process at least 48 hours in advance, the Cast Member will pre-schedule up to two DAS return times for each day of your visit. If you wait until you're at the park, you must schedule each DAS return time one-at-a-time.

Once DAS is linked to your pass, use the My Disney Experience app to schedule a return time for the attraction of your choice. You must be in the park already for this feature to be active.

Look for Disability Access Service on the menu (or walk to the attraction of your choice and ask the line attendant to

Insider's Tip!

Guests are supposed to return their wheelchairs to the rental location within each park before going to the parking lot. However, many guests ignore this requirement and take their rental wheelchairs out to their cars. This means you can often find rental wheelchairs in the disabled parking lot later in the day, which you could theoretically take and use for the rest of the day, thus avoiding the fee for the entire day if you only need a wheelchair for a few hours.

Insider's Tip!

If you know you'll need a wheelchair or scooter during your vacation, it's often much less expensive to rent one from an outside vendor. There are plenty in the Orlando area who will drop your scooter or wheelchair off at your hotel for you. Some of the larger companies who provide rentals include: Apple Scooter (applescooter.com), Best Price Mobility (bpmobility.com), Buena Vista Scooter Rentals (buenavistascooters), CARE Medical Equipment (caremedicalequipment.com), and ScooterBug (scooterbugmobilityrentals.com). Shop around, though. You may find even better prices!

assist you). A list off attractions available for DAS will appear with their current estimated wait times. Click on the attraction of your choice, check the box next to the name of each member of your party joining you, and request to join the queue.

You will receive a return time that is ten minutes less than the current estimated standby time.

NOTE: Rides with very long wait times may not appear in the list. Ask for assistance from the attraction attendant if an attraction you wish to experience doesn't appear on the list.

When your assigned time arrives, simply return to the ride with your party. You will each scan your passes and be allowed to go through the Lightning Lane queue.

You may only use DAS for one ride at a time, so don't expect to go from ride to ride collecting return times to be used one after the other. However, you can still reserve Lightning Lane times with your park ticket, and you can visit other attractions with shorter wait times or relax elsewhere in the park while waiting for your assigned time to go on the ride.

NOTE: For attractions that require a virtual queue, such as Remy's Ratatouille Adventure, you must join a virtual queue before you can use DAS.

Disabled Guests Who Need Frequent Breaks

Disney received some negative comments when they implemented the current DAS system. The major criticism of the system was that it no longer allowed people who had such severe illnesses or disabilities that they could only visit the park for a short period of time each day to experience a full day's worth of attractions in that time.

Disney now states that it will provide special accommodations for people suffering from these types of illnesses or disabilities. However, it will be on a case by case basis. More importantly, you will need to plead your case in person at Guest Relations. Disney doesn't make those special accommodations prior to a guest's visit.

Disney can't require a doctor's note for your illness or disability. However, if you're requesting these types of special accommodations that most disabled guests don't get and your illness or disability is not obvious, it would be helpful for you to bring a note from your doctor that briefly explains that you have a time limitation in the parks. Remember, you are not required to disclose the exact nature of your illness or disability!

Guests with Mobility Disabilities

Your mobility issue may range from needing a cane to needing a wheelchair. In fact, you may start out your day at the theme park walking, then find you need a scooter or wheelchair as the day goes on.

All Disney parks offer scooters and wheelchairs for rent, but doing so will cost you an additional fee. Wheelchair rentals are $12 per day or $10 per day if you rent for multiple days. Scooters (also called electric conveyance vehicles) are $50 per day plus a $20 deposit. They don't allow you to pre-reserve rentals. Fortunately, there are usually plenty available.

However, if you're staying on-property, you can get a wheelchair to use for free at your hotel (with a $315 deposit). Be sure to reserve your wheelchair with your hotel in advance if you need one, as there is limited availability.

Disney Transportation: Fortunately, all of Disney's on-site transportation, including boats, monorails, and buses, are designed to accommodate standard-sized wheelchairs and scooters. Space is limited on each vehicle, though, so you may find you need to wait for the next vehicle if there are others in wheelchairs or scooters in line before you.

Unusually long or wide wheelchairs and scooters may not fit on standard transportation. If you have a non-standard mobility device, you should contact Disney in advance of your trip to find out if you need to make other arrangements for transportation.

Swimming Pools: On a final note, Florida law requires each hotel to provide a chair at their swimming pools to give guests with mobility limitations the ability to easily get into and out of the water. You should find these chairs at all hotels, not just on Disney property.

However, we've noticed that some off-property pools have only met the minimum requirements of this law by installing a single chair for use at one of their pools, but not necessarily for all of their pools and hot tubs. All Disney resorts have a chair for each swimming pool and hot tub on property. Be sure to check before booking your hotel if this is an issue for you.

Going on Rides: Not all Disney rides will accommodate a wheelchair or scooter, particularly the thrill rides. You will need to transfer from your wheelchair or scooter to the ride in many cases. If that's not an option for you, here is a list of the attractions you will be able to visit and still sit in your wheelchair or scooter:

Magic Kingdom

- Jungle Cruise
- Walt Disney's Enchanted Tiki Room
- Country Bear Jamboree
- Raft to Tom Sawyer Island
- The Hall of Presidents
- Liberty Square Riverboat
- Mickey's PhilharMagic
- Walt Disney's Carousel of Progress
- Monsters, Inc. Laugh Floor

Epcot

- Advanced Training Lab
- Innoventions (Excluding The Sum of All Thrills)
- The Seas Pavilion
- Turtle Talk with Crush
- Bruce's Shark World
- Journey Into Imagination with Figment
- ImageWorks – The "What If" Labs
- Disney & Pixar Short Film Festival
- Mexico Folk Art Gallery
- Stave Church Gallery
- Reflections of China
- House of Whispering Willows
- The American Adventure
- America Gardens Theatre
- Bijutsu-kan Gallery
- Gallery of Arts and History
- Impressions de France
- O Canada!

Special Travel Considerations

Hollywood Studios

- The American Idol Experience
- Indiana Jones Epic Stunt Spectacular!
- Muppet Vision 3D
- Star Wars Launch Bay
- Star Wars: Rise of the Resistance
- Walt Disney Presents
- Voyage of the Little Mermaid
- Disney Junior - Live on Stage!
- Beauty and the Beast - Live on Stage
- Fantasmic!

Animal Kingdom

- Tree of Life Garden
- Discovery Island Trails
- It's Tough to be a Bug!
- Festival of the Lion King
- The Boneyard
- Dino-Sue
- Fossil Fun Games
- Finding Nemo - The Musical
- Gorilla Falls Exploration Trail
- Wildlife Express Train
- Flights of Wonder
- Maharajah Jungle Trek
- Conservation Station

Blizzard Beach

- Tike's Peak

Transfer Required. Here is a list of attractions for which you must transfer from your wheelchair or scooter. (NOTE: Some of these rides require you to transfer to another wheelchair at the ride, others directly onto the ride vehicle.)

Magic Kingdom

- Main Street Vehicles
- Big Thunder Mountain Railroad
- Splash Mountain
- Haunted Mansion
- The Barnstormer
- Prince Charming Regal Carrousel
- Dumbo the Flying Elephant
- Mad Tea Party
- Astro Orbiter
- Tomorrowland Speedway
- Walt Disney World Railroad
- The Magic Carpets of Aladdin
- "it's a small world"
- The Many Adventures of Winnie the Pooh
- Under the Sea ~ Journey of the Little Mermaid
- Enchanted Tales with Belle
- Buzz Lightyear's Space Ranger Spin
- Pirate's of the Caribbean
- Space Mountain
- Seven Dwarfs Mine Train

Epcot

- Soarin' Around the World
- Mission: SPACE
- The Sum of All Thrills
- Frozen Ever After
- Spaceship Earth
- The Seas with Nemo & Friends
- Living with the Land
- Behind the Seeds
- Gran Fiesta Tour Starring the Three Caballeros

Hollywood Studios

- The Twilight Zone Tower of Terror
- Toy Story Midway Mania!
- Slinky Dog Dash
- Alien Swirling Saucers
- *Millenium Falcon:* Smugglers Run
- Toy Story Midway Mania!
- Star Tours – The Adventures Continue
- Rock 'n' Roller Coaster Starring Aerosmith

Animal Kingdom

- Kali River Rapids
- Expedition Everest – Legend of the Forbidden Mountain
- Kilimanjaro Safaris

- TriceraTop Spin
- Affection Section

Blizzard Beach

- Slush Gusher
- Teamboat Springs
- Toboggan Racers
- Snow Stormers

- Runoff Rapids
- Cross Country Creek
- Chairlift
- Melt-Away Bay
- Ski Patrol Training Camp

Typhoon Lagoon

- Castaway Creek
- Crush 'n' Gusher
- Typhoon Lagoon Surf Pool
- Ketchakiddee Creek
- Miss Adventure Falls

Here is a list of attractions that will require you to walk (and in some cases climb steps) or be assisted by others in your party:

Magic Kingdom

- Swiss Family Treehouse
- Tom Sawyer Island
- Peter Pan's Flight
- Tomorrowland Transit Authority PeopleMover

Blizzard Beach

- Summit Plummet
- Downhill Double Dipper

Typhoon Lagoon

- Keelhaul Falls
- Mayday Falls
- Gangplank Falls
- Humunga Kowabunga
- Storm Slides
- Bay Slides

Parades and Shows: Guests with DAS or who are using a wheelchair or scooter have reserved seating areas at parades and inside theaters. Ask the queue attendant where to line up to get to this seating area, as there is typically a separate waiting area to get you seated early.

It's important to note that not all disabled seating is prime seating. You will usually have front row or close to front row viewing at parades. However, some of the theaters are designed with stadium seating and no direct route to the lower seats, so if you're in a wheelchair or scooter, you'll be seated in the very back (or highest) rows. Fantasmic! is one of the shows where you'll be seated far from the action. If you have some mobility, discuss your seating options with the queue attendant.

Service Animals

Disney has a liberal policy on trained (or in-training) service animals and does allow them in the parks. This is a wonderful option for guests who are unable to navigate the theme parks without assistance. They even allow service animals on certain attractions!

However, this doesn't mean you should dress up the family dog or even a comfort dog as a service dog to bring him to the park. We occasionally see people with their dogs in the parks who have clearly not been trained to be in a theme park environment. Unfortunately, the sights, sounds, smells, and numerous children trying to pet the dogs make it an overwhelming and potentially frightening environment for a dog not specifically trained as a service animal. Please be considerate of your animal's comfort and needs, and leave the dog at home or in a kennel if you don't need it with you as a service animal.

The facilities for service animals are limited, but there are places in each theme park for service dogs to use as a toilet. We've included the list of designated areas here. (The official Disney policy allows the service animal to do its business in any outdoor area, provided you pick up after it and leave the area clean.)

Magic Kingdom

- Next to Pirates of the Caribbean in Adventureland
- Near Tom Sawyer Island in Frontierland
- Next to Liberty Tree Inn in Liberty Square
- On the Path Behind The Barnstormer in Fantasyland
- Near the Space Mountain Restrooms in Tomorrowland

Epcot

- Next to the Restrooms Outside of MouseGear in Future World East
- Next to the Imagination! Restrooms in Future World West
- Next to the Restrooms in the United Kingdom Pavilion
- Across from the Restrooms in the Norway Pavilion

Hollywood Studios

- In Front of First Aid
- Next to the ABC Sound Studio Restrooms

Animal Kingdom

- Next to the Restaurantosorus Restrooms in DinoLand USA
- Next to the Maharajah Jungle Trek Restrooms in Asia
- Next to the Conservation Station Entrance in Rafiki's Planet Watch

Now the important stuff: the rides! You can take your service animal on many attractions. You will use an alternative entrance, such as those for wheelchairs, if available at the attraction. The queue attendant will direct you as you approach the line.

However, service animals aren't allowed on all rides, as it wouldn't be safe for the animal on certain attractions. For these restricted rides, check with the queue attendant for options. You may need to do a ride swap where one person waits with the service animal while the other goes on the ride, or the attendant may have a portable kennel available for the duration of the ride.

Here is the list of restricted rides:

Magic Kingdom

- Splash Mountain
- Big Thunder Mountain Railroad
- Peter Pan's Flight
- The Barnstormer
- Space Mountain

Epcot

- Mission: SPACE
- Test Track
- Soarin'
- Sum of All Thrills

Hollywood Studios

- Rock 'n' Roller Coaster Starring Aerosmith
- The Twilight Zone Tower of Terror
- Star Tours – The Adventure Continues
- Star Wars: Rise of the Resistance
- *Millenium Falcon:* Smugglers Run
- Alien Swirling Saucers
- Slinky Dog Dash

Animal Kingdom

- Affection Section at Rafiki's Planet Watch
- Kali River Rapids
- Expedition Everest – Legend of the Forbidden Mountain
- DINOSAUR

We've yet to see service cats or pigs or any other type of animal other than dog at the parks, but theoretically the above information would apply to them, as well.

Guests with Visual Impairments

If you or someone in your party has a visual impairment, head to Guest Relations immediately upon entering a park. In addition to a large braille map located at each Guest Relations, you can pick up an Audio Description Device and/or a Braille Guidebook for the park. (Availability for these devices is limited.)

Audio Description Device: This is a handheld device that provides you with audio description of scenery and action in certain attractions. You will be required to pay a $25 deposit when you pick up the device, which will be returned to you when you drop it back off at Guest Relations. You will need to pick up a new device each day of your visit.

Here is a list of attractions where you can use the Audio Description Device:

Magic Kingdom

- Buzz Lightyear's Space Ranger Spin
- Haunted Mansion
- "it's a small world"
- The Many Adventures of Winnie the Pooh
- Mickey's PhilharMagic
- Peter Pan's Flight
- Pirates of the Caribbean
- Tomorrowland Transit Authority PeopleMover

- Under the Sea ~ Journey of the Little Mermaid
- Walt Disney's Carousel of Progress
- Walt Disney's Enchanted Tiki Room

Epcot

- The American Adventure
- Disney & Pixar Short Film Festival
- Gran Fiesta Tour Starring the Three Caballeros
- Impressions de France
- Journey Into Imagination With Figment

- Living with the Land
- Frozen Ever After
- O Canada!
- Reflections of China
- The Seas with Nemo & Friends
- Spaceship Earth

Hollywood Studios

- Beauty and the Beast – Live on Stage
- Disney Junior – Live on Stage!
- Indiana Jones Epic Stunt Spectacular!
- Muppet Vision 3D
- Toy Story Midway Mania!
- Voyage of The Little Mermaid
- Walt Disney Presents

Animal Kingdom

- Finding Nemo – The Musical
- It's Tough to be a Bug!
- Maharajah Jungle Trek
- Gorilla Falls Exploration Trail

Braille Guidebook: You can pick up one of these guidebooks at Guest Relations in each park, which has descriptions of the attractions, dining, and shops for that particular park. As with the Audio Description Device, you will need to pay a $25 deposit each time you pick up a book, which you will get back when you return the book to Guest Relations at the end of the day. You will need to pick up a new book each day of your visit.

Guests with Hearing Impairments

Part of what makes Disney so magical is the music and dialogue of its characters, so we're pleased that Disney has tools to help people with hearing impairments get the full experience of the attractions.

Handheld Devices: You can pick up a Handheld Device from Guest Relations upon entering each park. Handheld Devices include two services: Assistive Listening and Handheld Captioning. Use of the device is free, but there is a $25 deposit that will be refunded when you return the device at the end of the day.

If your hearing loss is mild or moderate, the Assistive Listening service can be a great option for you. You use headphones with the device, and it acts as a sound amplifier (much like a hearing aid) for some of the attractions.

For other attractions, or if you are unable to hear the amplified sounds through the Assistive Listening service, turn on the Handheld Captioning. The text of what the characters are saying will scroll across the screen to help you easily understand. Handheld Captioning is available at attractions that don't have a fixed closed or reflective captioning system, such as the moving rides.

The free Disney park map you obtain upon entering each theme park shows an ear symbol for attractions with Assistive Listening services available and an "HC" symbol for those with Handheld Captioning services available.

Captioning: Disney offers either closed captioning or reflective captioning in attractions set in theaters. Check in with the queue attendant upon entering the line for any of these attractions, so they can

seat you in a location where you can easily view the captions.

The free Disney park map you obtain upon entering each theme park shows an "RC" symbol for attractions with reflective captioning and a "CC" symbol for attractions with closed captioning.

Sign Language Interpretation: Live shows at the Disney parks have sign language interpreters available, but the interpreters rotate throughout the shows and theme parks. You should request a schedule at least a week in advance of your trip by calling (407) 824-4321 or (407) 827-5141 (TTY). Generally speaking, interpreters are available at the parks on the following days:

- Magic Kingdom: Mondays and Thursdays
- Epcot: Fridays
- Hollywood Studios: Sundays and Wednesdays
- Animal Kingdom: Tuesdays and Saturdays

You can also request a sign language interpreter at least 14 days in advance by calling those same numbers for other live shows at the resorts, such as the Hoop-Dee-Doo Musical Revue. Again, be sure to contact Disney well in advance to schedule these services. They will verify your schedule with you prior to your trip.

Other Tools: Some Disney Cast Members speak sign language, which is noted on those Cast Member's name tags. However, it is not common enough to expect a sign language interpreter to always be on-hand.

When all else fails, Cast Members have notepads and pens handy to communicate with you. You can also pick up a free notepad and pen from Guest Relations to make sure you always have a way of communicating with people.

Companion Restrooms

All restrooms have at least one larger stall designed to accommodate wheelchairs. Most restrooms within the Disney theme parks also have companion restrooms. These are perfect if you have a disability that requires someone to assist you when using the toilet.

You may have a short wait to use one of these companion restrooms, as they're commonly used by families with small children. However, it's usually quick, as guests are respectful of people with special needs and tend to bypass companion restrooms even if that means they must wait in line.

Non-English Speaking Guests

Walt Disney World welcomes guests from all over the world. For the most part, getting around the parks requires very little communication. However, if English is not your first language, you may find it difficult to understand the attractions and get full enjoyment out of your vacation.

Disney Show Translators: There are handheld devices called Ears to the World that you can pick up at Guest Relations upon entering each park to help translate certain attractions from English to the following languages:
- French
- German

Special Travel Considerations

- Japanese
- Portuguese
- Spanish

These devices are free to use, but you must provide a $25 deposit per day, which is returned to you when you turn in the device at the end of each day. The Disney Show Translators work on the following attractions:

Magic Kingdom
- The Hall of Presidents
- Haunted Mansion
- Jungle Cruise
- Tomorrowland Transit Authority PeopleMover
- Walt Disney World Railroad

Epcot
- The American Adventure
- Journey into Imagination with Figment
- Living with the Land
- Mission: SPACE
- O Canada!
- Reflections of China
- Test Track

Hollywood Studios
- Muppet*Vision 3D
- The Twilight Zone Tower of Terror
- Walt Disney Presents

Animal Kingdom
- DINOSAUR
- It's Tough to be a Bug!
- Kilimanjaro Safaris

Part of the Disney success is our ability to create a believable world of dreams that appeals to all age groups. The kind of entertainment we create is meant to appeal to every member of the family.

- Walt Disney

Romance, Celebrations, and Nightlife

Disney isn't just for kids. In fact, it's a very popular destination for singles and couples who want to have fun and romance in a low-pressure environment. Children are nearly everywhere on Disney property, but we find the family atmosphere actually allows people to relax by removing some of the intimacy stressors involved with dating, such as feeling you need to grope each other just because everyone else in a nightclub is doing that same thing.

Don't worry, though. There are plenty of opportunities for alone time and romance on Disney property. Take it from some of our authors who actually got married and honeymooned on-property!

Disney Weddings & Vow Renewals

We may as well start this section with the most romantic thing Disney has to offer: fairytale weddings! What woman doesn't want to dress up as a princess and have her happily ever after with her very own prince charming?

Disney offers wedding packages, each with a wedding coordinator, that you can customize.

To determine the starting price range, you must first decide on a venue. That's because hte more popular and romantic locations come with a premium price, and a minimum amount you must spend on extras.

Of course, you must also consider the number of guests you plan to invite, as some venues are limited in size.

Just remember, the sky's the limit with Disney weddings. In our experience, Disney will allow you to add any special touch to your package...for a price.

Packages generally include at least one live musician who plays at your wedding. In fact, you can request one or two special songs, which the musician will gladly learn for you with enough advanced notice!

Memories

For a very basic package or vow renewal with up to four guests, you can expect to spend around $2,500 plus tax and gratuities. For the price, you get a choice of: three hotel settings (We especially like the beach setting at Polynesian Resort with the castle in the background.); the bride's bouquet; a photographer and 20 prints; a violinist; and a few extras. This is a great option for those with small families or those seeking to elope, as Florida has no requirement for a witness, unlike many states in the United States.

In reality, your Disney dream wedding is likely to cost you *conservatively* in the $25,000-$35,000 range (much more if you want the coveted Cinderella Castle venue). You can speak to a wedding coordinator to find out all of the options available and the cost to get them.

If you're planning a Disney wedding, vow renewal, or special honeymoon package (or if you just want to play around and dream about it), head to disneyweddings.com/florida/pricing or call (321) 939-4610.

Rogue/Guerilla Weddings

Let's face it: Disney wedding prices are way too high for the average person planning a wedding, and the one venue everyone wants (Cinderella's Castle) will set you back a minimum of $75,000!

We don't personally know anybody who has had a rogue wedding on Disney property, but a couple did reportedly get married on Pirate's of the Caribbean inside of the Magic Kingdom!

Be forewarned: our understanding is that anybody who is caught getting married on Disney property without going through Disney Fairy Tale Weddings will be removed from the premises immediately. It's certainly a subject for much debate and discussion, though.

Ideas that have come up include renting a boat on Seven Seas Lagoon to hold the ceremony in front of Magic Kingdom or having the ceremony on a monorail train. Others have suggested doing a quick, plain-clothes ceremony at the base of Cinderella's Castle. There is no requirement for a witness in Florida, so if you can find an officiant willing to perform the unauthorized ceremony in a very quick fashion, we imagine it could be done.

If you choose to do something like this, we take no responsibility for your actions or the ire you're likely to draw from others who went through the proper channels. Rogue weddings are at your own risk!

Disney Dating & Romantic Celebrations (Engagements & Anniversaries)

Creating a romantic moment at Disney can be difficult with the presence of so many strangers and children. Fortunately, people who choose Disney as a destination are generally more fun-loving and less concerned about private moments.

In addition to the theme parks, Walt Disney World has some exciting dating venues. Why not start your evening with dinner and dessert at Beaches & Cream Restaurant at Disney's Beach Club

Resort, then walk to Fantasia Gardens for miniature golf? With both places within an easy walk of Disney's BoardWalk, ending the evening by watching Epcot's fireworks from the BoardWalk makes for a perfect date.

Another excellent option is a fantastic Southern meal at Boatwright's Dining Hall, located at Port Orleans Riverside Resort, followed by a horse-drawn carriage ride around the resort property. You can end the evening with live jazz music and drinks at Scat Cat's Lounge, a short walk away at Port Orleans French Quarter Resort.

The most important element of creating a perfect moment at Disney is understanding what your partner enjoys. With its wide variety of hotels and dining options, chances are Disney has a perfect fit for everyone.

Romantic Special Events

Nothing says romance like fireworks … except perhaps adding to the celebration and having dessert along with the fireworks! Epcot, Magic Kingdom, and Hollywood Studios offer amazing desserts with their fireworks packages at particularly excellent viewing locations.

The **Harmonious Sparkling Dessert Party** at Epcot is offered on limited nights. You will be seated along World Showcase Lagoon to enjoy desserts and wine during Epcot's popular Harmonious fireworks show. A party of two can enjoy this romantic event for $98, including taxes and gratuity.

The **Tomorrowland Terrace Fireworks Dessert Party** is one of the Magic Kingdom's romantic fireworks options. While the crowds are clamoring for a standing view of the castle fireworks, you'll be seated at Tomorrowland Terrace Restaurant, enjoying a variety of gourmet desserts and beverages. This event is available nightly, though no wine is served. A party of two will pay $118 (tax and gratuity included) for this experience. The party books well in advance, so reservations are a must!

For even more romance, consider **Ferrytale Fireworks: A Sparkling Dessert Cruise**. Imagine floating on a serene lake, while enjoying fireworks, treats, and the company of only a handful of other guests. In fact, this may be the best option if you're planning to propose on-property! This experience will set you back $198 (tax and gratuity included) for two people. You get to keep a souvenir plate and glow glass to commemorate the occasion.

In Hollywood Studios, you can get a priority standing location in front of the Chinese Theater during the **Star Wars : A Galactic Spectacular Dessert Party**. Specialty drink options include alcoholic beverages for adults. For that special evening, expect to spend $138 (tax and gratuity included) for two people.

Romantic Hotels

If romance is on your mind, a stay in any Moderate or Deluxe hotel will help set the mood. These properties are much quieter than the Value resorts. Choose based on the theme. For instance, animal lovers will find the breathtaking views at Animal Kingdom Lodge to be ideal. However, if seclusion is what you're after The Cabins at Fort Wilderness or Alligator Bayou at Port Orleans Riverside are excellent choices.

If you're planning on staying on Disney property during your romantic celebration, there are a few hotels we recommend that offer excellent opportunities to sneak away together:

- Wilderness Lodge Resort's pool is romantic but can be noisy. A short walk takes you to a beach and secluded wilderness trail, complete with wild deer.

- Similarly, The Cabins at Fort Wilderness offer easy access to the wilderness trail in a quiet location away from others.
- Port Orleans Riverside Resort has peaceful and beautiful grounds with southern mansion-style buildings surrounding a winding river. Ask for a room in Alligator Bayou for the most secluded location on the property.
- Animal Kingdom Lodge offers a setting where you never need to leave your room. The entertainment is built in with its rooms that overlook a zoo-like setting, complete with wild animals.
- Our absolute favorite romantic lodging is the new on-the-water bungalows at Disney's Polynesian Villas & Bungalows hotel. With water surrounding you on one side, a white sand beach on the other, and nightly views of fireworks, this location is sure to set the mood.

Romantic Eats

While most restaurants on-property are likely to be noisy, there are a few places of refuge. For that quiet evening with your significant other, consider one of the following:

- Coral Reef (Epcot)
- The terrace at the Rose & Crown (Epcot)
- Corner booths at The Hollywood Brown Derby (Hollywood Studios)
- Upstairs tables at Monsieur Paul (Epcot)
- An alfresco table at Tutto Italia (Epcot)
- A fireside table at Tutto Gusto Wine Cellar (Epcot)
- A lakeside table at Spice Road Table (Epcot)

- Rooftop dining at Topolino's Terrace (Riviera Resort)
- Waterfront dining at Paddlefish (Disney Springs)
- A window table at California Grill (Contemporary Resort) for an incredible view of fireworks
- Victoria & Albert's (Grand Floridian; Reserve the chef's table for a very exclusive experience)

Eating later will improve your chances for a quiet meal, but remember that children are everywhere (except the two night clubs at Disney's BoardWalk). Children still awake during late hours tend to be tired and fussy.

Ask for a seat away from families to keep the noise levels down. If possible, the host will accommodate you. You can also ask if a nearby lounge serves food from the restaurant. Always ask to look through a restaurant before eating if you are concerned about the atmosphere.

In-Room Celebrations

Nothing says romance like an in-room couple's massage. See our section on Spas for the locations these services are offered.

Disney Floral and Gifts sells in-room packages ranging from chocolates and flowers to glass slippers and tiaras to create a perfect setting for your loved one to feel like a romantic princess. Expect to spend $300 - $400 when creating this perfect moment.

Alternatively, pick up your own gourmet chocolates from Ghirardelli's at Disney Springs and flowers from a local grocery store to create a less expensive, but no less perfect, setting yourself.

Character Meet & Greets and Character Dining

There is nothing more fun for children of all ages than meeting Disney characters. The short visits are great for laughs and good memories. It is optimized to allow you to get the experience on camera or video.

But for children, the most important component will be getting authentic autographs from their favorite characters. This is a fun keepsake that most children will not only love collecting, but will cherish for a long time after their trip.

Character Types and Varieties

Characters come in two varieties: referred to as either "fur" or "face". Fur characters have full-body costumes that completely cover their heads. These include Mickey, Minnie, and the rest of the animal characters, as well as some human-like characters, such as Russell. Most fur characters don't speak, as Disney long-ago determined it would be too difficult to train Cast Members to replicate their distinctive cinematic voices.

Fur characters manage to communicate quite effectively using lots of gestures. Try carrying on a conversation with them. It's a lot of fun and very easy. Blow them a kiss and make them blush!

Face characters are those with uncovered faces, such as princes, princesses, and fairies. Face characters are generally less frightening to children than furs, since they are more like regular people. These characters will speak to guests. They stay so well "in character" that the experience of meeting them can be the highlight of the trip for your little one.

Most kids tend to appreciate face characters more than fur, since they are able to interact and talk with them and engage in a way the muted animal-costumed

Insider's Tip!

If you are staying at a Disney resort, ask your front desk about which characters you can expect to see during your stay.

"fur" characters cannot. Almost all kids report a more fun experience with face characters, but the fur characters are trained to make gestures and be animated, giving hugs and handshakes.

How Many Characters are There?

There are dozens of opportunities to meet characters throughout the Disney parks and resorts. Only about 60 different characters (20%) actually interact and mingle with guests at regularly scheduled, in-park meets, though there are actually over 250 costumed characters at the World.

Insider's Tip!

Even though those events required special admission, during especially festive times every park will have other special characters that don't require separate admission. Ask a Cast Member to see if anyone unusual is on-hand.

You will not be able to meet some characters unless you are at a dining experience (although there are ways to see some of these characters from a distance, if you want to at least get a photograph). There are about another dozen characters that can only be met during special premium-admission events. Some appear very rarely, and others only appear during seasonal celebrations. The remaining characters

are limited to parades and shows, and are seldom seen mingling with guests.

Insider's Tip!

The best advice for guests is to just be enthusiastic. The characters will make the encounter magical for you. Let your eager child know it's okay to touch, pat, and hug the characters. They can expect big hugs in return!

Characters found at regular greeting locations and dining events will vary their costumes based on the type of event and location. For instance, Goofy at the Land pavilion (Epcot) is dressed as a farmer. At Pete's Silly Sideshow (Storybook Circus,) you will see Donald Duck, Goofy, Minnie, and Daisy Duck dressed for their circus and sideshow roles. During special events, such as a Christmas celebration,

Insider's Tip!

It is also a very good idea to have your children prepared to interact by asking questions. Think of something that relates to the story about the character, since they must remain *in character* at all times! Be ready to help your young child answer questions posed by the characters. The longer you can keep the experience fun for children and spectators, and not become awkward for the character, the better. They will remain engaged, and spend more time, with you and your child during the meet and greet or at the meal. After waiting for the experience, use the time accordingly.

Insider's Tip!

If you want to get an autograph, you will need to bring your own autograph book and pen. The character will sign autographs if you or your child simply holds the autograph book up where it can be clearly seen. As we mention below, the vision of the fur character is more limited, so holding the book directly in front of their face when asking them for their autograph will facilitate this process. Also keep in mind that fur characters have a harder time than most simply trying to hold onto those pens, so try to find a pen that's at least as thick as a marker.

you will see the entire gang in holiday costumes.

Premium Experiences

Special character experiences that require additional admission include Character Dining opportunities (either in parks or at Deluxe resorts). They also include events like the Pirates and Pals Fireworks Show.

You might also see specialty characters at Mickey's Not-So Scary Halloween Party (Magic Kingdom) in September

Insider's Tip!

Don't wait to buy your autograph book until you get to one of the parks. Disney charges a pretty hefty premium for these books, and we can almost guarantee your child will want one. Stop by Target or Walmart to pick up an autograph book for a fraction of the cost. Your child will love getting his/her favorite characters to sign it!

and October and Mickey's Very Merry Christmas Party in November and December. As mentioned previously, the parks close early for these two events, and they require separate guest admission. Some dates sell out well in advance.

Children Meeting Characters

The first thing to remember is that youngsters do not understand that characters are not real and will become very excited the instant they see them. Therefore, you need to be ready to take pictures and get video each time you see them interact, and especially the first time, when it is new to them.

Proper Character Etiquette. Be Considerate!

There are attendants working with each character. They have full control of the situation – it's the attendant's job to make sure that guests don't behave inappropriately. This includes improper touching, grabbing, inappropriate language, or other behavior. It also includes making sure every guest follows simple rules of etiquette. (The number of attendants varies based on the location. There are typically at least three: one at the front of the line, one at the back of the line, and one backstage helping performers change in and out of their costumes.)

Here are some things to keep in mind to make the process enjoyable and free of worry.

Insider's Tip!

During peak periods (and when it is quite hot) there are usually two or three Cast Members who are trading off a character role, and they will be back at work very shortly. So when they say that Minnie is going to be back in five minutes after she powders her nose, that is exactly what they mean, and a very fresh Minnie will be returning.

No Cutting in Line!

Insider's Warning!

You and your child will be ignored and turned away if you try approaching a character out of turn. Make sure your child understands proper line etiquette and about taking turns, or this may cause disappointment when they are rejected. Even if the attendant wanted to make an exception, cutting in line will not be tolerated by other guests no matter how desperate the child is to see a character. Even trying to do so is tactless and disrespectful to other guests waiting patiently for their chance to meet the character.

Be Nice!

Pluto looks just like a huge "walking plush toy" to children. Tell them that Pluto loves getting scratched behind his ears and that Donald loves getting smooched on his beak. Tigger loves to bounce and watch his new friends bounce, too!

Tell youngsters to be nice to the characters and that they will be very nice in return. Please prevent them from pulling on a character's ears, nose, tongue or tail. It can damage the costume, and pushing or pulling could cause the character to lose his balance.

Work Breaks

Characters only mingle for a few minutes at a time before they have to take a break. Minnie may need a snack or a restroom break, and during the hot summer months, she may be desperate for a short respite from the heat. The costumes get unbelievably hot and, for health reasons, characters are only allowed to remain at a meeting spot for a certain time period.

Attendants might "remind" a character of something to signal that it is time for a scheduled break, such as, "Tigger... have you had your bouncing lessons yet?" When they do have to leave, it may only be about five minutes or so for them to return. Waiting in a long line, it may be a little disappointing to have to wait even longer while a character takes his break.

When it is announced that a character is leaving the group, there is no use trying to delay him any longer than they are allowed. Do not grab a character to get him to stop for you. It's very important that they leave when the Cast Member attendant tells them it is time to do so. Ask the attendant for the expected time for their break and be patient for them to get back. Don't ruin your day and the experience of other guests by showing your frustration and causing a scene. (It is interesting to note that it is usually the parents rather than children who seem to be most impolite and impatient!)

Hot Characters Even on Cold Days

It is exceedingly rare that a character might pass out from the heat or dehydration, although it remains a very real risk if the breaks are not strictly enforced.

Comment from a Disney Character Cast Member:

"The costumes are extremely hot, since there are no fans or ventilation systems of any kind. During the hot summer, it gets so dangerously hot that each outdoor shift only lasts 20 minutes before the performer has to be brought inside and another performer is sent out. In these situations, there are typically three performers working the same character. An average summer work day would be eight rotations of 20 minutes on set and 40 minutes off.

When it cools off, the shifts change to two performers rotating 30 minutes on and 30 off. Even so, overheating and dehydration are always major concerns. We sweat so much that during each and every break we could easily drink a full liter of water."

Group Photos of Unrelated Characters

Even if you see two characters in close proximity and you want to get a group photo with both of them, it is almost impossible to do so. Disney's reasoning is that if they allow it once, then everyone will want a similar picture taken. To avoid disruptions, it is not allowed.

Insider's Tip!

When you are still home, find an online video of your child's favorite characters greeting other children. Talk about how tall the characters are and that the mean-sounding Cruella is really not so evil after all.

Insider's Tip!

If you find your children might be nervous about an upcoming meeting, as you're waiting in line to meet a character, talk about the interaction you see other children having. Use words like "silly" and "sweet" to dispel their fears. When it is your turn, be patient and allow the character to coax the child forward, and comment again about "how silly the character is" or mention "how sad the child is making Donald." You will often see the character play along with great effect.

While it might make for a cute picture, it would also slow down the process. When there is more than one character in a location, it is designed to move people through faster. Anything that impedes the flow would only make for a lot of unhappy kids because there was not enough time for them to meet their loved characters. Getting one picture with each individual character is a lot faster. There is one *kind* of exception, such as when characters are designed to be together for a meeting. Some examples of this are Chip 'N Dale or Cinderella's stepsisters and their mother, who are regularly together.

Characters Holding Children is Forbidden

The characters are often asked, "Can Mickey hold my child?" The answer is an unequivocal "No!" The greeter will warn you that the characters can be a little clumsy. No one wants Pooh dropping a child on his head! The chance for an awesome picture simply does not outweigh the risk when the characters interact with thousands of children every day.

Perhaps, if asked *really nicely*, the character might kneel down really low – or even sit right on the floor to get down to their level – and they might even allow the child to sit on their lap.

Children's Fear of Characters

Beware of how character meetings can scare children rather then be fun for them. Many children are afraid of the evil "face villains" (Cruella, Anastasia, and Drizella) simply because of their monstrous demeanor. Additionally, characters are often much larger than children expect. While some kids may be frightened because the characters are larger in life than they might have imagined, most will still be in awe.

Because they may have trepidation at the enormous size of some of the characters, discuss this in advance so that the kids know what to expect. Goofy, for example, is always over six feet tall. Looming high above, he can be intimidating – even for adults!

If you have more than one adult in your party, have one approach the character first, while the other waits with the child to show your child there is nothing to fear. Start the interaction with a short chat, and then ask if the child wants to join in.

If your children get cold feet at first, ask the attendant if you can step out of the queue for a few minutes and let your youngsters watch other kids interact with the character for a while. They will usually relax. If you stay within view of the Cast Member assisting the meet-and-greet, you can then ask for your child's turn without having to stand in line once again.

What Not to Do

If your child seems a little timid about approaching a character, don't force the issue. This may make matters worse. Most kids will readily approach characters they are interested in meeting. Remember not to thrust your child towards a character, or force them into the interaction if he or she is really frightened. You will only get videos or pictures of a crying, screaming child, and these do not make good memories. You don't want a photo of a terrified child in tears as proof your child really met with Mickey Mouse.

Character and Greeter Training

Dealing with scared children is a topic that is covered in depth during the character training process. Cast Members are told to get down on one knee and bring their arms close to their bodies to make themselves appear as small as possible. They are taught to not make any sudden movements, but instead use very small, inviting hand motions, and hope for the best. Sometimes youngsters overcome their fear and venture closer, sometimes it doesn't work at all.

Greeting attendants often come up with little phrases to try to enhance or personalize the guest experience and disarm nervous youngsters. Perhaps she will exclaim, "Tigger's feeling extra bouncy today, 'cause he just ate an entire cake!" Of course, if anyone is wearing a special Disney pin indicating a special celebration, that will also help break the ice with the character.

You should find that it only takes one or two encounters for most children to warm up to (most) all the characters. It is rare that it doesn't eventually happen, except for the always-scary Captain Hook! You may be surprised to find that your child still views an interaction as a magical treat, even if it isn't a complete success in your mind.

Fur Characters and Children Safety

As a parent, be aware of the limited visibility (and peripheral vision) fur characters possess. Most can only see a small area in front of them, and it's very difficult to feel things through the thick costumes. Make sure your child doesn't try approaching a character from behind or from the side to prevent the chance that the character could accidentally knock your child over!

Characters try not to move their feet much during interactions with children to keep from accidentally hurting your child. Keep a close eye out and be prepared to move quickly if it looks like a character might be about to bump into your child.

In most cases, there is a character attendant who will make sure the character sees your child. Feel free to get the character's attention and point to your child, though, or even hold your child up in front of the character, until you get some acknowledgment. **Tell the character your child's name and start a dialogue**.

Characters Stay "In Character"

The first rule of Character interaction is that they remain in character. While it is a great idea to prepare questions for each character you meet, they stay in character and answer according to what their character would know.

Don't ask them any questions that are out of line or might require them to break character. They can not do it, as they are

Insider's Tip!

While helpful most of the time, relying on character greeting information from any Cast Member may lead to confusion and frustration. Cast Members have special guides that are not available to guests. If they do not reach for it and do not seem completely certain of their answer, double check what they tell you. Guest Relations is the best place to get current character information.

Insider's Tip!

A Disney Cast Member who works as a character created a great website (kennythepirate.com) with a lot of relevant and interesting information. Updated regularly, "The Master List of Walt Disney World Character Locations" has a complete list of all characters, even those that are extremely rare and difficult to meet. Readers who are really interested in the character side of Disney can discuss character meet-and-greets. He also offers – for a reasonable cost – a character locator app (characterlocator.com).

trained to maintain the integrity of the performance. They will only talk about issues they would have personal understandings about and that they can relate to, pertaining to the era or place that the character is from, etc.

If you get see the Snow White, she will talk about her evil stepmother and mean sisters. If you see villains, don't expect them to be particularly "nice." For instance, when someone would tell the Evil Queen from Snow White to smile for a picture her terse reply would be, "I don't have to smile. I am beautiful." She might also ask little girls why they don't curtsy; didn't their parents teach them the correct way to greet a queen. Finally, don't be surprised to see Cruella doing things like hurriedly signing her autograph and then dropping pens and books on the ground, or Cinderella's step sisters saying mean things about her.

Where to Find the Characters

If your child, or even you, would like to meet your favorite Disney character, the daily Entertainment Schedule is available in the Times Guide at the gate. It lists the location where you can find each character throughout the day and when they will be available. Refer to it when you get to the park and keep it handy as you go about your day.

Current Information

The following represents **pre-COVID** information, to give readers an idea of who they can expect if they visit when the parks are at normal capacity.

Character appearances are intermittent during the times listed in your Times Guide. Scattered around parks, you may encounter characters who are not on the official lists and who blend in with the theme of various lands. Their appearance times aren't usually published in the times guides, but Cast Members or Guest Relations should be able to tell you when you might meet up with Mayor Weaver, or one of the other characters. Having the chance to interact with them just might make your day a little more magical. Likewise, if you are looking for a specific character, check with Guest Relations as soon as you arrive inside the park.

Times Guides are published every five days and include character greeting times and locations. A character meet-and-greet may be available continuously throughout the day or at specific times. If you pass a Greeting Location, you will often see the signboard that reflects the times you can expect to see the characters.

When to Meet the Characters

Refer to the Character Greeting Times in the My Disney Experience app. This will

Insider's Tip!

ABest Time to Meet: A good time for the meet-and-greets is when any parade or fireworks show is going on.

give you specific directions and times if any special events are taking place.

Guest Relations (such as City Hall at the Magic Kingdom) and other Cast Members have phone numbers they can contact to learn when and at what locations everyone will be making appearances. If you, or your child, have been dying for a photo with a favorite character, check the Times Guide and then double check with Guest Relations when you arrive at the park.

The fun of meeting live Characters, in person, including Mickey and Tinker Bell starts the second you walk into the Magic Kingdom and travel through the tunnels into Town Square. We will share all the information about this meeting point shortly.

Arrival

Plan to be at any of the outdoor meet-and-greet locations about 10 minutes before the character's expected arrival time, and be one of the first in the queue. Let others arriving know that you are waiting, so that they don't try to push their way in front of you.

Once the Cast Member Greeter knows a line is forming, they should quickly take control to make sure it is orderly. If you are walking through a park and see a queue line that has formed prior to the character's arrival, or if the line goes into an area you cannot see into, double check with the Cast Member before waiting in line to avoid being disappointed after waiting for any period of time to find that the character you got in line to see is not the one you were expecting at that location.

This section provides a complete listing of all the characters currently scheduled to appear through each park. Before we list them all, we will provide some tips about the process and what to expect.

Insider's Tip!

Some guests take Disney coloring books to be signed, while others have home-made autograph books. These allow children to get excited long in advance of their trip, and the characters will appreciate the extra thought. Warning: you cannot expect two back-to-back pages to survive intact, because the ink from a good pen will bleed through.

Tips for Getting Character Autographs and Great Photographs

Autographs, videos, and photographs of a special meeting with a child's favorite character make great keepsakes for children to look through long after the trip has ended. Signatures reflect the character's persona (e.g. Aladdin signs in curvy, Arabic-styled letters, reminiscent of the movie logo; The Queen of Hearts carries a red pen and will only sign in red; Eeyore draws a little rain cloud, etc.).

Getting an autograph book is a great idea, as they provide an incentive to be able to linger for just a little while extra to extend a meeting. We will explain shortly how to maximize the value of your visit.

Timid kids don't actually have to go up to the characters to get signatures, but can stay safely in the arms of their parents. Shy children don't actually have to say anything, either. If they want autographs, simply having the book in their hands will be enough of a signal to the characters.

Be ready with pens and autograph books, have your cameras on (and the lens cap off) and video cameras rolling to capture as much of the action as possible when it's your turn. It is also a great idea to put your name and address or hotel in the autograph book so that if you lose it,

you have a chance of getting it back. If you want a specific page signed, hand the book to the character already open to the page and in an upright manner.

Some people prefer to have a blank page opposite each autograph in order to paste a photo of the meet and greet alongside the autograph and turn the autograph book into a scrapbook. Other guests will return for an additional visit after having printed photos from a prior meeting, such as from the PhotoPass photographs that you can have printed in each park. They can then have an actual photograph of the guest meeting the character available for signature on the subsequent encounter. Characters make a big deal out of seeing "themselves" in a previous photo.

A variation of this is to use a portrait-sized photograph of a character. It can be a generic one found on-line, or it might be a scene from a movie that can be printed out. Finally, a cartoon image or even a coloring book image works great for your souvenir autograph collection. Another great idea is to bring individual 8" x 10" photo mats for the characters to sign. Once you get home, you can put a picture with it to display.

Remember that some characters have thick gloves that limit their dexterity. Big, thick ink pens are best for autograph books and other paper products. The Sharpie brand offers a "fat" felt tip writer in many color options and is particularly good for writing on other items such as hats, shirts, banners, and posters. While characters are allowed to sign clothing items, they cannot sign anything while it is being worn. Keep in mind that ballpoint pens do not write well on most fabrics. Use an ink color that contrasts heavily with the color of the background material, which is important for materials as well as the picture signing mentioned above.

Character Meet & Greets and Character Dining

Another option for autograph books is using fat crayons. Two advantages of them are that you don't have to worry about the colors running out of ink and children can use them at other times during the trip without making a huge mess. (Penway crayons are available at Walgreens, located all around Orlando. Crayola sells their "My First Pack" crayons.)

A couple of other variations that have met with success include large-format picture books. Others have purchased large photo albums (that will eventually house the printed pictures) and place simple (large) index cards that can slide in and out easily. It lets the kids determine the order in which they will place the eventual photographs.

Photographs and Videos

When taking photos, don't worry about having them all well-posed, with everyone looking squarely into the camera and smiling on cue. Some of the cutest pictures you will find will be of a small child staring up in wonder at the life size Pooh standing over her. There is nothing cuter than a little boy blushing when his "crush" starts talking to him. Be spontaneous and capture the process.

Magic Kingdom

In addition to the characters you will read about, remember that some characters randomly stroll around the park. And don't forget the high-caliber Magic Kingdom bands that play at fixed locations and stroll about the park. These Cast Members are highly-skilled musicians. Look for the banjo, dixieland, and steel drum bands.

Indoor, Climate Controlled Locations

We will first detail and describe the permanent, indoor character locations

that are continuously available throughout the day, until about 30 minutes prior to parks' closing. (Outdoor locations have set times throughout the day. Characters are available in those locations for less than an hour at a time.)

Town Square Theater

There are two indoor meeting locations just inside the park within Main Street's Town Square Theater. As you pass under the Main Street Walt Disney World Railroad station and enter the park, these meeting locations are on the right. This is a cool, indoor environment with a queue that moves reasonably fast. Because of its unique process, your family will get a little more time for photographs and autographs, and each guest gets some one-on-one time to chat either backstage with Mickey or with Tinker Bell in her Magical Nook. They are available all day long, from the time the park opens until about an hour before closing.

Previously known as Town Square Exposition Hall, the Town Square Theater venue has been re-imagined as a turn-of-the-Twentieth-Century theater with posters proclaiming Mickey Mouse the star of a magic show.

A glistening marquee with gold-leaf trim and sparkling lights entices guests from the promenade. Adjoining the meet-and-greet location on either side are the Box Office Gifts merchandise shop and Tony's Town Square Restaurant.

Entering the lobby you encounter beautiful plush curtains with gold rope tiebacks, polished-brass chandeliers, and a huge tile floor mosaic of the Town Square Theater logo.

Beyond the lobby, guests pass through an ornate archway to enter one of two queues to meet either Magician Mickey Mouse or Tinker Bell. Shortly, we will

Insider's Note!

If you heard about the amazing, talking Mickey, we are sorry to say that Walt Disney World discontinued this feature from the Magic Kingdom meet-and-greet.

discuss where to meet Mickey's friends and where princesses can be located.

Backstage Magic with Mickey Mouse

Entering the queue for Mickey, magical posters that feature Mickey's various magic acts come to life, enhancing the journey into the backstage corridors of the theater.

Mickey greets guests in his backstage rehearsal room, which is designed as a classic theater environment replete with posters from Mickey's magical career, steamer trunks, and stage props. The wood floor and ceiling are all well detailed. One wall is brick, the others are papered in Mickey's red and black colors.

Watch in awe as Mickey Mouse demonstrates his magic with a card trick, a disappearing dove, or possibly a rabbit coming out of a hat. The greatest magic of all is the hug from Mickey Mouse himself.

Make sure you tell Mickey (and any character you meet) if it is a special day, as he loves to wish congratulations.

Tinker Bell's Garden Theater

You will find Tinker Bell's Garden Theater right next to Mickey. Wander through a dimly lit magic portal where guests "magically" shrink down to the size of a fairy and get transported to Tinker Bell's Magical Nook. Here, you will have an opportunity to meet the pint-sized pixie.

Tinker Bell is a face character and provides a fun and bubbly encounter. Be sure to explain to the little ones that they are being shrunk down to her size. You can point out all of the amazing oversized items in the nook to convince your child that they have, in fact, become as small as fairies. These items include giant playing cards (perhaps taken from Mickey's magic act just steps away), a giant spool of thread, and even blades of grass looming overhead.

After meeting Mickey or Tinker Bell, guests exit through a retail location, Curtain Call Collectibles. This is a shop with design elements reflecting a backstage theater shipping and receiving area. Decorations include large, barn-like doors through which props and set pieces might pass.

Pete's Silly Sideshow (Storybook Circus)

Mickey's four best pals are on-hand throughout the day to meet with guests. Dressed in their 19th-century garb (and ready to perform in their circus and sideshow roles), there are two meeting queues.

You can either meet: 1) the duo of Donald and Goofy (as The Astounding Donaldo, the most charming of snake charmers, and The Great Goofini, circus stuntman extraordinaire); or 2) the pair of Minnie and Daisy (as Minnie Magnifique, a Parisian poodle trainer, and Madame Daisy Fortuna, a mysterious gypsy fortuneteller).

Ariel's Grotto (New Fantasyland)

Tucked away near the back of the new Fantasyland addition is The Little Mermaid ride inside of Prince Eric's castle. Just next door is Ariel's Grotto where you can meet The Little Mermaid herself.

The setting is designed to look like you are walking into caverns inside the seaside cliffs. After you wind your way into the grotto, you get the opportunity to meet Ariel in her full mermaid regalia. She even has a tail!

Enchanted Tales with Belle (New Fantasyland)

While not technically a meet-and-greet, guests who participate in this performance do get the opportunity to meet the lovely Belle after the show. Keep in mind, though, that only those who participate get the princess photo opportunity.

This retelling of the love story takes place in Beast's castle after a short trip through a magical portal from Belle's cottage. The setting incorporates much of the ornate décor seen in the Beauty and the Beast film, as you might expect inside a French fairy tale castle.

Anybody who wishes to be part of the show can volunteer. Some children and adults are given prominent roles, but anybody who wants to be included will receive a part in the production.

Princess Fairytale Hall (Fantasyland)

No trip to Cinderella's castle would be complete without meeting its resident princess at Princess Fairytale Hall. This location has two separate queues: one for Cinderella with Elena, the other for Rapunzel with a different visiting princess. (The visiting princesses vary based on availability.)

Each queue is similarly decorated with wall art from famous fairy tales. One of the most iconic pieces of décor is the open book inside of each of the two meet-and-greet locations. It is open to a page from the original Disney fairy tale: Snow White.

Outdoor Characters and Live Performances

At opening time, a number of the characters are always on hand to greet guests. If you arrive first thing in the morning, expect that there will be various characters throughout Town Square for photographs and autographs from 9 a.m. to early afternoon most days.

These often include Marie, Pluto, Mary Poppins, or even a princess, such as Snow White or Aurora. Check the Times Guide as you enter the park for specific character information that day.

If you prefer a different (and very humorous) character, Gaston loves to show off his powerful muscles to guests outside of his tavern each day in Fantasyland.

Alice and The Mad Hatter are also often on-hand near the *Mad Tea Party* ride in Fantasyland, just as you may find Peter and Wendy welcoming guests near *Peter Pan's Flight*.

Perhaps no outdoor meet-and-greet is as popular as Merida, though. The feisty princess has her own *Fairytale Garden* venue, and little ones can try their hands at archery after meeting her!

Seasonal Variations

There are seasonal variations that feature unique characters, character costuming, and changes in venues. For instance, Santa Claus and Santa Goofy can be expected around the Christmas holidays, and Mr. and Mrs. Easter Bunny can be found in the Town Square Courtyard in the weeks leading up to Easter on Main Street U.S.A. from 9 a.m. to approximately 5 p.m.

Character fans should also take note that on Valentine's Day, the Disney Princess meet-and-greets feature their princes. Seeing them together has always been quite rare.

While the Peter Pan and Wendy meet-and-greet is in the queue area of Peter Pan's Flight, during periods of congestion, such as during the week of Easter and Christmas, they commonly move to the bridge at the entrance to Adventureland.

Citizens of Main Street (Town Square and Main Street U.S.A.) 30 minutes

There are many sharply-dressed Citizens of Main Street that you might run into anywhere from City Hall in Town Square to the Central Plaza at the end of Main Street, U.S.A. They are not listed in your Times Guide, but various citizens mingle with guests most days, just soaking up the Florida sun and basking in the ambiance the town's atmosphere has to offer.

They are typically available for about 30 minutes every hour, giving them time to take breaks and cool down. (Since they are face characters, they cannot simply be substituted with another Cast Member.) You cannot be sure who will be available on any particular day. However, most of them, especially the Mayor and Fire Chief, will be around for special holidays, including Easter and Christmas.

The following is not a wholly complete list of these characters, so if you see anyone who is meandering the streets and shops along Main Street, dressed in attire from the late 1800's to turn-of-the-century, it is a safe guess that they are part of the Main Street Citizens troupe. You will certainly want to meet this group.

Expected Times

9:45 a.m.

10:45 a.m.

11:45 a.m.

1:00 p.m.

2:00 p.m.

Main Street Trolley Show

Some of the Main Street Characters utilize their joyous voices and dancing abilities to take part in a singing and dancing routine that starts at the second-floor of the train platform and on the ground floor at Town Square on Main Street. Each morning some of these citizens arrive at the park riding aboard a horse-drawn trolley, stopping in designated locations where they begin their performance with a short song and dance routine in the center of the street.

After one of their routines, the performers hop on the horse drawn streetcar, progressing to various locations where they stop and perform their way "right down the middle of Main Street, U.S.A." They move along the streetcar tracks from Town Square, down to the plaza in front of Cinderella's Castle and back to the fire station at Town Square where the performers go backstage. Their performance runs several times throughout the day, and the first one usually begins 45 minutes after the park opens. Each trip takes about 20 minutes. The show is seasonal. Check the Times Guide.

The Citizens of Main Street

- Andrew Bition
- Beatrice Starr
- Chief Smokey Miller, Main Street Volunteer Fire Department
- Constance Purchase
- Dewey Cheatem, Esquire works for the city council, and his motto is "do we cheat 'em? And how?" Rumor has it that Dewey no longer meets fans.
- Eunice McGilliacutty
- Francis Fermata is the resident Matchmaker of Main Street USA! She is the Etiquette Columnist for the Main St. Gazette
- Hank Bunting

- Hildegard Olivia Harding is part of the suffragette movement on Main Street USA and proudly wears a banner supporting the rights for women to unite.
- Inga DePoint Lively and comical, Inga is part of the suffragette movement on Main Street U.S.A., who along with her other quirky friends, campaign against Mayor Weaver!
- Mabel Mae Benaught is the President of the Main Street Social Society. Mabel claims to be in the know, but assures that she is not a gossip. ["Have we met? Well maybe, and maybe not."]
- Mayor Christopher George Weaver is the "official officiant for most things official"
- Penelope Prose
- Sheila Shufflehop
- Victoria Trumpetto

Dapper Dans (Main Street, U.S.A)

The Dapper Dans is an authentic (a capella) barbershop quartet. The four-piece harmony group appears throughout the day up and down Main Street and inside the barbershop. The Dapper Dans perform wearing their trademark straw hats, bowties, striped vests, and tap shoes adorned with spatterdashes (spats). Listen to their beautiful harmony, singing uplifting classics in their very unique style. After they finish their set, you may see talented guests invited to sing with them for an additional song. Take the time to watch their enjoyable performance.

They will often ride the Horse-Drawn Streetcars and may sometimes ride along with guests (or give a personal concert to them as a very special treat). See the vehicles on Main Street section to learn more. These vehicles pick up and drop off guests for a one-way ride from either end of Main Street (just below the Main Street Train Station and right in front of Cinderella's Castle). Around 5 p.m., you will see them take part in the Flag Retreat in Town Square.

Rare Characters and Special Appearances

There are rare characters that are often sought out by visitors who know to ask. They can make your visit even more memorable.

Of course, Santa shows up at all the parks and at Disney Springs each year. Very special Christmas-time characters are out to share the different holiday cultures at Epcot. Some characters that may only appear once a year include Shang (right before Christmas parade) or Shan-Yu (Epcot). And in the past Megara, has popped in a couple of times a year.

A rare, random meet, like seeing Mushu in Epcot might happen from time to time. Maybe you'll get lucky and find Governor Ratcliffe in Animal Kingdom.

Newly-appointed characters (trainees) use locations around Epcot to train with attendants and Photopass photographers. Therefore, you may have a chance to meet with someone new and very special. (Expect them to be nervous!)

Epcot Training is random, open to all guests, and can occur at any time or not at all. They are most common between 11 a.m. and 3 p.m.

Annual Special Events

On occasion, Disney schedules a non-recurring special event that showcases hard-to-find characters. There is typically at least one special themed event during the year, such as a park remaining open all night to celebrate a movie opening.

These experiences are quite popular, so if you want to attend special occasions like these, get tickets and plan to arrive early in the day.

During these occasions, you can expect many rare-to-find characters. The following is a list of many of those who have made appearances at these events:

- Hades and Meg, who alternated with Pain and Panic, from "Hercules".
- The Bowler Hat Guy from "Meet the Robinsons"
- Cruella De Vil
- Captain Hook
- Captain Jack Sparrow
- Evil Queen
- Maleficent
- Dr. Facilier
- Jafar
- Lots-O and Big Bad Wolf from "Toy Story 3"
- Queen of Hearts
- Stromboli from "Pinocchio"

There are also (rare) free events available outside the parks to meet special characters. For instance, the Car Masters Weekend, which was held annually until 2014 at Downtown Disney (now Disney Springs), was open to any visitor to the area and featured characters from the popular Cars films. In September 2016, the Coca Cola Polar Bear was added to its store and became the first regular character (other than Santa Claus) at Disney Springs.

Guests have also had the chance to meet rare, unannounced characters who only make sporadic and random appearances each day. For example, you might chance upon Wendell from the Country Bears, Clarabelle Cow and Horace Horsecollar, and all the Brers if you are lucky enough to see the Frontierland Hoedown at the Magic Kingdom. Immediately following their entertaining show, the characters have time for a brief meet-and-greet.

Character Meals

You can also enjoy a character meal at one of the resort hotels on a day you won't be at a park in order to give kids a meaningful memory of the off "rest" days. During these meals, you will meet two to five characters who mingle one at a time.

Enjoying your character meal on the day of your arrival is an excellent way to start your trip. Some kids are so excited to see Mickey that they won't settle down until they do, and a character meal is a great first way to introduce them to the magic. You may also plan the meal on your final day, giving a special send-off you will always remember.

Be prepared with questions to ask each character; they stay in character and will answer accordingly. Help your young child answer questions posed by the characters to keep them engaged longer.

- Have children near aisles for easy access from the dining room.
- Parents should sit against a wall, if possible, to keep an eye out for the characters and to enhance the pictures you will take (e.g., rather than having a wall or seatback in the picture, you will have the entire restaurant as your backdrop).
- Have cameras uncased, autograph books open with pens ready.
- Start pictures as soon as they approach, not just a posed photograph after autographs. You are paying a hefty premium for a character meet-and-greet at a restaurant. Take as many pictures and videos as you can to ensure that you have perfect memories.

Get to the restaurant early so that you can eat your meal prior to the characters showing up. Linger over a final dessert or refreshment. You do not want to be running to the buffet, having to keep an eye out for when the characters are getting to your table.

Ask for help from restaurant Cast Members if the characters inadvertently bypass your table or you otherwise miss the encounter. Any Cast Member will make sure you all are properly introduced.

Make sure you know which characters to expect. Don't hesitate to speak to someone if you were not able to meet a character, but do so in a polite and courteous manner. You are more likely to get a positive response if you treat the Cast Members with respect than if you are rude or demanding.

The "and friends" with meet-and-greets and character meals is to allow flexibility on Disney's part as to who might be available (due to mini-parades of characters, stage shows, etc.). Reconfirm all character meals, as the characters attending may change unexpectedly. Contact (407) WDW-DINE to verify which characters are expected to attend. If your child expects Cinderella and Pocahontas, for instance, seeing Mulan and Mary Poppins may be disappointing.

Warning: Advanced reservations are required for character meals. Your credit card will be charged a fee if you can't make it and do not cancel at least 24 hours in advance.

Unique among the reservations for character dining opportunities is Cinderella's Royal Table in Magic Kingdom. This meal requires prepayment and reserves an actual table, unlike others which simply give you advanced priority seating.

Insider's Tip!

If you are going to eat a character breakfast, try to get reservations as early as possible in the day. If you can get a reservation before the park opening time, you will be able to enjoy being one of the first into the park as well (admission still required) through a special line at turnstiles. Alternatively, enjoying a character lunch or dinner allows you to visit the park early in the morning to enjoy the shorter queues, and you will have a relaxing meal during the hottest and busiest times of the day.

Where to Find Characters

Magic Kingdom

The most iconic Disney characters call Magic Kingdom home. Guests can easily spend an entire day of their vacation meeting princesses and classic cartoon characters there.

Look for special shows that feature fan favorites throughout the park.

Interactive Character Experience:
Captain Jack Sparrow's Pirate Tutorial (Across from Pirates of the Caribbean, Adventureland)

#INCREDIBLESSuperDanceParty (Near Space Mountain, Tomorrowland)

Enchanted Tales with Belle (Fantasyland)

Epcot

You can find a variety of characters throughout World Showcase, including many princesses and some of the hard-to-find princes. Certain locations occasionally host special characters-in-training, such as The American Adventure and International Gateway. Check in these locations to see if a rare-to-find character may be out.

There is also a special meet-and-greet within Innoventions open only to Disney Chase card holders.

Insider's Tip!

Keep in mind that there is very little for small children to do at Epcot, so character meet-and-greets tend to have long queues. Lightning Lane reservations are not available for most meet-and-greets here, so plan to wait in each queue about 30 minutes for each character.

BONUS Insider's Tip!

Epcot has three spots to scope out that MAY occasionally have characters "in rehearsal": 1) International Gateway area near the shops; 2) American Adventure near huge gate to the left, when facing the pavilion or 3) World Showplace.

Hollywood Studios

Disney's Hollywood Studios is a great place to find characters from animated shows and movies. Several times during the day, certain characters emerge from the center of the park, and spread around the immediate area for meet and greets.

There is also a special meet-and-greet within Star Wars Launch Bay open only to Disney Chase card holders.

Interactive Character Experience:
Jedi Training: Trials of the Temple (Near Tatooine Traders, Echo Lake)

Animal Kingdom

One of the best and least crowded places to see characters is at Animal Kingdom when the park first opens. Guests usually head straight for the rides, leaving character lines open.

Animal Kingdom is home to some rare characters, including Pocohontas, Tarzan, and characters from The Jungle Book and Lion King.

Character Meet & Greets and Character Dining

Character Dining Experiences

Land	Restaurant	Characters (May be Substituted)	Character to Guest Ratio: (The Lower the 2nd Number, the Better)
Magic Kingdom			
Fantasyland	Be Our Guest	Beast (Dinner Only)	Unknown
Fantasyland	Cinderella's Royal Table	Cinderella, Ariel, Aurora, Snow White, Jasmine (rare)	1 to 26
Main Street, U.S.A	The Crystal Palace	Winnie the Pooh, Tigger, Eeyore, Piglet	1 to 67 (Breakfast); 1 to 89 (Dinner)
Epcot			
Future World, Land Pavilion	The Garden Grill	Mickey, Chip n Dale, Pluto	1 to 46
World Showcase, Norway Pavilion	Akershus Royal Banquet Hall	Ariel, Aurora, Belle, Cinderella, Jasmine, Mulan, Snow White or Mary Poppins	1 to 54
Hollywood Studios			
Echo Lake	Hollywood & Vine	Doc McStuffins, Handy Manny, Jake, Sofia the First (Breakfast) or Minnie and Friends (Lunch, Dinner)	1 to 71
Animal Kingdom			
Africa	Tusker House Restaurant	Donald, Mickey, Goofy, Daisy	Unknown
Disney Resorts			
BoardWalk Inn	Trattoria al Forno	Ariel & Eric, Rapunzel & Flynn Rider (Breakfast Only)	Unknown
Contemporary Resort	Chef Mickey's	Mickey, Minnie, Pluto, Donald, Goofy (The Fab Five)	1 to 56
Four Seasons	Ravello	Mickey, Minnie, Goofy	Unknown
Grand Floridian Resort	1900 Park Fare	Mary Poppins, Alice in Wonderland, the Mad Hatter, Winnie the Pooh and Eeyore	1 to 54 (Breakfast): 1 to 44 (Dinner)
Grand Floridian Resort	Disney's Perfectly Princess Tea	Princess Aurora, Miss Rose Petal	Unknown
Grand Floridian Resort	Wonderland Tea Party	Mary Poppins, Alice in Wonderland, Mad Hatter, Pooh, Eeyore	Unknown
Polynesian Village Resort	'Ohana	Stitch, Lilo, Mickey, Pluto (Breakfast Only)	1 to 57
Riviera	Topolino's Terrace	Mickey, Minnie, Donald, Daisy (Breakfast Only)	Unknown
Wilderness Lodge	Storybook Dining at Artist Point	Snow White, Evil Queen, Seven Dwarfs	Unknown

Magic Kingdom Meet-and-Greets

Park Land	Disney Character(s)
Adventureland	Aladdin & Jasmine
Fantasyland	Alice
Fantasyland	Ariel
Enchanted Tales with Belle	Belle
Tomorrowland	Buzz Lightyear
Frontierland	Chip n Dale
Fantasyland	Cinderella & Elena
Frontierland	Country Bears
Storybook Circus	Daisy Duck & Minnie Mouse
Storybook Circus	Donald Duck & Goofy
Fantasyland	Fairy Godmother
Fantasyland	Gaston
Fantasyland	Lady Tremaine & Ugly Stepsisters
Liberty Square	Mary Poppins
Fairytale Garden	Merida
Town Square	Mickey Mouse (Talking)
Town Square	Minnie Mouse
Fantasyland	Peter Pan
Town Square	Pluto
Adventureland	Rafiki
Fantasyland	Rapunzel & Tiana
Town Square	Snow White
Town Square	Stitch
Town Square	Tinker Bell
Fantasyland	Winnie the Pooh & Tigger
Tomorrowland	iCan the Showbot

Character Meet & Greets and Character Dining

Epcot Meet-and-Greets

Park Land	Disney Character(s)
United Kingdom	Alice
Norway	Anna & Elsa
France	Aurora
Innoventions West	Baymax
France	Belle
Legacy Plaza	Daisy Duck
Mexico	Donald Duck
Character Spot	Goofy
Morocco	Jasmine
Innoventions West	Joy & Sadness
United Kingdom	Mary Poppins
Innoventions West	Mickey & Friends* *Available only to Disney Chase bank card holders.
Character Spot	Mickey Mouse
Character Spot	Minnie Mouse
China	Mulan
World Showcase Plaza	Pluto
Germany	Snow White
Norway	Vikings
France	Princess Aurora

Hollywood Studios Meet-and-Greets

Park Land	Disney Character(s)
Star Wars Launch Bay	BB-8
Pixar Place	Buzz Lightyear & Woody
Star Wars Launch Bay	Chewbacca
Commissary Lane	Chip n Dale
Animation Courtyard	Doc McStuffins
Chinese Theater Courtyard	Donald Duck
Chinese Theater Courtyard	Goofy
Pixar Place	Green Army Men
Indiana Jones Stunt Spectacular	Indiana Jones & Friends* *Available at main stage after some shows.
Animation Courtyard	Jake
Star Wars Launch Bay	Jawas
Star Wars Launch Bay	Kylo Ren
Red Carpet Dreams	Mickey Mouse & Minnie Mouse
Star Wars Launch Bay	Star Wars Friends* *Available only to Disney Chase bank card holders.
Echo Lake	Olaf
Animation Courtyard	Pluto
Animation Courtyard	Sofia the First
Walt Disney Presents (Formerly One Man's Dream)	Star-Lord & Groot
Star Wars Launch Bay	Stormtroopers
Main Entrance	Various Characters* *Somewhat random meet of Fantasmic characters.

Animal Kingdom Meet-and-Greets

Park Land	Disney Character(s)
Asia	Baloo & King Louie
Conservation Station	Doc McStuffins
DinoLand	Donald Duck
Discovery Island	Flik
DinoLand	Goofy & Pluto
Discovery Island	Mickey Mouse & Minnie Mouse
Discovery Island	Pocahontas
Rafiki's Planet Watch	Rafiki
Discovery Island	Russell

Thank you for purchasing this guidebook. We appreciate our readers and value your support, as we strive for excellence in our materials.

Please take the time to rate or review this book.

Like and follow us on Facebook:

https://www.facebook.com/DisneyWorldMadeEasy

Share your love of Disney with us by joining our
Mickey's Not So Secret Disney World Fan Group
on Facebook:

https://facebook.com/groups/mickeysfangroup

Made in the USA
Monee, IL
24 January 2023

26103842R00230